Anonymous

Proceedings of the Grand Encampment of the Independent Order of

Odd Fellows

of the state of Connecticut. From its institution, April 20, 1843 to its annual session,

February 20, 1866, inclusive

Anonymous

Proceedings of the Grand Encampment of the Independent Order of Odd Fellows
of the state of Connecticut. From its institution, April 20, 1843 to its annual session, February 20, 1866, inclusive

ISBN/EAN: 9783337218355

Printed in Europe, USA, Canada, Australia, Japan

Cover: Foto ©Suzi / pixelio.de

More available books at **www.hansebooks.com**

PROCEEDINGS

OF THE

GRAND ENCAMPMENT

OF THE

Independent Order of Odd Fellows

OF THE

STATE OF CONNECTICUT,

FROM

ITS INSTITUTION, APRIL 20, 1843,

TO

ITS ANNUAL SESSION, FEBRUARY 20, 1866, INCLUSIVE.

PRINTED BY ORDER OF THE GRAND ENCAMPMENT.

NEW HAVEN:
PRINTED BY THOMAS J. STAFFORD.

1867.

INTRODUCTION.

The Patriarchal Branch of Odd Fellowship was not introduced into Connecticut until two years after the Lodges, and
not until a year after the Grand Lodge had been instituted.
Sassacus Encampment was instituted August 19, 1841, and
Oriental, Sept. 13, of the same year. No other Encampment
having arisen, seven Past Officers from these two were invested
with the powers of a Grand Encampment, on the twentieth of
April, 1843. The following June an Encampment was instituted by dispensation at Norwich ; and in July, 1844, a fourth
Encampment was instituted at New London. Up to this
period, the Patriarchal Branch had progressed very slowly.
In the next year, however, (1844,) four Encampments were
instituted ; in 1845, two ; in 1846, one ; but in 1847, four ; in
1848, one—making fifteen Encampments, and a constituency
of 549 under the jurisdiction of the Grand Encampment, the
highest point to which it has ever attained. In 1849, Midian
Encampment, No. 7, at Hartford, was expelled for contumacy.
From this point there was a continual decrease until 1863,
when there existed only five Encampments and 201 members.
Here commenced a revival, and at the close of the year 1866,
there were six Camps and 336 members, an increase of one Encampment (No. 10 revived) and 135 members ; and at the
present writing, July, 1867, there are 8 Encampments and 461
members, and from the interest everywhere manifested, there
is great reason to expect a considerable increase before the
close of the year.

INDEX.

I. O. O. F.

TO ALL WHOM IT MAY CONCERN.

We JOHN A. KENNEDY, Most Worthy Grand Sire of the Grand Lodge of the INDEPENDENT ORDER OF ODD FELLOWS, of the United States of America, and the jurisdiction of the Order thereunto belonging,

FRIENDSHIP, LOVE AND TRUTH,

Know, Ye, That by virtue of the power in us vested, we do hereby authorize and empower our trusty and well beloved Past Chief Patriarchs R. S. HINMAN, THOMAS C. BORDMAN, JOHN OSBORN, WILLIAM E. SANFORD, SAMUEL BISHOP, CHARLES W. BRADLEY, RICHARD S. PRATT, their successors duly and legally elected, to constitute a Grand Encampment in the City of New Haven, and State of Connecticut, to be known and hailed by the title of GRAND ENCAMPMENT OF THE STATE OF CONNECTICUT.

And we do further authorize and empower our said trusty and well beloved brethren and their Successors, to admit and make members according to the ancient usages and customs of the Order, and not contrariwise ; with full power and authority to hear and determine all and singular, matters and things relating to the Order within the jurisdiction of said Grand Encampment according to the rules and regulations of the GRAND LODGE of the UNITED STATES. *Provided always*, That the said above named brethren, and their successors pay due respect to the GRAND LODGE OF THE UNITED STATES, and the ordinances thereof, otherwise this Dispensation to be of no force or effect ; and provided also, that this Dispensation shall be approved by the said Grand Lodge at their next meeting thereof.

L. S.

Given under our Hand and Seal, at the City of New York in the State of New York this nineteenth day of April, Anno Domini, one thousand eight hundred of and forty three.

JOHN A. KENNEDY,
Grand Sire.

INSTITUTION

OF THE

GRAND ENCAMPMENT,

OF THE

STATE OF CONNECTICUT.

New Haven, Thursday, April 20, 1843.

M. W. Past Grand Patriarch and P. G. M. Wilson Small, of the city of New York, by virtue of a dispensation from M. W. John A. Kennedy, Grand Sire, proceeded to institute, "The Grand Encampment of the State of Connecticut," composed of the following Patriarchs, viz:

P. C. P. and *P. H. P.* ROBINSON S. HINMAN, of	Encampment No.	1
P. C. P. and *H. P.* WILLIAM E. SANFORD,	do.	" "
P. C. P. SAMUEL BISHOP,	do.	" "
P. C. P. and *P. H. P.* JOHN OSBORN,	do.	" "
P. C. P. and *P. H. P.* CHARLES WM. BRADLEY,	do.	" 2
P. C P. and *P. H. P.* RICHARD S. PRATT,	do.	" "
P. C. P. and *H. P.* THOS. C. BORDMAN,	do.	" "

The said Patriarchs having been fully instructed in the Grand Encampment Degree ; the chair called for nominations for the several officers of the Grand Encampment, when the following nominations were made, viz.:

Robinson S. Hinman, for *Gr. Patriarch.*
Charles W. Bradley, *G. H. Priest.*
Richard S. Pratt, *G. Senior Warden.*
William E. Sanford, *G. Scribe.*
Samuel Bishop, *G. Treasurer.*
Thos. C. Bordman, *G. J. Warden.*

The Grand Encampment proceeded to ballot for the several Grand Officers, and the said above mentioned Patriarchs were severally declared duly elected to said offices.

M. W. P. G. P. Small, assisted by M. W. G. P. Hinman, then conferred the Degree of P. C. P. on P. C. P. Charles W. Bradley, Richard S. Pratt, Wm. E. Sanford, Samuel Bishop and Thomas C. Bordman, and the Degree of P. H. P. upon P. H. P. Charles William Bradley, Richard S. Pratt, and Isaac Judson.

On motion of P. C. P. Sanford, it was

Resolved, That the M. W. G. Patriarch draw an order on the R. W. G. Treasurer, for such sum as shall be necessary to defray the expenses of opening the R. W. Grand Encampment.

On motion of P. C. P. Sanford, it was

Resolved, That the thanks of this R. W. Grand Encampment be and are hereby tendered to our worthy friend and brother, P. G. P. and P. M. E. H. P. and P. G. M. Wilson Small, for attendance and instructions to us at the Institution of this Grand Encampment.

On motion of P. C. P. and P. H. P. Bradley, it was

Resolved, That a committee of three be appointed to prepare and report a form of a Constitution and By-Laws for this Grand Encampment, and also for the subordinate Encampments.

The chair appointed G. M. E. H. P. Charles Wm. Bradley, G. Scribe William E. Sanford, and G. S. Warden Richard S. Pratt, said committee.

On motion, the Grand Encampment voted to work under the form of the Constitution of the R. W. Grand Encampment of the State of New York, until the adoption of a Constitution by themselves enacted.

P. H. P. Isaac Judson, and C. P. and P. H. P. William J. Thompson were instructed in the Grand Encampment Degree, and took their seats.

The M. W. Grand Patriarch, appointed P. H. P. Isaac Judson, Grand Sentinel, and P. H. P. and C. P. William J. Thompson, Deputy Grand Sentinel.

M. W. P. G. P. and P. G. M. Small then duly installed all the G rand Officers in their respective Grand Offices.

No further business appearing, the Grand Encampment closed in ample form.

Attest, WILLIAM E. SANFORD,
Grand Scribe.

ANNUAL SESSION.

NEW HAVEN, JULY, 14, 1843.

The Grand Encampment of the State of Connecticut was opened in due form.

PRESENT.

M. W. ROBINSON S. HINMAN, *Grand Patriarch.*
M. E. C. W. BRADLEY, *G. H. Priest.*
R. W. ISAAC JUDSON, *G. S. W. p. t.*
R. W. WILLIAM E. SANFORD, *G. Scribe.*
R. W. SAMUEL BISHOP, *Grand Treasurer.*
R. W. JOHN L. DEVOTION, *G. J. W. p. t.*
W. WM. J. THOMPSON, *G. S. p. t.*

The records of last meeting were read and approved.
The M. W. Grand Patriarch presented the following report :

To the R. W. Grand Encampment of the State of Connecticut, ⎱
       Friendship, Love and Truth, ⎰

The undersigned has the honor to report, that during the recess, since the meeting of the Grand Encampment, a petition was received from seven Patriarchs residing in Norwich, Connecticut, for an Encampment to be opened in that city, to be known and hailed as " Palmyra Encampment," No. 3.

The subscriber granted a dispensation on the 12th day of June, 1843, and on the 15th day of said June, he, assisted by the M. E. High Priest Bradley, R. W. G. Scribe Sanford, and R. W. G. Treasurer Bishop, proceeded to institute the said Encampment, under the style and title of Palmyra Encampment, No. 3, to be located at Norwich, according to the most ancient usages, and not contrariwise. The following Patriarchs were elected officers for the present term, which will expire at the first meeting in January, viz. John L. Devotion, Chief Patriarch ; Giles M. Eaton, High Priest ; William L. Brewer, Senior Warden ; John A. Lathrop, Scribe ; Rufus L. Fanning, Treasurer ; Edward W. Eells, J. Warden. We then initiated two candidates according to ancient custom, and raised them to the Degree of the Royal Purple.

From the character of the brethren who have commenced the good work, and the spirit of the members of the order in that city, Palmyra Encampment bids fair to make a flourishing and very respectable Encampment.

The petition is laid before your Right Worthy body for your approval, and that a charter may be granted to said Encampment.

All which is respectfully submitted.

R. S. HINMAN, *G. Patriarch.*

To the M. W. Grand Patriarch of the Grand Encampment, I. O. O. F., of the State of Connecticut:

The undersigned, members of the Order, in regular standing, residing at Norwich, in the State of Connecticut, being sincerely desirous of extending the Order in its benificent operations, do most respectfully petition for a Charter for a Subordinate Encampment, to be located in the city of Norwich, and county of New London, in the State of Connecticut, and to be hailed by the style and title of " PALMYRA ENCAMPMENT, No. 3," I. O. O. F.

And your petitioners will feel themselves more closely bound in F. L. and T.

JOHN L. DEVOTION, of Oriental Encampment, No. 2
G. M. EATON,   do.   do.   "
J. A. LATHROP,   do.   do.   "
W. L. BREWER,   do.   do.   "
JNO. T. WAIT,   do.   do.   "
EDWARD W. EELLS,   do.   do.   "
RUFUS L. FANNING,   do.   do.   "
NORWICH, JUNE 10, 1843.

On motion it was *Voted,* That a charter be granted to Palmyry Encampment, No. 3, of Norwich.

On motion of G. M. E. H. P. Bradley, the following resolution was adopted :—

Resolved, That charters be granted to Sassacus Encampment, No. 1, of New Haven ; and Oriental Encampment, No. 2, of East Haddam, respectively ; and that the said Encampments be allowed to retain in their archieves, the charters received from the Grand Lodge of the United States, subject to the order of this Grand Encampment.

On motion, *Voted,* That C. P. John L. Devotion be added to the committee on the Constitution and By-Laws ; and that said committee be continued to the next session of this Grand Encampment.

A semi-annual return was received from Sassacus Encampment, No. 1 ; which was accepted and ordered on file.

C. P. Devotion presented a copy of the Constitution and By-Laws, adopted by Palmyra Encampment, No. 3 ; which was approved and ordered on file.

The following resolution presented by G. M. E. H. P. Bradley, was adopted:

Resolved, That no subordinate Encampment under the jurisdiction of this Grand Encampment be allowed to initiate any member into their said Encampment, unless the candidate has been a member of a subordinate Lodge for at least six months. *Provided,* That the Grand Patriarch shall have power at all times to suspend this rule at his discretion.

The Grand Patriarch called for the nomination of officers for the ensuing year ; when

G. S. William E. Sanford, was nominated for *Grand Patriarch.*

S. W. Richard S. Pratt,	"	"	*G. H. Priest.*
G. Sentinel Isaac Judson,	"	"	*G. S. Warden.*
C. P. John L. Devotion,	"	"	*Grand Scribe.*
G. T. Samuel Bishop,	"	"	*Grand Treasurer.*
D. G. Sentinel Wm. J. Thompson,		"	*G. J. Warden.*
P. G. Patriarch R. S. Hinman,		"	*G Representative.*

On balloting, the aforementioned Patriarchs were severally elected to the offices to which they were nominated.

The officers were then duly installed into their respective offices.

A bill, amounting to seven dollars, for contingent expenses, was presented by P. G. P. Hinman, and ordered to be paid.

No further business appearing, the Grand Encampment closed in ample form.

Attest,   JOHN L. DEVOTION,
Grand Scribe.

<div style="text-align:center">~~~~~~~~~~~~~~</div>

SEMI-ANNUAL SESSION

NEW HAVEN, JANUARY 12, 1844.

The R. W. Grand Encampment of the State of Connecticut convened this day, and was opened in ample form.

PRESENT.

M. W. WILLIAM E. SANFORD, *Grand Patriarch.*
R. W. ISAAC JUDSON, *G. S. Warden.*
R. W. JOHN L. DEVOTION, *G. Scribe.*
R. W. SAMUEL BISHOP, *G. Treasurer.*
R. W. WM. J. THOMPSON, *G. J. Warden.*
  W. BELA LORD, *C. P.*
  W. J. M. ANDRUS, *H. P.*

The minutes of last meeting read and approved.

Grand Treasurer Bishop offered the following resolution, which was adopted.

Resolved, That the Grand Treasurer be authorized to borrow of the Grand Lodge of Connecticut, the sum of one hundred dollars, at six per cent interest per annum.

The following bills were laid before the Grand Encampment, and the same ordered to be paid ; viz :

2

Estate of R. S. Hinman,	-	-	-	$65 50
John Galpin,	-	-	-	-	3 50
William E. Sanford,	-	-	-	-	1 25

The semi-annual report of Palmyra Encampment, No. 3, was presented, and the same accepted and ordered on file.

The following communication from the R. W. Grand Lodge of the State of New York, informing of the expulsion of Perseverance, Lodge No. 17, of the city of New York, for refusing to comply with the mandates of said Grand Lodge, was read and ordered on file :—

I. O. O. F.

Office of the Grand Secretary, Grand Lodge, State of New York,
City of New York, May 5th, 1843.

In Grand Lodge of New York, May Session, 1843.

To the R. W. Grand Encampment of the State of Connecticut, F. L. and T.

Officers and Representatives :

You are hereby notified that Perseverance Lodge, No. 17, of the City of New York, has been *expelled* from communion with the Order, for refusing to comply with the mandates of the R. W. Grand Lodge.

You are therefore requested to notify the several Encampments under your jurisdiction, of the expulsion of said Lodge.

By order,   JNO. G. TREADWELL.
Grand Secretary.

The following communication from the R. W. Grand Lodge of the United States, was read and ordered on file :—

I. O. O. F.

Office of Corresponding and Recording Secretary, R. W.
G. L. U. S., Baltimore, December 20, 1843.

EXTRACT FROM THE JOURNAL OF SEPTEMBER SESSION, 1843.

"*Resolved*, That the Grand Secretaries and Grand Scribes of the several Grand Lodges and Grand Encampments be requested under revision of their Grand Lodges and Grand Encampments, to make out accurate lists of the names and dates of the institution of every Lodge and Encampment under their jurisdiction ; to report the dates at which they came under the jurisdiction of the State Grand Encampments and Grand Lodges —the dates of suspensions, expulsions and reinstatements—and to submit the same to the Grand Corresponding Secretary at least three months previous to the next Annual Communication.

"*Resolved*, That the Grand Corresponding Secretary be directed to procure two appropriate books to be kept as Registers —one for the Lodges and the other for the Encampments under their jurisdiction. That he cause all the Lodges and Encampments in communion with this Grand Lodge to be entered and registered in said books—numbering each of them according to seniority, as the same shall appear from the reports above required and from the documents in his office.

" *Resolved,* That hereafter, in all cases of grant of charter or dispensation by the Grand Lodges, or Grand Encampments— they shall immediately report the same to the Grand Corresponding Secretary, who shall enter the same in the general register, with its proper number, which shall be immediately communicated to the State Grand Lodge, or Grand Encampment, to be inserted in their charter, in addition to its State Number— as G. R——. And that as soon as the appropriate numbers of Lodges or Encampments now in existence shall be declared, they shall in like manner be added to the respective charters.

" *Resolved,* That the Grand Corresponding Secretary be directed to communicate the above to the several Grand Lodges and Encampments."

To   *R. W. G. S. of G. E. of Connecticut.*

Dear Sir and Brother :

In obedience to the aforegoing resolutions you are requested to furnish the information therein required at the earliest practicable moment,   Very respectfully,

Your ob't Serv't,

JAMES L. RIDGELY, *C. S.*

Grand Scribe Devotion, offered the following resolutions, which was adopted.

Resolved, That when a candidate has been rejected by an Encampment, he shall not be received by any Encampment under the jurisdiction of this Grand Encampment, in a less time than one year from the time of such rejection. All applications for initiation unto the Patriarchal branch of the order, must in all cases be made to the nearest Encampment to which such applicant or applicants reside ; nor shall any application for initiation be received by any Encampment which will tend to defeat the provisions of this resolution.

Resolved, That the Grand Scribe be directed to transmit copies of these resolutions to all the Encampments under this jurisdiction.

The committee on Constitution and By-Laws, reported that they were not prepared to lay before the Grand Encampment a Constitution or any By-Laws for adoption at the present session, and asked that the time for reporting the same be extended to the next session ; which was granted.

Grand Treasurer Bishop offered the following resolution, which was adopted :

Resolved, That the Grand Scribe be directed to inform the

Grand Secretary of the Grand Lodge of the United States, that this Grand Encampment has a charter without a seal.

On motion of Grand Treasurer Bishop, a committee of two was appointed to draft appropriate resolutions on the death of Grand Representative HINMAN. Grand Treasurer Bishop and Grand Scribe Devotion was appointed that committee.

The semi-annual report of Sassacus Encampment, No. 1, was presented ; accepted and ordered on file.

The committee appointed to draft resolutions on the subject of the death of Grand Representative Hinman, submitted the following Preamble and Resolutions, which were unanimously adopted :

Whereas, The members of this R. W. Grand Encampment have heard, with profound regret, of the death of our much esteemed brother, ROBINSON S. HINMAN, therefore

Resolved, That the members of this Grand Encampment do sympathize deeply with the friends of the deceased, in their recent loss.

Resolved, That in the death of our highly and much respected brother, the order has sustained a loss of one of the ablest champions of its rights and interests, and the community of a citizen whose courtesy and affability had won the confidence and esteem of all who knew him.

G. M. E. H. P. Charles W. Bradley, offered the following resolution, which was unanimously adopted ; viz :—

Resolved, That when any candidate has been rejected by an Encampment, he shall not be received by any other Encampment under the jurisdiction of this Grand Encampment in a less time than one year from the time of such rejection. All applications for initiation into the Patriarchal branch of the Order, *must,* in all cases, be made to the nearest Encampment to which such applicant or applicants reside—nor shall any application for initiation be *received* by any Encampment which will tend to defeat the provisions of this resolution.

The Grand Treasurer made a report which was accepted.

Hitchcock & Stafford's bill for $30 75, was read, and on motion, was referred to a committee consisting of Grand Treasurer Bishop and H. P. Andrus, with instructions to procure the seal of this Grand Encampment, and settle said bill on the best terms. Said committee were also instructed to settle the account with Sassacus Encampment, No. 1.

No further business offering, the Grand Encampment closed without day, according to the most ancient and honorable customs of the order.

Attest, JOHN L. DEVOTION,
Grand Scribe.

ANNUAL SESSION.

NEW HAVEN, JULY 12, 1844.

The R. W. Grand Encampment of Connecticut, I. O. O. F., convened this day, being the regular annual session, and opened in ample form.

PRESENT.

M. W. WILLIAM E. SANFORD, *Grand Patriarch.*
R. W. JOHN L. DEVOTION, *Grand Scribe.*
R. W. SAMUEL BISHOP, *Grand Treasurer.*
W. BELA LORD, *P. C. P.* and *P. H. P.*
W. WILLIAM L. BREWER, *C. P.*
W. JONATHAN M. ANDRUS, *C. P.*
W. PRELATE DEMICK, *H. P.*
W. JOHN A. LATHROP, *H. P.*

The minutes of last session were read and approved,

The Grand Patriarch stated that he had, since the last session of the Grand Encampment, received a petition from eight Patriarchs of the Royal Purple degree, residing in the city of New London, praying for a charter to open and constitute an Encampment in that place. On the first day of April, 1844, he granted a dispensation, subject to the approval of the Grand Encampment, for opening Unity Encampment, No. 4, and deputized R. W. Grand Scribe, John L. Devotion, and C. P. Giles M. Eaton, who proceeded to the city of New London, on the 22d day of April last, and instituted said Encampment according to the most ancient customs of the order.

The following report of their doings on that occasion was presented by the Grand Patriarch, and on motion it was *Voted,* That the doings of the Grand Patriarch be approved, and that a charter be granted to Unity Encampment, No. 4, of New London.

I. O. O. F.

FRIENDSHIP, LOVE, AND TRUTH.

NORWICH, JULY 5, 1844.

The undersigned respectfully report, that by authority of the within Dispensation, they proceeded to Institute " UNITY ENCAMPMENT, No. 4," I. O. O. F., in the city of New London, on the 23d day of April last, according to the most ancient and honorable customs of the Order.

The following named Patriarchs were elected officers for the present term, which will expire with the month of June ; viz :

Henry Champlain, *Chief Patriarch.*
A. C. Lippitt, *High Priest.*
O. F. Smith, *Senior Warden.*
John Ewen, Jr., *Scribe.*
Calvin Lester, *Treasurer.*
G. W. Brown, *Junior Warden.*
We then initiated eight brothers of " Thames Lodge, No. 9 ;"
four of whom were in a solemn and impressive manner, exalted
to the degree of the Royal Purple.

From the high standing of those into whose hands this branch
of the Order has fallen, in New London, we are led to believe
that this subordinate will prove to be an ornament to our confed-
eracy.   J. L. DEVOTION,
                                GILES M. EATON.

Semi-annual reports from Saccacus Encampment, No. 1, and
Palmyra Encampment, No. 3, were presented and ordered on
file :

The following communication from the Grand Corresponding
Secretary of the Grand Lodge of the United States, was read and
ordered on file :—

I. O. O. F.

Office of Cor. & Rec. Secretary, R. W. G. L. U. S.,
Baltimore, July 6, 1844.

DEAR SIR & BROTHER,
     Your communication on behalf of Grand Encampment
of Connecticut, has been duly received.   In reply, I have to say,
that the omission to attach the seal must have been inadvertent
on the part of the Grand Messenger, whose duty it is, by law,
to prepare such documents ; its omission will not, however, affect
the work of the Encampment, and may be cured at any time
that it is placed in our possession ; I presume the Grand Representative will be here in September, when it will be adjusted.
                    Yours in F. L. and T.,
                        JAS. L. RIDGLEY, *C. S.*
To J. L. DEVOTION, ESQ.,

The Grand Treasurer presented a report relating to the financial affairs of the Grand Encampment ; accepted and ordered
on file.

R. W. Grand Scribe, John L. Devotion, from the committee
appointed at a previous session, reported the following Constitution, By-Laws and Rules of Order, for the government of this
R. W. body, and also a Constitution for subordinate Encampments under this jurisdiction, which were read and unanimously
adopted.

CONSTITUTION

OF THE

RIGHT WORTHY GRAND ENCAMPMENT,

OF THE

I. O. O. F. OF CONNECTICUT, ADOPTED JULY 12, 1841.

ARTICLE I.

SECTION 1. THE R. W. Grand Encampment of Patriarchs of the Indedendent Order of Odd Fellows. of the State of Connecticut, is the Supreme tribunal of all Encampments of Patriarchs in said State.

It possesses by virtue of its charter from the Grand Lodge of the United States, the full power of granting charters to Encampments, and of suspending and taking away the same for proper cause; to pass laws for the regulation and working of Subordinate Encampments; to receive, hear and decide finally, all appeals from them or their members; redress grievances and complaints arising therein; and to do all other acts promotive of the interest of Patriarchs of the order, not in derogation of the Constitution or Laws of the Grand Lodge of the United States, nor inconsistent with the Constitution and Laws of this State, or of the United States.

SEC. 2. The Grand Encampment shall be composed of the past Chief Patriarchs and past High Priests in membership in the Encampments subordinate to this Grand Encampment; and the present Chief Patriarchs and High Priests of said Subordinate Encampments, after they have been duly installed.

SEC. 3. Any member of this Grand Encampment, may by a vote of two-thirds of the members present of the Grand Encampment, be fined, reprimanded, suspended or expelled, for conduct unbecoming a Patriarch.

SEC. 4. All questions before the Grand Encampment shall be decided by a majority of votes given, except on amendments to this Constitution, the adoption and amendment of By-Laws, Rules of Order, and the trial of a member, which shall require a vote of two-thirds of the members present. And no vote in balloting shall be counted, unless given for a candidate in nomination.

ARTICLE II.

SEC. 1. The elective officers of the Grand Encampment shall be,

    1st. Most Worthy Grand Patriarch.

    2d. Most Excellent Grand High Priest.

    3d. Right Worthy Grand Senior Warden.

    4th. Right Worthy Grand Scribe.

    5th. Right Worthy Grand Treasurer.

    6th. Right Worthy Grand Junior Warden.

    7th. Right Worthy Grand Representative to the Grand Lodge of the United States.

And the appointed officers shall consist of

    8th. Worthy Grand Sentinel.

    9th. Worthy Deputy Grand Sentinel, who shall be appointed by the Most Worthy Grand Patriarch, annually, and such others as the By-Laws may require.

SEC. 2. The elective Officers shall be elected annually by ballot. The election and installation shall take place at the regular Annual Session.

SEC. 3. The Most Worthy Grand Patriarch and Most Excellent Grand High Priest shall be chosen from among the Past Chief Patriarchs or Past High Priests. Any other member of the Grand Encampment shall be eligible for the other Grand Offices.

SEC. 4. All vacancies occurring in the Grand Offices shall be filled in the manner of the original selection, and for the residue of the term.

ARTICLE III.

Duties of Grand Officers.

SEC. 1. The Grand Patriarch shall preside at all sessions of the Grand Encampment: he shall preserve order, and decide all questions of order, (an appeal may be had from such decisions to the Grand Encampment.) He may appoint any Grand Officer *pro tem.* in case of the absence or disqualification of the regular Grand Officer: he may order special sessions of the Grand Encampment whenever he may deem proper ; he shall appoint all committees, unless otherwise ordered by the Grand Encampment: he shall in all cases, except on an appeal from his own decision, give the casting vote when the Grand Encampment is equally divided. In cases of emergency, he may grant dispensations to Subordinate Encampments in all such matters as he may deem promotive of the interest of the order, not inconsistent with the usages thereof.

SEC. 2. The M. E. Grand High Priest shall preside and act in the absence of Grand Patriarch. In case of the office of

Grand Patriarch becoming vacant, by any cause, he shall have the full powers of Grand Patriarch until the next regular session, and the vacancy being filled. It shall be his duty to perform according to his office, at the installation of the Grand Officers.

Sec. 3. The Grand Senior Warden shall assist the Grand Patriarch in presiding and preserving order. And in the absence of the Grand Patriarch and M. E. High Priest, he shall preside.

Sec. 4. The Grand Scribe shall attend all regular and special sessions of the Grand Encampment, and record the proceedings: he shall notify the members of the Grand Encampment of all special sessions. He shall prepare charters granted for Subordinate Encampments ; and perform such other duties as may be required by the Constitution and Laws of the Grand Encampment.

Sec. 5. The Grand Treasurer shall receive and take charge of all funds belonging to the Grand Encampment, and pay all orders passed by the Grand Encampment, when properly attested : he shall make a report of the receipts and expenditures annually, and submit his books of accounts for examination, whenever required : he shall give bond with surety to the two first named Grand Officers, for the faithful discharge of his duties.

Sec. 6. The Grand Junior Warden shall open and close the Grand Encampment according to his office ; and he shall introduce into the Grand Encampment all new members, after their credentials have been found correct.

Sec. 7. The Grand Sentinel shall have charge of the inner entrance to the Grand Encampment, and permit none to enter or depart without the proper formalities.

Sec. 8. The Deputy Grand Sentinel shall have charge of the outer entrance, and assist the Grand Sentinel in the performance of his duties.

ARTICLE IV.

Sec. 1. There shall be two regular sessions of the Grand Encampment in each year, the first shall be held on the Thursday following the second Wednesday of July, and be styled the *Regular Annual Session ;* the other shall be held on the Thursday following the second Wednesday of January, and be styled the *Regular Semi-annual Session.*

Sec. 2. Special sessions shall be held at the call of the Grand Patriarch.

Sec. 3. The Grand Encampment may adjourn from time to time, until the business of any session is completed.

3

Sec. 4. All sessions of the Grand Encampment shall be held in the City of New Haven.

ARTICLE V.

Sec. 1. Seven R. P. D. Patriarchs, or more, in good standing in the order, and members of Lodges subordinate to the Grand Lodge of the State of Connecticut, may petition the Grand Encampment in writing, for a charter to constitute an Encampment of Patriarchs; which petition must be accompanied by the sum of *Thirty Dollars,* as the Charter fee. Should the Charter be granted, the Grand Patriarch, or such other qualified Patriarch as he may delegate, shall open the Encampment and present the Charter. Travelling expenses, if any are incurred, to be borne by the Encampment opened.

Sec. 2. The terms of the Subordinate Encampments shall consist of at least six regular sessions, commencing with the first regular sessions in July and January. All terms shall be completed on the day the succeeding one commences.

Sec. 3. The Subordinates shall at the end of each term, report to the Grand Encampment, at its next regular session, the names of the Patriarchs initiated—admitted by card—reinstated —and of those exalted to the R. P. Degree—the number on whom degrees have been conferred—the names of Patriarchs withdrawn by card—deceased—suspended or expelled—the names of brothers rejected—the result of the election of Officers —the number of P. C. P. and P. H. P—the amount of all monies due the Grand Encampment—*and the time of their meetings.*

Sec. 4. At the annual session, each subordinate Encampment shall, in addition, report a complete list of its members, arranged according to rank in the Encampment.

Sec. 5. Each Encampment, subordinate to this Grand Encampment, shall pay semi-annually, *ten per cent.* on the minimum rates fixed by this Grand Encampment, on all sums received for initiations, depositing cards, degrees and dues.

Sec. 6. Should any Subordinate Encampment for two regular sessions of the Grand Encampment, neglect or refuse to make its returns and pay its dues, the members from such Encampments shall not be entitled to vote, until the returns are made, and dues paid. And should such subordinate Encampment continue for two years, to neglect or refuse, its charter shall be forfeited.

ARTICLE VI.

Sec. 1. Any proposal to alter, amend, suspend or annul this Constitution, or any part thereof, must be proposed at a regular session in writing ; and if approved by four members, the Grand Scribe shall, within thirty days thereafter, notify each Subordinate Encampment under this jurisdiction, of the proposition. And, if at the next regular session, it is adpoted by two-thirds of the members present, it shall prevail, and become a part of the Constitution ; otherwise it shall not.

Sec. 2. This Grand Encampment is fully authorized to adopt or amend at any regular session, such By-Laws and Rules of Order, as two-thirds of the members present may approve.

ARTICLE VII.

Sec. 1. Seven members shall constitute a quorum for business, provided, there is present a representation from two Subordinates.

BY-LAWS

OF THE

RIGHT WORTHY GRAND ENCAMPMENT,

I. O. O. F., OF CONNECTICUT.

ARTICLE I.

Sec. 1. The R. W. Grand Encampment of Patriarchs of the State of Connecticut, will assemble at the sessions held in January at 2 o'clock, P. M., and at the sessions held in July at 2 o'clock, P. M., and may adjourn from time to time until the business of the session is completed.

Sec. 2. Should a quorum be present, the Grand Officers provided by the Constitution to preside, shall proceed to open the Grand Encampment within thirty minutes of the time of meeting. But should there not be a quorum at the expiration of the time, the members assembled may adjourn the meeting until such time as they judge expedient, not exceeding twenty-four hours.

Sec. 3. When all the Grand Officers provided by the Constitution for presiding at the meeting are absent, the chair may be taken by a Past Grand Patriarch, should any be present, otherwise, by any member who may be called to it by a majority of the members present.

Sec. 4. All the meetings of the Grand Encampment for business and receiving members, shall be held in the Grand Encampment Degree. And for conferring the Past official Degree, shall be held in those Degrees respectively.

ARTICLE II.

Sec. 1. In all cases where an Encampment shall have been suspended or expelled, or its Charter shall have been forfeited, the charter, funds, books, properties and effects of all kinds, shall revert to the Grand Encampment. And it shall be the duty of the last installed officers of such Encampment, to deliver immediately to the Grand Patriarch, or the brother deputed by him to receive them, such funds and other effects as the Encampment may have claim to.

Sec. 2. Each Subordinate Encampment under this jurisdiction, shall have a proper Seal. And all official communications shall be sealed therewith.

Sec. 3. The following shall be the form of a certificate of a member of the Grand Encampment:

—— Encampment, No. ——, I. O. O. F.

To the R. W. Grand Encampment ⎱
of Connecticut, I. O. of O. F.   ⎰

This is to certify that [C. P. or H. P.]   was elected and installed [C. P. or H. P.] of this Encampment, on the —— day of ——, 18 , and is therefore entitled to a seat as a member of the Grand Encampment, agreeable to the provisions of the Constitution.

In testimony whereof, We hereunto affix our hands,
[**L. S.**]   and the Seal of our Encampment, this —— day of —— 18 .

—— ——, *C. P.*
—— ——, *H. P.*

Attest,   —— ——, *Scribe.*

Sec. 4. The following shall be the form of a certificate of a P. C. P. and P. H. P.:

—— Encampment, No. ——, I. O. O. F.

To the R. W. Grand Encampment ⎱
of Connecticut, I. O. of O. F.   ⎰

This is to certify that [C. P. or H. P.] —— has served his term of office as [C. P. or H. P.] in this Encampment, term ending —— 18 , and is therefore entitled to the past official degree of [C. P. or H. P.]

In testimony whereof, We hereunto affix our hands,
[**L. S.**]   and the Seal of our Encampment, this —— day of —— 18 .

—— ——, *C. P.*
—— ——, *H. P.*

Attest,   —— ——, *Scribe.*

RULES OF ORDER.

I.—ORDER OF BUSINESS.

After a quorum shall be ascertained to be present, the following shall be the order of business, viz :

1. The Grand Patriarch shall request the brethren to clothe themselves in proper regalia, and direct the Grand officers and members to take their respective stations.

2. The G. J. W. will report on the safe condition of the Grand Encampment.

3. The Grand Patriarch will call up the Grand Encampment while the G. H. P. performs the duties of his office.

4. Proclamation will be made of the opening of the Grand Encampment.

5. The minutes of the last session read, and if no objection be made to any part thereof, they shall stand approved without vote.

6. New members admitted and instructed.

7. Committees report by seniority.

8. Unfinished business acted on by priority.

9. New business.

10. Closing, (or adjournment,) in form.

The order of business, as here arranged, may, at any time, for a particular occasion, be changed or dispensed with, by a special two-third vote of the Grand Encampment.

II. OF DECORUM.

During the continuance of the meeting, the most decorous silence must be observed ; the officers and members retaining their respective seats, and no one leaving the room without the permission of the M. W. Grand Patriarch, nor entering without the consent of the R. W. Grand Senior Warden.

Every officer and member shall be designated in debate, or otherwise, by his proper office or title, according to his standing in the order.

· No member shall be permitted to vote or speak, unless clothed in regalia appropriate to his rank and station.

III.—OF THE CHAIR.

The Grand Patriarch while presiding, shall state every question coming before the Grand Encampment, and immediately before putting it to vote, shall ask : "*Is the Grand Encampment ready for the question ?*" He shall pronounce the votes and decisions of the Grand Encampment, on all subjects.   His decisions

on all questions of order shall be without debate, unless entertaining doubts on the point, he invite it.   And he shall have the
privilege of speaking only on such questions from the chair.
When his decision has been appealed from, the question shall be
put thus : *" Will the Grand Encampment sustain the chair in
its decision ?"*

IV.—OF DEBATE.

Every member when he speaks or offers a motion, shall rise
and respectfully address the chair, and when he has finished he
shall sit down.

While speaking, he shall confine himself to the question under
debate, avoiding all personality and indecorous language, as well
as any reflection upon the Grand Encampment or its members.

Should two or more members rise to speak at the same time,
the chair shall decide which shall be entitled to the floor.

No member shall disturb another in his speech, unless to call
him to order.

If a member while speaking, shall be called to order, at the
request of the chair, he shall cease speaking and take his seat
until the question of order is determined, when, if permitted, he
may again proceed.

No member shall speak more than once on the same question,
until all the members wishing to speak, shall have had an opportunity to do so ; nor more than twice without permission
from the chair.   But no member shall have the privilege of
speaking more than once on a question of order, after appeal
from the decision of the chair.

V.—OF QUESTIONS AND VOTES.

When any communication, petition, or memorial is presented,
before it is read, or any vote taken on it, a brief statement of its
contents shall be made by the introducer or the chair, and after
it has been read, a brief notice of the purport shall be entered on
the journal.

No motion shall be subject to action, until seconded and stated
by the chair ; and at the desire of any member, shall be reduced
to writing.

When a blank is to be filled, the question shall be taken first
upon the highest sum or number, and the longest time proposed.

Any member may call for a division of a question when the
sense will admit of it.

When a question is before the Grand Encampment, no motion shall be received, unless to adjourn, the previous question, to
lay on the table, to postpone indefinately, to postpone to a certain time, to refer, or to amend.   And these shall have precedence in the order herein arranged ; the three first of which
shall be decided without debate.

After any question, except one of indefinate postponement has been decided, any two members who voted in the majority, may at the same or next succeeding meeting, move for a reconsideration thereof.

The previous question can be called for by two members, if seconded by a majority, and shall be put in this form,—" *Shall the main question be now put ?*"—if carried, all amendments not already adopted, shall be precluded, and the main question be taken without debate.

When one-fifth of the members rise in favor of taking a question by ayes and nays, they shall be ordered to be so recorded.

Every member present shall vote on any question before the Grand Encampment, unless he is personally interested in the result, or has been excused by the Grand Encampment, or is othwise incapacitated.

CONSTITUTION

OF THE

SUBORDINATE ENCAMPMENTS,

OF THE

I. O. O. F. OF CONNECTICUT, ADOPTED JULY 12, 1844.

PREAMBLE.

For the purpose of ensuring uniformity in the Patriarchal Order within this jurisdiction, the Grand Encampment of the State of Connecticut, the Supreme tribunal of all Encampments of Patriarchs within its limits, without whose sanction and control, no Encampment can exist, ordains the following Articles as the Constitution of the Subordinate Encampments of Patriarchs.

ARTICLE I.

This Encampment shall be constituted by at least *seven* members of the R. P. Degree, and shall be hailed and entitled, ——

Encampment, No. ——, I. O. O. F. of Connecticut, and shall possess the full powers and privileges of a Subordinate Encampment, holding a legal, unreclaimed and valid Charter, duly granted and formally presented by the Grand Encampment of the State of Connecticut.

ARTICLE II.

OF MEMBERSHIP.

First Section—Admissions, &c.

Clause 1. No person shall be initiated into this Encampment, who is not a scarlet degree member of a Subordinate Lodge under the jurisdiction of the Grand Lodge of Connecticut, nor for a less sum than ten dollars, which shall include all the Degrees.

Clause 2. The name of a person offered for initiation, must be proposed in writing, by two members, stating the Lodge of which he is a member, and his residence, which must be entered on the record, and the subject referred to three Patriarchs for investigation, who shall report at the succeeding regular* meeting—when the candidate may be balloted for, with ball ballots, and if *one* black ball appears against him, he shall be rejected, and so declared.

Clause 3. A Patriarch of the Order wishing to become a member, shall present his card from the Encampment of which he was formerly a member, which shall be referred to a committee of three, and in other respects disposed of as provided by clause second, for other applicants : and on being admitted, shall pay a sum of not less than five dollars.

Second Section—Contributions and Benefits.

Clause 1. The regular contributions to the Encampment fund shall not be at less rate than twenty-five cents per month, to be determined by the By-Laws ; and the Encampment shall suspend all members who refuse or neglect payment of the sums so determined, for twelve months.

Clause 2. It shall be optional with this Encampment to pay benefits to its members : but when any is paid, it shall be such amount as shall be fixed upon by the By-Laws, and no Patriarch, shall be entitled to benefits who is indebted to the Encampment for dues over six months.

Clause 3. In case of the death of a Patriarch who shall be qualified as provided by Clause 2d, there shall be allowed from

---

* Amended by striking out " regular," so as to read, " at the succeeding meeting," &c.

the Encampment, a sum not less than fifteen dollars, to defray the expense of burial, which shall be paid over without delay to the deceased brother's nearest of kin. The C. P. in the absence of competent relations, shall assist in taking charge of the funeral, and receive account of disbursments.

Third Section—Penalties and Trials.

Clause 1. Any Patriarch who shall violate any of the principles of the order, or offend against these Articles or the By-Laws, shall be subject to be fined reprimanded, suspended or expelled, as the By-Laws may direct, ancient usage require, or the Encampment determine.

Clause 2. Every member shall be entitled to a fair trial for any offense involving reprimand, suspension, or expulsion; but no member of this Encampment shall be put on trial, unless charges, duly specifying his offense, be submitted in writing to the Encampment by two or more brothers of the Order, except when made liable by non-payment to the Encampment, or when suspended, or expelled, by the Lodge of which he is member.

Clause 3. When charges have been preferred against a Patriarch in proper manner, or any matters of grievance between Patriarchs be brought before the Encampment, they shall be referred to a special committee of five members, who shall, if possible, be chosen from among the peers of the implicated Patriarch; and they shall, with as little delay as the case will admit, summon the parties, and examine and determine the matter in question; and if not involving the expulsion or suspension of a member, or no appeal be taken from their decision to the Encampment, it shall be final without further action from the Encampment. Should the committee be convinced of the necessity of suspending or expelling a member, they shall submit a motion for the purpose to the Encampment for action.

Clause 4. When a motion for the expulsion or suspension of a Patriarch shall have been submitted in due form, it shall be announced at the regular monthly Session when submitted, and made the special order of business for the next regular monthly Session: and the accused shall be summoned to be in attendance at the Encampment on the time when it may have been determined to consider the question; at which time, whether the implicated Patriarch be present or not, the Encampment may proceed to consider and determine it; two-thirds of the members present voting in favor of the motion, it shall be carried;—and the Encampment shall be fully competent while such motion is under consideration, to vary the penalty from the original motion.

Clause 5. When the decision of the Committee appointed under Clause 3d, for the adjustment of grievances, shall not be satisfactory to all parties, either of those interested shall have

4

the privilege of appeal to the Encampment: and at the time appointed for trying the appeal, the committee shall present to the Encampment in writing the grounds on which their decision was founded, and the parties shall have the privilege of being heard before the Encampment, and the Encampment shall determine the correctness of the decision of the committee by a majority of votes present.

Clause 6. Any Patriarch feeling aggrieved by the decision of the Encampment against him, is entitled to an appeal to the Grand Encampment for a new trial; if informality or want of fairness be shown on the former trial. On the command of the Grand Encampment, the Patriarch may be tried anew for the same offence.

Clause 7. Any Patriarch having been suspended or expelled, notice thereof shall be sent to all the Encampments under the jurisdiction of the Grand Encampment of Connecticut; and a Patriarch who has been legally expelled, shall not be again admitted to membership, without the consent of the Grand Encampment.

ARTICLE III.

OF OFFICERS.

First Section—Elective and appointed Officers.

Clause 1. The elective Officers of the Encampment shall consist of a C. P., H. P., S. W., Scribe, Treasurer, and J. W., who shall serve a regular term each. However, when deemed necessary, the Encampment may elect in addition, an Assistant Scribe to serve for one year.

Clause 2. The appointed officers shall be a Gn, Ge, 1st W., 2d W., 3d W., 4th W., 1st G. of T., 2d G. of T., 1st S. of N., and 2d S. of N., who shall serve a regular term each.

Second Section—Duties of Officers.

The duties of the various officers shall be, as laid down in the charges of their office, and as specified by these Articles, and the By-Laws of the Encampment.

Third Section—Election, &c.

Clause 1. No Patriarch shall be eligible for C. P. or H. P. unless he has been elected to and discharged the duties of some other elective office; nor shall any Patriarch be eligible to the other elective offices until he has been appointed to, and discharged the duties of some appointed office. And all officers shall be eligible for re-election except the C. P. and H. P., who shall not be when any qualified Patriarchs are in nomination, until one term after passing the chairs respectively. And a majority of all the valid votes shall be necessary to election.

Clause 2. The nomination and election of the elective officers shall take place, on the last regular monthly session in each term. And the installation of the officers shall take place at the first regular monthly session in the succeeding one.

Clause 3. Any officer absenting himself for more than three successive Sessions, his seat may be declared vacant by a vote of the Encampment. And all vacancies shall be filled in the manner of the former selection, to serve the residue of the term; and officers so serving shall be entitled to the full honors of the term.

ARTICLE IV.

SESSIONS, TERMS, AND RETURNS.

First Section —Sessions.

Clause 1. The first regular Sessions held in each month, shall be styled the " regular monthly Sessions :" and those succeeding, shall be styled the " regular adjourned Sessions."*

Clause 2. Seven Patriarchs shall constitute a quorum for business : which shall be transacted in the R. P. Degree.

Second Section—Terms.

Regular semi-annual terms, consisting of not less than one regular Session in each month, shall commence on the first regular Session of July· and January only : and all terms shall end on the day on which the succeeding ones commence.

Third Section—Returns.

Clause 1. It shall be the duty of the last past officers to prepare and forward to the Grand Encampment immediately, on the installation of the Officers, the result of the elections, and a regular report of the work of the term, including the names of those initiated, admitted by card, admitted, advanced and exalted—rejected—withdrawn by card—suspended or expelled, and the cause thereof—reinstated and deceased—the whole number in membership—the amount of receipts—and the result of the election of Officers, accompanied by whatever amount may be due to the Grand Encampment.

Clause 2. It shall be the duty of the Encampment also to forward to the Grand Encampment in like manner, up to the first day of July annually, a full return of the members of the Encampment ranked according to the Degrees attained, and a statement of the number of Patriarchs relieved by the Encamp-

---

* Amended—see page· 30. ·

ment in the past year : the number of widowed families relieved—the number of Patriarchs buried—with the amount of moneys applied to each of these purposes—designating the amount paid for the education of orphans.

Fourth Section—Forfeiture of Charter.

Should this Encampment fail to make its returns, as required by the Third Section of this Article, for two years, it shall thereby forfeit its Charter and become extinct, unless by a vote of the Grand Encampment it be otherwise ordered, and it shall be the duty of the last installed officers to transmit or surrender to the Grand Patriarch, (or such other Patriarch as may be appointed by the Grand Encampment to receive them,) the charter, books, papers, furniture and funds of the Encampment.

ARTICLE V.

DEGREES.

First Section—Eligibility for Degrees.

Every Patriarch shall be eligible for degrees immediately on being initiated, but not more than three degrees shall be conferred on a Patriarch at the same Session, unless the most urgent necessity be proved, and two-thirds of the members present vote in favor thereof.

Second Section—Rates of Degrees.

No candidate shall be initiated until he has paid a sum of not less than ten dollars which shall entitle him to all the degrees.

ARTICLE VI.

AMENDMENTS &c.

First Section—Amendments.

Clause 1. When doubts arise of the true meaning of any part of these Articles, it shall be determined by the Grand Encampment.

Clause 2. These Articles nor any part thereof, shall not be altered, amended, suspended or annulled, except on motion made in the Grand Encampment.

Second Section—By-Laws.

This Encampment shall stand fully invested with power to adopt such By-Laws and resolutions from time to time, as may be deemed expedient, provided they do not in any wise contravene any part of these Articles, the Laws and Constitution of the Grand Encampment, or the principles of the Order.

The Grand Patriarch called for the nomination of officers for the ensuing year ; when the following nominations were made,

For *Grand Patriarch,* John L. Devotion, of No. 3.
" *G. M. E. H. P.* J. M. Andrus, of No. 1.
" *G. S. Warden,* William L. Brewer, of No. 3.
" *G. Scribe,* Prelate Demick, of No. 1.
" *G. Treasurer,* Samuel Bishop, of No. 1.
" *G. J. Warden,* John A. Lathrop, of No. 4.
" *G. Rep. to G. L. U. S.* William E. Sanford, of No. 1.

The Grand Patriarch appointed Grand Treasurer Bishop, and P. C. P. Henry Champlain, tellers.

The Grand Encampment proceeded to ballot for the several Grand officers, and the above mentioned Patriarchs were severally elected to the offices for which they were nominated.

The officers were then duly installed into their respective offices.

The following resolutions offered by R. W. Grand Scribe Demick, was unanimously adopted :

Resolved, That the Grand Patriarch be authorized to procure the printing of two hundred copies of the Constitution, By-Laws and Rules of Order of this Grand Encampment, and the Constitution for subordinate Encampments, and that he procure such other printing as he may deem necessary, and draw on the treasurer for the payment of the same.

On motion of Grand Treasurer Bishop, it was

Resolved, That the R. W. G. Representative be authorized to draw on the treasurer for the sum of thirty-five dollars, to defray his expenses in attending the Grand Lodge of the United States.

On motion of G. S. W. William L. Brewer, it was

Resolved, That the Grand Representative be directed to procure such books of the Grand Lodge of the United States as he may think proper for this Grand Encampment, and that he be authorized to draw an order on the treasurer for the payment of the same.

On motion, the Grand Scribe was directed to inform Oriental Encampment, No. 2, that no returns have been received by this Grand Encampment, and request that they will comply with the Constitution.

William E. Sanford's bill for one dollar and twenty-five cents ; and J. L. Devotion's bill for fifty cents, were presented and ordered paid.

No further business appearing, the Grand Encampment closed in ample form, according to the most ancient and honorable customs of the Order.

Attest,   P. DEMICK,
                               Grand Scribe.

SPECIAL SESSION.

New Haven, August 27, 1844.

The R. W. Grand Encampment of the State of Connecticut, I. O. O. F., convened this day in special session, and opened in ample form.

PRESENT.

M. W. JOHN L. DEVOTION, *Grand Patriarch.*
M. E. JONATHAN M. ANDRUS, *G. H. Priest.*
R. W. PRELATE DEMICK, *G. Scribe.*
R. W. SAMUEL BISHOP, *Grand Treasurer.*
M. W. WILLIAM E. SANFORD, *P. G. Patriarch.*
R. W. ISAAC JUDSON, *P. G. S. Warden, p. t.*
R. W. BELA LORD, *P. C. Patriarch.*

The object of the session having been stated by R. W. Grand Scribe, the Grand Representative elect, William E. Sanford, tendered his resignation of said office ; and on motion of Grand Treasurer Bishop, it was *Voted,* That his resignation be accepted.

On motion of P. G. Patriarch William E. Sanford,

Resolved, That the Grand Encampment, proceed to the nomination and election of Grand Representative to the Grand Lodge of the United States. Whereupon, the Grand Patriarch called for nominations; P. C. P. Bela Lord, then nominated Grand Treasurer Samuel Bishop, for said Representative. No other nominations being made, a ballot was taken, and Grand Treasurer Bishop was declared duly elected Grand Representative to the Grand Lodge of the United States.

The following amendments to the Constitution of subordinate Encampments enacted and ordained at the last annual session of this Grand Encampment, were offered by Grand Scribe P. Demick, and unanimously adopted :

In Article II. section 1, clause 2d, page 24, 5th line of said clause, (as printed,) strike out the word " *regular.*"

In Article IV. section 1, clause 1, page 27, (as printed,) 3d line of said clause, strike out the words, " *the regular,*" and insert after " adjourned," " *and special.*" It will then read, ' *shall be styled, adjourned and special sessions.*"

No further business offering, on motion of Grand Treasurer Bishop, the Grand Encampment was closed in ample form.

Attest,   P. DEMICK,
                                          Grand Scribe.

SEMI-ANNUAL SESSION

New Haven, January 9th, 1845.

The R. W. Grand Encampment, I. O. O. F. of Connecticut, convened this day, being the semi-annual session, and was opened in ample form.

PRESENT.

M. W. JOHN L. DEVOTION, *Grand Patriarch.*
M. E. JONATHAN M. ANDRUS, *Grand High Priest.*
R. W. WILLIAM L. BREWER, *Grand S. Warden.*
R. W. PRELATE DEMICK, *Grand Scribe.*
R. W. SAMUEL BISHOP, *Grand Treasurer.*
M. E. CHARLES W. BRADLEY, *Grand High Priest.*
W. BELA LORD, *P. C. P.* and *P. H. P.*

The minutes of last session were read and approved.

N. C. Hall, *H. P.* of No. 1 ; Edward W. Eells, *H. P.* of No. 3 ; J. Greenwood, Jr., *P. C. P.*, and Munson H. Shepard, *P. H. P.* and *C. P.* of No. 5 ; Thos. C. Simpson, *H. P.*, and Origen Utley, *C. P.*, and Erastus H. Booth, *P. C. P.* of No. 6 ; A. M. Gordon, *C. P.*, and John W. Johnson, *H. P.* of No. 7, presented their credentials and were instructed in the Grand Encampment degree, and took their seats as members.

The Grand Patriarch submitted his Semi-annual Report, **as** follows:

R. W. Grand Officers and Patriarchs :

We are again assembled for the purpose of legislating for the Order here committed to our charge.

It is with no ordinary pleasure that I inform you of the continued prosperity of this branch of our Order ; at no time since its establishment in this State, has it been in a more flourishing condition.

On the 19th day of August, I received a petition from seven Patriarchs residing in the town of Danbury, county of Fairfield, for an Encampment to be located at that place, and known and hailed by the style and title of " Devotion Encampment, No. 5, I. O. O. F." I accordingly granted a Dispensation, subject to your approval, and on the 28th day of Aug., accompanied by R. W. Grand Senior Warden Brewer, and R. W. Grand Treasurer Bishop, I proceeded to institute the same, according to the most ancient ceremonial of the order. —— were on this occasion exalted to the Royal Purple degree.

On the 26th day of September, I received a petition from seven qualified Patriarchs, for an Encampment to be located at

Middletown, in the county of Middlesex. I granted a Dispensation, subject to your approval, and on the 27th day of the same month, I proceeded to institute the same, under the style and title of "SOWHEAG ENCAMPMENT, No. 6, I. O. O. F." On this occasion, I received the assistance of C. P. Palmer, of Oriental Encampment, No. 2, and Patriarch Converse, of Palmyra Encampment, No. 3 ; one brother was advanced to the degree of the Royal Purple.

On the 7th day of December, I received another petition from seven Patriarchs residing in the city of Hartford, for an Encampment, to be located in that city, and known and hailed by the style and title of "MIDIAN ENCAMPMENT, No. 7, I. O. O. F." I accordingly granted a Dispensation, subject to your approval, and on the 24th day of the same month, assisted by P. C. P. Booth and H. P. Simpson, of Sowheag Encampment, No. 6, and Patriarch Converse of Palmyra Encampment, No. 3, I proceeded to institute the same, according to the established usages of the order. On this occasion, six brothers were solemnly and impressively admitted to a knowledge of the sublime degree of the Royal Purple.

I would suggest to you, the propriety of making some provision for the appointment of some qualified Patriarch, whose duty it shall be to superintend the order in their respective Encampment, and install the officers.

JOHN L. DEVOTION,
Grand Patriarch.

Grand Treasurer Bishop offered the following resolution, which was unanimously adopted, viz :

Resolved, That the doings of the M. W. Patriarch be approved by this Grand Encampment, and charters granted to Devotion Encampment, No. 5, of Danbury ; Sowheag Encampment, No. 6, of Middletown ; and Midian Encampment, No. 7, of Hartford.

Semi-annual reports were received from Sassacus Encampment, No. 1 ; Oriental, No. 2 ; Palmyra, No. 3 ; Devotion, No. 5 ; and Sowheag, No. 6, each accompanied by the amount due the Grand Encampment, as per said reports. No report or dues were received from Unity Encampment, No. 4, of New London.

The Grand Patriarch appointed Grand Senior Warden Brewer, and Patriarchs Simpson and Eells a *Committee of Finance,* and Patriarch John Greenwood, Jr., *G. Sentinel,* and Patriarch E. H Booth, *D. G. Sentinel.*

The Grand Senior Warden offered the following resolution, which was unanimously adopted ; viz :

Resolved, That so much of the Grand Patriarch's report as relates to the appointment of some qualified Patriarch for each subordinate Encampment under this jurisdiction, to superintend the order, and install officers in their respective Encampments, be referred to a special committee of two.

On the passage of the above resolution, the Grand Patriarch appointed Grand Senior Warden Brewer, and Grand Sentinel Greenwood, that committee.

The committee of Finance submitted the following report, viz :

The Finance committee to whom was referred the accounts of Grand Treasurer Bishop, would respectfully report, That they have examined said accounts, and found them to be correct. They find a balance due the Grand Encampment of one hundred and nineteen dollars and sixty cents.

All which is respectfully submitted,

WILLIAM L. BREWER,	*Finance*
THOMAS C. SIMPSON,	*Committee.*
E. W. EELLS,	

The committee also recommended that the Grand Treasurer be authorized to pay the amount due the Grand Lodge.

Report and recommendation accepted.

The special committee raised on the resolution of G. S. W. Brewer, reported by submitting the following resolution, which was unanimously adopted:

Resolved, That there shall be appointed semi-annually, by the Grand Patriarch, from among the past chief Patriarchs or past High Priests, who are not holding office in their Encampment, a Deputy Grand Patriarch for each Encampment under this jurisdiction, whose duty it shall be to install officers and have a general supervision of the interests of the order, in their respective Encampments.

All which is respectfully submitted.

W. L. BREWER,
JOHN GREENWOOD, Jr.

Patriarch E. W. Eells, of No. 3, submitted the following resolution, which was unanimously adopted ;

Resolved, That all officers of this Grand Encampment, residing out of the city of New Haven, shall be allowed for travel and attendance at the sessions of the Grand Encampment, the same amounts as are provided for attendance on the Grand Lodge, by Art. V. of the By-Laws of the Grand Lodge of this State. *Provided however,* That no officer of this Grand Encampment shall receive pay for travel and attendance, whose expenses are paid by the Grand Lodge, or by the subordinate Lodge or Encampment of which he is a member.

The committee of Finance reported bills amounting to four dollars, twelve and half cents ; ordered paid.

5

The following resolution offered by Patriarch E. H. Booth, was unanimously adopted;

Resolved, That in all elections throughout this jurisdiction, no blank shall be counted, or in any manner regarded as a vote or ballot. And all ballots having on them the name of any person not in regular nomination, shall be treated as blanks, and wholly disregarded; so that the regular nominated candidate having a clear majority of ballots, cast for regular nominated candidates, shall be declared duly elected.

On motion, *Voted,* that the cypher as arranged by the M. W. Grand Patriarch, be adopted as the cypher of this Grand Encampment.

On a call for the sense of the Grand Encampment, the Grand Representative was instructed to attend on the anticipated extra session of the Grand Lodge of the United States, should it be holden.

On motion, it was ordered by this Grand Encampment, that no Patriarch shall be installed into office, or occupy any official seat or station in any Encampment under this jurisdiction, while charges are standing against him, which have been legally preferred, and which involve suspension or expulsion.

On motion of Patriarch M. A. Shepard, the following resolution was adopted; viz:

Resolved, That should the chair of Chief Patriarch become vacant in consequence of charges preferred against a Chief Patriarch, the said chair shall be assumed in person or by proxy by the Deputy Grand Patriarch, until such time as the Chief Patriarch is restored, or the chair filled by a subsequent election.

The Grand Patriarch announced the appointments of Deputy Grand Patriarch, as follows; viz:

Isaac Judson, of Sassacus Encampment, No. 1.
R. S. Pratt, of Oriental   "   No. 2.
Wm. L. Brewer, of Palmyra   "   No. 3.
Henry Champlain, of Unity   "   No. 4.
J. Greenwood, Jr. of Devotion   "   No. 5.
E. H. Booth, of Sowheag   "   No. 6.
          of Midian   "   No. 7.

On motion, the Grand Scribe was directed to address Oriental Encampment, No. 2, requesting them to forward to this Grand Encampment, the sum of $11 57, supposed by them to be due to the Grand Lodge of the United States.

Also, to request Unity Encampment, No. 4, to forward to the Grand Scribe, their semi-annual report, due the 9th inst. together with the amount of dues.

No further business offering, the Grand Encampment closed in ample form, according to the most ancient and honorable customs of the order.

Attest,   PRELATE DEMICK,
                               Grand Scribe.

ANNUAL SESSION.

NEW HAVEN, JULY 10, 1845.

The R. W. Grand Encampment of Connecticut, I. O. O. F., convened this day, and opened in ample form.

PRESENT.

M. W. JOHN L. DEVOTION, *Grand Patriarch.*
M. E. JONATHAN M. ANDRUS, *G. H. Priest.*
R. W. WILLIAM L. BREWER, *G. S. Warden.*
R. W. PRELATE DEMICK, *G. Scribe.*
R. W. SAMUEL BISHOP, *G. Treasurer.*
R. W. NEWEL C. HALL, *G. J. Warden, p. t.*
W. JOHN GREENWOOD, Jr., *G. Sentinel.*
W. ERASTUS H. BOOTH, *D. G. Sentinel.*

Also P. G. P. William E. Sanford ; P. M. E. G. H. P. Chas. Wm. Bradley, and a numerous representation from subordinate Encampments.

The minutes of the last session were read and approved.

The committee on credentials, submitted the following report ; to wit :

To the R. W. Grand Encampment of Connecticut :

The Committee on credentials report,

That the following Patriarchs have presented certificates which are in due form ; they are therefore entitled to seats in this Grand Encampment ; viz :

H. P. Lucius A. Thomas, of No. 1.
H. P. John C. Palmer, of No. 2.
C. P. Junius M. Willey, of No. 2.
C. P. H. C. Bridgham, of No. 3.
H. P. David Young, of No. 3.
H. P. John S. Parmelee, of No. 6.
H. P. Aaron Morley, of No. 7.
C. P. A. B. Beers, of No. 8.
H. P. Samuel B. Brittan, of No. 8.

O. F. Smith, and Geo. W. Brown, are without certificates, but are returned by the D. G. Patriarch of Unity Encampment, No. 4, as having been installed into office in said Encampment, and as being entitled to seats in this Grand Encampment.

WM. L. BREWER, ⎫
M. A. SHEPARD, ⎬ *Committee.*
JONA. M. ANDRUS, ⎭

Report accepted, and the committee discharged.

On motion of P. M. E. G. H. P. Chas. W. Bradley,

Resolved, That C. P. Orrin F. Smith, and H. P. George W. Brown, of No. 4, be admitted to the Grand Encampment degree, and that they be directed to forward to the Grand Scribe their certificate, immediately on their return to their Encampment.

The aforementioned Patriarchs were then introduced, and admitted to the Grand Encampment degree, and took their seats as members of this body.

The G. S. Warden called the attention of the Grand Encampment, to the report of the M. W. Grand Patriarch, which was as follows :

Right Worthy Grand Officers and Patriarchs :

In accordance with former custom, I respectfully present you with a summary of my official acts, since our last session.

It is with pleasure that I inform you of the continued prosperity of the Encampments under your jurisdiction ; during the past year, four subordinates have been instituted, all of which are in a very flourishing condition.

In the month of January, I forwarded Dispensations to the several deputy Grand Patriarchs, empowering them to perform the duties therein named, until this day.

On the 14th day of April, I received a petition from seven Patriarchs, residing in the city of Bridgeport, in the county of Fairfield, for an Encampment to be located there. I granted a Dispensation subject to your approval, and on the 22d day of April, I instituted the same, under the style and title of " Mount Hermon Encampment, No. 8, I. O. O. F." On this occasion I received the assistance of M. E. Grand High Priest Andrus, R. W. Grand Scribe Demick, and a large number of Patriarchs from New Haven and Danbury. This Encampment commenced its existence under the most favorable circumstances.

I have this day received a petition from an Encampment to be located at Norwalk, in the county of Fairfield, to be known and hailed by the style and title of " ———— Encampment, No. 9, I. O. O. F.;" the same is herewith laid before you, and recommended to your favorable notice.

In conclusion, permit me to tender you my grateful acknowledgments for the kindness which I have received at your hands, during the period which I have had the honor of presiding over your deliberations ; on retiring from the distinguished position to which your partiality elevated me, I assure you that the many pleasing associations which are connected with the part I have taken in the important business of the Grand Encampment during the past year, will long be held in cherished remembrance ; nor shall I cease to remember the officers and members who have been so pleasantly associated with me ; be pleased to accept, individually, my best wishes for you happiness and prosperity, and the advancement of the Order under your supervision.

JOHN L. DEVOTION,
Grand Patriarch.

On motion, the report of the M. W. Grand Patriarch was accepted, and ordered to be entered on the proceedings of the Grand Encampment.

The R. W. Grand Treasurer submitted his report, with the certificate of the Finance committee, that they had examined the same and found it correct.

On motion, The Grand Treasurers' report was accepted, and ordered on file.

Semi-annual reports were received from all the subordinates, under this jurisdiction, and referred to the committee on returns Their report is as follows ; to wit:

To the R. W. Grand Encampment of Connecticut :
The committee on returns respectfully report,

That the following semi-annual returns, with the dues therein accredited to this Grand Encampment, are correct ; viz:

Sassacus Encampment, No. 1, dues thereon,	-	$15 15
Oriental	"	" 2,	"	- -	1 00
Palmyra	"	" 3,	"	- -	19 07
Urity	"	" 4,	" three rep'ts	48 14
Devotion	"	" 5,	"	- -	10 56
Sowheag	"	" 6,	"	- -	4 65
Midian	"	" 7,	"	- -	25 80
Mt. Hermon,	"	" 8	"	- -	11 00

$135 37

Respectfully submitted,

WILLIAM L. BREWER, ⎫
JNO. GREENWOOD, Jr. ⎬ *Committee.*
THOS. C. SIMPSON. ⎭

Several bills for travelling expenses to officers of this Grand Encampment, and for contingent expenses, amounting in the aggregate to $37 79 cents, were ordered paid,—the items being fully specified in the records.

On motion, The Grand Treasurer was authorized to settle with Sassacus Encampment, for rent due from this Grand Encampment.

The M. W. Grand Patriarch called for nominations of Grand officers for the year ensuing, when the following nominations were made:

For Grand Patriarch, Jonathan M. Andrus, of No. 1.
" *G. M. E. H. P.* Wm. L. Brewer, of No. 3.
" *G. S. Warden,* Munson A. Shepard, of No. 5.
" *G. Scribe,* Prelate Dimick, of No. 1.
" *G. Treasurer,* Samuel Bishop, of No. 1.
" *G. J. Warden,* John W. Johnson, of No. 7.
" *G. Rep. G. L. U. S. P. G. P.* John L. Devotion, of No. 3.

On motion, *Resolved,* That the Grand Encampment proceed to the election of Grand Officers.

The M. W. Grand Patriarch appointed as tellers, Orrin F. Smith, of No. 4, and John Greenwood, Jr. of No. 5.

The Grand Encampment proceeded to ballot for the several Grand Officers, and ¡the above mentioned Patriarchs were severally elected to the offices for which they were nominated.

On motion, the Grand Encampment proceeded to the installation of its Grand officers elect, and they were severally installed into their respective offices in ample form.

On assuming the chair, the M. W. Grand Patriarch announced the following appointments :

For *G. Sentinel,* George W. Brown, of	No.	4.
" *Dep. G. Sentinel,* David Young,	"	3.
John C. Palmer,	"	2.
Chauncey Burgess,	"	3.
George W. Brown,	"	4.
" " *G. Patriarchs,* M. A. Shepard,	"	5.
E. H. Booth,	"	6.
John W. Johnson,	"	7.
Samuel B. Brittan,	"	8.

The following resolution, submitted by P. M. E. H. P. Charles W. Bradley, was unanimously adopted ;

Grand Encamp. I. O. O. F. of Conn. July 10, 1845.

Resolved, That there be, and hereby is granted to the R. W. G. Scribe, an annual salary of twenty-five dollars, (conditioned on the faithful performance of his duties,) payable semi-annually.

On motion of P. G. P. John L. Devotion,

Resolved, That the D. Grand Patriarch, George W. Brown be and hereby is authorized to install the officers of Unity Encampment, No. 4, at such time as may suit the convenience of said Encampment.

Resolved, That the Grand Scribe be authorized to procure the printing of two hundred copies of the proceedings of this Grand Encampment, from its organization, to the close of the present session ; and that the Grand Patriarch be authorized to draw an order on the Grand Treasurer for the payment of the same ; and that a copy be forwarded every member of this Grand Encampment, and one to each subordinate under this jurisdiction.

On motion of Grand Sentinel J. Greenwood, Jr., it was

Resolved, That our R. W. Grand Representative be authorized to draw upon the Grand Treasurer, for his expenses to special, and also to regular Sessions of the Grand Lodge of the United States.

On motion of Patriarch Thomas C. Simpson of No. 6,

Resolved, That a committee of two be appointed by this Grand Encampment to report at its next Session, what is the proper regalia, to be worn by the several Grand Officers, and the members of this R. W. Grand Encampment, and also for the officers and Patriarchs of subordinate Encampments.

The M. W. Grand Patriarch announced on this committee P. G. P. John L. Devotion, of No. 3, and Patriarch T. C. Simpson of No. 6.

On motion of Patriarch N. C. Hall, it was

Resolved, That the R. W. Grand Scribe be directed to furnish Visiting and Final Cards, to the several subordinates, at the cost and expense of the same, whenever he shall receive orders for them from said subordinates.

On motion of the Grand Scribe, the sum of thirty-one dollars and twenty-five cents was appropriated, to pay the R. W. G. L. U. S., for Cards ordered by the G. Scribe, for the use of subordinates under this jurisdiction.

Resolved, That the further sum of twenty dollars be, and the same is hereby appropriated, to pay the dues from this Grand Encampment, to the R. W. G. L. U. S.

A petition was received from seven qualified Patriarchs, residing in Norwalk, Fairfield County, praying for a charter for a subordinate Encampment of Patriarchs, to be located at that place, and to be known and hailed by the style and title of —— Encampment No. 9, I. O. O. F. of Connecticut.

On motion of Patriarch Newel C. Hall, it was

Resolved, That a charter be granted to the said petitioners ; and that the same be presented to them by the Grand Patriarch, as soon as the constitutional provisions shall have been complied with.

The M. W. G. P. John L. Devotion, presented to the R. W. Grand Encampment the following Proclamation, which was read, and ordered on file.

I. O. O. F.

Office of the Grand Sire, R. W. G. L. U. S.,

To all to whom it may concern, I, Howell Hopkins, most worthy Grand Sire of the Grand Lodge of I. O. O. F, of the United States of North America, and the jurisdiction of the order thereunto belonging

Send Greeting.

Whereas, The Grand Lodge of the United States at a Session thereof, held at the city of Baltimore, on the 16th day of September, A. D. 1844, did by ballot elect a Committee of five, with full power to revise all the Lectures and Charges of the Order, and did then and there resolve that it is expedient that a Special Session of the Grand Lodge, should be called at the earliest possible period after the committee are prepared to make their report, for the purpose of considering the same. And

WHEREAS, the said Committee have duly notified me that they will be prepared to make their report on Tuesday the ninth day of September next ensuing the date thereof.

NOW KNOW YE, That I, HOWELL HOPKINS, most worthy Grand Sire as aforesaid, by virtue of the power and authority in me vested, do order and direct that a Special Session of the Grand Lodge of the United States of I. O. O. F. shall be held at the Odd-Fellow's Hall in the City of Baltimore, and State of Maryland, on Tuesday the ninth day of September, in the year of our Lord one thousand eight hundred and forty-five, then and there to take into consideration the report which shall be made by the Committee appointed to revise all the Lectures and Charges of the Order. And further, I do order and direct, that at the said Special Session, Petitions may be presented and acted upon, for the granting of Charters for Grand Lodges or Grand Encampments within the jurisdiction of the Grand Lodge of the United States.

In witness Whereof, I have hereunto set my hand and caused the Seal of the Grand Lodge of I. O. of O. F. of the United States of North America, to be affixed at the city of Baltimore, this thirteenth day of May, Anno Domini 1845, and of our Order in the United States of North America the 27th.

H. HOPKINS,
Grand Sire.

I. O. O. F.

Office of Cor. & Rec. Secretary,
Baltimore, June 2, 1845.

To the R. W. Grand Encampment of Connecticut.

In obedience to the Constitution of the Grand Lodge of the United States, the above Proclamation is transmitted through the proper officer of the Grand Encampment of Connecticut.

The great importance of the business to be transacted, it is hoped, will ensure the presence of every Grand Lodge and Grand Encampment under this jurisdiction.

Very truly and Fraternally
Yours, in F. L. T.
JAS. L. RIDGLEY, *C. S.*

No further business appearing, the Grand Encampment closed in ample form, according to the most ancient and honorable customs of the Order.

Attest,   P. DEMICK,
Grand Scribe.

GRAND ENCAMPMENT OF CONNECTICUT, I. O. O. F.

SEMI-ANNUAL SESSION.

New Haven, January, 15th, 1846.

The R. W. Grand Encampment of Connecticut I. O. O. F., convened this day in regular Semi-Annual Session.

PRESENT.

M. W. JONATHAN M. ANDRUS, *Grand Patriarch.*
M. E. WILLIAM L. BREWER, *Grand High Priest.*
R. W. MUNSON A. SHEPARD, *Grand S. Warden.*
R. W. PRELATE DEMICK, *Grand Scribe.*
R. W. SAMUEL BISHOP, *Grand Treasurer.*
R. W. JOHN W. JOHNSON, *Grand J. Warden.*
R. W. HENRY CHAMPLAIN, *Grand Sentinel, pro. tem.*
P. G. Patriarch William E. Sanford, and a due representation from the several subordinates under this jurisdiction.

By command of the M. W. G. Patriarch, the Grand Encampment was opened in ample form.

The Throne of Grace was addressed by the M. E. G. H. P. William L. Brewer.

The reading of the minutes of the last session, was ordered by the M. W. G. P., pending which, on motion, the further reading was dispensed with.

The M. W. G. P. announced the following committee on *credentials*, to wit: M. E. G. H. P. William L. Brewer, and Past Grand Patriarch William E. Sanford.

Semi-Annual Reports from the following subordinates were laid on the table : to wit,

No. 1. Dues to this Grand Encampment, $5 84. Paid.
" 3. do.   do.   12 57. do.
" 4. do.   do.   15 22. do.
" 5. do.   do.   10 30. do.
" 6. do.   do.   7 15. do.
" 8. do.   do.   11 10. do.
" 9. do.   do.   9 00. do.

            $71 18

No. 7. Reported verbally, that the dues to Grand Encampment were, - - $5 26 } Not
" There is also due for cards, - - 2 21 } Paid.

            $7 47

No Report or dues were received from No. 2.

The committee on credentials submitted their report, as follows, which was accepted:

'The committee on credentials having atttended to the duties assigned them, beg leave to report: That the following Patriarchs have presented certificates in due form, which entitle them to seats in this R. W. Grand Encampment, viz; from

No. 1. Daniel H. Moore, *H. P.*
" 4. A. S. Wightman, *C. P.*
" " C. C. Culver, *H. P.*
" 5. James R. Greenwood, *H. P.*
" " William W. Bedient, *C. P.*
" " James P. Sanders, *C. P.*
" 7. Henry L. Miller, *H. P.*
" 8. George S. Sanford, *H. P.*
" 9. James A. Quintard, *C. P.*
" " Peter L. Cunningham, *H. P.*
" " C. J. Gruman, *C. P.*

    Respectfully submitted,
      WILLIAM L. BREWER, } *Committee.*
      WILLIAM E. SANFORD, }

The R. W. Grand Treasurer, submitted his report of the State of Finances, exhibiting a balance in his hands of one hundred and eight dollars and thirty one cents, on which was endorsed the following certificate,

The Finance Committee find on examination the above account to be correct.
     WILLIAM L. BREWER,
      Committee of Finance.

The candidates for membership, as reported by the Committee on credentials, were, on motion, introduced by G. J. Warden, John W. Johnson, instructed in the Grand Encampment Degree, by the M. E. H. P. William L. Brewer, and took their seats as members of this R. W. Grand Encampment.

The M. W. G. P, then submmitted his Semi-Annual Report as follows :—

Right Worthy Grand Officers and Patriarchs:

Custom has made it necessary for me at this time to render an account of my official acts, since our annual session in July last.

It is my happy privilege to inform you of the continued prosperity of the Order within your jurisdiction; nothing has occurred to materially interrupt the harmony that has ever existed, since the establishment of the Patriarchal branch of our Order in this State.

Upon the third of September, I received a communication from Patriarch C. J. Gruman of Norwalk, informing me that the Patriarchs in that place were fully prepared to be constituted an Encampment agreeably to the provisions of a Charter granted at our last session ; and upon the 17th of September, I visited Norwalk, accompanied by R. W. G. S. Demick, and a number of Patriarchs of Mount Hermon Encampment, No. 8, and instituted the said Encampment under the style and title of " KAB-AOSA ENCAMPMENT, No. 9, I. O. O. F., according to the most ancient usage and custom of the Order. After the installation of the officers, five candidates were introduced and instructed in the first three degrees. A session was held in the evening, at which time the candidates were severally exalted to the sublime degree of the Purple.

From the spirit of the members of the Order in Norwalk, and the character of those who have taken hold of the Patriarchal branch of the Order there, we are led to anticipate that Kab-aosa will ere long occupy an enviable position among our subordinate Encampments.

Upon the 31st of October, I received a petition in due form, (unaccompanied by the Charter fee,) signed by seven Patriarchs residing in New London, for a Dispensation to constitute there an Encampment, to be known, hailed and styled " NEW LONDON ENCAMPMENT, No. 10, I. O. O. F."

Doubting the expediency of granting a Dispensation to constitute an Encampment where one already existed, I wrote to the petitioners, expressing the view I entertained, and requested them if still desirous of the Dispensation to forward the Charter fee, and their proposition would *be entertained.*

I received other communications, setting forth that another Encampment would be prejudicial to the best interest of the Order in New London, signed by Patriarchs standing high in the Order; and in view of all the circumstances, I did not regard it such an emergency as is contemplated by that Article of the Constitution, giving power to the Grand Patriarch to grant Dispensations to constitute subordinate Encampments. I therefore declined granting the Dispensation, and recommended the petitioners to this Right Worthy body. Should the petition be presented, you will take such action as the merits of the case, in your judgment require.

I must call your attention to a resolution passed in Grand Encampment, July 12, 1843, relative to the initiation into our Encampments, of members who have not been members of some subordinate Lodge, at least six months. I would suggest whether it would not be well to give the D. G. Patriarch " power at all times to suspend this rule," at their " discretion."

I have received a communication from the M. W. G. P. of Kentucky, asking for a copy of the proceedings of this Grand Encampment; also a communication from the R. W. Grand Scribe of the Grand Encampment of Maryland, enclosing a copy of the proceedings of their Grand Encampment, and a copy of their Constitution, asking a copy of our Constitution and proceedings, to be remitted to his address; also several other communications of no material interest to this R. W. body; all of which have been duly attended to, according to their several requests.   JONATHAN M. ANDRUS,
                                        Grand Patriarch.

On motion, the report of the M. W. G. P., was referred to a special Committee of three, to take into consideration, and report, what action ought to be taken thereon, by this G. Encampment.

The M. W. G. P., appointed on this Committee, P. G. P. William E. Sanford, of No. 1, P. C. P. J. Greenwood, Jr., of No. 5, P. C. P. O. Utley, of No. 6

The following bills were presented, audited, and ordered paid : bill of

Grand Scribe, compensation and postage, - -	$16 00
Grand Patriarch, for procuring books, - - -	6 13
Grand Representative, special and regular session,	54 00
Grand J. Warden, traveling expenses this session, -	6 00

On motion of Grand J. Warden, Johnson,

Voted, that, the G. S., or G. P., deliver the new work, to subordinates, when received, and collect the old work, to deliver them in person, or otherwise, and the expenses thereby incurred, be paid by this Grand Encampment.

The special Committee to whom was referred the report of
G. P. submitted the following;
The Committee to whom was referred the report of the M.
W. G. P. recommend to the Grand Encampments approval of the
course taken, with regard to the petition from New London, feeling satisfied from representations that have been made to them,
that our Order would not be benefitted by creating new Encampments in the same towns with Encampments now existing.
     With regard to the proposed alterations suggested in the re-
port, the Committee recommend that the subject remain in its
present state, until the Annual Session.
                    WILLIAM E. SANFORD, ⎫
                    JOHN GREENWOOD, Jr. ⎬ *Committee.*
                    O. UTLEY.   ⎭

     Patriarch, H. L. Miller of No. 7, moved to strike out so much
of the report of special Committee, as relates to the course of G.
P., in the matter of petition from New London, on which the
previous question was moved, sustained and the motion carried.
     The M. W. G. P., then presented the petition of Patriarchs
residing in New London, for a charter for an Encampment of
Patriarchs to be located in that city.
     P. G. P. William E. Sanford moved that the petitioners have
leave to withdraw their petition, which motion being under consideration, G. J. W. J. W. Johnson, moved to amend the same,
by continuing said petition to the next annual session of this
Grand Encampment. The amendment of Patriarch Johnson,
being in order before the Grand Encampment, was debated at
length, by Patriarchs A. M. Gordon, J. M. Willey, H. Champlain, A. S. Wightman, J. W. Johnson, H. L. Miller, William
E. Sanford, and others.
     The question was then taken on said amendment, and carried
in the affirmative, so the petition was continued to next session.
     The M. W. G. P., then instructed the Representatives, in the
Semi-Annual P. W.
     No further business offering, the Grand Encampment was
closed with the usual solemnities, and in ample form.
          Attest,   PRELATE DEMICK,
                                        Grand Scribe.

ANNUAL SESSION.

NEW HAVEN, JULY 9th, 1846.

PRESENT:

M. W. JONATHAN M. ANDRUS, *Grand Patriarch.*
M. E. WILLIAM L. BREWER, *Grand High Priest.*
R. W. MUNSON A. SHEPARD, *Grand S. Warden.*
R. W. PRELATE DEMICK, *Grand Scribe.*
R. W. SAMUEL BISHOP, *Grand Treasurer.*
R. W. JOHN W. JOHNSON, *Grand J. Warden.*
R. W. J. L. DEVOTION, *P. G. P.* and *G. R. G. L. U. S.*
W. DAVID YOUNG, *Grand Sentinel,* pro tem.
W. BELA LORD, *Deputy Grand Sentinel,* pro tem.
Also, P. G. P. William E. Sanford, and a numerous representation from Subordinate Encampments under this jurisdiction.

By command of M. W. Grand Patriarch, the R. W. Grand Encampment was opened in ample form.

The minutes of last session were read, and approved.

The M. W. Grand Patriarch appointed Patriarchs J. L. Devotion of No. 3, and H. L. Miller of No. 7, a committee on *credentials.*

Also, Patriarchs William E. Sanford of No. 1, and John Greenwood, Jr., of No. 5, a committee on Semi-Annual Returns.

The committee on credentials, having attended to the duties assigned them, submitted the following report, which was accepted.

To the R. W. Grand Encampment of Conn., I. O. O. F.
The Committee on credentials beg leave to report,
That they find the following named Patriarchs entitled to seats, as members of this Grand Encampment ; viz :
H. P. Elizur Hubbell, of Sassacus Encampment, No. 1.
H. P. H. Hobart Roath, of Palmyra   do.   No. 3.
C. P. Wm. F. Hoyt, of Devotion   do.   No. 5.
H. P. E. T. Farnham, of   do.   do.   No. 5.
H. P. E. B. Stevens, of Mt. Hermon   do.   No. 8.
H. P. Geo. W. Smith, of Kabaosa   do.   No. 9.
All which is submitted, in
Faith, Hope and Charity,
JOHN L. DEVOTION, } *Committee on*
HENRY L. MILLER, } *Credentials.*
NEW HAVEN, JULY 9, 1846.

On motion, the above candidates were introduced by G. J. Warden J. W. Johnson; and on motion of P. G. P. J. L. Devotion, Patriarch Philo M. Judson, was admitted without certificate ; he having passed the necessary chairs to entitle him to a seat, as appeared by returns, under seal of his Encampment. He was also vouched for by P. G. P. Devotion.

The candidates were then instructed in the Grand Encampment Degree, and took their seats as members.

The M. W. Grand Patriarch then submitted his Annual Report, as follows :—

Right Worthy Grand Officers and Patriarchs :

By permission of Divine Providence you are once more assembled in Grand Encampment, to deliberate upon, and enact such measures as will, in your judgment promote the interest of the Order under your jurisdiction.

On the 17th of February, a communication was received by me from Unity Encampment, No. 4, asking a suspension of the Rules, and authority to be given said Encampment to initiate into the Patriarchal Order, two brothers not otherwise eligible. Also upon the 21st of February, a similar request, and for the same purposes, was received from Midian Encampment, No. 7 ; also, upon the 5th of May, a communication of the same character was received from Mount Hermon Encampment, No. 8, all of which requests were severally granted, and authority given to receive and initiate the petitioning candidates.

Upon the 6th of March, the long expected reviewed work of the Order arrived, and was distributed among the Subordinate Encampments, in accordance with a vote passed at your Semi-Annual Session.

It may not be improper for me to here state, that I found very little doing in any of the Encampments that I visited ; some had given up all business at their stated meetings ; and some who had sent in the old work and were entirely destitute, were anxiously awaiting the arrival of the revised work. It was gratefully received, and no doubt exists in my mind, that its influence will be favorably felt throughout the Patriarchal branch of our beloved Order.

Upon the 23d of May, I received a petition in proper form, signed by seven Patriarchs under your jurisdiction, praying this R. W. body to grant them a charter for an Encampment to be located at Mystic, to be known, hailed and styled "Charity Encampment, No. 10, I. O. O. F. There being no apparent necessity for immediate action, I concluded to wait your Annual Session, and do herewith transmit the petition. I would respectfully recommend the petitioners to your favorable consideration.

Patriarchs, the time has arrived for me to retire from the position that I, through your kind indulgence have occupied during the last year; permit me to tender to you, one and all, my thanks for the kindness that has been shown me on all occasions—and allow me to assure you, that the many tokens of respect and confidence it has been my happiness to receive during the time I have presided in your councils, will be held in grateful rememberance. And I should be wanting in gratitude to those Patriarchs with whom I have been called to associate in the discharge of my official duties, did I neglect to assure them that their many kind attentions are, and ever will be held in cherished remembrance.

Finally, brothers, farewell! let Faith, Hope and Charity, be our guide. May we trust in the God of the Patriarchs, through all the vicissitudes of this uncertain life.

JONATHAN M. ANDRUS,

Grand Patriarch.

On motion of P. G. P. John L. Devotion, *Voted,* That the Report of the M. W. Grand Patriarch be entered on the Records.

R. W. G. Treasurer Bishop submitted his Report, which was accepted, and ordered on file.

On motion of P. G. P. Devotion, *Voted,* that a Charter be granted the petitioners for a new Subordinate Encampment, to be located at Mystic, New London County, to be known and hailed by the title of " CHARITY ENCAMPMENT, No. 10, I. O. O. F."

The Committee on returns having attended to the duties assigned them, submitted their report, which was accepted :—

To the R. W. Grand Encampment :

The undersigned Committee on Semi-Annual Returns, beg leave to report;

That the following Subordinates have made returns to this Grand Encampment, in due form, for the last six months ; viz :

Sassacus Encampment, No. 1,	dues paid,	- -	$10 02
Palmyra	"	" 3,	" - - -	14 41
Unity	"	" 4,	" - - -	20 00
Devotion	"	" 5,	" - - -	1 27
Sowheag	"	" 6,	" - - -	5 20
Midian	"	" 7,	" - - -	19 05
Mt. Hermon,	"	" 8,	" - - -	5 00
Charity	"	" 10,	for Charter, -	30 00

$104 95

The following bills were presented and referred to the Committee on Finance ; upon whose report they were ordered paid ; viz :

Jonathan M. Andrus, - - - - - - $22 25
P. Demick, - - - - - - - - - -   20 00
Bela Lord, - - - - - - - - - -   1 00

No returns were received from Kabaosa, No. 9, and none from Oriental, No. 2.

Oriental Encampment, No. 2, having failed to make any returns to this R. W. Grand Encampment for the last twelve months, Patriarch Young of No. 3, offered the following resolution, which was unanimously adopted ; to wit :

Resolved, " That Oriental Encampment, No. 2, be required to make their semi-annual reports for the terms ending January and July, 1846, to the Grand Scribe, within thirty days from the rising of this Grand Encampment.

On motion, *Voted,* That the Grand Encampment proceed to the nomination of Grand Officers, for the year ensuing.

Upon the call of the M. W. Grand Patriarch, the following nominations were made ; to wit :

For *M. W. Grand Patriarch,* William L. Brewer, of No. 3.
" *M. E. G. H. Priest,* Munson A. Shepard, of No. 5.
" *R. W. G. S. Warden,* John W. Johnson, of No. 7.
" *R. W. G. Scribe,* Prelate Demick, of No. 1.
" *R. W. G. Treasurer,* Samuel Bishop, of No. 1.
" *R. W. G. J. Warden,* Junius M. Willey, of No. 2.
" *R. W. G. Representative Grand Lodge of United States,* John Greenwood, Jr., of No. 5.

On motion, *Voted,* That the Grand Encampment proceed to election.   The M. W. Grand Patriarch appointed P. G. P. John L. Devotion, of No. 3, and Patriarch Henry L. Miller, of No. 7, tellers.

The ballots having been deposited, were counted by the tellers, when it appeared that William L. Brewer was unanimously elected Most Worthy Grand Patriarch, for the year ensuing, and he was declared so elected.

The balloting continued for each of the candidates in the above list of nominations, separately, and each was declared duly elected to the office for which he was nominated, as above.

On motion the Grand Encampment next proceeded to Install the Grand Officers elect, which having been done, the M. W. Grand Patriarch appointed

H. Hobert Roath, of No. 3, *Grand Sentinel.*
James S. Parmelee, of No. 6, *D. Grand Sentinel.*

2

Also, the following *D. G. Patriarchs*, viz.:
Sassacus, No. 1, Newel C. Hall.
Oriental,   " 2, Thomas C. Bordman.
Palmyra,   " 3, Theodore Raymond.
Unity,   " 4, Charles E. Hewit.
Devotion,   " 5, James R. Greenwood.
Sowheag, " 6, Thomas C. Simpson.
Midian,   " 7, Aaron Morley.
Mount Hermon, No. 8, George S. Sanford.
Kabaosa, No. 9, Peter L. Cunningham.

On motion of Patriarch Miller, of No. 7, a vote of thanks to the last Past Grand Patriarch, for the dignified, able, and impartial manner in which he has discharged the duties of his office, was unanimously passed.

The petition, (continued from last session,) of Patriarchs residing in New London, for a new Subordinate Encampment, to be located there, was by vote, taken up, and leave granted the petitioners to withdraw the same.

On motion, *Voted,* That the Grand Representative be requested to present his bill for the amount of his expenses in attending the ensuing session of the R. W. Grand Lodge of the U. S., to the Grand Scribe, and the Grand Scribe be authorized to draw an order on the Grand Treasurer for the payment of the same.

A. S. Wightman, D. G. P. of Unity Encampment, No. 4, stated, that at the last election of officers in said Subordinate Encampment, all the Patriarchs eligible to fill certain offices therein, declined their nominations thereto ;—that the said offices were subsequently filled by the election of Patriarchs who were not eligible thereto by the laws of said Subordinate ;—that he installed them, notwithstanding their ineligibility,—and asked whether this R. W. Grand Encampment would sanction the course he had taken ?

On motion of P. G. P. John L. Devotion, *Voted,* That the election and installation of ineligible Patriarchs were justifiable, under the circumstances stated; and that the official doings of D. G. P. Wightman in the matter aforesaid, be, and the same is hereby approved by this Grand Encampment.

Amendments to the Constitution of Subordinate Encampments under this jurisdiction. And to two *Resolutions of this R. W. Grand Encampment,* were adopted, as follows ; viz:

Article II. Sec. 1. Clause 1, was, on motion of Patriarch Miller, of No. 7, amended by striking out the word "*ten*" in the 4th line, and substituting therefor, the word "*six.*"

Article II. Sec. 1. Clause 2, was on motion of P. G. P. John L. Devotion, amended, by striking out the word "*one,*" in the seventh line, and substituting therefor, the word "*three.*"

Article V. Sec. 1, was on motion of —— ——, amended by striking out the word "*three*," in second line, and substituting therefor, the word, "*two ;*" and striking out the word "*ten*" in the seventh line, and substituting the word "*six*."

Resolution of Grand Encampment, adopted January 12, 1843, was on motion of Patriarch Miller, of No. 7, amended, by inserting after the words Grand Patriarch, in the fifth line, the words, "*or his Deputy.*"—[*See first printed Constitution, page* 24.]

Resolution of Grand Encampment, adopted January 12, 1844, was on motion of Patriarch Miller, of No. 7, admended, by inserting after the word "*by*," in the second line, "*that or.*"—[*See first printed Constitution, page* 24.]

On motion of G. J. Warden Willey, of No. 2, the Grand Scribe was instructed to procure the printing of two hundred and fifty copies of the proceedings of the last, and present sessions of this Grand Encampment, and that the said Scribe be authorized to draw an order on the R. W. Grand Treasurer for the payment of the same.

On motion, the Grand Scribe was further instructed to furnish one copy of said printed proceedings to each Subordinate under this jurisdiction, and one copy to each member of this Grand Encampment.

On a call of the Grand Encampment, the Grand Representative to the Grand Lodge of the United States, proceeded to instruct the members in the work of the Patriarchal Branch of the Order.

No further business offering, the Grand Encampment was closed in ample form, according to the most ancient ceremonials of the Order.   Attest,

P. DEMICK,
Grand Scribe.

GRAND ENCAMPMENT, I.O.O.F. OF CONNECTICUT.

SEMI-ANNUAL SESSION.

New Haven, January 14th, 1847.

The R. W. Grand Encampment, I. O. O. F. of Connecticut, convened this day, in Semi-Annual Session.

PRESENT:

M. W. WILLIAM L. BREWER, *Grand Patriarch,*
M. E. MUNSON A. SHEPARD, *Grand High Priest,*
R. W. JOHN W. JOHNSON, *Grand Senior Warden,*
R. W. PRELATE DEMICK, *Grand Scribe,*
R. W. SAMUEL BISHOP, *Grand Treasurer,*
R. W. JUNIUS M. WILLEY, *Grand Junior Warden,*
R. W. JOHN GREENWOOD, Jr., *Grand Rep. G. Lodge U. States,*
W. H. HOBART ROATH, *Grand Sentinel,*
W. J. S. PARMELEE, *Deputy Grand Sentinel,*

and a due representation from the several subordinates under this jurisdiction.

By command of the M. W. G. Patriarch, the Grand Encampment was opened in ample form.

The Throne of Grace was addressed by the M. E. Grand H. P.

The reading of the minutes of the last session was ordered and commenced, when, on motion, the further reading was dispensed with.

The M. W. G. Patriarch announced the following Committee on Credentials, viz: P. G. P. J. L. Devotion and G. J. Warden J. M. Willey.

Semi-Annual Reports from the following subordinates were laid on the table of the G. Scribe, viz:

Sassacus,	No.	1,	Dues to G. Encampment,	$	6.25
Oriental,	No.	2,	"	"	18.07
Palmyra,	No.	3,	"	"	12.05
Devotion,	No.	5,	"	"	4.00

Sowheag,   No. 6, Dues to G. Encampment, $ 1.87
Midian,   No. 7, "   "   18.04
Mount Hermon, No. 8, "   "   8.26
Kabaosa,   No. 9, "   "   10.43
Charity,   No. 10, "   "   8.08

Unity Encampment, No. 4, made no report, and paid no dues.

The Committee on Credentials submitted their report as follows:

To the R. W. Grand Encampment, I. O. O. F. of the State of Connecticut:

The Committee on Elections and Returns beg leave respectfully to report—That they have examined and found correct the credentials of the following named Patriarchs:

. From Sassacus Encampment, No. 1—Frederick Croswell.
    " Oriental, No. 2—John S. Dickinson.
    " Palmyra, No. 3—James D. Mowrey.
    " Devotion, No. 5—William A. Judd.
    " Sowheag, No. 6—Dennis Sage and T. P. Abell.
    " Midian, No. 7—Edson Fessenden and W. H. Sweetland.
    " Mount Hermon, No. 8—Gilson Landon, Joseph Crosby, and Dwight Morris.

We therefore recommend that they be admitted to the Grand Encampment degree.

JOHN L. DEVOTION, } *Com.*
J. M. WILLEY, }

The R. W. Grand Treasurer submitted his report of the state of the finances, which was referred to the Committee on Finance.

On motion of P. G. P. Devotion, the candidates for admission were introduced, instructed in the Grand Encampment degree, and took their seats as members.

The attention of the Grand Encampment was then called to the Report of the M. W. Grand Patriarch, which he submitted as follows:

To the R. W. Grand Encampment :—

PATRIARCHS,—I have the honor to report, that on the tenth day of November last, attended by P. G. P. John L. Devotion, W. Grand Sentinel H. Hobart Roath, Deputy G. P. Hewett, and twenty-five Patriarchs from Encampments Nos. 3 and 4, I proceeded to Mystic, where I instituted *Charity Encampment*, No. 10, I. O. O. F., according to the ancient and imposing ceremonial of the Order. On this occasion I presented the charter granted by this R. W. body at its last session.

The following named Patriarchs were elected to office, viz :—Grover G. King, Chief Patriarch; Benjamin F. Lewis, High Priest; Wm. Meeker, Senior Warden; Amos Clift, Scribe , John Holliday,

Treasurer, and Peleg Noyes, Junior Warden—who were then installed in ample form. We then initiated one brother, who was passed to the degree of the Golden Rule, and also raised to the sublime degree of the Royal Purple, in due and ancient form.

From my knowledge of the character and standing of the officers of Charity Encampment, and the great interest manifested by them in its work, I have no doubt of its ultimate success.

On the fourth day of November, I made an official visit to Midian Encampment, No. 7, for the purpose of giving instruction in the oral work of the Order. Deputy Grand Sentinel Parmelee, of No. 6, was present by appointment, for instruction in behalf of Sowheag Encampment. During my visit, a candidate was initiated and passed to the degree of the Golden Rule, with all the ceremony and imposing rites incident to this degree, and in a manner highly creditable to the members of this Encampment.

I take this occasion to express my sincere acknowledgments to the officers and members of No. 7, for the attention and politeness which I received at their hands.

There is, I am forced to say, a great want of uniformity in the *oral* work of subordinates under this jurisdiction. This is an evil of too great importance to pass unnoticed. Some action must be had, to bring about a strict and entire uniformity in this particular. Much of the indifference which is manifested in the Patriarchal branch of the Order, may be attributed to this source.

An application has been forwarded to me by the Scribe of Devotion Encampment, in behalf of that Encampment, for permission to change the location of said Encampment. It is their desire that their place of meeting for the future be at Bethel. I would recommend this their petition to your favorable consideration.

I would also call the attention of the Patriarchs to the expediency of abolishing, altogether, the semi-annual session of this Grand Encampment. It appears to me that the interests of the subordinates would be in no way sacrificed, and one great source of useless expense be avoided.

I would further suggest the propriety of so altering our Constitution as to allow none but Past C. P's and P. H. P's admission to this Grand Encampment.

All which is respectfully submitted.

WILLIAM L. BREWER, *G. Patriarch.*

On motion, the report of the M. W. G. P. was referred to a special committee of three, for distribution of subjects therein contained to appropriate committees.

The M. W. Grand Patriarch announced as this committee, Patriarchs J. W. Johnson, J. L. Devotion, and John Greenwood, Jr.

The following bills were presented, audited and ordered paid, viz:

Bill of Grand Scribe, compensation, postage and
     expenses,   -   -   -   - $18.18
" of G. Rep. to Grand Lodge U. States,   40.00
" of 4 years Rent due to Sassacus Encamp-
     ment for Hall, at $5 per annum,   -   20.00
    The Committee on Finance submitted the following report,
which was accepted :

To the Grand Encampment, I. O. O. F. of Connecticut:

The Finance Committee, having audited the accounts of the Grand
Treasurer, find them correct. There is in his hands a balance of
$15.17, to be carried to new account.
    All which is respectfully submitted.

                    GEO. S. SANFORD,   } *Com.*
                    ORIGEN UTLEY,   }

New Haven, Jan. 14, 1847.

    Patriarch Cunningham submitted the following resolution,
which was adopted :

Resolved, That the G. Scribe be authorized to procure, and
send to each of the several Encampments under this jurisdiction, two books, in addition to those they already have, for
the installation of their officers.

    The committee to whom was referred the Report of the M.
W. G. P. submitted the following, which was adopted :

To the R. W. Grand Encampment, I. O. O. F. of Connecticut :

The committee appointed to examine the Report of the M. W.
Grand Patriarch, and recommend such action as may be necessary for
the Grand Encampment, would recommend that a committee of three
be appointed on that part of said report relating to Devotion Encampment, No. 5,—that part in relation to the alteration of the Constitution, to a committee of four,—that the report be accepted and spread
upon the records.

    All which is respectfully submitted by

                    JOHN W. JOHNSON,   }
                    JOHN L. DEVOTION, } *Com.*
                    JOHN GREENWOOD, Jr. }

New Haven, January 14, 1847.

    The M. W. G. Patriarch announced as a committee on Devo-
tion Encampment, Patriarchs J. M. Andrus, Townsend P.
Abell, and James D. Mowrey ; and as a committee on the alteration of the Constitution, Patriarchs Frederick Croswell,
Junius M. Willey, J. P. Sanders, Wm. W. Bedient.

    On motion, the Grand Scribe was requested to furnish
blank reports to the several subordinates under this jurisdiction.

    On motion, Patriarchs F. Croswell, P. M. Judson, and Junius M. Willey, were appointed a committee to consider the expediency of establishing a plan of general education, by the Order of Odd Fellows, as suggested by the circular of G. Sec. Ridgley.

The committee to whom was referred so much of the M. W. G. Patriarch's Report as relates to Devotion Encampment, submitted the following, which was adopted:

To the R. W. Grand Encampment, I. O. O. F. of Connecticut:

The committee to whom the subject was referred, beg leave to report—That they have had the same under consideration, and would recommend that Devotion Encampment have leave to remove its place of meeting at any time after such removal is authorized by a two-third vote of said Encampment: *Provided* notice shall be given in said Encampment one month previous to the time of action, of the pending of said question.

All which is respectfully submitted.

J. M. ANDRUS,
T. P. ABELL,   } <i>Com.</i>
JAMES D. MOWREY,

The committee to whom that subject was referred, submitted their report, which was adopted.

To the R. W. Grand Encampment, I. O. O. F. of Connecticut:

The undersigned committee, to whom was referred so much of the M. W. G. P's message as refers to amendments of the Constitution, report—That in their opinion the amendments proposed by the M. W. G. Patriarch would, if adopted by this Grand Encampment, be conducive to the interests of the Order. They therefore offer the following resolution for the action of this Grand Encampment at its next regular session.

All of which is respectfully submitted in F., L. and T.

F. CROSWELL,
J. M. WILLEY,
J. P. SANDERS,   } <i>Com.</i>
WM. W. BEDIENT,

Resolved, That Art. I, Sec. 2, be amended by erasing all after the words " Grand Encampment" in the third line, and that the following be substituted for Art. IV, Sec. 1 :—The Regular Sessions of the Grand Encampment shall be held in each year on the Thursday following the 2d Wednesday of July.

The M. W. Grand Patriarch announced the appointment of Deputy Grand Patriarchs, as follows:

PRELATE DEMICK, Sassacus, No. 1.
THOMAS C. BORDMAN, Oriental, No. 2.
THOMAS L. STEDMAN, Palmyra, No. 3.
CHARLES E. HEWIT, Unity, No. 4.
JAMES R. GREENWOOD, Devotion, No. 5.

ORIGEN UTLEY, Sowheag, No. 6.
HENRY L. MILLER, Midian, No. 7.
GEORGE S. SANFORD, Mount Hermon, No. 8.
CHOLWELL J. GRUMAN, Kabaosa, No. 9.
GROVER G. KING, Charity, No. 10.

On motion, the Grand Encampment proceeded to give instruction in the work of the Order.

No further business offering, on motion, the Grand Encampment closed in ample form, and with the ancient ceremonials of the Order.

Attest,

PRELATE DEMICK, *Grand Scribe.*

ANNUAL SESSION.

NEW HAVEN, JULY 15, 1847.

The R. W. Grand Encampment, I. O. O. F. of the State of Connecticut, convened this day, at 2 o'clock P. M., according to the requisitions of its Constitution and By-Laws; but a quorum not being present, the meeting was adjourned until 7 o'clock P. M. At 7 o'clock, the Grand Encampment again convened, and after prayer by the G. H. Priest, the Encampment was opened in ample form.

PRESENT :

M. W. WILLIAM L. BREWER, *Grand Patriarch,*
M. E. MUNSON A. SHEPARD, *Grand High Priest,*
R. W. JOHN W. JOHNSON, *Grand Senior Warden,*
R. W. PRELATE DEMICK, *Grand Scribe,*
R. W. SAMUEL BISHOP, *Grand Treasurer,*
R. W. JUNIUS M. WILLEY, *Grand Junior Warden,*
R. W. JOHN GREENWOOD, JR., *Grand Representative,*

and the following members, viz: from

Sassacus, No. 1—J. M. Andrus, N. C. Hall, L. A. Thomas, Elizur Hubbell, F. Croswell.

Palmyra, No. 3—John L. Devotion, H. Hobart Roath, P. M. Judson.

Unity, No. 4—A. S. Wightman.

Devotion, No. 5—E. T. Farnum, Wm. A. Judd.

Sowheag, No. 6—O. Utley, J. S. Parmelee, D. Sage, T. P. Abell.

Midian, No. 7—A. M. Gordon, J. W. Johnson, Aaron Morley, H. L. Miller, Edson Fessenden, W. H. Sweetland.

Mount Hermon, No. 8—Geo. Sanford.

Kabaosa, No. 9—C. J. Gruman.

The reading of the minutes of last session was ordered by the Grand Patriarch, when, on motion, the further reading was dispensed with.

The Grand Patriarch appointed as a Committee on Credentials, Patriarchs J. M. Andrus, J. L. Devotion, and James P. Sanders.

The Grand Scribe reported that he had received semi-annual reports from the following subordinates, viz:

Sassacus, No. 1 ; Palmyra, No. 3 ; Unity, No. 4 ; Devotion, No. 5 ; Sowheag, No. 6 ; Midian, No. 7 ; Mount Hermon, No. 8 ; Kabaosa, No. 9 ; Charity, No. 10 ; Connecticut, No. 11 ; and annual reports from Nos. 1, 3, 4, 5, 6, 7, 9.

Patriarchs J. W. Johnson, J. S. Parmelee, and Aaron Morley, were appointed a committee on the reports of subordinates.

The Committee on Credentials submitted the following report, which was accepted :

To the R. W. Grand Encampment, I. O. O. F. of Connecticut :

The Committee on Credentials have attended to the duties assigned them, and find the following Patriarchs entitled to membership in this Grand Encampment, viz : from

Sassacus, No. 1—C. P. Eliphalet G. Storer, and H. P. Noah Chandler.

Palmyra, No. 3—C. P. James A. Hovey.

Unity, No. 4—C. P. Robert B. Jackson.

Midian, No. 7—C. P. O. D. Seymour, H. P. M. M. Merriman.

Kabaosa, No. 9—C. P. George W. Smith.

Charity, No. 10—C. P. William Meeker, H. P. Amos Clift.

Connecticut, No. 11—P. C. P. Ezra Clarke, Jr., P. C. P. A. C. Goodman, P. II. P. Elihu Geer, C. P. William B. Davis, H. P. R. G. Drake.

All which is respectfully submitted.

JONATHAN M. ANDRUS, } *Committee.*
J. L. DEVOTION,

The Grand Treasurer submitted his semi-annual report, which was referred to a committee consisting of Patriarchs J. M. Willey, H. Hobart Roath, and O. Utley.

The candidates for membership were then introduced and instructed in the Grand Encampment degree, and took their seats.

The Grand Patriarch submitted the following report :

To the R. W. Grand Encampment of Connecticut :

OFFICERS AND PATRIARCHS :—In presenting my annual report, allow me to congratulate you upon the continued prosperity and harmony of the Order in this jurisdiction. The silent, yet rapid increase of our institution, and the repeated practical demonstrations of its usefulness, should be to us a source of pride and satisfaction. In a society as large as ours, we are naturally led to expect great diversity of opinion, and the manifestation of partisan or sectional interests and feelings. In the hitherto total absence of any such manifestations, may we not confidently hope that the principles of the Order are exercising a controlling influence upon the conduct of its members. Let us, in the performance of our duties at this time, exemplify the virtues by which we profess to be governed, and by our prudence secure to the Order continued success.

Your attention is now called to a summary of my official acts since our semi-annual session.

On the 4th day of February, accompanied by D. G. Patriarch Theodore Raymond, of No. 3, I visited Unity Encampment, No. 4, of New London, for the purpose of giving instruction in the oral work of the Order. This Encampment was not represented at our last session, and the officers were not properly instructed in the unwritten work. Much credit is due to the members of this subordinate, for the interest they continue to manifest in the work of their Encampment.

On the 13th day of February, an application in due form of law was received from ten Patriarchs of Midian Encampment, No. 7, for a dispensation to open an Encampment to be located in the city of Hartford, to be known by the title of " Connecticut Encampment, No. 11, I. O. of O. F." The petitioners stated, somewhat in detail, the reasons which moved them in making this application. They also, at the same time, forwarded a communication signed by a number of Past Grands, brothers of the highest respectability and influence, recommending and urging me to grant the petition. The reasons offered by the petitioners were such as to me appeared to be entitled to consideration. I made full inquiry as to the character of the petitioners, such of them as were unknown to me. Inquiry was also made as to the number of brothers in that vicinity likely to support a second Encampment ; and having consulted such members of the Order as were in no way connected with the difficulties supposed to exist in Hartford, and upon whose judgment I could safely rely, I determined to grant a dispensation. On the 16th of February I notified the petitioners that a dispensation would be issued, and directed them to prepare for institution.

On the 22d day of February I was visited by a committee from Midian Encampment, consisting of the Grand Senior Warden Johnson, Deputy Grand Patriarch Miller, and Patriarch Eldredge. This committee presented a remonstrance from Midian Encampment, against the establishment of a new Encampment in the city of Hartford. From the earnest tone of the remonstrance, and more especially from the verbal representations made to me by this committee, I was induced to believe that my decision had been too hastily formed, and that great injury would result to the order by the establishment of a second Encampment in Hartford. The petitioners were immediately informed of my change of purpose, and were directed to suspend all preparation for the institution of their Encampment.

For the petition, remonstrance, and copies of correspondence, see document A, accompanying this report.

On the 1st day of March a communication was received from Patriarch Aaron C. Goodman and others, the former petitioners, in which they renewed their petition for a charter for an Encampment. The applicants stated that, relying upon my letter of the 16th of February, in which they were directed to prepare for institution, they had applied to and received from Midian Encampment, their cards of withdrawal, which cards they then held ; that they were unwilling to offer them for deposit, in order again to become members of said Encampment. They concluded their application by requesting that, in view of the conflicting statements, the Grand Patriarch would personally investigate the matter in the city of Hartford, where both parties could be present and be heard.

Accompanying this last petition was a memorial signed by fifty-nine members of the scarlet degree, residing in the city of Hartford. The memorialists stated, "that they were desirous of being initiated into the Patriarchal branch of the Order ; but, for reasons which they deemed satisfactory, and objections which were insuperable, they could not unite with the only Encampment then existing in the county of Hartford." They therefore respectfully asked that the prayer of certain qualified petitioners, for a new Encampment, to be located in the city of Hartford, might be granted.

These and other reasons, which will appear from the documents to be laid before you, caused me seriously to consider whether on this petition the interests of the Order did not demand *immediate* action ; whether, as your executive officer, I should perform my duty, did I refuse to listen to the application of so large a number of petitioners. A long time was to elapse before the session of the Grand Encampment, and great injury might come to the order by this apparent desire to avoid individual responsibility. My personal knowledge of the character and standing of many of the petitioners and memorialists, both as citizens and as members of the Order, forbade me to suppose they would persist in this application, without some cause of complaint. I accordingly wrote the petitioners and respondents of my determination to give the subject of this petition a thorough investigation, and that I should visit Hartford for that purpose on the 3d day of March. For papers connected with this part of my report, see document B.

On the evening of the 3d of March, the parties were heard at the hall of Charter Oak Lodge. At that time there was laid before me memorials from members of three Lodges, to wit, Charter Oak, Oak-

9

land, and Farmers and Mechanics, signed by sixty members of the Scarlet Degree. These memorials set forth, in substance, what has been recited from the first-mentioned memorial, with this addition,—" That there were nearly one thousand members of the Scarlet Degree in the county of Hartford, and that the establishment of a new Encampment in the city of Hartford would, in their judgment, be a benefit to the one already existing and to the Order in general."

Upon an application for a charter for an Encampment in any particular location, the first and principal inquiry should be, " Will the interests of the Order be advanced thereby ?" After a careful investigation of all matters connected with this petition, I became satisfied that the institution of a new Encampment in Hartford would *essentially advance* the interests of the Order in that section of the State.

On the morning of the 4th of March the petitioners were informed that their application for a dispensation had been granted, and that the Encampment would be instituted at such time and place, on the afternoon of that day, as they should designate. The Chief Patriarch of Midian Encampment was, at the same time, informed of the result of this application, and was invited, together with the other officers and Patriarchs of said Encampment, to be present and assist at the institution.

On the afternoon of the 4th of March, at the hall of Mercantile Lodge, assisted by Patriarch Skinner, of Winsted, I instituted an Encampment, to be known and styled as " Connecticut Encampment, No. 11, I. O. of O. F." The following Patriarchs were elected to office, to wit : Aaron C. Goodman, Chief Patriarch ; Elihu Geer, High Priest; William B. Davis, Senior Warden ; Isaac A. Bragaw, Scribe ; John Burt, Junior Warden ; who were then installed in ample form. The term of this Encampment closed on the first session of the present month.

In connection with this report of my proceedings in instituting Connecticut Encampment, your attention is called to a " Circular," received by the Grand Patriarch on the 7th inst. Said Circular was issued by Midian Encampment, and is dated March, 1847. It purports to contain " a statement of facts connected with the institution of Connecticut Encampment, No. 11," and was, by a vote of Midian Encampment, directed to be sent to the Grand Patriarch and each of the subordinate Encampments. See document C.

Prior to the institution of Connecticut Encampment, but subsequent to my letter to the officers of Midian Encampment informing them of my decision, a petition was received, signed by the Grand Senior Warden Johnson and six other members of this Right Worthy Body, residents of the city of Hartford, asking that a special session of the R. W. Grand Encampment might be called "at the earliest convenient opportunity, that the whole matter connected with the application for a new Encampment might be referred to that body. Accompanying that petition was another, signed by thirteen members of Midian Encampment, asking the Grand Patriarch to grant the

prayer of the petition above mentioned. I did not deem that occasion
such an emergency as would warrant me in calling a special session of
the Grand Encampment, and on the 29th day of March the petitioners
were informed that their petition would not be granted. See document D.

As the circumstances under which the dispensation for Connecticut Encampment was issued were somewhat peculiar, I have stated
at length my proceedings ; but in so doing I have endeavored simply
to state, not argue, the case, lest there might be imputed to me a design to dictate, or to forestall your opinion. The whole subject is
before you, and I trust it will receive at your hands that calm and
deliberate attention its importance demands.

I am happy to be able to inform the Grand Encampment of the
prosperous condition of Connecticut Encampment. It already numbers fifty-eight members, and is the most flourishing subordinate in
this jurisdiction. I would respectfully recommend that a charter be
granted to said Encampment.

*   *   *   *   *   *   *

On the 7th of April a communication was received from Devotion
Encampment, informing me of the action of that Encampment in relation to the removal of the same to Bethel. It appearing that Devotion Encampment had complied with the resolution passed at our
last session, prescribing the course to be pursued by them before the
location of said Encampment could be changed, I gave permission
to the officers of that Encampment to remove its location to the hall
of Howard Lodge at Bethel.

On the 28th of May, accompanied by the R. W. Grand Junior
Warden Willey and Past Grand Patriarch Devotion, I made an official visit to Charity Encampment, No. 10, at Lower Mystic. On
that occasion nine brothers of Stonington Lodge, No. 26, were initiated and passed to the Golden Rule Degree, two of whom were
also exalted to the Sublime Degree of the Royal Purple.

The officers and members of Charity Encampment are entitled to
great credit for the faithfulness and interest they continue to manifest in all things pertaining to their Encampment. No Encampment
in this jurisdition is better furnished with paraphernalia, regalia, &c.
necessary to carry on the work as it should be performed. This of
itself has tended in no small degree to keep up the interest so apparent in all the members. From the small number of brothers of the
Scarlet Degree in that vicinity, a rapid increase of numbers is not to
be expected ; but, from the character of its members, this Encampment, although comparatively small, is an ornament to the Order.

On the 25th of June, a petition was received from seven Patriarchs of Midian Encampment, residents of Winsted, for a dispensation to open an Encampment at Winsted, to be known and hailed as
" Winsted Encampment, No. 12, I. O. of O. F." The session of the
Grand Encampment being so near at hand, I declined acting upon
the application. The petition, which is in due form, and is accompanied by a recommendation from Midian Encampment, is herewith
submitted. I recommend the same to your favorable consideration.

· The statistical reports show a steady, but not rapid increase of members in the several subordinate Encampments. In this jurisdiction there are at present eleven subordinates, with three hundred and four contributing members.

The Grand Patriarch, in taking leave of the members of this Grand Encampment, must be permitted to express his thanks for the uniform kindness and courtesy which has always been extended towards him, and for the many tokens of regard and esteem he has received while in the discharge of his official duties.

W. L. BREWER, Grand Patriarch.

New Haven, July 15, 1847.

The following remonstrance was presented:

MIDIAN ENCAMPMENT, No. 7, I. O. O. F.,
July 5th, 1847.

At a regular session of Midian Encampment, No. 7, held at their Hall, on the evening of July 5th, 1847, the following resolutions were unanimously adopted:

Resolved, That the representatives of Midian Encampment to the R. W. Grand Encampment, to be holden at New Haven, on the 15th July inst., be, and they are hereby instructed to remonstrate against the granting of a charter to "Connecticut Encampment, No. 11," now holding sessions in this city, under a dispensation of the Grand Patriarch, said dispensation having been obtained by misrepresentation and fraud, and granted without a proper and impartial investigation on the part of the Grand Patriarch—its existence being against the peace, harmony, and prosperity of the Patriarchal branch of the Order.

Resolved, That a copy of the above resolution be furnished the Representatives of this Encampment, for presentation to the Grand Encampment, attested by the seal of this Encampment, and the signatures of the C. P. and Scribe.

Resolved, That the Representatives of this Encampment be instructed to use all lawful means to prevent so gross an act of injustice to Midian Encampment, from final consummation.

[L. S.]   O. D. SEYMOUR, *C. P.*
               JOHN B. ELDREDGE, *Scribe.*

Patriarch A. M. Gordon, of No. 7, moved that the remonstrance be referred to a special committee of three, with instructions to report at the next session of the Grand Encampment, and that the granting of a charter to Connecticut Encampment, No. 11, be deferred to the same session.

Motion amended, to refer to Committee of the Whole.

On the motion, as amended, the previous question was demanded and sustained—22 yeas, 7 nays.

The Grand Encampment then went into Committee of the Whole, on the remonstrance of Midian Encampment.

Patriarch Judson moved that the Committee report to the

Grand Encampment the following resolution, and recommend its adoption. Motion carried.

Resolved, That this Encampment approve of the doings of the M. W. Grand Patriarch, in the matter of instituting Connecticut Encampment, No. 11, and that a charter be granted to said Encampment.

On motion, the committee rose and reported to the Grand Encampment.

The resolution above reported was, on motion, adopted by the Grand Encampment.

Patriarch Thomas moved that Midian Encampment be allowed to present to this Grand Encampment, at its next session, any evidence relating to the institution of Connecticut Encampment.

Motion by Patriarch N. C. Hall, to amend by appointing a committee of three to examine the evidence and report to the Grand Encampment at its next session—lost.

Original motion prevailed.

By-laws of Connecticut Encampment, No. 11, presented and referred to a special committee for examination, consisting of Pats. J. A. Hovey, M. A. Shepard, and J. M. Andrus.

The Grand Encampment then proceeded to the nomination and election of officers.

There were nominated for

Grand Patriarch—Munson A. Shepard, T. P. Abell.

G. High Priest—Townsend P. Abell, J. W. Johnson.

G. S. Warden—J. M. Willey.

G. J. Warden—C. J. Gruman, Dennis Sage.

G. Representative—W. L. Brewer, N. C. Hall, N. Chandler.

Grand Scribe—P. Demick, R. G. Drake.

Grand Treasurer—S. Bishop.

Pat. Demick declined the nomination for G. Scribe.

On balloting, G. H. P. Munson A. Shepard had 19 out of 20 ballots, and was declared duly elected *Grand Patriarch.*

Pat. Townsend P. Abell had 20 out of 31 ballots, and was declared duly elected *Grand High Priest.*

G. J. W. Junius M. Willey had 13 out of 14 ballots, and was declared duly elected *Grand Senior Warden.*

Pat. R. G. Drake had all the ballots cast, and was declared duly elected *Grand Scribe.*

G. T. Samuel Bishop had all the ballots cast, and was declared duly elected *Grand Treasurer.*

Pat. C. J. Gruman had 19 out of 24 ballots, and was declared duly elected *G. Junior Warden.*

G. P. Wm. L. Brewer had 22 out of 31 ballots, and was declared duly elected *G. Representative.*

The committee to whom was referred the By-laws of Connecticut Encampment, made the following report :

To the R. W. Grand Encampment, I. O. O. F. of Connecticut :

The committee to whom was referred the By-Laws and Rules of Order adopted by Connecticut Encampment, No. 11, have examined and considered the same, and are of opinion that the same should be approved by this Encampment. They therefore recommend the adoption of the accompanying resolution.

All which is respectfully submitted by

> JAS. A. HOVEY, ⎞
> M.,A. SHEPARD, ⎠ *Committee.*

Resolved, That the By-Laws and Rules of Order adopted by Connecticut Encampment, No. 11, and which have been presented to this Encampment for approval, be, and the same hereby are, approved.

Report accepted and resolution adopted.

Motion to grant a charter for constituting Winsted Encampment, No. 12, as recommended in the Grand Master's report, was passed.

Motion by Pat. Thomas, that the report of the Grand Patriarch, with the accompanying documents, be printed with the proceedings of the Grand Encampment—passed.

The committee appointed at the last session to consider a plan of education, reported adversely to any action on the subject by the Grand Encampment.

The officers elect were then installed in ample form.

The Grand Patriarch made the following appointments :

W. WM. A. JUDD, *Grand Sentinel.*

W. A. S. WIGHTMAN, *D. Grand Sentinel.*

On motion, $2 were appropriated to pay Pat. John Kennedy for opening and lighting the Hall.

The amendments to Art. I, Sec. 2, and Art. IV, Sec. 1, of the Constitution of the Grand Encampment, proposed by a committee at the last session, p. 57, were called up for consideration.

Pat. Thomas moved to amend, by striking out " Thursday following the second Wednesday of July," in Art. IV, Sec. 1, and inserting " Tuesday next preceding the second Wednesday of July :" amendment adopted.

The section as amended is as follows :

Sec. 1. The Regular Sessions of the Grand Encampment shall be held in each year on the Tuesday next preceding the second Wednesday of July.

After some discussion, the whole subject was laid over to the next session.

The committee on returns of subordinates submitted the following report, which was accepted :

To the R. W. Grand Encampment, I. O. O. F. of Connecticut :

The Committee on Returns, to whom was recommitted their former report for correction, beg leave to report—That they would recommend the several sums hereinafter named, to be credited on the books of the Grand Encampment to the several subordinate Encampments, being the amount overpaid by said Encampments,* viz: Sassacus, No. 1 ; $0.40 ; Palmyra, No. 3, $2.16 ; Devotion, No. 5, $0.45 ; Sowheag, No. 6, $1.60 ; Midian, No. 7, $5.08 ; Mount Hermon, No. 8, $1.60; Kabaosa, No. 9, $3.60 ; Charity, No. 10, $4.80.

All of which is respectfully submitted.

> J. W. JOHNSON,   } *Com.*
> JAS. S. PARMELEE, }

Pat. R. G. Drake, Grand Scribe, tendered his resignation of the office, which was accepted.

The Grand Encampment then proceeded to the nomination and election of Grand Scribe. Whereupon Pat. LUCIUS A. THOMAS was nominated and elected Grand Scribe, and installed in ample form.

On motion, the Grand Scribe was directed to fill out and procure framed the charter of this Grand Encampment.

The following resolution was, on motion, adopted :

Resolved, That the thanks of this Grand Encampment be presented to P. G. P. Brewer, for his faithfulness and diligence in the discharge of his duties as G. P. for the past year.

Pat. Demick and the Grand Scribe were appointed a committee to procure blank charters for subordinate Encampments.

The Grand Scribe was authorized to procure a suitable case or chest for the books and papers of this Grand Encampment.

The Grand Scribe was directed to procure the printing of the usual number of copies of proceedings of last and present sessions of this Grand Encampment.

No further business offering, the Grand Encampment was closed in ample form.

Attest,

LUCIUS A. THOMAS, *G. Scribe.*

---

* The minimum of the initiation fee was reduced at the last annual session of the Grand Encampment, from ten to six dollars ; and many Encampments having paid ten per cent. on the original rates, the overplus was ordered to be carried to their credit respectively, as above.

DOCUMENTS ACCOMPANYING

THE

REPORT OF THE M..W. GRAND PATRIARCH,

ANNUAL SESSION, JULY, 1847.

DOCUMENT A.

To the M. W. G. Patriarch, Officers and Patriarchs of the R. W. Grand Encampment, I. O. O. F. of Connecticut:

The petition of the subscribers respectfully represents, that they are members in good standing of the Independent Order of Odd Fellows, having attained to the several degrees attached to their names respectively;—that they are sincerely desirous to extend the beneficent principles of the institution, and deeming that this laudable object may be promoted by granting their prayer, they ask that your honorable body would inquire into the facts set forth, and on finding them true, to issue a commission for the institution of Encampment, No.   I. O. O. F., either by dispensation or by charter—the said Encampment to be located in the city of Hartford.

The charter fee ($30) is herewith remitted.

AARON C. GOODMAN,   R. P. degree.
WM. B. DAVIS,   "   "
CHARLES SPENCER,   "   "
ISAAC A. BRAGAW,   "   "
JOHN BURT,   "   "
ELIHU GEER,   "   "
BENJAMIN STEVENS,   "   "
W. S. CRANE,   "   "
C. M. DARROW,   "   "
EZRA CLARK, JR.,   "   "
WM. RUSSELL, [withdrawn,] "   "
ERASTUS HUBBARD,   "   "

Members of Midian Encampment.

To the M. W. G. Patriarch of the R. W. Grand Encampment, I. O. O. F. of Connecticut:

Dear Sir and Brother,—The undersigned, members of Midian Encampment, No. 7, deem it proper to state that they are satisfied, from reasons which they will proceed to give, that the granting of the accompanying petition would greatly promote the interests and growth of the Patriarchal branch of our beloved Order in the city of Hartford.

In presenting this petition, the undersigned would say that past experience shows that the multiplying of subordinate Lodges in this city, has not, as far as our judgment goes, been productive of any advantage to one, to the detriment of another, but, on the contrary, has rather tended to an increase of members in all; and from the fact that several members of Subordinate Lodges in this city and vicinity are anxious to attain to the R. P. degree, but positively decline sending their propositions to Midian Encampment, while others, who have been proposed and accepted, decline presenting themselves for membership, on account of the rejection of members in good standing in the subordinate Lodges, (among which are two Past Grands of Mercantile Lodge,) by Midian Encampment, and for other causes which might be named, if time and space would admit.

The undersigned would further add, that the granting of their petition would, they believe, tend to excite a justifiable spirit of emulation among the Patriarchs, which would cause a much greater interest to be taken by them, and materially promote the growth of both Encampments.

There are now seven subordinate Lodges in Hartford county, (the population of which in 1840 was upwards of 55,000,) the most distant of which is but twelve miles from this place, and we think and know that there is a desire on the part of some of the members of these and other more distant Lodges, to join an Encampment, and will do so, should it be deemed expedient to grant our petition.

In conclusion, permit us to say that we sincerely believe that the granting of our petition will heal any little dissensions which may have arisen, and promote the welfare and best interests of our Order generally, in this city and vicinity, which we all have at heart.

Yours, in F., L. and T.

AARON C. GOODMAN,	BENJAMIN STEVENS,
JOHN BURT,	EZRA CLARK, JR.,
WM. B. DAVIS,	ISAAC A. BRAGAW,
C. M. DARROW,	ERASTUS HUBBARD,
W. S. CRANE,	WM. RUSSELL, [withdrawn.]
CHARLES SPENCER,	

HARTFORD, Feb. 12th, 1847.

M. W. G. P.:

Dear Sir,—We, the undersigned, members of the Independent Order of Odd Fellows, resident in Hartford, and having attained to the scarlet degree, being desirous to be initiated into the higher orders of Odd Fellowship, and feeling that there are objections to Midian Encampment which to us are insurmountable, would respectfully ask that a dispensation or charter for another Encampment be granted in this city, which they believe would tend greatly to promote the interests of the Order. They believe, also, that were another Encampment to be established in this city, very many gentlemen of high standing and character, who have hitherto kept aloof from the Order, would be induced to unite themselves with us.

For these, with other reasons which might be mentioned, we are induced to make the present application, in connection with another

10

which we understand is being forwarded to you for a dispensation or
charter for another Encampment in this city.

Respectfully yours, in F., L. and T.,

P. G. Leonard Wheeler,
P. G. L. B. Allyn,
P. G. A. N. Clark,
P. G. Wm. B. Ely,
P. G. Thos. Martin,
N. G. R. G. Drake.

Office of the G. Patriarch, I. O. O. F. of Connecticut, ⎰
Norwich, Feb. 16, 1847.   ⎱

To Aaron C. Goodman and William B. Davis:

Patriarchs,—A petition signed by you and ten Patriarchs of Midian Encampment, asking for a dispensation for an Encampment to be
located in the city of Hartford, has been received.

After some deliberation, I have determined to grant the prayer of
the petition. You will, therefore, at your earliest convenience, make
the necessary preparations, and inform me at what time you desire
the institution to take place. The Dispensation will be presented at
the institution of the Encampment.

It gives me great pleasure thus to have complied with your wishes,
and I trust that all your proceedings will be characterized by the
spirit which genuine Odd Fellowship dictates.

With sentiments of respect and esteem,

Yours, in F., H. and C.,

W. L. Brewer, *G. Patriarch.*

Hartford, February 17th, 1847.

*To Wm. L. Brewer, M. W. G. Patriarch of the Grand Encampment, I. O. O. F.
of Connecticut :*

Dear Sir and Brother,—It gives me pleasure to acknowledge the
receipt of your favor of yesterday's date, and to express my thanks
for the Dispensation you signified your intention of granting our new
Encampment.

It is now our intention, if you can favor us with your presence at
that time, and nothing should occur to prevent, to be in readiness for
institution on Wednesday, the 24th inst., say at 3 o'clock, P. M. after
which we can initiate new members in the evening.

Will you please signify to us, by return of mail, if the day named
meets your approbation, and if so, we will endeavor to make our arrangements accordingly, and give you notice at once.

With the highest sentiments of respect and esteem,

We remain yours, in F., H. and C.,

Aaron C. Goodman,

In behalf of the Petitioners.

P. S. The cars arrive here from Worcester and Springfield, about
2 o'clock P. M.

Office of the G. Patriarch, I. O. O. F. of Connecticut, }
Norwich, Feb. 22, 1847. }

To A. C. Goodman and other Patriarchs :

Brothers,—I have this day received a visit from a committee of Midian Encampment. I must say that I am now disposed to view the application of the petitioners in a very different light. Their statement of facts induces me to consider the petition as one which the G. Encampment alone ought to decide.

Meanwhile I must direct that all arrangements must be stayed.

I have furnished this committee with my opinions, to which you can refer in your Encampment.

To-morrow I will write you, and give more at length the reasons which have induced this change of opinion.

Respectfully yours, in F., L. and T.,
W. L. Brewer, *G. Patriarch.*

At a special session of Midian Encampment, No. 7, I. O. of O. F., held at their room on the evening of Feb. 20th, 1847, pursuant to a legal notice, the following preamble and resolutions were adopted, to wit :

Whereas, it having been rumored about our streets that efforts were secretly making to organize a new Encampment in this city, much to the surprise and astonishment of the members of this Encampment; and whereas, in order to consummate this movement without the knowledge or sanction of this Encampment, it is understood that a secret application has been made to the Grand Patriarch for a dispensation, and that deceptive representations have been made to that worthy and respectable officer, to induce him to favor this illadvised and factious movement—therefore it is

Resolved, That the rumored attempt to organize a new Encampment in this city does not receive the approval of Midian Encampment, it being perfectly well known that this Encampment has long been in a state of depression and weakness, from which it is just beginning to emerge, and yet needs the united efforts of the members of the Order to sustain it as it should be ; and also, that the establishment of a new Encampment here at this time would be disastrous to the peace and harmony of the Order in our city.

Resolved, That although it does not become the members of this Encampment to impugn the motives of the pioneers in this movement, be they who they may, yet we must be allowed to express our belief that the project was designed with no purpose of doing good to the Order, but rather to gratify personal feelings, and which, if allowed to succeed, can accomplish little else than to give " form and substance" to a factious and disorganizing spirit, the legitimate fruits of which will be unhappy feuds and discord.

Resolved, That in the opinion of this Encampment, the consummation of this project at the present time, would tend only to engender jealousies and schisms among the members of the Order in this city, and prove the prolific source of untold evil and mischief.

Resolved, That Patriarchs Miller, Johnson, and Eldredge, be a committee to present in person to the Grand Patriarch a certified copy of these resolutions, and in behalf of Midian Encampment respectfully to remonstrate against the establishment of another Encampment in this city.

Resolved, That a sum of money not exceeding twenty-five dollars be hereby appropriated from the funds of the Encampment, to defray the expenses of the committee above named, in the performance of their duty.

The above resolutions were discussed at considerable length, when, on motion of Patriarch Bragaw, it was

Voted, That the question on the adoption of these resolutions be taken by yeas and nays.

The question was then taken with the following result :

Yeas.—Patriarchs Button, Hale, Chapin, Strong, Eldredge, Sears, King, Woodhouse, Smart, Olmsted, Brown, A. Woodruff, Sweetland, Morley, Alexander, Miller, Johnson, Merriman, S. Woodruff—19.

Nays.—Patriarchs Clark, Bragaw, Goodman, Spencer, Davis, Hubbard, Darrow—7.

The vote was then declared by the C. P. to be *nineteen* in favor of the resolutions, and *seven* against them, and the resolutions adopted.

The above is a true copy of the proceedings of the Encampment.

E. FESSENDEN, *Chief Patriarch.*

M. M. MERRIMAN, *Scribe.*

To the Officers and Members of Midian Encampment, No. 7, I. O. O. F.:

The committee appointed to present to the Grand Patriarch the resolutions adopted by this Encampment, on the evening of February 20th, remonstrating against the establishment of a new Encampment in this city, have attended to their duty, and respectfully beg leave to report :

That on Monday last they repaired to Norwich, the residence of the Grand Patriarch, and after being very kindly and cordially received by that gentlemanly and worthy officer, they presented to him the doings of this Encampment in relation to the project of which for some days had been secretly ripening of establishing an *Opposition* Encampment in this city, which he examined with due attention—after which the committee laid before him, in a familiar and unrestrained manner, a candid statement of *facts* connected with the matter they had in charge—all of which the Grand Patriarch carefully considered and weighed, and then *decided* that there appeared to him just cause to postpone further action upon the subject until the next session of the Grand Encampment, at which time and place this question could be understandingly and definitively settled. This decision was communicated to your committee by the following note from the Grand Patriarch.

OFFICE OF GRAND PATRIARCH, ⎰
Norwich, February 22d, 1847. ⎱

To Messrs. J. B. Eldredge, H. L. Miller, and J. W. Johnson, Committee, &c.:

Brothers,—The remonstrance of Midian Encampment, presented by you against the institution of a new Encampment in the city of Hartford, accompanied as it has been by a long and full exposition of what you deem to be the true interests of the Order, in regard to the same, has induced me to defer any further action in relation to the application of the petitioners. I shall request the petitioners to suspend any further preparations, and will with great cheerfulness present their petition to the Grand Encampment at its next session.

Believe me, gentlemen, to be yours in F., L. and T.,

W. L. BREWER, *G. P.*

The interview which the committee had with the Grand Patriarch was a somewhat protracted one, and in view of the embarrassments which seemed to surround the question which was before him, the committee feel constrained to say, that the Grand Patriarch manifested a strong desire and determination not only to act with strict impartiality, and to do justice to all concerned in this matter, but also to do that which in his judgment would most promote the harmony and prosperity of the Order in this vicinity. Your committee need hardly add, that it affords them great satisfaction to be able to place before the Encampment these details of their proceedings; and they cannot close their report without publicly expressing for themselves personally the sentiments of heartfelt gratitude which they feel towards the Grand Patriarch for the truly *paternal* and *patriarchal* manner in which he has interposed to relieve them from a "*fearfully dangerous crisis.*"

All which is respectfully submitted.

JOHN B. ELDREDGE, ⎫
H. L. MILLER,   ⎬ *Committee.*
J. W. JOHNSON,   ⎭

Voted, That the thanks of this Encampment are due to the Grand Patriarch of the Grand Encampment, for the kind consideration bestowed upon the remonstrance presented by the committee against the institution of a new Encampment in this city, and his decision that the Grand Encampment of the State must decide upon the application of the petitioners at its annual session in July next.

Voted, That while we disapprove the apparent motive, *secrecy* and *haste,* of the Patriarchs who petitioned for a new Encampment, and who have withdrawn from us, yet we cordially invite them to return their cards, and again unite with us in our endeavors to increase our numbers and prosperity of this branch of our Patriarchal Order.

Voted, That   be a committee to purchase all the regalia, or materials for new regalia, which said petitioners have purchased for the use of their anticipated Encampment.

Voted, That if the petitioners refuse to sell the regalia, &c., and refuse to again unite with us, as members of this Encampment, we invite them to visit us at their pleasure, and we assure them of a kind reception among us as guests; and should the Grand Encampment see fit to grant them their request, we will tender to them the right hand of fellowship.

Mr. Brewer,

Dear Brother,—We send the doings of our Encampment of last evening, according to a vote unanimous to do so.

E. Fessenden, *C. P.*

Matthew M. Merriman, *Scribe.*

Brother Brewer,

Dear Sir,—The report of the committee was accepted, and the accompanying resolutions passed, without one dissenting vote, every Patriarch voting in favor of report and resolutions.

Yours, in F., L. and T.,

E. Fessenden, *C. P.*

———

DOCUMENT B.

To the Most Worthy Grand Patriarch of the Grand Encampment, I. O. O. F. of the State of Connecticut :

The undersigned having, while Patriarchs of Midian Encampment, No. 7, I. O. O. F., petitioned the Grand Patriarch to institute them as an Encampment, in the city of Hartford, do now, as Patriarchs withdrawn from said Encampment and holding their cards, renew their said petition.

The undersigned beg leave most respectfully to recite their proceedings in the premises, and to lay before the Most Worthy Grand Patriarch additional reasons for his reconsideration of their prayer.

On the 17th day of February inst., the petitioners received from the Grand Patriarch a communication in answer to their memorial, whereby they were greatly encouraged with the hope of their speedy institution, and did, upon the recommendation of the Grand Patriarch, immediately proceed to order a considerable amount of expensive regalia and fixtures, all of which were in the rapid process of completion when the letter of the Grand Patriarch, of the 22d inst., (directing a suspension of further movements in the matter,) was received. On the evening preceding that on which the last named official document of the Grand Patriarch came to hand, the petitioners, together with another Patriarch, numbering ten in all, did, at a special meeting of Midian Encampment, called for that purpose, ask and receive their several cards of withdrawal from said Midian Encampment, which said cards they now hold.

Your petitioners further represent, that they are sincerely desirous of being again connected with the Patriarchal branch of their beloved Order, but that they are unwilling to offer their cards for deposite in said Midian Encampment; and although they exceedingly regret the alternative, they will feel themselves obliged to remain in perpetual separation from that department of Odd Fellowship, should the Grand Patriarch finally refuse the prayer of their petition. Of the justice of their first representations, made to the Grand Patriarch, they are still convinced, and three days hence they beg leave to add memorials of other qualified petitioners, as evidence of an extensive desire for their institution, and a pledge of their success.

The undersigned respectfully request that, in view of the facts and additional evidence herewith presented, the Grand Patriarch will, at his earliest convenience, personally investigate this whole matter in the city of Hartford, and that finding the allegations herein set forth to be true, he will proceed to grant their prayer, and to institute them as an Encampment, with full powers, under the authority wherewith he is invested by the Right Worthy Grand Encampment of Connecticut.

Dated at Hartford City, Feb. 27th, 1847.

A. C. GOODMAN,	JOHN BURT,
ELIHU GEER,	CHARLES SPENCER,
WM. B. DAVIS,	EZRA CLARK, JR.,
ISAAC A. BRAGAW,	C. M. DARROW.
BENJ. STEVENS,	

To the Most Worthy Grand Patriarch of the Grand Encampment, I. O. O. F. of Connecticut :

The memorial of the subscribers respectfully represents, that they are members of Mercantile Lodge, No. 8, of the Independent Order of Odd Fellows, under the jurisdiction of the R. W. Grand Lodge of Connecticut ; that they have attained to the scarlet degree, and are in good standing ; that they are desirous of being initiated into the Patriarchal branch of said Order, and that for reasons which they deem satisfactory, and for objections which are insuperable, they cannot unite with the only Encampment of Odd Fellows now existing in the county of Hartford—praying that the Most Worthy Grand Patriarch will favorably consider the petition of sundry Patriarchs (late of Midian Encampment) for a new Encampment, now pending before him, and that he will grant the prayer of their said petition.

Dated at Hartford, this 27th day of Feb., 1847.

LEONARD WHEELER,	SAMUEL H. PORCH,
WM. E. SUGDEN,	WILLIAM P. WOOLLEY,
R. VALLANT,	EMMONS RUDGE,
CHAS. P. BURR,	WARREN ROWLEY,
LORENZO DANIELS,	HARVEY HEBARD,
GEO. H. OLMSTED,	E. S. McCOLLUM,
H. SCHULZE,	WM. H. RISLEY,
A. N. CLARK,	E. KIMMELL,
CHAS. P. WELLS,	CHAS. D. NATT,
V. P. TAYLOR,	WM. MONTGOMERY,
LEOPOLD LITHANER,	F. C. STRICKLAND,
R. STOCKBRIDGE,	G. B. CAREY,
FREDERICK S. BROWN,	E. B. RICHARDSON,
JAMES G. WELLS,	E. D. TIFFANY,
LEVI STILES,	HENRY H. BARBER,
LEWIS W. GOODSELL,	E. S. GILBERT,

Frederick H. Redfield,	W. Bigelow, Jr.,
Wm. B. Ely, P. G.	S. H. Clarke,
George A. Wright,	H. E. Goodwin,
Joseph Winship,	L. B. Allyn, P. G.,
James H. Webb,	Moses Church,
William Camp,	Thos. Martin, P. G.,
Chas. R. Wadsworth,	H. J. Sawyer,
Thos. Winship,	Albert G. Cooley,
R. G. Drake, N. G.	Erastus Granger,
Sandford S. Underwood,	C. N. Humphrey,
West W. Russell,	Wm. J. Babcock,
J. K. Southmayd,	Elisha Moore,
E. D. Morley,	C. A. Avery.
Henry Middleton,	

Office of the G. Patriarch, &c., }
Norwich, March 1st, 1847. }

To A. C. Goodman and others, petitioners:

Brothers,—Your communication of the 27th February has been received. In view of the various and conflicting statements which have been made to me, I am in doubt what course ought to be pursued. I have but one object in view, and that is the good of the Order.

I shall defer any answer to your petition until I can give the whole subject a personal investigation, and shall have heard the parties, and all the facts in the case. Nothing short of this will warrant me in giving a further opinion.

For this purpose, I shall be in Hartford on Wednesday next. Enclosed you have copies of all your communications, in case you may not have retained them. I have informed the committee of Midian Encampment, who visited me, of the renewal of your petition, and have enclosed them copies of all the statements made by you, that they may be prepared to answer them. You will therefore prepare for a final hearing of your application on Wednesday evening next.

Yours, &c.,   W. L. Brewer, *G. P.*

To the Most Worthy Grand Patriarch of the Grand Encampment, I. O. O. F.
of the State of Connecticut:

The memorial of the subscribers respectfully represents, that they are members of Charter Oak Lodge, No. 2, of the Independent Order of Odd Fellows, under the jurisdiction of the Right Worthy Grand Lodge of Connecticut; that they have attained to the scarlet degree, and are in good standing; that they are desirous of being initiated into the Patriarchal branch of this Order; that they believe, as there is only one Encampment in this county, where we number nearly one thousand members of the scarlet degree, that the establishing of a new Encampment in this city will be a benefit to the one now existing, and to the Order in general; and therefore pray that the Most Worthy Grand Patriarch will favorably consider the petition of sundry Patriarchs (late of Midian Encampment) for a new Encampment,

now pending before him, and that he will grant the prayer of their
said petition.

Dated City of Hartford, this 27th day of Feb., 1847.

T. Sheldon, P. G.,	George Simons,
Stillman Niles,	Chas. W. Church,
Moses Burr,	C. Spencer,
Jos. Pratt, Jr., P. G.,	John Fairman,
Silas Farrington,	W. H. Pratt,
H. Waters,	M. P. Holt,
E. B. Miller,	Wm. H. Gilbert,
E. S. Woodward,	E. C. Kellogg, P. G.,
Horace Ensworth,	Benning Mann,
Stephen Strickland,	Walter Lewis.
Woodard Denn,	

*To the Most Worthy Grand Patriarch of the Grand Encampment, I. O. O. F. of
the State of Connecticut :*

The memorial of the subscribers respectfully represents, that they
are members of Farmers and Mechanics Lodge, No. 22, of the Independent Order of Odd Fellows, under the jurisdiction of the Right
Worthy Grand Lodge of Connecticut ; that they have attained to the
scarlet degree, and are in good standing ; that they are desirous of
being initiated into the Patriarchal branch of this Order ; that they
believe, as there is only one Encampment in this county, which is
the most populous one in the State, and where we number nearly one
thousand members of the scarlet degree, with a still rapid increase,
that the establishing of a new Encampment in the city of Hartford
will lead to the formation of other Encampments in this county, all
which will benefit the Order in general.   We, the petitioners, therefore pray that the Most Worthy Grand Patriarch will favorably consider the petitions of sundry Patriarchs (late of Midian Encampment)
for a new Encampment, now pending before him, and that he will
grant the prayer of their said petition.

Dated at Warehouse Point, this 27th day of Feb., 1847.

Lodawick Weller, P. G.,	Samuel Patchen,
Philip Tucker, N. G.,	R. H. Alling,
John Rewell,	John Abbe, 2d,
Benj. Pease,	Wm. J. Whipple, P. G.,
Noyes L. Parsons,	Levi Barnes,
Corydon O. Lord,	Lemuel E. Reed,
R. Thrall,	Stephen Adams,
Alonzo Day,	John C. Marley,
Justus D. Chapman,	Charles A. Chase,
E. Kingsbury,	John H. Inslee,
Horace Porter,	Norton M. Braman,
C. A. Lord, P. G.,	John C. Bush,
William Coomes,	Alexander Downie,
R. E. Bannon,	Joseph Kingsbury.
S. F. Fish,	

11

To the M. W. G. Patriarch of the G. Encampment, I. O. O. F. of Conn.:

The memorial of the subscribers respectfully represents, that they are members of Oakland Lodge, No. 25, of the Independent Order of Odd Fellows, under the jurisdiction of the Right Worthy Grand Lodge of Connecticut; that they have attained to the scarlet degree, and are in good standing; that they are desirous of being initiated into the Patriarchal branch of said Order, and that for reasons which they deem satisfactory, and for objections which are insuperable, they cannot unite with the only Encampment of Odd Fellows now existing in the county of Hartford—praying that the Most Worthy Grand Patriarch will favorably consider the petition of sundry Patriarchs (late of Midian Encampment) for a new Encampment, now pending before him, and that he will grant the prayer of their said petition.

Dated at Oakland, (Manchester,) this 27th day of Feb., 1847.

HENRY W. HUDSON, P. G.,   HENRY J. JOHNSON,
ALLEN DEMING,   ISRAEL H. PERRY,
JOSEPH CARROLL,   VALETTE D. PERRY, P. G.
GEO. ELLIOTT,   JAMES M. PERRY,
M. HUDSON, P. G.,   CHARLES FOX.
WELLS BUCKLAND,

DOCUMENT C.

OFFICE OF THE G. P., I. O. O. F. OF CONNECTICUT,
Hartford, March 4, 1847.

Patriarchs,—After a careful examination of all matters connected with your petition for a new Encampment to be located in this city, I have determined to grant the dispensation. Please inform me when it will suit your convenience, and at what place you will present yourselves for institution.

Yours, in the bonds of brotherhood,

W. L. BREWER, *G. Patriarch.*

To Aaron C. Goodman and others, petitioners.

HARTFORD, March 4th, 1847.

To Wm. L. Brewer, M. W. G. Patriarch of G. Encampment, I. O. O. F. of Conn.:

Dear Sir and Brother,—Your communication informing the petitioners for a new Encampment in this city, that their prayer is granted, is before me. In reply to your inquiries, when and where it will be convenient for us to be instituted, we would name Mercantile Hall, at 3 o'clock, this afternoon, as the place and time, if it meets your approbation.

Permit me to thank you for the patience with which you have heard us, and the promptness with which you have given your decision.

With sentiments of respect and esteem,

I remain yours, in F., H. and C.,

A. C. GOODMAN,

In behalf of the petitioners.

OFFICE OF G. PATRIARCH, &c., ⎱
Hartford, March 4, 1847. ⎰

To Edson Fessenden, Esq., C. P. of Midian Encampment:

Dear Sir and Brother,—After a careful and deliberate examination of the whole matter, I deem it my duty to grant the prayer of sundry qualified petitioners for a new Encampment to be located in this city. The institution of this Encampment will take place in Mercantile Hall, at 3 o'clock P. M. of this day, and I hereby invite the presence and assistance of the officers and other Patriarchs of Midian Encampment.

Be pleased to communicate my best wishes for the harmony and entire prosperity of the Encampment over which you have the honor to preside, with the ardent hope that the senior institution may cordially extend its fellowship to their offspring, and that no other rivalry may exist than that of a generous emulation, and a desire to excel in the fruits of Faith, Hope and Charity.

Yours, &c.,   W. L. BREWER, *G. P.*

CIRCULAR.

HARTFORD, March, 1847.

Patriarchs and Brothers—

At a meeting of Midian Encampment, No. 7, I. O. of O. F., held on the evening of the 15th inst., it was unanimously

Voted, That the following STATEMENT OF FACTS connected with the recent Institution of " *Connecticut Encampment,* No. 11," in this city, be printed and a copy be furnished to the Worthy Grand Patriarch and each subordinate Encampment under the jurisdiction of the Grand Encampment of this State.

On the 16th of February last a petition was presented to the Most Worthy G. P. in the city of Norwich by ten members of Midian Encampment, No. 7, all of them members of Mercantile Lodge, asking for a dispensation to open and constitute a new Encampment in this city. Said petition was presented in person through a Committee of their own number, who represented to the M. W. G. P. that the *movement was a secret at Hartford,* known only to the Petitioners and seven scarlet members of Mercantile Lodge residing in this city, who had three days previous, by letter, recommended that the petition be granted. The M. W. G. P., without consulting with any members of the Patriarchal branch of the Order in this city, and without delay or further inquiry, was pleased to grant the prayer of the Petitioners, and wrote to them to go forward with their arrangements for the Institution. Thus far all was a *profound secrecy,* and no member of the Order in this city, except the Petitioners, knew any thing of the proposed new Encampment. On the 17th of Feb., for the *first time* it came to the knowledge of the members of Midian Encampment that such a project was in contemplation. On the 20th, at a special meeting of Midian Encampment, a Remonstrance against the Institution of a new Encampment in this city was *unanimously* adopt-

ed, and a committee of three appointed to present the same in person
to the Most Worthy G. P. and to use all proper arguments to induce
a reconsideration of his decision, or at least *a delay until the meeting
of the Grand Encampment in July next.* The Committee were received by the Most Worthy G. P. and after a presentation of the Remonstrance, accompanied by facts relative to the origin of the movement of the Petitioners, the Most Worthy G. P. was pleased to inform the Committee that although it *was told him by the Committee
of the Petitioners that the movement was a secret one,* yet he was assured that only a very few members of Midian Encampment would
feel any opposition, and that with members of the Order generally it
would be popular and greatly promote the union and harmony of its
members, and especially increase the number and promote the usefulness of the Patriarchal branch of the Order. The Committee of
Midian Encampment then satisfied the Most Worthy G. P., *as they
supposed,* of the all-important fact, that the Petitioners and those who
recommended the establishment of a new Encampment here, *were
without exception members of Mercantile Lodge,* who had been un-
successful in their attempt to induce Midian Encampment to occupy
Mercantile Lodge Hall, at a rent of over One Hundred Dollars per
annum, and were therefore *determined to have an Encampment of
their own, which should occupy their Hall.*

. In view of the remonstrance of Midian Encampment and the facts
presented by its committee, the Most Worthy G. P. stated " *that he
was satisfied that it was a matter for the Grand Encampment alone to
decide,*" and that *he would take no further steps in the matter except to
" direct the Petitioners to stay all further preparations,"* and notify
them that the Grand Encampment alone must decide upon their application in July next—and at the same time declaring that " *he would
hear no further ex-parte testimony.*

With this assurance, and with a letter from the Most Worthy G.
P. addressed to the Petitioners, and another to Midian Encampment
Committee, expressing in plain and unmistakable terms the decision
of the Grand Patriarch, the latter returned home and made a report
of their doings to Midian Encampment. During the absence of
Midian Encampment Committee, however, the ten Petitioners for
a new Encampment had taken out their withdrawal Cards, which
fact induced Midian Encampment the same evening their Committee
reported, to pass a vote unanimously inviting them to return, and appointing a Committee to purchase any materials for new Regalia,
&c. which might be on their hands—and here it was hoped the matter would rest. But as the Petitioners had secretly fixed upon the
24th of Eebruary for Institution, and had borrowed Regalia, Cos-
tumes, &c. from a neighboring State, to be used on the occasion, evidently expecting to have been Instituted *without even the knowledge
of Midian Encampment,* they again sent a Committee to Norwich, and.
induced the Most Worthy G. P. *to visit Hartford and institute their
Encampment under the following circumstances!*

On the 2d day of March, Midian Encampment was notified that on the evening of the 3d inst. a hearing would be granted them and the Petitioners before the Most Worthy G. P. At the appointed hour the meeting was held, though *evidently only for form's sake*, and by permission of the G. P. about fifty members of Mercantile Lodge, who had within the two preceding days been induced to sign a paper stating that they had insuperable objections to joining Midian Encampment, were allowed to be present and take part in the proceedings, until the period arrived when disclosures pertaining to the *Encampment Degrees* were to be made, when they were *reluctantly* required to retire.

On the part of the Petitioners it was declared *in general terms*, both in written petition and in debate, that there were insuperable objections to Midian Encampment, but only *one* specific reason given as a cause of complaint against it. Their application was supported by 59 members of Mercantile Lodge, which is composed of about 250 members—about 18 members of Charter Oak Lodge, which numbers over 300, and some 20 scarlet members each from Oakland Lodge, No. 25, and Farmers and Mechanics Lodge, No. 22, whose names were presented.

On the part of Midian Encampment it was shown that of the Petitioners some were restless spirits who had hindered the prosperity of the Encampment in times past, but who had recently lost their influence and discontinued their attendance—that none of the Petitioners had just cause of complaint or dissatisfaction, and that the only specification in their petition *was not true*—that of the Scarlet Degree members who had signed papers recommending a new Encampment, some *had been rejected by Midian Encampment for good and sufficient reasons*, some had signed on urgent persuasion as *a personal favor* to the Petitioners, without any wishes or feelings of their own to move them, some avowedly to encourage *opposition* and promote *strife* and *discord*, and many under an entire misapprehension of the matter in issue. It was most fully shown that the project had its origin with those who were dissatisfied because they had lost their influence in Midian Encampment, and been resisted and outnumbered in their perverse desire to carry on *improper* and *indecent practices*, in conferring the R. P. Degree, who had been moved to immediate action in the matter of a new Encampment because Midian Encampment had declined to occupy Mercantile Lodge Room at the enormous rent of $110 or $115, choosing rather to occupy another Hall at a greatly reduced rent.

In view of the above facts, which were abundantly substantiated, the members of Midian Encampment humbly besought the Most Worthy G. P. to delay a decision of the matter until the Grand Encampment, in July, could take the application into careful and candid consideration, and act as should seem to them just and equitable, and for the best interest of the Order, in both branches, in this city. But should he think it unjust towards the Petitioners to delay until that time, the G. P. was respectfully requested to call *a special session* of the Grand Encampment, to hear and decide at an earlier day.

At this stage of the proceedings, the meeting on the evening of the 3d inst. was adjourned.   At an early hour, on the following day, although the decision of the Most Worthy G. P. was not made known, it was feared from some indications that he was about to consummate the institution of the new Encampment, and such Patriarchs of Midian Encampment as were thus impressed, renewed their humble petition in due form, that a *special session* of the Grand Encampment might be called.   Thus matters stood, until about 2 o'clock P. M., when, to the great surprise and grief of the members of Midian Encampment, their C. P. received a note from the Most Worthy G. P., informing them that in *one hour*, at 3 o'clock P. M., *the new Encampment would be instituted in Mercantile Lodge Hall*, which letter was followed by another saying that *the matter of calling a special session* of the Grand Encampment was one of *great importance, requiring time to deliberate*, and that when duly considered a reply would be forwarded by mail from his residence at Norwich.   As no reply has yet been received, we are bound to suppose the Most Worthy G. P. is yet *gravely considering the subject ! ! !*

Thus was this measure consummated, after passing through its various phases, in nineteen days from the first application to the G. P., and in twelve days after it was first known to the members of this Encampment, and in opposition to the wishes of *every member of this Encampment, and contrary to their united, honest, and solemn convictions of right and justice.*

We state these facts to you, Patriarchs, not to engender strife and discord, but under a serious and heartfelt sense of duty to ourselves, to you, and to the Order.   We claim, and we are able and ready to show, that *no good cause* of dissatisfaction existed, and that it was *to gratify Mercantile Lodge with an Encampment of their own*, that the thing was sought—that while it may increase the *number* of Patriarchs in this city, it must and will inevitably *build up and perpetuate a wall of separation*, that destroys harmony, and defeats the very objects of the institution of the Patriarchal, and indeed of both branches of our beloved Order ; and further, that there was no such *emergency* as the Grand Encampment contemplated when by *usage* (not by its Constitution) it authorizes its G. P. to give Dispensations to Patriarchs who petition for new Encampments *during the recess* of the Grand Encampment.

With this simple statement of facts, we await the future with unabated zeal and devotion to the cause of Odd Fellowship among ourselves, throughout the State, and throughout the world.

E. Fessenden, *C. P. Midian Encampment.*

M. M. Merriman, *Scribe.*

DOCUMENT D.

To the M. W. Grand Patriarch of the G. Encampment, I. O. O. F. of Conn.:

We, the undersigned, officers and members of the Grand Encampment of Connecticut, I. O. O. F., in view of the late decision of the M. W. Grand Patriarch, in relation to the petition of certain Patriarchs for a second subordinate Encampment to be located in this city, and believing that such a decision at this time will be productive of untold evils to the whole Order in our midst, and particularly the patriarchal branch of the Order, and having in view the harmony, growth, and prosperity of Midian Encampment, and the whole Order in this city, would respectfully ask of the M. W. Grand Patriarch that a special session of the Grand Encampment of Connecticut, I. O. O. F., be called at the earliest convenient moment, in order that certain facts may be presented to that R. W. Grand Body, and that a full hearing of the matter at issue may be had.

Dated at Hartford, this 4th day of March, Anno Domini, one thousand eight hundred and forty-seven.

JOHN W. JOHNSON, *G. S. Warden,*
A. M. GORDON, *P. C. P.,*
AARON MORLEY, *P. C. P.,*
E. FESSENDEN, *C. P.,*
HENRY L. MILLER, *P. H. P.,*
WM. H. SWEETLAND, *H. P.,*
SAML. WOODRUFF, *P. H. P.*

To the M. W. Grand Patriarch of the G. Encampment, I. O. O. F. of Conn.:

We, the undersigned, officers and members of Midian Encampment, No. 7, I. O. O. F., in view of the late decision of the M. W. G. P. of Grand Encampment of Connecticut, I. O. O. F., in relation to the petition of certain Patriarchs for a second subordinate Encampment, to be located in this city, and believing that such a decision at this time will be the production of great and lasting injury to the harmony, growth, and prosperity of the whole Order in our midst, and especially the Patriarchal branch of the Order, and having in view the welfare and harmony of the Order in our city, and especially of Midian Encampment. No. 7, I. O. O. F., would respectfully ask of the M. W. Grand Patriarch, that a special session of the Grand Encampment of Connecticut, I. O. O. F., be holden at the earliest possible convenient opportunity, in order that the whole matter at issue, and now pending, may be presented, and a full hearing be had.

Dated at Hartford, this 4th day of March, 1847.

EDWARD BUTTON,	CALVIN NORTHROP,
OLIVER D. SEYMOUR,	JOSEPH BROWN,
WILLIAM OLMSTED,	M. M. MERRIMAN,
JOEL SPERRY,	H. K. SIMS,
JOHN B. ELDREDGE,	JOS. W. BLALE,
WM. H. CHAPIN,	JOHN SMART,
GEO. KING,	N. S. WEBB.
ABIJAH WOODRUFF,	.

OFFICE OF THE G. PATRIARCH, &c., {
Hartford, March 5, 1847. }

To J. W. Johnson, Esq., R. W. G. S. Warden, and others, petitioners :

Patriarchs,—Your petition, requesting that a special session of the R. W. G. Encampment may be called, has been received. The subject is one which demands great deliberation. I shall take time for reflection, and will reply to the petition after my arrival at Norwich.
Yours, &c.,   W. L. BREWER, *G. P.*

OFFICE OF THE G. PATRIARCH, I. O. O. F. OF CONNECTICUT, {
Norwich, March 29, 1847. }

To J. W. Johnson, Esq., R. W. G. Senior Warden, and others, petitioners :

Patriarchs,—The petition which it was your pleasure to present to me on the 4th of the present month, asking that a special session of the G. Encampment might be called, has received my most serious consideration. I have also consulted many members of the G. Encampment in relation to the same. The result of my deliberations is, that I do not deem it expedient to call a special session of the G. Encampment at this time. It is thought not to be such an emergency as will warrant the G. Patriarch in so doing.

Please accept, Brothers, assurances of my highest regard.
Sincerely yours,
W. L. BREWER, *G. P.*

Abstract of Annual Returns of Subordinate Encampments under the jurisdiction of the Grand Encampment, I. O. O. F. of Connecticut, for the year ending July, 1847.

Name.	Initiated.	Adm. by Card	Reinstated.	Rejected.	Withdrawn.	Suspended.	Whole No.	Receipts.	Am't on hand.	Dues to G. E.	No. relievd.	Am't for same.	Total benefits.
Sassacus, No. 1,	5	0	0	0	0	18	63	$105.70	$286.70	$16 42	0	$ 00	$ 00
Oriental,* 2,	7	0	0	0	0	0	17	00	00	6 50	0	00	00
Palmyra, 3,	12	0	0	0	2	1	75	155.00	694 48	27.55	2	20.00	20.00
Unity, 4,	1	0	0	0	0	0	63	91.37	00	16 24	7	42.00	42.00
Devotion, 5,	2	0	0	0	4	0	23	55.91	00	9.59	0	00	00
Sowheag, 6,	4	0	0	0	0	0	28	78.82	68.02	8.15	5	72.00	72.00
Midian, 7,	31	1	0	1	11	0	67	188.30	147.31	26.17	1	12.00	12.00
MountHermon,†8,	9	0	0	0	2	0	35	69.34	50.00	13.59	0	00	00
Kabaosa,† 9,	14	0	0	0	0	0	31	118.51	00	16.42	0	00	00
Charity,† 10,	12	0	0	0	0	0	21	143 95	00	9.59	0	00	00
Connecticut, 11,	47	11	0	0	0	0	58	480.00	53.25	29.20	0	00	00
Total,	144	12	0	1	19	19	481	1486 90	1299.76	179.42	15	146.00	146.00

* No report of last term.   † No returns of relief.

GRAND TREASURER'S ACCOUNT.

Grand Encampment, I. O. O. F., in account with S. Bishop, G. T.

Dr.   Jan. 14, 1847, To cash paid W. L. Brewer,   - - - $9.00
    "   "   "   "   M. A. Shepard,   - - -   6.00
    "   "   "   "   W. L. Brewer,   - - -   2.90
    "   "   "   "   P. Demick,   - - - -   18 18
    "   "   "   "   J. W. Johnson,   - - -   5.00
    "   "   "   "   J. S. Parmelee,   - - -   5.00
    "   "   "   "   J. Greenwood, Jr.,   - -   40.00
    "   "   "   "   Sassacus Encampment,   -   20.00
    "   "   "   "   J. Kennedy,   - - - -   1.00
    "   "   To balance to new account,   - - -   5.64

                                       $112.72

Cr.   Jan. 14, 1847, By balance from old account, $15.17
    "   "   " cash received of G. S.,
              January Session, - - -   97.55
                                   $112.72

The Committee of Finance have examined the above account, and find it correct.

         J. M. Willey,
         H. Hobart Roath, } *Committee of Finance.*
         O. Utley,

SUBORDINATE ENCAMPMENTS,

Belonging to the jurisdiction of the Grand Encampment, I. O. O. F. of Connecticut.

Name.		Where held.	County.	Time of meeting.	Instituted.
Sassacus,	No. 1,	New Haven,	New Haven,	First Friday.	August 19, 1841.
Oriental,	2,	East Haddam,	Middlesex,	First Friday.	September, 1841.
Palmyra,	3,	Norwich,	New London,	First and third Friday.	June 15, 1843.
Unity,	4,	New London,	New London,	First and third Thursday.	April 22, 1844.
Devotion,	5,	Bethel,	Fairfield,	First and third Friday.	August 28, 1844.
Sowheag,	6,	Middletown,	Middlesex,	First Tuesday.	September 27, 1844.
Midian,	7,	Hartford,	Hartford,	First Monday.	December 24, 1844.
Mount Hermon,	8,	Bridgeport,	Fairfield,	First and third Friday.	April 22, 1845.
Kabaosa,	9,	Norwalk,	Fairfield,	First Wednesday.	September 17, 1845.
Charity,	10,	Mystic,	New London,	First Tuesday.	November 10, 1846.
Connecticut,	11,	Hartford,	Hartford,	First Thursday.	March 4, 1847.

OFFICERS AND MEMBERS

OF THE

GRAND ENCAMPMENT, I. O. O. F. OF CONNECTICUT.

OFFICERS FOR 1847-8.

M. W. MUNSON A. SHEPARD,	*Grand Patriarch.*
M. E. TOWNSEND P. ABELL,	*Grand High Priest.*
R. W. JUNIUS M. WILLEY,	*Grand Senior Warden.*
R. W. LUCIUS A. THOMAS,	*Grand Scribe.*
R. W. SAMUEL BISHOP,	*Grand Treasurer.*
R. W. CHOLWELL J. GRUMAN,	*Grand Junior Warden.*
R. W. WILLIAM L. BREWER,	*Grand Representative.*
W. WILLIAM A. JUDD,	*Grand Sentinel.*
W. ALLEN S. WIGHTMAN,	*Deputy Grand Sentinel.*

PAST GRAND PATRIARCHS.
ROBINSON S. HINMAN, 1843.
WILLIAM E. SANFORD, 1843–4.
JOHN L. DEVOTION, 1844–5.
JONATHAN M. ANDRUS, 1845–6.
WILLIAM L. BREWER, 1846–7.

PAST GRAND HIGH PRIESTS.
CHARLES W. BRADLEY, 1843.
WILLIAM E. SANFORD, 1843–4.
JONATHAN M. ANDRUS, 1844–5.
WILLIAM L. BREWER, 1845–6.
MUNSON A. SHEPARD, 1846–7.

DEPUTY GRAND PATRIARCHS.

No. 1, L. A. THOMAS.	No. 7. EDSON FESSENDEN.
No. 2, —— ———	No. 8, DWIGHT MORRIS.
No. 3, H. HOBART ROATH.	No. 9, G. W. SMITH.
No. 4, ROBERT B. JACKSON.	No. 10, G. G. KING.
No. 5, WM. A. JUDD.	No. 11, AARON C. GOODMAN.
No. 6, DENNIS SAGE.	

MEMBERS.

Sassacus, No. 1, New Haven.

Wm. E. Sanford, April 20, 1843.
Samuel Bishop, April 20, 1843.
Robinson S. Hinman, April 20, 1843.
Isaac Judson, April 20, 1843.
Bela Lord, Jan. 12, 1844.
Jonathan M. Andrus, April 12, 1844.
Prelate Demick, July 12, 1844.
N. C. Hall, Jan. 9, 1845.

L. A. Thomas, July 10, 1845.
Daniel H Moore, Jan. 15, 1846.
Elizur Hubbell, July 9, 1846.
F. Croswell, Jan. 14, 1847.
Truman Hart, Jan. 14, 1847.
Eliphalet G. Storer, July 15, 1847.
Noah Chandler, July 15, 1847.

Oriental, No. 2, East Haddam.

Chas. W. Bradley, April 20, 1843.
Richard S. Pratt, April 20, 1843.
Thos. C. Bordman, April 20, 1843.

J. C. Palmer, July 10, 1845.
J. M. Willey, July 10, 1845.
John S. Dickinson, Jan. 14, 1847.

Palmyra, No. 3, Norwich.

John L. Devotion, July 14, 1843.
Wm. L. Brewer, July 12, 1844.
John A. Lathrop, July 12, 1844.
Edward W. Eells, Jan. 9, 1845.
H. C. Bridgham, July 10, 1845.

David Young, July 10, 1845.
H. Hobart Roath, July 9, 1846.
P. M. Judson, July 9, 1846.
James D. Mowrey, Jan. 14, 1847.
James A. Hovey, July 15, 1847.

Unity, No. 4, New London.

O. F. Smith, July 10, 1845.
George W. Brown, July 10, 1845.
Allen S. Wightman, Jan. 15, 1846.

C. C. Culver, Jan. 15, 1846.
Robert B. Jackson, July 15, 1847.

Devotion, No. 5, Danbury.

J. Greenwood, Jr., Jan. 9, 1845.
Munson A. Shepard, Jan. 9, 1845.
James R. Greenwood, Jan. 15, 1846.
William W. Bedient, Jan. 15, 1846.

James P. Saunders, Jan. 15, 1846.
Wm. F. Hoyt, July 9, 1846.
Ethel T. Farnum, July 9, 1846.
Wm. A. Judd, Jan. 14, 1847.

Sowheag, No. 6, Middletown.

Thomas C. Simpson, Jan. 9, 1845.
Origen Utley, Jan. 9, 1845.
Erastus H. Booth, Jan. 9, 1845.

John S. Parmelee, July 10, 1845.
Dennis Sage, Jan. 14, 1847.
Townsend P. Abell, Jan. 14, 1847.

Midian, No. 7, Hartford.

A. M. Gordon, Jan. 9, 1845.
John W. Johnson, Jan 9, 1845.
Aaron Morley, July 10, 1845.
Henry L. Miller, Jan. 15, 1846.

Edson Fessenden, Jan. 14, 1847.
Wm. H. Sweetland, Jan. 14, 1847.
M. M. Merriman, July 15, 1847.
O. D. Seymour, July 15, 1847.

Mount Hermon, No. 8, Bridgeport.

A. B. Beers, July 10, 1845.
S. B. Brittan, July 10, 1845.
George S. Sanford, Jan. 15, 1846.
E. B. Stevens, July 9, 1846.

Gilson Landon, Jan. 14, 1847.
Joseph Crosby, Jan. 14, 1847.
Dwight Morris, Jan. 14, 1847.

Kabaosa, No. 9, Norwalk.

James A. Quintard, Jan. 15, 1846.
P. L. Cunningham, Jan. 15, 1846.

Cholwell J. Gruman, Jan. 15, 1846.
George W. Smith, July 9, 1846.

Charity, No. 10, Mystic Bridge.

Wm. Meeker, July 15, 1847.

Amos Clift, July 15, 1847.

Connecticut, No. 11, Hartford.

Ezra Clarke, Jr., July 15, 1847.
R. G. Drake, July 15, 1847.
Wm. B. Davis, July 15, 1847.

A. C. Goodman, July 15, 1847.
Elihu Geer, July 15, 1847.

SEMI-ANNUAL SESSION.

NEW HAVEN, Jan. 13, 1848.

The R. W. Grand Encampment, I. O. O. F. of Connecticut, convened this day in regular session, at 2 o'clock P. M.

PRESENT :

M. W. MUNSON A. SHEPARD, *Grand Patriarch,*
M. E. TOWNSEND P. ABELL, *Grand High Priest,*
R. W. JUNIUS M. WILLEY, *Grand Senior Warden,*
R. W. LUCIUS A. THOMAS, *Grand Scribe,*
R. W. SAMUEL BISHOP, *Grand Treasurer,*
R. W. CHOLWELL J. GRUMAN, *Grand Junior Warden,*
R. W. WILLIAM L. BREWER, *Grand Representative,*
ELIPHALET G. STORER, *Grand Sentinel, pro tem.*

After prayers by the Grand High Priest, the Grand Encampment was opened in ample form.

The Grand Scribe proceeded to read the proceedings of last session, when, on motion, the further reading was dispensed with, the proceedings having been printed.

The Grand Patriarch appointed a committee to examine the credentials of candidates for admission to membership in the Grand Encampment, consisting of P. G. P. Wm. E. Sanford and Pat. J. W. Johnson, who submitted the following report :

To the R. W. Grand Encampment of Connecticut :

The Committee on Elections would report as correct the following named Patriarchs :

C. P. Samuel H. Harris,	of Sassacus,	No.	1.
H. P. Lucius Peck,	" "	"	1.
P. H. P. L. D. Allen,	" Unity,	"	4.
C. P. W. B. Casey,	" Sowheag,	"	6.
H. P. Calvin Northrop,	" Midian,	"	7.
C. P. E. S. Quintard,	" Kabaosa,	"	9.
C. P. John H. Mills,	" Winsted,	"	12.
H. P. J. J. Twiss,	" "	"	12.
C. P. Joseph Olmsted, Jr.,	" Hinman,	"	13.
H. P. Robert M. Abbe,	" "	"	13.
C. P. Robert H. Lockwood,	" Wascussee,	"	14.

All of which is respectfully submitted.

WM. E. SANFORD,
JOHN W. JOHNSON.

Whereupon the above named candidates were admitted and instructed in the work of the Grand Encampment.

The Grand Patriarch submitted the following report:

To the R. W. Grand Encampment:

OFFICERS AND PATRIARCHS:—We are again assembled in Grand Encampment, for the purpose of legislating for the Order entrusted to our care. In conformity with the usage in this State, I present you with a synopsis of my official acts since our last session, and make such suggestions for your consideration as occur to me, requiring your attention.

On the 28th day of October, I instituted Winsted Encampment, No. 12, I. O. O. F., and presented the charter granted at the last session. After the institution, five brothers were initiated and exalted to the R. P. degree, and one admitted by card, when the following Patriarchs were elected to office, viz :—J. H. Mills, C. P. ; J. J. Twiss, H. P. ; S. R. Weller, S. W. ; William S. Phillips, Scribe ; Orlando Pease, Treas. ; William S. Wetmore, J. W. ; and were installed in ample form.

On the 22d day of October, I received a petition from seven Patriarchs residing in the village of Warehouse Point, for an Encampment to be located at that place, by the name of Hinman Encampment, No. 13, I. O. O. F. Said petition was accompanied by recommendations from G. S. W. Willey, D. G. P. Goodman, and by Connecticut Encampment, No. 11. I accordingly granted a dispensation, subject to your approval, and on the 29th day of October, assisted by P. H. P. J. H. Waite, of Middlesex Encampment, No. 9, of Massachusetts, Patriarchs Goodrich, Ely, and Burt, of Connecticut Encampment, No. 11, and Patriarchs Gilman and Wilder, of Midian Encampment, No. 7, I instituted the same, and installed the following named officers, viz : Joseph Olmsted, Jr., C. P. ; R. M. Abbe, H. P. ; R. Thrall, S. W. ; J. D. Chapman, Scribe ; C. A. Lord, Treas. ; C. A. Chase, J. W. Three brothers were initiated and advanced to the R. P. degree. This Encampment now numbers eighteen members ; and from their intelligence, their standing in the community, and their zeal in Odd Fellowship, I cannot but predict for them a series of prosperity.

On the 23d day of October, I received a petition from seven Patriarchs residing in Stamford, for an Encampment to be located in that place, to be known and hailed by the name of Wascussee Encampment, No. 14, I. O. O. F. Said petition being accompanied by a recommendation from Kabaosa Encampment, No. 9, I granted a dispensation, subject to your approval, and on the 26th day of November, accompanied by P. H. P. E. T. Farnum, I repaired to Stamford and instituted the Encampment. The following named Patriarchs were elected and installed into office, viz :—R. H. Lockwood, C. P. ; H. N. Hudson, H. P. ; Chauncey Ayres, S. W. ; J. P. Tobias, Scribe ; Edward Caperon, Treas. ; J. T. Pratt, J. W. From my acquaintance with the character and standing of the officers of this Encampment, and the acknowledged high reputation of Rippowam Lodge, from which it must mainly derive its support, I have no doubt of its ultimate success.

I have this day received a petition, accompanied by the charter fee, for an Encampment to be located in Bristol. Said petition is signed by seven members of Connecticut Encampment. I would recommend the petition to your favorable consideration.

On the 15th of November, at the request of the officers of Hinman Encampment, I made an official visit to Midian Encampment, for the purpose of investigating some reported irregularities; but, on inquiry, I found nothing of which I could take notice.

I would suggest the necessity of so altering the Constitution of this Grand Encampment, and the Constitution of Subordinates, as hereafter to admit none but Past Chief Patriarchs and Past High Priests to the privileges of the Grand Encampment; to make it obligatory upon the subordinates to acknowledge the principle of benefits; and to confine the appointment of D. G. P. to the P. C. P. I believe these alterations are required by the Digest of the Laws, as adopted by the Grand Lodge of the United States. I would also suggest the propriety of providing by law for the appointment of the various standing committees of this R. W. body.

                              M. A. SHEPARD, *G. Patriarch.*
New Haven, January 13, 1848.

The Grand Scribe submitted the following report :

To the R. W. Grand Encampment :

In compliance with a now established custom of the Order, I herewith present a report of such matters within the province of the Grand Scribe, as the Grand Encampment may need cognizance of.

To the proceedings of the two last sessions, (which were published in compliance with a vote of the last session,) I prepared and appended an abstract of the reports of subordinate Encampments for the past year, together with a list of officers, past officers, and members of the Grand Encampment.

In the reports of subordinates, so much imperfection exists as to render difficult any attempt to present a view of the condition and progress of the Order. Until the last annual session, none of the subordinates reported the amount paid for benefits, and then but partial returns were made. Another important item is likewise deficient in the reports, and not provided for by any law, viz : the amount of funds on hand. These, with the amount of receipts, furnish data from which can be ascertained, with considerable precision, the ratio of income and expense in the Order, and enable us to arrive at accurate conclusions as to the proper amount of premiums or benefits which Encampments can pay their members without impairing their funds. A lamentable remissness has existed in the Order, ever since its establishment, in regard to the acquirement of statistical information relating to the income, expenses, and amount of premiums, in the various branches of the Order; no steps, so far as I can learn, have been taken to further this important object.

In all other institutions for insurance, and particularly that of life insurance, facts and other data have been carefully treasured up from year to year, through a long period. Thus arranged, they enable the various bodies thus engaged to calculate the chances of loss of life, or even property, with a near approximation to certainty. Had the same care been bestowed on facts so easily collected in our Order, and they collated from year to year, much of the disappointment so often met with in the newly established branches of our Order, would have been avoided, and a larger fund, and a wider extended useful-ness, would have been the portion of our venerated institution.

I recommend such enactments as will enable us to collect the defi-cient information of the past, and secure precision and punctuality for the future.

In arranging the list of members, I found much uncertainty from the imperfection of our early records, and probably many errors exist therein, which can only be corrected by the recollections of the mem-bers. I shall be glad to avail myself of any information which will assist me in making the list complete and correct.

Since the last session, I have opened a set of books, embracing the accounts between the Grand Encampment and its subordinates, from the institution of this R. W. body. As no such accounts had hitherto been kept, some doubt existed as to their accuracy ; I have, therefore, transmitted to each subordinate a copy of its account for adjustment From the want of such accounts, at the last session, the report of a committee appointed to examine the semi-annual re-ports in regard to the amounts to be credited to the several Encamp-ments, was incorrect in some particulars, as will be seen by refer-ence to the accounts.

I deem it necessary to say here, that in thus referring to various deficiencies and irregularities, I do not think them attributable to the fault of any of the officers who have preceded me, and hope it may not be so construed. Those officers have probably done all that could have been expected of them under the circumstances. The difficulty, in my apprehension, is attributable to other causes. The Grand Encampment has held its sessions immediately after those of the Grand Lodge, when both the officers and members, fatigued by attendance on its sessions, have found neither time nor inclina-tion to give the business that care and attention which it demanded. The low state of this branch of the Order in the State, in compari-son with the other, I have no doubt is attributable, in a good degree, to this source. I respectfully recommend the adoption of the propo-sition now before us, to fix the time of the sessions of the Grand Encampment anterior to that of the Grand Lodge.

I have, according to direction, completed the charter of this Grand Encampment, and had it suitably mounted. I have also procured a book-case suited to our wants.

I would also recommend that the Grand Scribe be authorized to publish the proceedings immediately after each session, instead of annually. The difference in cost will be trifling, and the convenience to the subordinates will be very great.

Lucius A. Thomas, *G. Scribe.*

The reports of the G. Patriarch and G. Scribe were accepted and referred to a special committee consisting of P. G. P. Brewer, G. S. W. Willey, and Pat. Utley.

The Grand Treasurer presented his semi-annual report, which was referred to a committee consisting of G. S. W. Willey and Pats. Utley and Crosby, who reported it correct.

The semi-annual reports of subordinates were referred to a special committee consisting of Pat. Croswell, G. J. W. Gruman, and Pat. Abbe.

Br. D. W. Patterson, of Owego Lodge, No. 204, of the State of New York, applied for dispensation allowing him admission to the Patriarchal branch of the Order, within the jurisdiction of this G. Encampment, which was accompanied by permission and recommendation of the G. Patriarch of the G. Encampment of New York.

On motion, the G. Patriarch was authorized to grant a dispensation to Br. Patterson.

The committee on the reports of the G. Patriarch and G. Scribe submitted the following report, which was accepted and committee discharged:

To the R. W Grand Encampment of Connecticut:

The Committee to whom was referred the reports of the M. W. G. Patriarch and G. Scribe, beg leave respectfully to report—That they would recommend that the following select committees of three members each be raised upon the subjects hereinafter named, to wit :

Upon so much of the M. W. G. Patriarch's report as relates to Charters for new Encampments ;

Upon so much of the G. Patriarch's report as relates to the alteration of the Constitution of Grand Encampment ;

Upon so much of the report of the R. W. G. Scribe as relates to the Reports of Subordinates.

All which is respectfully submitted, in Faith, Hope, and Charity.

W. L. Brewer,
J. M. Willey, } *Committee.*
O. Utley,

The Grand Patriarch appointed P. G. P. Sanford and Pats. Goodman and Clarke, of No. 11, Committee on Charters for new Encampments ; G. Scribe Thomas, G. S. W. Willey, and Pat. E. G. Storer, Committee on the alteration of the Constitution of Grand Encampment ; and G. H. P. Abell and Pats. Johnson and Olmsted, Committee on the Reports of Subordinates.

The following memorials were presented :

To the R. W. Grand Encampment of the State of Connecticut:

The memorial of the subscribers respectfully represent, that they are members of Farmers and Mechanics Lodge, No. 22, I. O. O. F., under the jurisdiction of the Right Worthy Grand Lodge of the State of Connecticut, that they have attained to the Scarlet Degree of the Order and are in good standing, that they are desirous of being initiated into the Patriarchal branch of the Order, and that for reasons which they deem satisfactory, and for objections which are "*insuperable*," they cannot unite with Hinman Encampment, located in Warehouse Point, Ct. And therefore pray that they may be permitted to unite with Midian Encampment in the city of Hartford.

Broadbrook, Dec. '47.

(Signed)   HORATIO N. BARROW, C. V. PECKHAM, JOHN CLARK, ALFRED E. DAY, JONAS HOLMES.

To the R. W. Grand Encampment of the State of Connecticut :

The memorial of the subscribers respectfully represent, that they are members of Pine Meadow Lodge, No. 39, I. O. O. F., under the jurisdiction of the Right Worthy Grand Lodge of the State of Connecticut, that they have all attained to the Scarlet Degree of the Order and are in good standing, that they are desirous of being initiated into the Patriarchal branch of the Order, and that for reasons which they deem satisfactory, (and for objections which are insuperable,) they cannot unite with Hinman Encampment, located in Warehouse Point, and do therefore pray that they may be permitted to unite with Midian Encampment in the city of Hartford.

Dec. 10, 1847.

(Signed)   DANIEL CRAGG, RAMSAY DOUGLASS, JAMES DOUGLASS.

To the R. W. Grand Encampment of the State of Connecticut:

The memorial of the subscribers respectfully represents, that they are members of Thompsonville Lodge, No. 45, of the Independent Order of Odd Fellows, under the jurisdiction of the Right Worthy Grand Lodge of the State of Connecticut ; that they have attained to the Scarlet Degree of the Order, and are in good standing ; that they are desirous of being initiated into the Patriarchal branch of the Order, and that for reasons which they deem satisfactory, and for objections which are "*insuperable*," they cannot unite with Hinman Encampment, located at Warehouse Point, and therefore pray that they may be permitted to unite with Midian Encampment in the city of Hartford.

Signed,   G. W. MARTIN, GEORGE C. OWEN, P. G., JOHN HALLAS, JAS. WORTHINGTON, JOHN OATES, DAVID HALLAS, JOHN SECKELL, V. G., NATHANEAL KING, THOS. M. KNIGHT, JOHN LAUERWEIN, JAMES WYLLIE, MATTHEW ANDERSON, A. J. TINKHAM, JERE D. EGLESTON, JOHN KENYON, MANNING WHEELOCK, JAMES BIDWELL, THOMAS SMALL, I. T. PEASE, DONALD GRAHAM, JACHIN ILLINGWORTH, DAVID L. PEELER, WM. BROOKES, H. C. BAGG.

After some discussion, it was moved, that the petitioners have leave to withdraw : carried, 21 to 4.

The By-Laws of Nos. 11 and 12, and amendments to By-Laws of No. 8, were submitted and referred to a committee consisting of G. S. W. Willey, Pat. Utley, and P. G. P. Brewer.

Pat. Gordon, of No. 7, called in question the right of the Grand Scribe to leave out from the printed abstract any portion of the records of the Grand Encampment, as appeared in the record of last session, p. 63. The Grand Patriarch decided it to be at the discretion of the G. Scribe. Pat. Gordon offered a resolution to that effect, which was deemed unnecessary, and the subject indefinitely postponed.

The committee appointed to examine the By-Laws of subordinates submitted the following report, which was accepted :

To the R. W. Grand Encampment :

The select committee to whom was referred the By-Laws of subordinates, beg leave to ask, that the committee be continued to the next regular session, that a more full examination may be had of the documents placed in their hands.

All which is respectfully submitted, in F., H. and C.

J. M. WILLEY, } Committee.
O. UTLEY, }

The following committee reported :

To the R. W. Grand Encampment :

The select committee to whom was referred so much of the report of the M. W. G. Patriarch as relates to the alteration of the Constitution, beg leave respectfully to report—That in the opinion of the committee, a complete and thorough revision of the Constitution is required ; and as the time during which this Grand Encampment will be in session will not be sufficient to enable the committee to give due consideration to so important a subject, they would submit the following resolution.

All which is respectfully submitted, in F., H. and C.

L. A. THOMAS, }
J. M. WILLEY, } Committee.
E. G. STORER, }

Resolved, That a committee of three be appointed, with instructions to revise the Constitution and By-Laws in accordance with the Digest and decisions of the Grand Lodge of the U. S.

Report accepted, resolution adopted, and G. Sec. Thomas, Pat. F. Croswell, and P. G. P. William E. Sanford appointed the committee, as recommended in the resolution.

The following proposition to amend the Constitution of the Grand Encampment, was submitted :

The undersigned hereby propose that the Constitution and By-Laws of the Grand Encampment be amended so as to conform to the laws and decisions promulgated by the Grand Lodge of the United States.

L. A. Thomas, of No. 1,
J. M. Willey, of No. 2,
W. L. Brewer, of No. 3,
Joseph Olmsted, Jr., of No. 13.

The committee on returns of subordinates made the following report, which was accepted:

To the R. W. Grand Encampment:

The undersigned, Committee on Returns, respectfully report— That they have examined the returns of the following subordinate Encampments, and find them correct, viz: Sassacus, No. 1; Palmyra, No. 3; Unity, No. 4; Sowheag, No. 6; Mount Hermon, No. 8; Kabaosa, No. 9; Connecticut, No. 11. There were no returns presented from Nos. 2, 7, and 10.

Respectfully submitted, by

Fred. Croswell,
R. M. Abbe, } *Committee.*
C. J. Gruman,

New Haven, January 13, 1848.

The following amendments to the Constitution of the Grand Encampment, laid on the table at a previous session, [see pp. 57 and 66,] were called up for consideration, viz:

To amend Art. I, section 2, by erasing all after the words "Grand Encampment," in the third line, making the section as follows:

Sec. 2. The Grand Encampment shall be composed of the Past Chief Patriarchs and Past High Priests in membership in the Encampments subordinate to the Grand Encampment.

To amend Art. IV, section 1, by substituting the following:

Sec. 1. The regular sessions of the Grand Encampment shall be held in each year on the Tuesday next preceding the second Wednesday of July [*and January.*]

On motion, Sec. 1 was amended by adding after July, " *and January.*"

After some debate, the amendments were unanimously adopted.

The committee on so much of the G. Patriarch's report as relates to Charters for subordinates, made the following report, which was accepted, and the Charters therein named granted:

To the R. W. Grand Encampment:

The Committee on New Charters have examined the petitions for Encampments to be located at Bristol, at Warehouse Point, and at

Stamford, and recommend that Charters in accordance with the laws of this Grand Encampment be granted for that purpose.

All which is respectfully submitted.

WM. E. SANFORD, *Chairman of Com.*

Pat. Harris, of No. 1, submitted the following resolution, which was adopted:

Resolved, That Art. II, clause 7th, of the Constitution for Subordinate Encampments, be amended by inserting after the word " suspended," in the first line of said clause, the following words : *" except for non-payment of dues."*

G. Sec. Thomas submitted the following resolution, which passed :

Resolved, That hereafter subordinate Encampments be required to pay ten per cent. on all receipts, instead of on the minimum rates fixed by the Grand Encampment.

G. Sec. Thomas moved that clause 2d, section 2d, Art. II, Constitution for Subordinates, be amended by striking out the words, "It shall be optional with this Encampment to pay benefits," which was decided in the negative.

On motion, the Grand Scribe was directed to procure one hundred copies of the Digest of the Laws of the Order, and supply them to members of the Order at 37½ cents each.

On motion, the Grand Scribe was directed to print an abstract of the proceedings at the close of each session.

No further business appearing, the Grand Encampment adjourned.

LUCIUS A. THOMAS, *Grand Scribe.*

15

GRAND TREASURER'S ACCOUNT.

Grand Encampment, I. O. O. F., in account with S. Bishop, G. T.

DR.	July 16, 1847,	To cash paid	J. S. Parmelee, - - -	$5.00
"	"	"	" P. Demick, - - - -	16.00
"	"	"	" J. W. Johnson, - - -	5.00
"	"	"	" N. H. Roath, - - -	9.00
"	"	"	" Wm. L. Brewer, - -	9.00
"	"	"	" Wm. L. Brewer, - -	5.95
"	"	"	" Wm. H. Stanley, - -	9.01
"	"	"	" E. B. Smith, - - - -	75
"	"	"	" M. A. Shepard, - - -	6.00
Nov. 3,	"	"	" G. L. U. S. for Dues,	20.00
Oct. 27,	"	"	" G. Rep. Brewer, - -	50.00
"	"	"	" G. L. U. S. for Books,	6.00
Jan. 13, 1848,	"	"	" J. Kennedy, - - - -	2.00
"	"	To balance to new account, - - -		58.20

                         $201.91

CR.	July 16, 1847,	By balance from old account,					$5.64
"	"	" Cash for dues of No. 1,					10.57
"	"	"	"	"	"	" 3,	15.50
"	"	"	"	"	"	" 4,	16.13
"	"	"	"	"	"	" 5,	5.59
"	"	"	"	"	"	" 6,	7.88
"	"	"	"	"	"	" 7,	24.10
"	"	"	"	" cards for	" 7,	2.21
"	"	"	"	" dues of	" 8,	6.93
"	"	"	"	"	"	" 9,	11.85
"	"	"	"	"	"	" 10,	6.31
"	"	"	"	"	"	" 11,	29.20
"	"	"	"	" Charter	" 11,	30.00
"	"	"	"	"	"	" 12,	30.00

                         $201.91

     The undersigned, Committee of Finance, have examined the above account, and find it correct.

                 J. M. WILLEY,⎫
                 O. UTLEY, ⎬ *Com. of*
                 J. CROSBY, ⎭ *Finance.*

Abstract of the Returns of Subordinate Encampments, for the term ending January, 1848.

Name.	Initiated.	Adm. by Card.	Reinstated.	Rejected.	Withdrawn.	Suspended.	Expelled.	Whole No.	Died.	Receipts.	Am't on hand.	Dues to G. E.
Sassacus, No. 1, . . .	15	0	0	0	1	3	0	74	0	$226.37	$463.00	$21.14
Oriental, 2, . . .	0	0	0	0	0	0	0	17	0	19.00		1.90
Palmyra, 3, . . .	4	0	0	0	0	0	0	83	0	119.37		10.33
Unity, 4, . . .	1	0	0	0	0	1	0	62	1	57.87	69.67	5.39
Devotion, 5, . . .	5	0	0	0	0	1	0	25	0	68.91		6.89
Sowheag, 6, . . .	2	0	0	0	0	0	0	30	0	47.63		4.76
Midian,* 7, . . .												
Mount Hermon, 8, . . .	2	1	0	0	0	2	0	36	0	56.50		4.85
Kabaosa, 9, . . .	11	0	0	0	6	0	†1	36	0	142.56		10.35
Charity,* 10, . . .												
Connecticut, 11, . . .	6	0	0	0	7	0	0	57	0	102.37		7.81
Winsted,‡ 12, . . .												
Hinman,‡ 13, . . .												
Wascusee,‡ 14, . . .												
Total, . . .	46	1	0	0	14	7	1	420	1	$840.58	$532.67	$73.42

* No. reports.   † Conduct unbecoming an Odd Fellow and a man.
‡ First term not finished.

☞ No reports of relief have been received.

NOTICE.

The following enactments of the Grand Encampment at the last session, require the attention of subordinate Encampments.

The time at which the Grand Encampment holds its sessions, has been altered to the Tuesday next preceding the second Wednesday of July and January.

The Grand Encampment is to be composed only of Past Chief Patriarchs and Past High Priests, and not those officers elect, as heretofore.

The dues of subordinate Encampments will be ten per cent. on all receipts, and not on the minimum rates, as heretofore.

The Grand Encampment will therefore hold its next session at New Haven, Tuesday, the 11th day of July, at 2 o'clock P. M.

Lucius A. Thomas, G. Scribe.

GRAND ENCAMPMENT, I.O.O.F. OF CONNECTICUT.

ANNUAL SESSION.

New Haven, July 11, 1848.

The R. W. Grand Encampment, I. O. O. F. of Connecticut convened this day in annual session.

PRESENT:

M. E. TOWNSEND P. ABELL, *G. H. P., Acting Grand Patriarch,*
R. W. WILLIAM E. SANFORD, *Grand High Priest, pro tem.*
R. W. JUNIUS M. WILLEY, *Grand Senior Warden,*
R. W. LUCIUS A. THOMAS, *Grand Scribe,*
R. W. SAMUEL BISHOP, *Grand Treasurer,*
R. W. CHOLWELL J. GRUMAN, *Grand Junior Warden,*
R. W. WILLIAM L. BREWER, *Grand Representative G. Lodge U. S.*
W. AARON MORLEY, *Grand Sentinel, pro tem.*
W. ALLEN S. WIGHTMAN, *Deputy Grand Sentinel,*

and a representation from the several subordinates under this jurisdiction.

By command of the M. W. Grand Patriarch, the Grand Officers took their stations, and after the Throne of Grace had been addressed by the M. E. Grand High Priest, the Grand Encampment was opened in ample form.

The reading of the minutes of the last session was, on motion, dispensed with.

The following Patriarchs were then appointed a committee on credentials, viz : P. G. P. Wm. L. Brewer, Pats. Origen Utley and Ezra Clark, Jr. ; who submitted the following report :

To the R. W. Grand Encampment of Connecticut :

The Committee on Elections would report as correct the following named Patriarchs :

Charles Hull, A. Chichester, F. Ball, A. Stevens, and H. N. Bennett,	of Devotion,	No.	5.
H. E. Bissell,	" Kabaosa,	"	9.
John Burt,	" Connecticut,	"	11.
Chauncey Ayres,	" Wascussee,	"	14.
G. W. Bartholomew and Adna Whiting,	" Montevideo,	"	15.

All of which is respectfully submitted.

Wm. L. Brewer,
Ezra Clark, Jun. } *Committee.*
O. Utley,

The report was accepted, and the above named candidates introduced and properly instructed.

The acting Grand Patriarch submitted the following report :

To the R. W. Grand Encampment :

OFFICERS AND PATRIARCHS,—Under the protection of a benignant Providence, we are again assembled, in annual session, to ponder upon the lessons of our past experience, find our present bearings, and legislate for the future.

It has been customary for our Grand Patriarchs, on occasions similar to this, to submit a succinct statement of their official proceedings through the preceding term. The exigence which has placed me in this chair, renders my present duty susceptible of an easy discharge.

The subordinate Encampments have been officially informed, by a circular from the Grand Scribe, of the death of our Most Worthy Grand Patriarch, Munson A. Shepard, on the 29th day of February last. It is probably unnecessary that I should review the circumstances of his sickness and death, or enlarge upon the excellencies of his character, or the regularity of his life. By those to whom he was the best known, he was the most esteemed ; and the members of this branch of our Order need the persuasions of no highly-wrought eulogy to convince them that in the early departure of our late Grand Patriarch, we have reason to lament the loss of a consistent, intelligent, and devoted supporter of our Institution. I would respectfully recommend the adoption of some suitable expression of our feelings of respect and affection for the memory of our late M. W. Grand Patriarch.

The official business coming before me has been limited, and in the main unimportant. A charter had been granted by my predecessor to certain Patriarchs and Brothers in Bristol ; and on the 7th of March, I empowered Pat. Wm. B. Davis, D. G. P., of Hartford, to open and institute an Encampment, on the 15th day of March, in Bristol. Accordingly, on the last named day, D. G. P. Davis, assisted by P. C. P. John W. Johnson, of No. 7, and Patriarchs E. D. Tiffany, H. Hubbard, C. F. Howard, A. Ferry, and C. P. Brown, of No. 11, instituted in Bristol, Ct., an Encampment, to be known and styled as Montevideo Encampment, No. 15, I. O. O. F. The following Patriarchs were elected to office and installed in regular form : G. W. Bartholomew, C. P.; Adna Whiting, H. P. ; E. Foster, S. W.; H. L. Welch, Scribe ; F. Lamb, Treas.; R. Ferry, J. W. At the evening session, nine brothers were admitted to membership, and duly exalted to the R. P. degree. The prospects of this new Encampment are represented as being very encouraging. The brethren in Bristol received and entertained their guests with the greatest courtesy and kindness. Their virtues and zeal will not fail to secure a due measure of success.

In consequence of some oversight, the appointment of Deputy Grand Patriarchs was not made at the last sesion, and I recently issued an order empowering the Chief Patriarchs to install their succeeding officers into their respective chairs for the current term.

The committee to whom was referred the constitution and by-laws for revision, I understand have attended to their duty, and are prepared to submit an elaborate and carefully digested report. It is to be hoped that its adoption will very greatly subserve the interests of this branch of the Order in this jurisdiction, and largely add to its stability and usefulness.

TOWNSEND P. ABELL, A. G. P.

The report of the acting Grand Patriarch was accepted, and on motion referred to a special committee, consisting of Past G. Patriarchs Andrus and Brewer, and Patriarch Clark.

On motion, a resolution was adopted directing the chairs of the principal officers of the Grand Encampment to be hung in mourning during the present session, in token of sorrow for the death of our Most Worthy Grand Patriarch; and Patriarchs Harris and Storer were appointed a committee to carry the same into effect.

The Grand Treasurer submitted his report, which was referred to the Committee on Finance.

The following petition of members of Oriental Encampment, No. 2, was presented and read:

To the R. W. Grand Encampment of the State of Connecticut, I. O. O. F. :

The undersigned, Patriarchs of Oriental Encampment, No. 2, I. O· O. F., located at East Haddam, in said State, do respectfully represent, that in our opinion the best interests of said Encampment would be promoted by changing the location from said East Haddam to the borough of Essex, in the town of Saybrook; and that said Encampment, at a meeting specially held for that purpose, on the 23d day of June, 1848, passed a resolution in favor of such change of location, with entire unanimity. We therefore pray that your R. W. body will take our case into consideration, and on finding the allegations herein stated to be true, take measures to establish said Encampment at Essex; and your petitioners, as in duty bound, will ever pray. Dated at East Haddam, this 30th day of June, A. D. 1848.

J. C. Palmer, *P. C. P.*	Wm. S. Tyler, *P. C. P.*
R. S. Pratt, *P. C. P.*	Nathan Tyler, Jr., *P. C. P.*
T. C. Bordman, *P. C. P.*	E. W. Pratt,
W. B. Smith,	James H. Pratt, *C. P.*
George Douglass,	Alpheus S. Spencer, *H. P.*
D. B. Warner, *P. C. P.*	J. M. Willey, *P. C. P.*

The above petition was, on motion, referred to a special committee, consisting of Patriarchs J. W. Johnson, Wm. E. Sanford, and E. G. Storer.

The committee appointed at the last session to revise the constitution and by-laws of the Grand Encampment, made the following report:

To the R. W. Grand Encampment of Connecticut:

The committee appointed at the last session to revise the constitution and laws of this R. W. body, respectfully report, that they have attended to the duty assigned them, and herewith submit the result of their labors. They have diligently compared them with the Digest set forth by the Grand Lodge of the United States, and with the former enactments and decisions of this Grand Encampment, and have incorporated such parts as seemed needful to make our code clear and explicit. Owing to the familiarity of most of our members with the formulas of the Grand Lodge of this State, the committee deemed it a matter of some moment to assimilate the arrangement of laws and the order of business, as nearly as was compatible with the difference in the two bodies. All which is respectfully submitted.

L. A. THOMAS,
FRED. CROSWELL, } *Committee.*
WM. E. SANFORD,

The constitution and by-laws, as reported, were then taken up for consideration.

Art. III, sec. 4, Constitution of Grand Encampment was amended by filling blank in last line but one with *fifty.* Art. V, sec. 1, Constitution of Subordinates, was amended by striking out all after the word Encampment, in fourth line. Sec. 2 was amended by substituting the words *one half* for *two thirds*, in third line.

Constitution and By-Laws of Grand Encampment, as amended, were then adopted—ayes 25, nays 3.

Constitution of Subordinates, as amended, was adopted—ayes 21, nays 4.

P. G. P. Brewer submitted the following resolution, which was adopted:

Resolved, That the Constitution and By-Laws adopted at this session for the government of the Grand Encampment, shall take effect immediately.

The committee on the Grand Patriarch's report submitted the following:

To the R. W. Grand Encampment of Connecticut:

The committee to whom was referred the report of the M. W. G. Patriarch, beg leave to recommend that a select committee of three members be raised upon so much as relates to the death of our Most Worthy Grand Patriarch. All of which is respectfully submitted.

WM. L. BREWER,
J. M. ANDRUS, } *Committee.*
EZRA CLARK, Jr.

The report was accepted, and Patriarchs Ayres, Farnam, and Andrus, were appointed on the committee therein recommended.

The following petition of members of Charity Encampment, No. 10, was presented and read:

To the R. W. Grand Encampment, I. O. O. F. of the State of Connecticut, to be holden at New Haven, on Tuesday, the 11th day of July, A. D. 1848:

The petition of the subscribers respectfully represents, that they are Patriarchs and members in regular standing of Charity Encampment, No. 10, under your jurisdiction, located at the village of Lower Mystic, in the town of Stonington ; that it would be for the convenience of a large portion of the members of said Encampment, to change the place of meeting of said Encampment, from said village of Lower Mystic to Stonington borough ; that said Encampment has decided upon such change, by nearly a unanimous vote, provided the consent of your R. W. body can be obtained ; and that it would be for the good and welfare of the Patriarchal branch of the Order in this section of the State if such change could be secured. They therefore pray your R. W. body to take their case into consideration, and the facts herein stated being found true, to order and direct that said Encampment be removed to Stonington borough, as herein before stated.   Dated at Stonington, this 23d day of June, A. D. 1848.

CALVIN G. WILLIAMS,	WM. H. BRYANT,
D. B. POTTER,	THOMAS W. NOYES,
C. H. SMITH, 2d,	JOHN G. CLIFT,
R. C. HANCOX,	LEMUEL B. PARK,
HORACE LEWIS,	WILLIAM MEEKER,
STANTON SHEFFIELD,	AMOS CLIFT,
HENRY ALCORN,	WILLIAM KEENEY,
JAMES McDONALD,	J. R. HALLADAY.
PELEG NOYES,	

On motion, the above petition was referred to the committee appointed on the petition of Oriental Encampment, No. 2.

On motion of Pat. Hovey, it was resolved that a committee of three be appointed to ascertain whether any members were present who are not entitled to vote in this Grand Encampment.   The G. P. appointed Pats. Hovey, Willey, and Storer on said committee.

The committee on the petition of Oriental Encampment, No. 2, made the following report:

To the R. W. Grand Encampment, I. O. O. F. of Connecticut :

The undersigned committee, to whom was referred the petition of twelve members of Oriental Encampment, No. 2, to have the location of their Encampment changed from East Haddam to the borough of Essex, in the town of Saybrook, ask leave to report, that in their opinion the interests of Oriental Encampment would be greatly pro-

moted by the change sought for. The committee therefore recommend that the prayer of the petitioners be granted. Respectfully submitted.
WM. E. SANFORD,
J. W. JOHNSON, } *Committee.*
E. G. STORER,

The report was accepted, and the following resolution, introduced by P. G. P. Brewer, was adopted :

Resolved, That the location of Oriental Encampment, No. 2, be and the same is hereby changed, from East Haddam to the borough of Essex, in the town of Saybrook.

The same committee made the following report on the petition of Charity Encampment, No. 10, which was accepted, and the accompanying resolution adopted :

To the R. W. Grand Encampment, I. O. O. F. of the State of Connecticut:
The undersigned committee, to whom was referred the petition of seventeen members of Charity Encampment, No. 10, to have the location of their Encampment changed from the village of Lower Mystic to the borough of Stonington, ask leave to report, that in their opinion the interests of Charity Encampment would be greatly promoted by the change sought for. The committee therefore recommend the adoption of the following resolution. Respectfully submitted.
WM. E. SANFORD,
J. W. JOHNSON, } *Committee.*
E. G. STORER,

Resolved, That the location of Charity Encampment, No. 10, be and the. same is hereby changed, from the village of Lower Mystic to the borough of Stonington.

On motion, the following resolution was adopted :

Resolved, That the Grand Patriarch be requested to take immediate steps to carry into effect the above resolutions relative to Oriental and Charity Encampments.

The Grand Encampment then adjourned to 8 o'clock P. M.

At 8 o'clock P. M. the Grand Encampment met pursuant to adjournment.

Pat. Hovey, from the committee appointed to ascertain whether any members were present not entitled to vote in the Grand Encampment, reported, verbally, that there were none. Report accepted.

The committee on so much of the acting G. P's report as relates to the death of the late Most Worthy Grand Patriarch, reported the following preamble and resolutions, which were unanimously adopted :

Whereas it has pleased Almighty God, in his wise Providence, to remove from us, by death, our distinguished head and eminently beloved brother, MUNSON A. SHEPARD, Grand Patriarch of this Grand Encampment; therefore,

Resolved, That the Order of Patriarchs at large has sustained a loss of one of its brightest ornaments, and the Grand Encampment of Connecticut in particular mourns for the zealous and efficient officer whom it one year ago called to preside over its deliberations.

Resolved, That we revere and cherish the memory of our departed brother, as a faithful Odd Fellow, who had become endeared to his associates by his activity, his exemplary courtesy, and practical benevolence.

Resolved, That we hereby tender our cordial sympathies to the relatives and friends of the deceased.

Resolved, That as a token of respect to the memory of our deceased Grand Patriarch, the following biography of his life be spread on the journal of this Grand Encampment.

All of which is respectfully submitted.

CHAUNCEY AYRES,
ETHEL T. FARNUM, } *Committee.*
JONA. M. ANDRUS,

MUNSON A. SHEPARD was born in Danbury, Ct., in the year 1812. In early life, his advantages for intellectual culture were very limited, being confined to an occasional attendance at the district school. He early manifested, however, an unusual taste for historical reading, as well as for the investigation of subjects of a more abstruse nature ; and his leisure hours were devoted to the perusal of such works as were within his reach, of a historical and metaphysical character ; so that, at the termination of his apprenticeship as a hatter, his mind was stored with an amount of useful information rarely obtained by young men pursuing the same avocation, and laboring under similar disadvantages.

From the period of his majority till within a few months of his decease, he was engaged in the business to which he had been apprenticed, and met with various success. His early habits prevailed in maturer years, and his leisure hours were still devoted to study. In fact, his modest and retiring manners almost compelled him to seek amusement in the closet, rather than in company, and in the formation of the usual social alliances. No circumstance so much contributed to interrupt this long cherished seclusion, and to *bring out* the social, moral, and intellectul powers of the man, as his union, but a few years since, with the Independent Order of Odd Fellows. It may be said, that from the period of his initiation, he became an altered man ; less retiring and more communicative ; less secluded and more alive to the enjoyment of social intercourse. Odd Fellowship opened to him a new field of action, and it need hardly be said that he entered it with ardor, since he succeeded in attaining its highest honors. Those who knew him well, will consider it no undue eulogy to assert that he was master of its *work*, and it may also be truly said that he was the embodiment of its principles.

It cannot be too strongly insisted that Odd Fellowship exerted a benign influence upon his whole character. At the period of his union with the Order, he was at least hesitating in reference to the cardinal doctrines of the Christian religion. After passing through various transmutations, common to minds like his, he settled down upon the firmest belief in its great and leading truths. Is it assuming too much, to claim that the high moral tone of Odd Fellowship, its enlarged and comprehensive views of benevolence, and its touching sympathies, had at least a share in the production of this result? We think not.

Some three years since, Brother Shepard commenced the study of Medicine in a systematic manner, and devoted that part of his time, not occupied in his regular business, exclusively to its pursuit. As he advanced, he became enthusiastic in the study of medical science, and his proficiency was sufficient, at the period of his attendance upon lectures in the medical department of Yale College, to gain for him the highest esteem of the Professors in that Institution. After obtaining a license to practice, he had returned home, and had already concluded to locate himself in a town a few miles distant, for the practice of his profession. On the 12th of February, 1848, he was seized with the disease then epidemic in Danbury, (Erysipelatous Fever,) and died in ten days from the attack, after having suffered the severest agonies of that terrible malady. During his last days, he arranged all his temporal affairs, with his usual precision, perfectly conscious that he could not survive long, and bearing his afflictions with the fortitude of a stoic.

The Grand Encampment then proceeded to the nomination and election of Grand Officers for the year ensuing. P. G. Patriarchs Andrus and Brewer were appointed tellers. On balloting, the following Patriarchs were duly elected, and so declared, viz :

Lucius A. Thomas, of No. 1, *Grand Patriarch.*
Junius M. Willey, of No. 2, *Grand High Priest.*
Cholwell J. Gruman, of No. 9, *Grand Senior Warden.*
Prelate Demick, of No. 1, *Grand Scribe.*
Samuel Bishop, of No. 1, *Grand Treasurer.*
William B. Davis, of No. 11, *Grand Junior Warden.*
Townsend P. Abell, of No. 6, *G. Representative to G. L. U. S.*
The Grand Officers elect were then installed in ample form.
The G. P. appointed Pat. E. T. Farnum, of No. 5, *G. Sentinel.*
Members from Hinman Encampment, No. 13, remonstrated against the proceedings of Midian Encampment, No. 7, in initiating brothers belonging to the jurisdiction of said Hinman Encampment.

On motion, the Grand Encampment resolved itself into a committee of the whole, Pat. Hovey in the chair.

P. G. P. Brewer submitted the following resolutions, which were adopted by the committee:

Resolved, That the officers of Midian Encampment, No. 7, be and hereby are directed to pay to the Treasurer of Hinman Encampment, No. 13, the whole amount of fees received by said Midian Encampment for the initiation of all those members who belonged at the time of their admission to the jurisdiction of Hinman Encampment.

Resolved, That in case of the refusal of the officers of Midian Encampment to comply with the foregoing requisition within three months from the date of the passage of this resolution, the charter of said Midian Encampment shall be annulled.

Resolved, That the M. W. Grand Patriarch and R. W. Grand Scribe be and are hereby directed to furnish a certificate of membership, under seal of this Grand Encampment, to all such members of Midian Encampment as in their judgment have not violated the laws of this Grand Body.

Resolved, That in case said Midian Encampment shall be expelled by virtue of the foregoing resolutions, the Grand Scribe shall give immediate notice thereof to the several Grand Encampments under the jurisdiction of the Grand Lodge of the United States.

On motion, the committee rose, and reported to the Grand Encampment, recommending the adoption of the above resolutions; whereupon, the report was accepted, and the resolutions adopted unanimously.

On motion of G. H. P. Willey, the following resolution was adopted:

Resolved, That the sum of twenty-five dollars be paid to Past G. Scribe Thomas, in addition to his regular salary, for his services during the past year.

The following bills, having been approved by the Committee on Finance, were ordered paid:

L. A. Thomas, salary and postage,	$25.50
T. P. Abell, mileage and postage,	6.85
C. J. Gruman, mileage,	5.50
Wm. L. Brewer, mileage,	9.00
T. J. Stafford, printing,	28.10
John Kennedy, care of room,	3.00

On motion, a resolution was passed directing the G. Scribe to procure the printing of the usual number of copies of the proceedings of the present session, with the Constitution and By-Laws of the Grand Encampment, and Constitution of Subordinates.

No further business appearing, the Grand Encampment was closed in ample form.

PRELATE DEMICK, *G. Scribe.*

17

GRAND TREASURER'S ACCOUNT.

Grand Encampment, I. O. O. F. in account with S. Bishop, G. Treas.

DR.   Jan. 13, 1848, To cash paid T. P. Abell, ... $5.00
   " " " " C. J. Gruman, ... 5.50
   " " " " J. Kennedy, ... 2.00
   " " " " Croswell & Jewett, . . 2.71
   " " " " Peck & Stafford, . . . 33.00
   " " " " Bassett & Bradley, . . 2.00
   " " " " S. M. Bassett, ... 3.25
   " " " " L. A. Thomas, ... 17.12
 Feb. 25, " " " J. B. Bowditch, . . . 7.00
 " 28, " " " G. Lodge U. S. Digests, 25.00
      To balance to new account, ... 81.77

                 $184.35

CR.   Jan. 13, 1848, By balance from old account, $58.20
   " " cash for dues of No. 1, . 19.74
   " " " " " 2, . 2.00
   " " " " " 3, . 10.33
   " " " cards, " 3, . 1.50
   " " " dues, " 4, . 5.51
   " " " " " 6, . 3.16
   " " " " " 8, . 3.23
   " " " " " 9, . 9.37
   " " " " " 11, . 7.81
   " " " cards, " 11, . 2.00
   " " " charter, " 13, . 30.00
   " " " " " 14, . 30.00
   " " " cards, Uncas Lodge, 1.50

                 $184.35

 The Committee on Finance have examined the above account, and find it correct.

       J. M. WILLEY, }
       O. UTLEY,   } *Com. on Finance.*

Abstract of Semi-annual Returns of Subordinate Encampments under the jurisdiction of the Grand Encampment, I. O. O. F. of Connecticut, for the term ending July, 1848.

Name	Initiated	Adm. by Card	Reinstated	Rejected	Withdrawn	Suspended	Expelled	Deceased	Whole No.	Receipts	Am'nt on hand	Dues to G. Enc.	No. br's relieved	Am'nt for same	Families reliev'd	Am'nt for same	Brothers buried	Am'ut for same	Total benefits pd.
Sassacus, No. 1,	29	1	0	0	0	0	0	0	91	$284.00	614.00	$28.40	0						
Oriental, 2,	0	0	0	0	0	0	0	0	17	9.00		.90	0						
Palmyra, 3,	2	0	0	0	0	0	0	0	80	77.75		7.77	6	$34.00					$34.00
Unity, 4,	0	0	0	0	0	0	0	0	60	50.50		5.05	0						
Devotion, 5,	0	0	0	0	0	0	0	1	31	107.93		10.79	0						
Sowheag, 6,	8	0	0	0	0	0	1	0	46	132.28		13.22	0						
Midian,* 7,																			
Mount Hermon, 8,	14	0	0	0	0	1	0	0	36	53.62		5.46	0						
Kabaosa, 9,	1	0	0	0	0	1	0	1	35	22.25		2.22	0						
Charity,* 10,																			
Connecticut, 11,	11	7	0	0	7	0	0	0	61	243.12		24.31	2	$27.00					27.00
Winsted, 12,	11	1	0	0	0	0	0	0	19	110.53		11.05	0						
Hinman, 13,	16	7	0	0	0	0	0	0	26	184.53		15.65	0						
Waeeussee, 14,	15	7	0	0	0	0	0	0	22	196.21		19.62	0						
Montevideo, 15,	18	1	0	0	0	0	0	0	25	189.00		18.90	0						
Total,	125	16	0	0	7	6	1	2	549	$1660.72	614.00	163.24	8	$61.00					$61.00

* No reports.

SUBORDINATE ENCAMPMENTS,

Belonging to the jurisdiction of the Grand Encampment, I. O. O. F. of Connecticut.

Name.		Where held.	County.	Time of Meeting.	Instituted.
Sassacus,	No. 1,	New Haven,	New Haven,	First Friday.	August 19, 1841.
Oriental,	2,	Essex borough,	Middlesex,	First Friday.	September, 1841.
Palmyra,	3,	Norwich,	New London,	First and third Friday.	June 15, 1843.
Unity,	4,	New London,	New London,	First and third Thursday.	April 22, 1844.
Devotion,	5,	Bethel,	Fairfield,	First and third Friday.	August 28, 1844.
Sowheag,	6,	Middletown,	Middlesex,	First Tuesday.	September 27, 1844
Midian,	7,	Hartford,	Hartford,	First Monday.	December 24, 1844.
Mount Hermon,	8,	Bridgeport,	Fairfield,	First and third Friday.	April 22, 1845.
Kabaosa,	9,	Norwalk,	Fairfield,	First Wednesday.	September 17, 1845.
Charity,	10,	Stonington,	New London,	First Tuesday.	November 10, 1846.
Connecticut,	11,	Hartford,	Hartford,	First Thursday.	March 4, 1847.
Winsted,	12,	Winsted,	Litchfield,	First Wednesday.	October 28, 1847.
Hinman,	13,	Warehouse Point,	Hartford,	2d and 4th Wednesday.	October 29, 1847.
Wascussee,	14,	Stamford,	Fairfield,	First and third Friday.	November 26, 1847.
Montevideo,	15,	Bristol,	Hartford,	First and third Thursday.	March 15, 1848.

GRAND ENCAMPMENT, I. O. O. F. OF CONNECTICUT.

OFFICERS FOR 1848-9.

M. W. LUCIUS A. THOMAS,	*Grand Patriarch.*
M. E. JUNIUS M. WILLEY,	*Grand High Priest.*
R. W. CHOLWELL J. GRUMAN,	*Grand Senior Warden.*
R. W. PRELATE DEMICK,	*Grand Scribe.*
R. W. SAMUEL BISHOP,	*Grand Treasurer.*
R. W. WILLIAM B. DAVIS,	*Grand Junior Warden.*
W. ETHEL T. FARNUM,	*Grand Sentinel.*
R. W. TOWNSEND P. ABELL,	*G. Rep. to G. L. U. S.*

PAST GRAND PATRIARCHS.

WILLIAM E. SANFORD, 1843-4.
JOHN L. DEVOTION, 1844-5.
JONATHAN M. ANDRUS, 1845-6.
WILLIAM L. BREWER, 1846-7.

PAST GRAND HIGH PRIESTS.

RICHARD S. PRATT, 1843-4.
JONATHAN M. ANDRUS, 1844-5.
WILLIAM L. BREWER, 1845-6.
TOWNSEND P. ABELL, 1847-8.

MEMBERS.

Sassacus, No. 1, New Haven.

William E. Sanford, April 20, 1843.	Daniel H. Moore, Jan. 15, 1846.
Samuel Bishop, April 20, 1843.	Elizur Hubbell, July 9, 1846.
Isaac Judson, April 20, 1843.	Fred. Croswell, Jan. 14, 1847.
Bela Lord, Jan. 12, 1844.	Truman Hart, Jan. 14, 1847.
Jonathan M. Andrus, April 12, 1844.	Eliphalet G. Storer, July 15, 1847.
Prelate Demick, July 12, 1844.	Noah Chandler, July 15, 1847.
Newel C. Hall, Jan. 9, 1845.	Samuel H. Harris, Jan. 13, 1848.
Lucius A. Thomas, July 10, 1845.	Lucius Peck, Jan. 13, 1848.

Oriental, No. 2, Essex Borough.

Richard S. Pratt, April 20, 1843.	Junius M. Willey, July 10, 1845.
Thomas C. Bordman, April 20, 1843.	John S. Dickinson, Jan. 14, 1847.
John C. Palmer, July 10, 1845.	

Palmyra, No. 3, Norwich.

John L. Devotion, July 14, 1843.	David Young, July 10, 1845.
William L. Brewer, July 12, 1844.	H. Hobart Roath, July 9, 1846.
John A. Lathrop, July 12, 1844.	Philo M. Judson, July 9, 1846.
Edward W. Eells, Jan. 9, 1845.	James D. Mowrey, Jan. 14, 1847.
H. C. Bridgman, July 10, 1845.	James A. Hovey, July 15, 1847.

Unity, No. 4, New London.

Henry Champlain, July 12, 1844.
O. F. Smith, July 10, 1845.
George W. Brown, July 10, 1845.
Allen S. Wightman, Jan. 15, 1846.

C. C. Culver, Jan. 15, 1846.
Robert B. Jackson, July 15, 1847.
I. D. Allen, Jan. 13, 1848.

Devotion, No. 5, Bethel.

John Greenwood, Jr., Jan. 9, 1845.
James R. Greenwood, Jan. 15, 1846.
William W. Bedient, Jan. 15, 1846.
James P. Saunders, Jan. 15, 1846.
William F. Hoyt, July 9, 1846.
Ethel T. Farnum, July 9, 1846.

William A. Judd, Jan. 14, 1847.
Charles Hull, July 11, 1848.
A. Chichester, July 11, 1848.
F. Ball, July 11, 1848.
A. Stevens, July 11, 1848.
H. N. Bennett, July 11, 1848.

Sowheag, No. 6, Middletown.

Thomas C. Simpson, Jan. 9, 1845.
Origen Utley, Jan. 9, 1845.
Erastus H. Booth, Jan. 9, 1845.
John S. Parmelee, July 10, 1845.

Dennis Sage, Jan. 14, 1847.
Towsend P. Abell, Jan. 14, 1847.
W. B. Casey, Jan. 13, 1848.

Midian, No. 7. Hartford.

A. M. Gordon, Jan. 9, 1845.
John W. Johnson, Jan. 9, 1845.
Aaron Morley, July 10, 1845.
Henry L. Miller, Jan. 15, 1846.
Edson Fessenden, Jan. 14, 1847.

William H. Sweetland, Jan. 14, 1847.
M. M. Merriman, July 15, 1847.
O. D. Seymour, July 15, 1847.
Calvin Northrop, Jan. 13, 1848.

Mount Hermon, No. 8, Bridgeport.

A. B. Beers, July 10, 1845.
S. B. Brittan, July 10, 1845.
George S. Sanford, Jan. 15, 1846.
E. B. Stevens, July 9, 1846.

Gilson Landon, Jan. 14, 1847.
Joseph Crosby, Jan. 14, 1847.
Dwight Morris, Jan. 14, 1847.

Kabaosa, No. 9, Norwalk.

James A. Quintard, Jan. 15, 1846.
P. L. Cunningham, Jan. 15, 1846.
Cholwell J. Gruman, Jan. 15, 1846.

George W. Smith, July 9, 1846.
E. S. Quintard, Jan. 13, 1848.
H. E. Bissell, July 11, 1848.

Charity, No. 10, Stonington.

William Meeker, July 15, 1847.

Amos Clift, July 15, 1847.

Connecticut, No. 11, Hartford,

Ezra Clark, Jr., July 15, 1847.
R. G. Drake, July 15, 1847.
William B. Davis, July 15, 1847.

A. C. Goodman, July 15, 1847.
Elihu Geer, July 15, 1847.
John Burt, July 11, 1848.

Winsted, No. 12, Winsted.

John H. Mills, Jan. 13, 1848.

J. J. Twiss, Jan. 13, 1848.

Hinman, No. 13, Warehouse Point.

Joseph Olmsted, Jr., Jan. 13, 1848.

Robert M. Abbe, Jan. 13, 1848.

Wascussee, No. 14, Stamford.

Robert H. Lockwood, Jan. 13, 1848.

Chauncey Ayres, July 11, 1848.

Montevideo, No. 15, Bristol.

George W. Bartholomew, July 11, 1848.

Adna Whiting, July 11, 1848.

CONSTITUTION

OF THE

RIGHT WORTHY GRAND ENCAMPMENT,

OF THE

I. O. O. F. OF CONNECTICUT, ADOPTED JULY 11, 1848.

~~~~~ ~~~~~~~ ~~~~~~~

ARTICLE I.

POWERS

SECTION 1. The R. W. Grand Encampment of Patriarchs of the Independent Order of Odd Fellows of Connecticut, is the Supreme tribunal of all Encampments of Patriarchs in said State.

SEC. 2. It possesses, by virtue of its charter from the Grand Lodge of the United States, the full power to grant charters for Encampments, and to suspend and take away the same for proper cause; to pass laws for the regulation and working of subordinate Encampments; to receive, hear, and decide finally, all appeals from them or their members; redress grievances and complaints arising therein; and to do all other acts promotive of the interest of Patriarchs of the Order, not in derogation of the Constitution or Laws of the Grand Lodge of the United States, nor inconsistent with the Constitution and Laws of this State or of the United States.

Seal.

SEC. 3. The Grand Encampment shall have a suitable seal, which shall be attached to all official documents issued by its authority.   •

————

ARTICLE II.

MEMBERS.
Qualifications.

SEC. 1. The Grand Encampment shall be composed of the past Chief Patriarchs and past High Priests in membership in the Encampments subordinate to this Grand Encampment.

Certificate.

Sec. 2. Each past officer, upon presenting himself for admission to membership, must be furnished with a certificate in the following form :

——— Encampment, No. —.

To the R. W. Grand Encampment, I. O. O. F. of Connecticut.

This is to certify that Patriarch   has served
as Chief Patriarch (or High Priest) for the term ending   18
and is therefore entitled to membership in your Right Worthy body.

In testimony whereof we hereunto affix our hands and the seal of
[seal.]   our Encampment, this   day of   18

C.·P.
Scribe.

———

ARTICLE III.

GRAND OFFICERS.

Sec. 1. The Officers of the Grand Encampment shall be,
Most Worthy Grand Patriarch ;
Most Excellent Grand High Priest ;
Right Worthy Grand Senior Warden ;
Right Worthy Grand Scribe ;
Right Worthy Grand Treasurer ;
Right Worthy Grand Junior Warden,
who shall be elected annually by ballot ; and Worthy Grand Sentinel, who shall be appointed by the Most Worthy Grand Patriarch.

Sec. 2. The election and installation of officers shall take place at the annual session in July.

Sec. 3. All vacancies occurring in the Grand Officers shall be filled in the manner of the original election, and for the residue of the term.

Grand Patriarch.

Sec. 4. The Grand Patriarch shall preside at all sessions of the Grand Encampment ; he shall preserve order, and decide all questions of order—subject, however, to an appeal to the Grand Encampment. He may appoint any Grand Officer, *pro tem.*, in case of the absence or disqualification of the regular Grand Officer ; he may order special sessions of the Grand Encampment whenever he may deem proper ; he shall appoint all committees, unless otherwise ordered by the Grand Encampment ; he shall, in all cases except on an appeal from his own decision, give the casting vote when the Grand Encampment is equally divided. In cases of emergency, he may grant dispensations to subordinate Encampments, in all such matters as he may deem promotive of the interest of the Order, not inconsistent with the usages thereof.

Grand High Priest.

SEC. 5. The Grand High Priest shall preside and act in the absence of the Grand Patriarch. It shall be his duty to perform according to his office, at the installation of the Grand Officers. In case the office of Grand Patriarch becomes vacant, he shall have the full powers of Grand Patriarch until the next regular session, when the vacancy shall be filled.

Grand Senior Warden.

SEC. 6. The Grand Senior Warden shall assist the Grand Patriarch in presiding and preserving order; and in the absence of the Grand Patriarch and Grand High Priest, he shall preside.

Grand Scribe.

SEC. 7. The Grand Scribe shall attend all regular and special sessions of the Grand Encampment, and record the proceedings; he shall keep the accounts between the Grand Encampment and its subordinates, report all delinquencies, receive all moneys coming to the Grand Encampment therefrom, give receipts therefor, and pay the same over to the Grand Treasurer immediately, taking his receipt for the same; he shall notify the members of the Grand Encampment of all special sessions; he shall prepare charters granted for subordinate Encampments; he shall transmit to the Grand Secretary of the Grand Lodge of the United States, immediately on the institution of a subordinate Encampment, the name, number, date of charter or dispensation, and location of such Encampment, and also the same information on the suspension or expulsion of an Encampment; he shall have charge of the seal, and all books and papers belonging to the Grand Encampment, and perform such other duties as may be required by the Grand Encampment; and for the faithful performance of the duties of his office, he shall be entitled to receive *fifty* dollars annually from the funds of the Grand Encampment.

Grand Treasurer.

SEC. 8. The Grand Treasurer shall receive and take charge of all funds belonging to the Grand Encampment, and pay all orders passed by the Grand Encampment, when properly attested; he shall make a report of the receipts and expenditures annually, and submit his books of accounts for examination whenever required; he shall give bond, with surety, to the two first named Grand Officers, for the faithful discharge of his duties.

18

Grand Junior Warden.

SEC. 9. The Grand Junior Warden shall open and close the Grand Encampment, according to his office; and he shall introduce into the Grand Encampment all new members, after their credentials have been found correct.

Grand Sentinel.

SEC. 10. The Grand Sentinel shall have charge of the entrance to the Grand Encampment, and permit none to enter or depart without the proper formalities.

Mode of Election.

SEC. 11. Candidates for office may be nominated at any time previous to the election. Each elected officer must be voted for separately by ballot, and each must receive a majority of all the votes given, to be elected. All votes given for persons not in nomination, shall be counted as blanks, and in case, at any election, there shall be more blanks than regular votes, then a new nomination shall be made.

Installation.

SEC. 12. The Grand Officers shall be installed at such time during the session as the Grand Encampment may determine. The present Grand Patriarch, or any past Grand Patriarch, may install the Grand Patriarch elect, who shall install the other Grand Officers.

SEC. 13. All Grand Officers shall be installed to serve until the next annual session, and the installation of their successors.

ARTICLE IV.

GRAND REPRESENTATIVE.

Election.

SEC. 1. At the annual session in July, in each alternate year, there shall be elected, in the same manner as the officers of the Grand Encampment, a Grand Representative, who must be a Past Grand and a member of the Grand Encampment, to represent this Grand Encampment in the Grand Lodge of the United States, to serve for two years from the commencement of the session of the Grand Lodge of the United States next succeeding his election.

Duties.

SEC. 2. It shall be the duty of the Grand Representative to attend the sessions of the Grand Lodge of the United States which may be held during the term for which he is elected, and faithfully represent the wishes of this Grand Encampment therein ; and should he be unable to attend, he shall nominate as a substitute such member of the Grand Encampment as the Grand Patriarch shall approve. The Grand Representative shall be entitled to receive from the funds of the Grand Encampment, fifty dollars for each session of the Grand Lodge of the United States which he may attend.

ARTICLE V.
STANDING COMMITTEES.

SEC. 1. At each session there shall be appointed the following Standing Committees, viz :—Committee on Credentials ; Committee on the State of the Order ; Committee on Finance.

Committee on Credentials.

SEC. 2. The Committee on Credentials shall consist of three members, who shall be appointed by the Grand Patriarch, or the incumbent of the chair at the time of opening the session, and whose duty it shall be to examine and report, without delay, on the eligibility of members.

Committee on the State of the Order.

SEC. 3. The Committee on the State of the Order shall consist of three members, and shall be nominated by the Grand Patriarch and approved by the Grand Encampment. It shall be the duty of this Committee to examine and report on the semi-annual returns of the subordinates—on the laws and rules of subordinate Encampments, when presented to the Grand Encampment for its approval—on all propositions for amending the Constitution of subordinate Encampments, and on all resolutions pertaining to the general interests of the Order.

Committee on Finance.

SEC. 4. The Committee on Finance shall consist of three members, who shall be nominated by the Grand Patriarch and approved by the Grand Encampment, and whose duty it shall be to examine and report on all accounts and claims against the Grand Encampment, previous to their being passed for payment ; to examine the accounts of the Grand Treasurer, semi-annually ; and to suggest such measures of finance as they may deem expedient.

ARTICLE VI.
SESSIONS, VOTES, &c.

Sec. 1. The regular sessions of the Grand Encampment shall be held in each each year, on the Tuesdays next preceding the second Wednesdays of July and January; and special sessions shall be held at the call of the Grand Patriarch; during either of which, the Grand Encampment may adjourn from time to time, until the business of the session is completed. All sessions of the Grand Encampment shall be held in the city of New Haven, and in the G. E. degree.

Annual and Semi-annual Sessions.

Sec. 2. At the annual and semi-annual sessions, the subordinates shall have their reports, returns, and sums due, presented, as required by these articles; new members shall be admitted to their seats, and all manner of business within the power of the Grand Encampment, may be transacted.

Special Sessions.

Sec. 3. At special sessions, no business shall be transacted except that for which the session is called, which shall be distinctly stated in the notification to members; but no business, at a special session, shall be so acted on as to involve the expenditure of money.

Quorum.

Sec. 4. The Grand Encampment shall not be opened, unless there be present a representation from at least two subordinates, consisting of not less than ten members.

Votes.

Sec. 5. All questions before the Grand Encampment shall be determined by a majority of the votes given by the members present.

Dues.

Sec. 6. Each subordinate Encampment shall pay semi-annually to the Grand Encampment ten per cent. on the whole amount of their receipts for the term last past.

ARTICLE VII.
REMOVALS, SUSPENSIONS, AND EXPULSIONS.

Sec. 1. Any Grand Officer may be removed from his office for conduct unworthy of his standing in the Order, or for inattention to the duties of his office.

Sec. 2. Any member being guilty of conduct in derogation of the character of the Order, on being regularly convicted, shall be fined, reprimanded, suspended, or expelled, at the discretion of the Grand Encampment.

SEC. 3. Every officer and member shall be entitled to a fair trial, for any offence involving removal, suspension, or expulsion ; but no member shall be but upon trial, unless charges specifying his offence shall be submitted to the Grand Encampment in writing, by a member thereof.

SEC. 4. When charges have been preferred against an officer or member in due form, they shall be referred to a special committee of five, (none of whom shall belong to the same subordinate Encampment with the accused,) who shall immediately notify the parties ; and after one month therefrom, they shall meet and proceed to examine the evidence in the case, (all of which shall be in writing.) and make report thereon to the Grand Encampment. And it shall be the duty of said Committee to furnish the accused a copy of their report, in writing, at least one month before the next regular session of the Grand Encampment, at which session the case shall be heard and decided. And every member so accused and tried shall be allowed to be heard in his own defence, when the case is before the Grand Encampment. *Provided,* that such member shall not be allowed to vote in the Grand Encampment during the time of his trial.

SEC. 5. No officer or member shall officiate in the Grand Encampment during the time occupied in his trial, nor be present when the question is taken on the report or resolution offered by the committee. Should the Grand Patriarch be under charges, a past Grand Patriarch, if any be present, shall preside, while any question arising therefrom shall be under consideration.

ARTICLE VIII.

AMENDMENTS.

SEC. 1. Any proposal to alter, amend, suspend, or annul this Constitution, or any part thereof, must be proposed at a regular session, in writing; and if approved by four members, the Grand Scribe shall, within thirty days thereafter, notify each subordinate Encampment under this jurisdiction, of the proposition. And if, at the next regular session, it is adopted by two thirds of the members present, it shall prevail, and become a part of the Constitution ; otherwise it shall not.

SEC. 2. This Grand Encampment is fully authorized to adopt or amend, at any regular session, such By-Laws and Rules of Order as two thirds of the members present may approve.

BY-LAWS

OF THE

GRAND ENCAMPMENT, I.O.O.F. OF CONNECTICUT.

ARTICLE I.

RELATING TO GRAND ENCAMPMENT.

Time of Meeting.

SEC. 1. The R. W. Grand Encampment shall convene, at its regular sessions, at two o'clock P. M., and may adjourn from time to time, until the business of the session is completed, unless otherwise specially ordered by a vote of the Grand Encampment.

Opening of Grand Encampment.

SEC. 2. Within thirty minutes of the time of meeting, the presiding officer shall proceed to open the Grand Encampment, should there be a quorum present; and at the expiration of that time, should there not be a quorum, the members assembled may organize informally, and adjourn the meeting to such time as they may determine upon.

Absence of Officers.

SEC. 3. When all the Grand Officers provided by the Constitution for presiding at the meeting are absent, the chair may be taken by a Past Grand Patriarch, should any be present; otherwise by any member who may be called to it by a majority of the members present.

ARTICLE II.

RELATING TO SUBORDINATES.

Application for Charter.

SEC. 1. Seven R. P. degree Patriarchs, or more, in good standing in the order, and members of Lodges subordinate to the Grand Lodge of the State of Connecticut, may petition this Grand Encampment, in writing, for a charter to constitute an Encampment of Patriarchs; which petition must be accompanied by the sum of *Thirty Dollars*, as the charter fee, and the withdrawal cards of the petitioners. Should the charter be granted, the Grand Patriarch, or such other qualified Patriarch as he may delegate, shall open the Encampment and present the charter. Traveling expenses, if any are incurred, to be paid by the Encampment opened.

Cards to Members of Extinct Encampments.

SEC. 2. Members of an extinct Encampment, who were in good standing at the time of its dissolution, as may appear by the records of such Encampment, or who may have paid all arrearages then due to the Grand Encampment, shall, upon application to the Grand Scribe, receive a certificate, under the seal of the Grand Encampment, to enable them to make application for membership in another Encampment : *Provided*, that no such certificate shall be given to a member of a suspended or expelled Encampment, unless ordered by a special vote of the Grand Encampment.

Funds.

SEC. 3. The funds and properties of subordinate Encampments, having been raised for the purpose of relieving sick and distressed Patriarchs, and other charitable uses in the Order, shall not be divided in any manner among the members individually, or between one Encampment and another that may branch from it ; but shall remain, for its legitimate purposes, the property of the Encampment, so long as its charter is unreclaimed, and seven members remain in good standing.

RULES OF ORDER.

I. *Order of Business.*

AFTER a quorum shall be áscertained to be present, the following shall be the order of business, viz :

1st. The Grand Patriarch shall request the brethren to clothe themselves in proper regalia, and direct the Grand Officers and members to take their respective stations.

2d. The Grand J. W. will report on the safe condition of the Grand Encampment.

3d. The Grand Patriarch will call up the Grand Encampment, while the G. H. P. performs the duties of his office.

4th. Proclamation will be made of the opening of the Grand Encampment.

5th. The minutes of the last session read, and if no objection be made to any part thereof, they shall stand approved without vote.

6th. New members admitted and instructed.

7th. Committees to report by seniority.

8th. Unfinished business acted on by priority.

9th. New business.

10th. Closing (or adjournment) in form.

The order of business, as here arranged, may, at any time, for a particular occasion, be changed or dispensed with, by a special two-third vote of the Grand Encampment.

II. *Of Decorum.*

During the continuance of the meeting, the most decorous silence must be observed : the Officers and members retaining their respective seats, and no one leaving the room without the permission of the M. W. Grand Patriarch, nor entering without the consent of the R. W. Grand Senior Warden.

Every Officer and member shall be designated in debate, or otherwise, by his proper office and title, according to his standing in the Order.

No member shall be permitted to vote or speak, unless clothed in regalia appropriate to his rank and station.

III. *Of the Chair.*

The Grand Patriarch, while presiding, shall state every question coming before the Grand Encampment, and immediately before putting it to vote, shall ask : "*Is the Grand Encampment ready for the question ?*" He shall pronounce the votes and decisions of the Grand Encampment, on all subjects. His decisions on all questions of order shall be without debate, unless entertaining doubts on the point, he invite it. And he shall have the privilege of speaking only on such questions from the Chair. When his decision has been appealed from, the question shall be put thus : "*Will the Grand Encampment sustain the Chair in its decision ?*"

IV. *Of Debate.*

Every member, when he speaks or offers a motion, shall rise and respectfully address the Chair, and when he has finished he shall sit down.

While speaking he shall confine himself to the question under debate, avoiding all personality and indecorous language, as well as any reflection upon the Grand Encampment or its members.

Should two or more members rise to speak at the same time, the Chair shall decide which shall be entitled to the floor.

No member shall disturb another in his speech, unless to call him to order.

If a member, while speaking, shall be called to order, at the request of the Chair he shall cease speaking and take his seat until the question of order is determined, when, if permitted, he may again proceed.

No member shall speak more than once on the same question, until all the members wishing to speak shall have had an opportunity to do so ; nor more than twice without permission from the Chair. But no member shall have the privilege of speaking more than once on a question of order, after appeal from the decision of the Chair.

V. *Of Questions and Votes.*

When any communication, petition, or memorial is presented, before it is read, or any vote taken on it, a brief statement of its contents shall be made by the introducer or the Chair, and after it has been read a brief notice of the purport shall be entered on the journal.

No motion shall be subject to action, until seconded and stated· by the Chair ; and at the desire of any member, shall be reduced to writing.

When a blank is to be filled, the question shall be taken first upon the highest sum or number, and the longest time proposed.

Any member may call for a division of a question when the sense, will admit of it.

When a question is before the Grand Encampment, no motion shall be received, unless to adjourn, the previous question, to lay on the table, to postpone indefinitely, to postpone to a certain time, to refer or to amend. And these shall have precedence in the order herein arranged ; the three first of which shall be decided without debate.

After any question, except one of indefinite postponement, has been decided, any two members who voted in the majority may, at the same or next succeeding meeting, move for a reconsideration thereof.

The previous question can be called for by two members, if seconed by a majority, and shall be put in this form—" *Shall the main question be now put ?*"—if carried, all amendments not already adopted shall be precluded, and the main question be taken without debate.

When one-fifth of the members rise in favor of taking a question by ayes and nays, they shall be ordered to be so recorded.

Every member present shall vote on any question before the Grand Encampment, unless he is personally interested in the result, or has been excused by the Grand Encampment, or is otherwise incapacitated.

19

CONSTITUTION

FOR THE

SUBORDINATE ENCAMPMENTS

OF THE

I. O. O. F. OF CONNECTICUT, ADOPTED JULY 11, 1848.

PREAMBLE.

FOR the purpose of insuring uniformity in the Patriarchal Order within this jurisdiction, the Grand Encampment of the State of Connecticut, the supreme tribunal of all Encampments of Patriarchs within its limits, ordains the following Articles as the Constitution for Subordinate Encampments.

ARTICLE I.

POWERS AND LIABILITIES.

How Constituted.

SECTION 1. Every subordinate Encampment shall be constituted by at least *seven* members of the R. P. degree, and shall possess all the powers and privileges of a subordinate Encampment, upon the presentation of a charter, duly granted by the Grand Encampment of Connecticut.

By-Laws.

SEC. 2. Each Encampment shall stand fully invested with power to adopt such By-Laws and resolutions, from time to time, as may be deemed expedient, provided they do not in any wise contravene any part of these articles, the Laws and Constitution of the Grand Encampment, or the principles of the Order.

Forfeiture.

SEC. 3. Should any subordinate Encampment, for two regular sessions of the Grand Encampment, neglect or refuse to make its returns and pay its dues, the members from such Encampment shall not be admitted into the Grand Encampment until the returns are made and dues paid; and should such subordinate Encampment continue for two years so to neglect or refuse, its charter shall be forfeited.

Effects Revert to Grand Encampment.

Sec. 4. In all cases where an Encampment shall have been suspended or expelled, or its charter shall have been forfeited, the charter, funds, books,' properties, and effects of all kinds, shall revert to the Grand Encampment. And it shall be the duty of the last installed officers of such Encampment, to deliver immediately to the Grand Patriarch, or the brother deputed by him to receive them, such funds and other effects as the Encampment may have claim to.

Seal.

Sec. 5. Each subordinate Encampment under this jurisdiction shall have a proper seal, and all official communications shall be sealed therewith.

ARTICLE II.

MEMBERSHIP.

Qualifications.

Sec. 1. No person shall be initiated into an Encampment, unless he is a member of a subordinate Lodge under the jurisdiction of the Grand Lodge of Connecticut, and has attained to the scarlet degree.

Fees.

Sec. 2. Each Encampment shall specify in its By-Laws the amount of the fee of admission, which shall not be less than six dollars, to be paid before initiation, and which shall entitle the candidate to all the degrees.

Admission.

Sec. 3. The name of a person offered for initiation, must be proposed in writing, by two members, stating the Lodge of which he is a member, and his residence, which must be entered on the record, and the subject referred to three Patriarchs for investigation, who shall report thereon, when the candidate shall be balloted for with ball ballots, and if *three* black balls appear against him, he shall be rejected, and so declared; but if the ballot is clear, or if less than three black balls appear, he shall be declared elected.

Applications.

Sec. 4. All applications for initiation into the Patriarchal branch of the Order, *must*, in all cases, be made to the nearest Encampment to which the applicant resides.

Deposit of Card.

SEC. 5. A patriarch of the Order, wishing to become a member, shall present his card from the Encampment of which he was formerly a member, which shall be referred to a committee of three, and in other respects disposed of as provided by section third for other applicants ; and on being admitted shall pay a sum not less than five dollars.

Rejections.

SEC. 6. When a candidate has been rejected by any Encampment, his proposition shall not be received by any other Encampment under this jurisdictin, in less than one year from the time of such rejection.

Degrees.

SEC. 7. Every brother shall be eligible for the degrees immediately on being elected ; but not more than two degrees shall be conferred at the same session, unless the most urgent necessity be proved, and two thirds of the members present vote in favor thereof.

ARTICLE III.
CARDS.
Visiting Cards.

SEC. 1. Any member who is free from charges on the books of the Encampment, and in good standing, may, on application to the Encampment, or to the Chief Patriarch and Scribe, receive a visiting card, by paying his dues to the time for which such card is granted, and paying such amount therefor as the by-laws shall direct ; and when the time has expired for which the card is granted; it shall be returned to the Encampment.

Traveling Card.

SEC. 2. When any Patriarch desires to withdraw his membership from the Encampment, he may make application at a regular session ; and if he is free from all charges on the books, and a majority of the members present agree thereto, he shall be entitled to a traveling or final card, which dissolves his connection with the Encampment.

Recalling Card.

SEC. 3. Each Encampment has power to recall or annul, for good cause, any card granted by them.

Relief to be Endorsed on Card.

SEC. 4. When relief is extended to a Patriarch by an Encampment of which he is not a member, the amount shall be endorsed upon his card, and the Encampment to which he belongs notified thereof.

ARTICLE IV.
OFFICERS.
Elective Officers.

SEC. 1. The elective officers of the Encampment shall consist of a Chief Patriarch, High Priest, Senior Warden, Scribe, Treasurer, and Junior Warden, who shall serve a regular term each. When deemed necessary, the Encampment may elect, in addition, an Assistant Scribe, to serve for one year.

Appointed Officers.

SEC. 2. The appointed officers shall be a Sentinel, Guide, 1st, 2d, 3d, and 4th Watches, who shall be appointed by the Chief Patriarch; 1st and 2d Guards of the Tent, who shall be appointed by the High Priest.

Duties of Officers.

SEC. 3. The duties of the various officers shall be as laid down in the charges of their office, the work of the Order, and the By-Laws of the Encampment.

Qualifications.

SEC. 4. No Patriarch shall be eligible for Chief Patriarch or High Priest, unless he has been elected to and discharged the duties of some other elective office ; nor shall any Patriarch be eligible to the other elective offices, until he has been appointed to and discharged the duties of some appointed office, except for the first term of an Encampment, when any R. P. member shall be eligible.

Nomination and Election.

SEC. 5. The nomination and election of officers shall take place on the last regular monthly session in each term. And the installation of the officers shall take place at the first regular monthly session in the succeeding one.

Ballot.

SEC. 6. Each elective officer shall be voted for separately by ballot, and each must receive a majority of all the votes given, to be elected. All votes given for persons not in nomination, shall be counted as blanks ; and in case, at any election, there shall be more blanks than regular votes, then a new nomination shall be made.

Absentees.

SEC. 7. Any officer absenting himself for more than three successive sessions, his seat may be declared vacant by a vote of the Encampment. And all vacancies shall be filled in the manner of the former election, to serve the residue of the term ; and officers so serving shall be entitled to the full honors of the term.

ARTICLE V.

CONTRIBUTIONS AND BENEFITS.

Contributions.

SEC. 1. Each member shall contribute to the Encampment a sum not less than three dollars a year, to be determined by the By-Laws; which, with the initiation fees, fines, &c., shall constitute the funds of the Encampment.

Weekly Benefits.

SEC. 2. The amount of weekly benefits to be paid to sick and disabled members shall be determined by the By-Laws; but in no case shall the amount per week exceed one half of the amount of dues paid per year.

Funeral Benefit.

SEC. 3. On the death of a Patriarch, who shall not be disqualified as by Sec. 4, there shall be allowed by the Encampment a sum not less than fifteen dollars, to assist in defraying the expense of burial; which shall be paid, without delay, to the deceased Patriarch's widow, or nearest of kin. The C. P., in the absence of competent relations, shall assist in taking charge of the funeral, and receive account of disbursements.

Non-Payment of Dues.

SEC. 4. No Patriarch shall be entitled to benefits, who is indebted to the Encampment for dues over six months; and the Encampment shall suspend all members who refuse or neglect the payment of their dues for twelve months.

ARTICLE VI.

PENALTIES AND TRIALS.

Penalties.

SEC. 1. Any Patriarch who shall violate the principles of the Order, or offend against these Articles or the By-Laws, shall be fined, reprimanded, suspended, or expelled, as the By-Laws may direct, ancient usage require, or the Encampment determine.

Charges.

SEC. 2. Every member shall be entitled to a fair trial for any offence involving reprimand, suspension, or expulsion; but no member of the Encampment shall be put on trial, unless charges, duly specifying his offence, be submitted in writing to the Encampment by two or more Patriarchs, except when made liable by non-payment to the Encampment, or when expelled or suspended by the Lodge of which he is a member.

Committee.

SEC. 3. When charges have been preferred against a Patriarch in proper manner, or any matters of grievance between

Patriarchs be brought before the Encampment, they shall be referred to a special committee of five members, who shall, if possible, be chosen from among the peers of the implicated Patriarch; and they shall, with as little delay as the case will admit, summon the parties, and examine and determine the matter in question; and if not involving expulsion or suspension, and no appeal be taken from their decision to the Encampment, it shall be final, without further action. Should the committee be convinced of the necessity of suspending or expelling a member, they shall submit a motion for that purpose to the Encampment.

Action on Motion of Committee.

Sec. 4. When a motion for the expulsion or suspension of a Patriarch shall have been submitted in due form, it shall be announced, and made the special order of business for the next regular monthly session of the Encampment, and the accused shall be duly summoned to be then and there in attendance; at which time, whether the implicated Patriarch be present or not, the Encampment may proceed to consider and determine the question. Two thirds of the members present voting in favor of the motion, it shall be carried; and the Encampment shall be fully competent, while such motion is under consideration, to vary the penalty from the original motion.

Appeal from Decision of Committee.

Sec. 5. When the decision of the committee appointed under Sec. 3, for the adjustment of grievances, shall not be satisfactory to all parties, either of those interested shall have the privilege of appeal to the Encampment; and at the time appointed for trying the appeal, the committee shall present to the Encampment, in writing, the grounds on which their decision was founded, and the parties shall have the privilege of being heard before the Encampment, which shall determine the correctness of the decision of the committee, by the vote of a majority of the members present.

Appeal to Grand Encampment.

Sec. 6. Any Patriarch feeling aggrieved by the decision of the Encampment against him, is entitled to an appeal to the Grand Encampment for a new trial, if informality or want of fairness be shown on the former trial. On the command of the Grand Encampment, the Patriarch may be tried anew for the same offence.

Notice of Appeal.

Sec. 7. Whenever an appeal shall be taken by any member to the Grand Encampment, notice thereof, stating the grounds of such appeal, shall be served upon the Encampment of which the appellant is a member, at least two weeks before the session of the Grand Encampment.

Notice to other Encampments.

Sec. 8. When a Patriarch has been expelled or suspended, (except for non-payment of dues,) notice thereof shall be sent to all the Encampments under the jurisdiction of the Grand Encampment of Connecticut; and a Patriarch who has been legally expelled, shall not be again admitted to membership, without the consent of the Grand Encampment.

ARTICLE VII.

SESSIONS, TERMS, AND RETURNS.

Sessions.

Sec. 1. The first regular session held in each month shall be styled the "monthly session;" and those succeeding shall be styled "adjourned or special sessions."

Sec. 2. Seven Patriarchs shall constitute a quorum; and all business shall be transacted in the R. P. degree.

Terms.

Sec. 3. Semi-annual terms, consisting of not less than six monthly sessions, shall commence on the first regular sessions of July and January only; and all terms shall end on the day on which the succeeding ones commence.

Returns.

Sec. 4. It shall be the duty of the last past officers to prepare and forward to the Grand Encampment, immediately on the installation of their successors, the result of the elections, and a regular report of the work of the term, including the names of those initiated, admitted by card, advanced and exalted, rejected, withdrawn by card, suspended or expelled, and the cause thereof, reinstated and deceased, the whole number in membership, the amount of receipts, amount of funds on hand, number of Patriarchs relieved, number of widowed families relieved, number of Patriarchs buried, with the amount applied to each of these purposes, designating the amount paid for the education of orphans—accompanied by whatever sum may be due to the Grand Encampment.

ARTICLE VIII.

AMENDMENTS.

This Constitution or any part thereof shall not be altered, amended, suspended or annulled, except on motion made in the Grand Encampment.

PROCEEDINGS

OF

GRAND ENCAMPMENT, I.O.O.F. OF CONNECTICUT.

SEMI-ANNUAL SESSION.

New Haven, Jan. 9th, 1849.

The R. W. Grand Encampment, I. O. O. F., of Connecticut, convened this day in semi-annual session.

PRESENT:

M. W. LUCIUS A. THOMAS, *Grand Patriarch,*
M. E. JUNIUS M. WILLEY, *Grand High Priest,*
R. W. ORIGEN UTLEY, *Grand Senior Warden, pro. tem.*
R. W. PRELATE DEMICK, *Grand Scribe,*
R. W. SAMUEL BISHOP, *Grand Treasurer,*
R. W. A. C. GOODMAN, *Grand Junior Warden, pro. tem.*
R. W. TOWNSEND P. ABELL, *Grand Rep. to G. Lodge U. S.*
W. SAMUEL H. HARRIS, *Grand Sentinel, pro. tem.*

and a representation from subordinates under this jurisdiction.

By command of the M. W. Grand Patriarch, the Grand Officers took their stations, and after the Throne of Grace had been addressed by the M. E. Grand High Priest, the Grand Encampment was opened in ample form.

The Grand Scribe commenced reading the minutes of the last session, when, on motion, the further reading was dispensed with by vote of the Grand Encampment.

The following Patriarchs were then appointed a Committee on Credentials, viz.: G. Rep. T. P. Abell and Pats. E. G. Storer and L. Peck, who submitted the following report:

To the R. W. Grand Encampment, now in session:

The Committee on Credentials would report as correct the following named Patriarchs :—

Jas. H. Leforge and W. H. Ellis, Sassacus, No. 1.
Calvin G. Williams, Charity, No. 10.
Orlando Pease and Benj. B. Woodford, Winsted, No. 12.
Ruel Thrall and Reuben P. Gage, Hinman, No. 13.
Erastus Foster and Ralph E. Terry, Montevideo, No. 15.

All of which is respectfully submitted.

T. P. ABELL,
E. G. STORER, } *Com.*
LUCIUS PECK,

The report was accepted, and the above named candidates introduced and properly instructed.

20

The M. W. Grand Patriarch submitted the following report, with the accompanying documents:

To the R. W. G. Encampment, I. O. Ó. F. of Ct.:

OFFICERS AND PATRIARCHS,—In extending to you the congratulations of the season, upon your assembling to deliberate upon the welfare of the Patriarchal branch of our Order in this State, I am gratified in being able to inform you, that within this jurisdiction perfect quiet and harmony prevails, if I may be allowed so to infer from the fact, that during the interval since our last session, no question of doubt or dispute has been presented for my consideration. The few acts left by the Grand Encampment for my completion have been fully and satisfactorily consummated.

The Grand Encampment having directed the locations of Oriental Encampment, No 2, and Charity Encampment, No. 10, to be changed in compliance with the requests of those subordinates, the one from East Haddam to Essex, and the other from Lower Mystic to Stonington, I issued authority to R. W. J. M. Willey, G. H. P., directing him to superintend the proposed removals, and upon their proper location, to declare them competent to proceed in their work. His return, declaring the fulfillment of his commission, which is herewith submitted, is full and satisfactory, and gives assurance that the change will be eminently serviceable to both those subordinates.

Resolutions were adopted at the last session directing Midian Encampment, No. 7, to pay to the Treasurer of Hinman Encampment, No. 13, the whole amount of fees received by said Midian Encampment for the initiation of all those members who belonged, at the time of their admission, to the jurisdiction of Hinman Encampment. And in case of the refusal of Midian Encampment to comply within three months, her charter was declared annulled.

Before the completion of the prescribed time, viz., about the 25th of September last, the officers of Midian Encampment surrendered to the Grand Scribe their charter and working books, accompanied with a statement of their grievances. I subsequently, through D. G. P. Wm. B. Davis, made a demand for their records, funds and other property. The demand was refused, and he informed that the property had been transferred to a new institution.

The Grand Scribe issued, under my direction, a notice to the various Grand Encampments, of the expulsion of Midian Encampment, in compliance with the resolution directing it. I also caused the same notice to be inserted in a circular transmitting to the subordinates in this jurisdiction the annual and semi-annual P. W., and promulged through the same channel the information that a Chief Patriarch is competent to install his successor in the absence of all designated officers, and of all P. C. Patriarchs, much inconvenience having arisen from a want of knowledge of that fact.

The Grand Lodge of the United States adopted a resolution directing the manner in which Encampments shall be notified of the cessation of membership of its Patriarchs in the Lodges to which they respectively belong. I commend it to your attention, as requiring some legislation for its consummation.

The Grand Lodge of United States, at its last session, adopted a resolution whose effect will be to prevent any State Grand Bodies from amending in any way their Constitutions, without the consent of that Body. A committee was also appointed to prepare and report to the next session of the Grand Lodge of United States, forms of Constitutions to be uniformly imposed upon the respective Grand Lodges and Grand Encampments in the United States, in place of those of their own adoption ; the effect of which will be to change our whole laws and customs, and place us under a new and untried régime. Both these acts I regard as encroachments upon our chartered rights, and as unwarrantable assumptions of power by the Grand Lodge of the United States. I respectfully recommend that this Right Worthy Body remonstrate against their consummation.

L. A. THOMAS, *Grand Patriarch.*

M. W. Lucius A. Thomas, Grand Patriarch of the R. W. Grand Encampment, I. O. O. F. of the State of Connecticut :

DEAR SIR AND BROTHER—Pursuant to instructions received from you under date of Aug. 4. 1848, I proceeded to Essex Borough on the 6th day of October last, and the charter, books, furniture, and other effects of Oriental Encampment, No 2, having been previously conveyed from East Haddam to said Borough of Essex, I called a special session of said Oriental Encampment in the Hall of Fenwick Lodge, No. 20, I. O. O. F., and then and there in due form declared said Encampment regularly removed according to the order of the R. W. Grand Encampment, to said Borough of Essex. I have the honor to report that said Encampment commenced its labors at its new home under exceedingly favorable auspices, and that on said occasion three members of Fenwick Lodge were received within the tent, and also in ancient form exalted to the degree of the Royal Purple.

Pursuant to similar instructions of the same date, I caused the books, furniture, charter, and effects of Charity Encampment, No. 10, to be removed from Lower Mystic to the Borough of Stonington, and on the 16th day of October last, its removal was legally consummated by public announcement of the fact at a special session of said Encampment in the Hall of Stonington Lodge, No. 26, I. O. O. F.

All which is respectfully submitted, in F., H. and C

JUNIUS M. WILLEY, *G. H. P. G. E. of Conn*

The report of the M. W. Grand Patriarch was accepted, and, on motion, referred to a special committee, consisting of G. Rep. Abell, G. H. Priest Willey, and Pat. Ellis.

The Grand Treasurer submitted his report, which was referred to the Committee on Finance, which committee was thereupon appointed by the M. W. Grand Patirarch, and consisted of Patriarchs O. Utley, E. G. Storer, and Lucius Peck.

The M. W. Grand Patriarch appointed G. H. Priest Willey, and Patriarchs O. Utley and J. R. Greenwood, a Committee on the State of the Order.

The special committee to whom was referred the report of

the M. W. Grand Patriarch, submitted the following report, which was accepted :

To the R. W. Grand Encampment, now in session :

The committee to whom was referred the G. Patriarch's semi-annual report, beg leave to report,—That they have had the same under consideration, and recommend that so much of said report as relates to Midian Encampment, together with the accompanying document from Midian Encampment, be referred to a committee of three :

That so much as relates to the resolution of the G. L. U. S. regarding the cessation of membership of Patriarchs in subordinate Lodges, be referred to a committee of three :

And that so much as relates to the action of the G. L. of the United States in regard to the Constitutions of the State Grand Bodies, be also referred to a committee of three.

All of which is respectfully submitted.

> T. P. ABELL, ⎫
> J. M. WILLEY, ⎬ *Com.*
> WM. H. ELLIS, ⎭

The following committees were then appointed, viz. : On so much of the said report as relates to the late Midian Encampment, No. 7, Patriarchs S. H. Harris, E. G. Storer, and O. Utley. On so much of said report as relates to the cessation of membership of Patriarchs in subordinate Lodges, G. H. Priest Willey, and Patriarchs J. R. Greenwood and B. B. Woodford. On so much as relates to action of the R. W. Grand Lodge of the United States, G. Rep. T. P. Abell, Pat. A. C. Goodman, and P. G. P. William E. Sanford.

The Committee on Finance submitted their report on the accounts of the Grand Treasurer, which was accepted.

The Committee on the State of the Order submitted the following report, which was accepted :

To the R. W. Grand Encampment of the State of Connecticut :

The Committee on the State of the Order, to whom was referred the semi-annual Reports of Subordinate Encampments, beg leave to report, that they have examined said reports, and find correct those from

> Sassacus Encampment, No. 1,
> Sowheag   "   " 6,
> Winsted   "   " 12,
> Hinman   "   " 13,
> Montevideo   "   " 15.

The Report from Wascussee Encampment, No. 14, is deficient in not stating the time of meeting of said Encampment.

No returns have been received from Nos. 2, 3, 5, 8, 9, 10 and 11.

All which is respectfully submitted in Faith, Hope, and Charity.

> J. M. WILLEY,   ⎫
> O. UTLEY,   ⎬ *Com.*
> JAS. R. GREENWOOD, ⎭

The Committee on the State of the Order also submitted the following report, which was accepted :

The Committee on the State of the Order to whom were submitted the By-Laws of subordinates, beg leave to report, that they have examined the By-Laws of Sassacus Encampment, No. 1, and find the same correct, and in conformity with the Constitution of the Grand Encampment and the Constitution of subordinates.

All of which is respectfully submitted in Faith, Hope, and Charity.

> J. M. Willey,
> O. Utley,   } *Com.*
> Jas. R. Greenwood,

The Committee on the State of the Order also submitted the following report, which was accepted, and the Constitution and By-Laws referred back to No. 15, for correction.

The Committee on the State of the Order, having examined the Constitution and By-Laws of Montevideo Encampment, No. 15, find that Art. 4, Sec. 1st, clause 1st, of the Constitution is copied incorrectly. Art. 2, Sec. 1st, and Art. 3, Sec. 5th, also Art. 6, Sec. 2d, of their By-Laws, are in confliction with the Constitution ; they would therefore recommend that said Encampment correct their By-Laws so as to correspond with the Constitution.

All of which is respectfully submitted.

> J. M. Willey
> O. Utley,   } *Com.*
> Jas. R. Greenwood,

On motion, the Grand Encampment adjourned to half past 6 o'clock, this evening.

HALF PAST 6 O'CLOCK P. M., Jan. 9, 1849.

Grand Encampment met pursuant to adjournment.

Present: M. W. Grand Patriarch, M. E. Grand H. P., Officers and Patriarchs.

The Grand Encampment proceeded to the business of the session.

The committee to whom the subject was referred, submitted the following report, which was accepted :

To the R. W. Grand Encampment, I. O. O. F. of Connecticut :

The committee to whom was referred so much of the M. W. Grand Patriarch's Report (together with the accompanying document) as relates to the late Midian Encampment, No. 7, respectfully Report—

That they have had the subject under consideration, and fully approve of the doings of the Grand Encampment and M. W. Grand Patriarch in the premises ; and while they deem the insubordination and conduct of the members of that Encampment most reprehensible and unworthy of Odd Fellows, they would recommend that no further action be taken in the matter, except that the names of the members of said Midian Encampment appended to the memorial, be published with the proceedings of this session of the Grand Encampment, as having been expelled from this branch of the Order.

Submitted in Faith, Hope, and Charity.

S. H. Harris, ⎫
E. G. Storer, ⎬ *Com.*
O. Utley,   ⎭

The committee to whom the subject was referred, submitted the following report, which was accepted, and the resolution adopted :

To the R. W. G. Encampment of the State of Connecticut :

The undersigned committee on so much of the Report of the M. W. G. Patriarch as relates to the " cessation of the membership of Patriarchs in subordinate Lodges," beg leave to report, that they have attended to the duties of their appointment, and recommend the passage of the following resolution.

All which is respectfully submitted in Faith, Hope and Charity.

J. M. Willey,   ⎫
Jas. R. Greenwood, ⎬ *Com.*
B. B. Woodford, ⎭

Resolved, That the Scribe of each Encampment shall furnish to the Secretary of each subordinate Lodge from which its members may be drawn, the names of such members of the Encampment as may be members of said Lodge.

Patriarch Harris submitted the following resolution, which was adopted :

Resolved, That the officers of this Grand Encampment, together with its Grand Representative, shall be allowed for travel and attendance at the regular sessions of the Grand Encampment, the same amounts as are provided for attendance on the Grand Lodge, I. O. O. F. of Connecticut. *Provided, however,* that no officer or Grand Representative of this Grand Encampment shall receive pay for travel and attendance, whose expenses are paid by said Grand Lodge, or by the subordinate Encampment or Lodge of which he is a member.

The committee to whom the subject was referred, submitted the following report, which was accepted, and the accompanying resolutions adopted :

To the R. W. Grand Encampment, now in session :

The committee to whom was referred so much of the Grand Patriarch's semi-annual report as relates to the action of the R. W. G. L. U. States, in prohibiting State Grand Encampments and Lodges from amending their Constitutions without the consent of said Supreme Body ; and also as relates to the action of the G. L. U. S. in providing for the enactment of a uniform Constitution for the several State Grand Bodies under her jurisdiction, have had the same under consideration and beg leave to report—

That in their judgment they can but consider said action of the

R. W. G. L., in these instances, as premature, inexpedient, and unjust, and must therefore operate deleteriously for the interests of the Order at large.

It is premature, inasmuch as no time or means were taken to consult the wishes and views of the jurisdictions most vitally interested in such legislation, and from which, it is possible, a general voice of protestation might have been heard.

It is inexpedient, because it is impossible that a uniform constitution should not conflict with the established customs, legislations, and experience of our State Grand Bodies, from which confusion and inefficiency must ensue.

It is unjust, because having grown up to maturity under laws of our own creating, and become acquainted with all their ramifications, bearings, and utilities, we should then be called upon to forego advantages thus secured to us, and enter upon a new and uncertain career; and because it is a direct violation of rights guarantied to us by charter, by custom, and by direct legislation.

We therefore recommend the adoption of the following resolutions. All of which is respectfully submitted.

T. P. ABELL,
A. C. GOODMAN, } *Com.*
W. E. SANFORD,

Resolved, That this Grand Encampment have learned with profound concern, that the G. L. U. S. have not only attempted to abrogate their rights of legislation in matters relating to their state jurisdiction, but have also proposed to set aside their Constitution, and impose upon them another without their consent.

Resolved, That we therefore respectfully protest against this proposed usurpation of power by the G. L. U. S. over the State Grand jurisdictions.

On motion, the Grand Scribe was authorized to procure a suitable chest for the use of the Grand Encampment.

On motion, the Grand Representative proceeded to give instruction in the work of the Order.

The following bills were presented, referred to the Committee on Finance, and by them approved, after which they were ordered paid.

M. W. Lucius A. Thomas, Grand Patriarch, for postage,	$1.00
Grand Representative T. P. Abell, for Mileage, . . .	5.00
Prelate Demick, for compensation, &c., ...	28.28
T. J. Stafford, for printing, ...	33.22
A. C. Heitmann, for bill of stationery, ...	2.93
John Kennedy, for care of room, ...	3.00

No further business offering, the Grand Encampment was closed in ample form.

Attest,

P. DEMICK, *Grand Scribe.*

GRAND TREASURER'S ACCOUNT.

Grand Encampment, I. O. O. F. in account with S. Bishop, G. Treas.

DR.	July 11, 1848, To cash paid T. P. Abell,			$6.85
"	"	" " J. Kennedy,		3.00
"	"	" " C. J. Gruman,		5.50
"	"	" " Wm. L. Brewer,		9.00
"	"	" " T. J. Stafford,		28.10
"	"	" " L. A. Thomas,		23.50
"	"	" " L. A. Thomas,		25.00
"	"	" " Dues G. L. U. S,		20.00
	Oct. 6, 1848,	" " G R. Abell,		50.00
	January, 1849, To balance to new account,			10.40

$181.35

CR.	July 11, 1848, By balance from old account,		$81.77
"	"	Dues Sassacus, No. 1,	28.40
"	"	" Oriental, " 2,	.90
"	"	" Palmyra, " 3,	7.77
"	"	" Unity, " 4,	5.05
"	"	" Devotion, " 5,	17.68
"	"	" Mt. Hermon, 8,	5.36
"	"	" Kabaosa, " 9,	2.22
"	"	" Winsted, " 12,	11.05
"	"	" Montevideo, 15,	18.90
"	"	" Cards,	2.25

$181.35

The Committee on Finance have examined the above account and find the same correct.

O. UTLEY,
E. G. STORER, } Com.
LUCIUS PECK, }

New Haven, Jan. 9, 1849.

~~~~~~~~~~~~~~~~~~~~~~~~~~~~~~~~~

The following are the names appended to the memorial of the late Midian Encampment, No. 7, ordered to be published (page 138) with the proceedings of this session of the G. Encampment, as having been expelled from this branch of the Order.

Henry Moore,	Hiram B. Case, P. G.,	Thomas M. Knight,
John B. Eldredge, P. G.,	Calvin Northrop, P. H. P.,	Wm. Olmsted,
Hezekiah K. Sears,	Geo. King,	Charles Collins,
Aaron Morley, P. C. P.,	E. Fessenden, P. C. P.,	C. V. Peckham,
Wm. E. Learned,	C. C. Strong,	Benjamin Pease,
James Worthington,	James Bidwell,	John Smart,
Abijah Woodruff, P. C. P.,	George W. Martin,	John J. Benton,
John Kitson,	Henry Clay Bagg,	John Fox,
Daniel L. Pealer,	John Kenyon,	John Lee,
John Seckett,	Thomas Small,	J. W. Johnson, P. C. P.,
J. D. Egleston,	George C. Owen,	O. Woodhouse, P. C. P.,
J. Wheelock, Jr,	John Scurvier,	W. H. Crowell, S. W.,
H. C. Brainard,	Donald Graham,	Geo. D. Jewett, H. P.,
J. Hallac, P. G.,	Matthew Anderson,	Francis Dana,
J. K. Parsons,	Wm. H. Chapin,	Joseph Pratt, Jr., P. G.,
Henry Hastings, P. G.,	Joseph Brown,	O. D. Seymour, P. C. P.,
L. Weller, P. G.,	H. L. Miller, P. G. M.,	W. P. Chamberlin,
E. Hubbard,	A. M. Gordon, P. C. P.,	Goodwin Chaffee,
M. M. Merriman, P.H.P.,	William Boardman, P. G.,	W. S. Crane,
A. Skaats,	J. L. Rice, P. G.,	J. C. Wakeley, P. G.,
W. H. Hoadley,	Horace Fox,	M. P. Holt,
Rawson Read, P. G.,	Horatio N. Barrow,	Samuel Alexander, Jr.,
L. H. Hamblin,	S. M. Dart,	Wells Adams,
H. A. Chapin,	S. Woodruff, P. H. P.,	John H. Inslee,
Joel Sperry,	A. S. Tinkham,	William Brooks.
James Levon,	A. Denison,	

GRAND ENCAMPMENT, I.O.O.F. OF CONNECTICUT.

.

ANNUAL SESSION.

NEW HAVEN, July 10th, 1849.

THE R. W. Grand Encampment, I. O. O. F. of Connecticut, convened this day in annual session.

PRESENT:

M. W. LUCIUS A. THOMAS, *Grand Patriarch,*
M. E JUNIUS M. WILLEY, *Grand High Priest,*
R. W. CHOLWELL J. GRUMAN, *Grand Senior Warden,*
R. W. PRELATE DEMICK, *Grand Scribe,*
R. W. SAMUEL BISHOP, *Grand Treasurer,*
R W. WILLIAM B. DAVIS, *Grand Junior Warden,*
R. W. TOWNSEND P. ABELL, *Grand Rep. to G. Lodge U. S.*
W. ETHEL T. FARNAM, *Grand Sentinel,*

and a representation from the several subordinates under this jurisdiction.

By command of the M. W. Grand Patriarch, the Grand Officers took their stations, and after the Throne of Grace had been addressed by the M. E. Grand High Priest, the Grand Encampment was opened in ample form.

The reading of the minutes of the last session was ordered, and the Grand Scribe commenced reading them; when, on motion of Patriarch Wm. E. Sanford, the further reading was dispensed with, by vote of the Grand Encampment.

The M. W. Grand Patriarch appointed Patriarchs Wm. E. Sanford of No. 1, Geo. S. Sanford of No. 8, and H. H. Roath of No. 3, Committee on Credentials.

Patriarchs J. M. Willey, Origen Utley, and Lucius Peck, were appointed Committee of Finance.

The Committee on Credentials submitted the following re-

port, which was accepted, and the candidates therein named
introduced and properly instructed.

To the R. W. Grand Encampment, now in session.

The Committee on Credentials would report that the following
Patriarchs have presented legal certificates, entitling them to the
Grand Encampment degree:

    A. C. Heitmann, P. C. P.,
    F. Turner, P. H. P.,   } of Sassacus, No. 1.
    Jas. Phelps, P. H. P., of Oriental, No. 2.
    A. Chichester, P. C. P., of Devotion, No. 5.
    Geo. G. Wheeler, P. C. P.,
    John L. Roberts, P. C. P., } of Mt. Hermon, No. 8.
    D. B. Potter, P. C. P., of Charity, No. 10.
    E. C. Kellogg, P. C. P., of Connecticut, No. 11.
    Jas. L. Lockwood, P. C. P., of Wascussee, No. 14.
    P. Wardwell, P. C. P.,
    Geo. F. Steele, P. H. P., } of Montevideo, No. 15.
    All of which is respectfully submitted.

          WM. E. SANFORD,
          GEO. S. SANFORD, } *Committee.*
          H. H. ROATH,

The M. W. Grand Patriarch submitted the following, being
his annual report:

Officers and Members of the Grand Encampment of Conn.

I greet you once again upon the return of the annual period of
your assembling, at which those whom you have invested with the
cares and responsibilities of office, return to you their authority and
give account of their stewardship.

I am hardly able, however, to congratulate you upon the progress
or extension of our branch of the order in this jurisdiction. During
the past year, our tents have been spread upon no new ground, and,
judging from the few reports which I have seen, small additions
have been made to those already occupied. It is for you to inquire
whether any defect exists in our organization or laws which needs
correction.

I have taken occasion, during the recess, to examine more at
length the subject to which I called your attention at the last session, to wit, the attempt of the Grand Lodge of the United States
to wrest from the State jurisdictions the right of constitutional
legislation; and I deem it my duty to revert once more to the subject.

When the Grand Lodge of the United States was formed, in
1824–5, the Grand Lodge of Maryland and U. S. surrendered the
original charter, received from England, "*to the States of Maryland, Massachusetts, Pennsylvania, and New York, and all other
States, Territories, and Districts, within the Union, wherein a Grand*

Lodge may be legally established,*—and they in turn surrendered certain of their powers for the mutual benefit of the whole, and framed the Grand Lodge of the United States, upon the model of our Federal Government.† " *It was,*" says G. Secretary Ridgely,‡ " *a body of exceedingly limited jurisdiction;*" its powers being defined, by G. Sire Kennedy, to be, "*providing for uniform work, general intercourse, and the administration of justice.*"§ In other words, it was to have the entire control of the work of the Order ; to enact laws by which visiting brothers were to be governed ; and to act as umpire, or court of errors, for deciding questions carried up by *permission*, or by *order* of State jurisdictions. These and the right to grant charters in States where Grand Lodges had not been already established, were all the powers claimed by its Constitution, which also contained a provision that no alteration should be made in the instrument, without the concurrence of two thirds the State jurisdictions, for which purpose six months' notice of all proposed amendments were to be given.‖

At the session of 1833, however, when there were present seven members from Maryland, and only two from other States, the Constitution was taken up, in violation of its own provisions, and entirely remodeled. The clause rendering them accountable to the State jurisdictions was left out, and another introduced, claiming " *original and exclusive jurisdiction in Oddfellowship.*"¶

An attempt was made, in 1834, to exercise this " *exclusive jurisdiction.*" The Grand Lodge of Ohio presented a copy of her Constitution, complimentarily, to the Grand Lodge of the U. States ; when, at the instance of Rep. Hopkins, of Pennsylvania, she was authoritatively " *directed to change the style and title.*" Rep. Ridgely, proxy for that State, " *solemnly protested against the right of the Grand Lodge of the United States to interfere with the Constitution of the Grand Lodge of Ohio.*"** This claim, at that time undeniable, was admitted, and for the next ten years no attempt was made to interfere with the legislation of State jurisdictions.

Prior to 1843, no Grand Lodge or Grand Encampment presented its constitution or laws for examination ; nor did the G. L. of U. S. even presume to give them an approval prior to that time. No law of the Grand Lodge of the United States existed prior to 1847,

---

* Journal of Proceedings, Vol. I, p. 65.
† " The constitution of our federal government, framed by the wisdom of the sages of the revolution—wherein twenty-four wheels revolve in one wheel, twenty-four empires in one empire, and twenty-four sovereignties in one sovereignty—acting together in one harmonious concert, the beauty of its symmetry and practical operation has commanded the gratitude of our countrymen and the applause of mankind. Upon this system has been reared the government of Oddfellowship ; and by it the order has been advanced, its interests promoted, and its prosperity secured."—Ibid, Vol. I, p. 65.
‡ Journal of Proceedings, Vol. I, p. 420.   § Ibid, Vol I, p. 397.
‖ Ibid, Vol. I, pp. 30, 31, 59, 60, 61.   ¶ Ibid, Vol. I, p. 109.
** Ibid, Vol. I, p. 139.

claiming any right to supervise or examine the Constitutions of State jurisdictions. Nor is there any law now in existence, which claims any right to alter, amend, or annul the constitutional enactments of State jurisdictions, except when they conflict with existing laws.*

The resolution, then, adopted at the last session of the G. Lodge of the United States, which declares that the laws of a State jurisdiction are not legally in force until sanctioned by the Grand Lodge of the United States,† as well as the projected plan for enacting Constitutions for State jurisdictions and annulling those of their own adoption,‡ are not only violations of the original compact on which the Grand Lodge of the United States was established, but are not even sanctioned by any of its own statutes or laws, and are in direct opposition to the usage of the Order for more than twenty years,—a period sufficient to establish it as ancient usage, if so vague an authority can be held of any weight.

Measures so manifestly at variance with the laws of the Order, so contrary to every principle of right, and so opposed to the spirit of the institutions under which we live, cannot be too strenuously resisted. It were far better that the order should crumble to pieces, than sink into a despotism. And while I would yield a willing and cheerful obedience to the Grand Lodge of the United States, in all things under her proper jurisdiction, I would firmly resist any attempt to encroach upon our rights and prerogatives. The links which bind us in the union of love and kindness, may adorn us as the voluntary bond of friendship; but when forced upon us, they become manacles, which should be rent and cast aside by all who do not wish to own themselves slaves.

The evils under which the Order in New York are now suffering have arisen entirely from the unlawful assumption and exercise of powers by the Grand Sire. Had the Order in that State been permitted to enact their own laws, as was their undoubted right, by the same rule that governs alike states and corporate bodies, under our free institutions, viz., the majority at the ballot boxes, the difficulties in that State would, long ere this, have settled into harmony and quiet. The noble stand which the majority of the Order in the State have taken against the usurpations of power by the Grand Sire and the Grand Lodge of the United States, must command the admiration of all lovers of freedom, and deserve our sympathies and our aid.

The Grand Scribe will lay before you a memorial from the Order in New York, which I commend to your earnest consideration. Should your views coincide with mine, I recommend that the Grand Encampment take such action and express such opinions as will convey to the Grand Lodge of the United States, and to the Order at large, our convictions and our determination.

						L. A. THOMAS, *G. Patriarch.*

---

* Digest, p. 41, 42.		† Journal, Vol. III, p 155.		‡ Ibid, Vol. III, pp. 154, 157.

The above report was accepted by the Grand Encampment, and, on motion referred to a committee of three, for distribution of the subjects, therein referred to, to appropriate committees.

Patriarchs Townsend P. Abell, William E. Sanford, and Adrian C. Heitmann, were appointed said committee.

The Grand Treasurer submitted his report, which was referred to the Committee of Finance; who subsequently reported that they had examined and found the same correct. On motion, it was voted, that the report be accepted.

Patriarchs Origen Utley, A. C. Goodman, and Lucius Peck, were appointed a Committee on the State of the Order.

Patriarch T. P. Abell, from the committee to whom was referred the Grand Patriarch's report, submitted the following report:

To the R. W. Grand Encampment of Conn.

The committee to whom was referred the report of the M. W. Grand Patriarch, have had the same under consideration, and beg leave to recommend—

That so much of said report as relates to the present condition of the Patriarchal branch of our Order in this jurisdiction, be referred to a committee of three:

That so much as relates to the encroachments of the Grand Lodge of the United States upon the State jurisdictions, be referred to a committee of three:

And that so much as relates to the condition of the Order within the jurisdiction of the State of New York, be also referred to a committee of three.

All of which is respectfully submitted.

T. P. ABELL,
WM. E. SANFORD, } *Committee.*
A. C. HEITMANN,

The above report was accepted, and the following committees appointed in accordance with the recommendation therein contained:

On so much as relates to the present condition of the Patriarchal branch of our Order in this jurisdiction, Patriarchs E. T. Farnam, F. Turner, and J. Phelps.

On so much as relates to the encroachments of the Grand Lodge of the United States upon the State jurisdictions, Patriarchs George S. Sanford, T. P. Abell, and H. Hobart Roath.

On so much as relates to the condition of the Order within the jurisdiction of New York, Patriarchs Wm. E. Sanford, A. C. Heitmann, and W. B. Davis.

A communication from the R. W. Grand Lodge of the

State of New York was received and referred to the Committe on so much of the M. W. Grand Patriarch's report as relates to the condition of the Order within the jurisdiction of New York.

On motion of Patriarch Origen Utley, the Grand Encampment proceeded to the nomination and election of Grand Officers for the year ensuing. On balloting, the following Patriarchs were declared duly elected :

> *M. W.* Junius M. Willey, *Grand Patriarch.*
> *M. E.* Cholwell J. Gruman, *Grand High Priest.*
> *R. W.* William B. Davis, *Grand Senior Warden.*
> *R. W.* Prelate Demick, *Grand Scribe.*
> *R. W.* Samuel Bishop, *Grand Treasurer.*
> *R. W.* Origen Utley, *Grand Junior Warden.*

The Grand Officers elect were then installed into their respective chairs, in ample form.

On motion, the Grand Encampment adjourned to half past 7 o'clock this evening.

Tuesday, July 10th, 7½ P. M.

The Grand Encampment met pursuant to adjournment. Present, the Grand Officers and Members.

The M. W. Grand Patriarch having announced that the Grand Encampment was ready to proceed with the business of the session,

Patriarch Chichester, of No. 5, offered the following resolution, which was adopted, after his reasons for moving it had been set forth :

Resolved, That Devotion Encampment, No. 5, have the permission of this Grand Encampment to remove the location of said Encampment from Bethel to Danbury ; and whenever the Grand Patriarch shall be duly apprised that two thirds of the members present and voting, at a meeting called for that purpose, are in favor of . the same, he shall empower them to remove.

Patriarch F. Turner, from the committee on that subject, submitted the following report, which was accepted, and the accompanying resolution adopted :

To the R. W. Grand Encampment of Connecticut.

The special committee on so much of the M. W. Grand Patriarch's report as relates to the present condition of the patriarchal branch of our Order in this jurisdiction, beg leave to report, that they hear with deep regret the statement therein made, that this Order is not as flourishing at this time as it has been in former years. They hardly believe that anything may be done by this Grand body further than to recommend to the several representatives here present, to use their influence in their respective Encampments to arouse the dormant energies of their own members to a more healthy action. They will therefore offer the subjoined resolution.

All of which is respectfully submitted.

E. T. FARNAM, ⎞
F. TURNER,   ⎬ *Committee.*
J. PHELPS,   ⎠

Resolved, That the R. W. Grand Scribe be directed to address to the several subordinate Encampments in this State, a request to exert their influence to awaken the slothfulness of the members of Lodges around them, and induce as many as they can to join the Order of Patriarchs.

The M. W. Grand Patriarch announced the appointment of Patriarch D. B. Potter to the office of Grand Sentinel.

Patriarch Geo. S. Sanford, from the committee on that subject, submitted the following report, with the accompanying resolutions; which report was accepted, and the resolutions *unanimously* adopted:

To the R. W Grand Encampment, now in session.

The committee to whom was referred so much of the G. Patriarch's semi-annual report as relates to the encroachments of the Grand Lodge of the United States on the State jurisdictions, have had the same under consideration, and beg leave to recommend the adoption of the subjoined resolutions.

All of which is respectfully submitted.

GEO. S. SANFORD,   ⎞
T. P. ABELL,,   ⎬ *Committee.*
H. HOBART ROATH,   ⎠

Resolved, That the Grand Lodge of the United States was modeled after the Federal Government; that it possesses only such powers as were delegated by the State jurisdictions, by and through which it was formed.

Resolved, That the power to revise the constitutions and laws of State jurisdictions, has never been conceded to that body by tho State jurisdictions; that for twenty years after the formation of the Grand Lodge of the United States, no attempt was made to exercise any such power; and that until the publication of the Digest, in 1847, it never was claimed by that body.

Resolved, That tho attempt to legislate for State jurisdictions, by enacting constitutions for their government, is in violation of the compact upon which the Grand Lodge of the United States was formed, unsanctioned by its own statutes or laws, and should be strenuously resisted by every State jurisdiction.

Resolved, That the Grand Representative from this R. W. body, be instructed to present to the Grand Lodge of the United States a copy of these resolutions.

Patriarch A. C. Heitmann, from the committee to whom the subject was referred, submitted the following report, and accompanying resolutions. The report was accepted, and the resolutions *unanimously* adopted.

To the R. W. Grand Encampment, I. O. O. F. of Conn.

The committee to whom was referred so much of the M. W. G. Patriarch's report as relates to the condition of the Order in New York, together with the communication from the R. W. Grand Lodge of New York, beg leave to report,—

That they have examined and carefully considered the subjects referred to them, and are of opinion that the hearty sympathies of this R. W. body, as well as of the Order at large in this jurisdiction, are with our oppressed brethren of New York.

The whole question being so well understood by the members in general, and having been so ably commented on by the M. W. Grand Patriarch, your committee do not deem it necessary to make any lengthened argument, and will therefore recommend the adoption of the following resolutions.

Respectfully submitted.

WM. E. SANFORD,
A. C. HEITMANN,   } *Committee.*
WM. B. DAVIS,

Resolved, That the Constitution adopted by the R. W. G. Lodge of New York, at its November session, 1847, was adopted by a constitutional majority, and became the legal constitution of that State, and is binding upon that jurisdiction until repealed by legal and constitutional measures by that body.

Resolved, That neither the Grand Sire, nor the Grand Lodge of the United States, possessed any power to amend, annul, or suspend the said Constitution, or in any way interfere in the premises.

Resolved, That the R. W. G. Representative of this Grand Encampment be and he is hereby instructed to bring this question before the R. W. Grand Lodge of the United States, at its session in September next; and he is hereby further instructed to introduce, advocate, and vote for such resolutions as will tend to recognize as the legal jurisdiction, the R. W. Grand Lodge of New York working under the Constitution adopted at the November session, 1847, of that body, in accordance with the recommendation of the R. W. Grand Lodge of the United States.

Resolved, That the communication from the R. W. Grand Lodge of New York be spread upon the records, and published with the proceedings of this session.

The following communication from R. W. Grand Representative Abell, was read, and on motion, his resignation was accepted.

To the R. W. Grand Encampment.

Officers and Members :—The undersigned, feeling duly grateful for the favors and indulgence he has received at your hands, begs leave very respectfully to resign the office of Grand Representative to the Grand Lodge of the United States.

TOWNSEND P. ABELL.

On motion, the Grand Encampment then proceeded to the nomination and election of a Grand Representative, to fill the vacancy occasioned by the resignation of Patriarch Abell; and on balloting, P. G. P. WILLIAM E. SANFORD was declared duly elected to that office.

The following bills, having been approved by the Finance Committee, were ordered paid, viz :

T. J. Stafford, for Printing, &c.	$12.25
Lucius Peck, for Chest,	6.50
John Kennedy, for care of room, &c.	3.00
P. Demick, G. Scribe, for compensation, postage, &c.	27.49
C. J. Gruman, for attendance,	5.50
Wm. B. Davis, "	5.00
E. T. Farnam, "	6.00
T. P. Abell, "	5.00

On motion of Pat. Utley, the Grand Scribe was directed to address communications to those subordinates that are delinquent in forwarding Reports and dues.

Pat. F. Turner offered the following resolution, which was unanimously adopted :

Resolved, That the thanks of this Grand Encampment are due, and hereby tendered, to Past Grand Pat. LUCIUS A. THOMAS, for the able manner in which he has conducted the affairs of this Grand Body, and the dignified and impartial manner in which he has presided over its deliberations during the year now closed.

No further business offering, the Grand Encampment adjourned without day, and closed in ample form.

Attest,

P. DEMICK, *Grand Scribe.*

GRAND TREASURER'S ACCOUNT.

Grand Encampment, I. O. O. F., in account with S. Bishop, G. T.

DR.   Jan. 9, 1849, to cash paid T. P. Abell, ... $5.00
  "   "   "   "   J. Kennedy, ...   3.00
  "   "   "   "   T. J. Stafford, ...   33.22
  "   "   "   "   L. A. Thomas, ...   1.00
  "   "   "   "   P. Demick, ...   28.28
  "   "   "   "   A. C. Heitmann,   . . .   2.93
  "   "   "   "   Balance to new account,   .   36.79
                                                    ————
                                                    $110.22

CR.   Jan. 9, 1849, By balance from old account, $10.40
  "   "   "   Dues   "   No. 11, .   24.31
  "   "   "   "   "   "   8,   3.42
  "   "   "   Digests,   10.75
  "   "   "   Dues   "   "   15,   14.84
  "   "   "   "   "   "   13,   19.06
  "   "   "   "   "   "   12,   8.56
  "   "   "   "   "   "   6,   9.45
  "   "   "   "   "   "   4,   6.61
  "   "   "   "   "   "   1,   2.82
                                            ————
                                            $110.22

The Committee of Finance have examined the above accounts, and find them correct.

J. M. WILLEY, ⎫
O. UTLEY, ⎬ *Finance Committee.*
LUCIUS PECK, ⎭

NEW HAVEN, July 10th, 1849.

GRAND ENCAMPMENT, I. O. O. F. OF CONNECTICUT.

OFFICERS FOR 1849-50.

M. W. JUNIUS M. WILLEY,	*Grand Patriarch.*
M. E. CHOLWELL J. GRUMAN,	*Grand High Priest.*
R. W. WILLIAM B. DAVIS,	*Grand Senior Warden.*
R. W. PRELATE DEMICK,	*Grand Scribe.*
R. W. SAMUEL BISHOP,	*Grand Treasurer.*
R. W. ORIGEN UTLEY,	*Grand Junior Warden.*
W. D. B. POTTER,	*Grand Sentinel.*
R. W. WILLIAM E. SANFORD,	*G. Rep. to G. L. U. S.*

PAST GRAND PATRIARCHS.	**PAST GRAND HIGH PRIESTS.**
WILLIAM E. SANFORD, 1843–4.	RICHARD S. PRATT, 1843–4.
JOHN L. DEVOTION, 1844–5.	JONATHAN M. ANDRUS, 1844–5.
JONATHAN M. ANDRUS, 1845–6.	WILLIAM L. BREWER, 1845–6.
WILLIAM L. BREWER, 1846–7.	TOWNSEND P. ABELL, 1847–8.
LUCIUS A. THOMAS, 1848–9.	JUNIUS M. WILLEY, 1848–9.

MEMBERS.

Sassacus, No. 1, New Haven.

William E. Sanford, April 20, 1843.	Fred. Croswell, Jan. 14, 1847.
Samuel Bishop, April 20, 1843.	Truman Hart, Jan. 14, 1847.
Isaac Judson, April 20, 1843.	Eliphalet G. Storer, July 15, 1847.
Bela Lord, Jan. 12, 1844.	Noah Chandler, July 15, 1847.
Jonathan M. Andrus, April 12, 1844.	Samuel H. Harris, Jan. 13, 1848.
Prelate Demick, July 12, 1844.	Lucius Peck, Jan. 13, 1848.
Newel C. Hall, Jan 9, 1845.	James H. Leforge, Jan. 9, 1849.
Lucius A. Thomas, July 10, 1845.	William H. Ellis, Jan. 9, 1849.
Daniel H. Moore, Jan. 15, 1846.	Adrian C. Heitmann, July 10, 1849.
Elizur Hubbell, July 9, 1846.	François Turner, July 10, 1849.

Oriental, No. 2, Essex Borough.

Richard S. Pratt, April 20, 1843.	Junius M. Willey, July 10, 1845.
Thomas C. Boardman, April 20, 1843.	John S. Dickinson, Jan. 14, 1847.
John C. Palmer, July 10, 1845.	James Phelps, July 10, 1849.

Palmyra, No. 3, Norwich.

John L. Devotion, July 14, 1843.	David Young, July 10, 1845.
William L. Brewer, July 12, 1844.	H. Hobart Roath, July 9, 1846.
John A. Lathrop, July 12, 1844.	Philo M. Judson, July 9, 1846.
Edward W. Eells, Jan. 9, 1845.	James D. Mowrey, Jan. 14, 1847.
H. C. Bridgman, July 10, 1845.	James A. Hovey, July 15, 1847.

Unity, No. 4, New London.

Henry Champlain, July 12, 1844.
O. F. Smith, July 10, 1845.
George W. Brown, July 10, 1845.
Allen S. Wightman, Jan. 15, 1846.

C. C. Culver, Jan. 15, 1846.
Robert B. Jackson, July 15, 1847.
L. D. Allen, Jan. 13, 1848.

Devotion, No. 5, Bethel.

John Greenwood, Jr., Jan. 9, 1845.
James R. Greenwood, Jan. 15, 1846.
William W. Bedient, Jan. 15, 1846.
James P. Saunders, Jan. 15, 1846.
William F. Hoyt, July 9, 1846.
Ethel T. Farnum, July 9, 1846.

William A. Judd, Jan. 14, 1847.
Charles Hull, July 11, 1848.
A. Chichester, July 11, 1848.
F. Ball, July 11, 1848.
A. Stevens, July 11, 1848.
H. N. Bennett, July 11, 1848.

Sowheag, No. 6, Middletown.

Thomas C. Simpson, Jan. 9, 1845.
Origen Utley, Jan. 9, 1845.
Erastus H. Booth, Jan. 9, 1845.
John S. Parmelee, July 10, 1845.

Dennis Sage, Jan. 14, 1847.
Townsend P. Abell, Jan. 14, 1847.
W. B. Casey, Jan. 13, 1848.

Mount Hermon, No. 8, Bridgeport.

A. B. Beers, July 10, 1845.
S. B. Brittan, July 10, 1845.
George S. Sanford, Jan. 15, 1846.
E. B. Stevens, July 9, 1846.
Gilson Landon, Jan. 14, 1847.

Joseph Crosby, Jan. 14, 1847.
Dwight Morris, Jan. 14, 1847.
George G. Wheeler, July 10, 1849.
John L. Roberts, July 10, 1849.

Kabaosa, No. 9, Norwalk.

James A. Quintard, Jan. 15, 1846.
P. L. Cunningham, Jan. 15, 1846.
Cholwell J. Gruman, Jan. 15, 1846.

George W. Smith, July 9, 1846.
E. S. Quintard, Jan. 13, 1848.
H. E. Bissell, July 11, 1848.

Charity, No. 10, Stonington.

William Meeker, July 15, 1847.
Amos Clift, July 15, 1847.

Calvin G. Williams, Jan. 9, 1849.
D. S. Potter, July 10, 1849.

Connecticut, No. 11, Hartford.

Ezra Clark, Jr., July 15, 1847.
R. G. Drake, July 15, 1847.
William B. Davis, July 15, 1847.
A. C. Goodman, July 15, 1847.

Elihu Geer, July 15, 1847.
John Burt, July 11, 1848.
E. C. Kellogg, July 10, 1849.

Winsted, No. 12, Winsted.

John H. Mills, Jan. 13, 1848.
J. J. Twiss, Jan. 13, 1848.

Orlando Pease, Jan. 9, 1849.
Benjamin B. Woodford, Jan. 9, 1849.

Hinman, No. 13, Warehouse Point.

Joseph Olmsted, Jr., Jan. 13, 1848.
Robert M. Abbe, Jan. 13, 1848.

Ruel Thrall, Jan. 9, 1849.
Reuben P. Gage, Jan. 9, 1849.

Wascussee, No. 14, Stamford.

Robert H. Lockwood, Jan. 13, 1848.
Chauncey Ayres, July 11, 1848.

James L. Lockwood, July 10, 1849.

Montevideo, No. 15, Bristol.

George W. Bartholomew, July 11, 1848.
Adna Whiting, July 11, 1848.
Erastus Foster, Jan. 9, 1849.

Ralph E. Terry, Jan. 9, 1849.
P. Wardwell, July 10, 1849.
George F. Steele, July 10, 1849.

DUES TO THIS GRAND ENCAMPMENT,

Have been received as follows, viz :

From Sassacus,   No. 1, for term ending July 1st, 1849, $9.00
 "   Oriental,   " 2, "   "   "   "   "   5.40
 "   Palmyra,   " 3, "   "   "   "   "   3.35
 "   Unity,   " 4, "   "   "   "   "   1.17
 "   Devotion,   " 5, " *estimated* for *year* ending July, '49, 15.00
 "   Sowheag,   " 6, " term ending July 1st, 1849,   15.19
 "   Mt. Hermon, " 8, "   "   "   "   "   5.80
 "   Kabaosa,   " 9, "   "   "   "   "   6.57
 "   Charity,   " 10, "   "   "   "   "   9.41
 "   Connecticut, " 11, "   "   "   "   "   8.26
 "   Wascussee,   " 14, " two terms ending July 1st, 1849, 5.94
 "   Montevideo, " 15, " term   "   "   "   7.95
 "   C. J. Gruman, for Digest,   .38

There are now due to this Grand Encampment, the Reports of

Oriental,   No. 2, for the term ending Jan., 1849, and dues thereon.
Palmyra,   " 3, "   "   "   "   "   " dues only.
Devotion,   " 5, " *two* terms "   July, " Reports only.
Kabaosa,   " 9, " the term "   Jan., " and dues thereon.
Charity,   " 10, "   "   "   "   "   "   "   "
Connecticut, " 11, "   "   "   "   "   " Report only.
Winsted,   " 12, "   "   "   "   "   " and dues thereon.
Hinman,   " 13, "   "   "   "   "   "   "   "   "

♦ APPENDIX.

GRAND LODGE OF THE STATE OF NEW YORK, I. O. O. F.

CITY OF NEW YORK, JUNE 25, 1849.

To the Grand Lodges and Encampments in the United States.

OFFICERS AND BRETHREN :—Your attention for a season is respectfully asked in behalf of your brethren of the Order in the State of New York, adhering to the Grand Lodge working under the Constitution adopted in November, 1847.

The rights and privileges of that Grand Lodge have been assailed in a manner which, if submitted to by the Order at large, will destroy the freedom and independence of State Grand bodies, and impair the usefulness and perpetuity of Odd Fellowship.

We regard our Order in this country as an institution of the present, not of the past. Its earliest existence, and its continued history, can be traced by its recorded journals. Its charges, regulations, and lectures, as well as its constitutions and laws, owe their origin to American, and not foreign legislation. It is entirely separated from the English Orders, and we cannot, and should not, refer to them for any illustration of our principles.

As an American institution, its principles of government should be founded upon, and expounded by, those principles which belong to a free republican country. Those principles are, that all governments exist by the consent of, and for the benefit of, the governed, who, by their responsible representatives, legislate for the good of the whole, under restrictions contained in written constitutions and laws.

Our constitutions and laws, therefore, contain the provisions and limitations by which the many confer upon the few, who are the agents and servants of the whole, those powers of legislation which, in so large and widely extended an Order, cannot be exercised by all. They are the grants of power ; and whatever is not so granted, must be considered as withheld by, and belonging to, the whole. Any exercise of power not specifically granted by our constitutions and laws, and not necessarily belonging to specially delegated powers, is usurpation. If, without special authority, one power in our Order is usurped by our agents and servants, the whole may be so usurped ; and then Odd Fellowship, instead of being an institution moving in harmony with the genius of a free government, will be one of despotism, commanding us as members to obey that which as citizens we abhor, and would resist.

The Order in New York has suffered from this usurpation, as the following facts will prove :

1st. In August, 1846, at the annual session of our Grand Lodge, which was attended by representatives from all parts of the State, the old constitution was considered so defective, that, by a vote of 129 to 13, a convention was called to revise and submit a new constitution for adoption.

2d. After the constitution had been thus revised and submitted, and before its final approval by the Lodges, in December, 1846, at an adjourned quarterly session, when but few were present, except from the city of New York, the action of the annual session was illegally rescinded, and the session closed.

3d. At the first meeting of the next quarterly session, held in February, 1847, a motion was regularly made and seconded to reconsider the action in December. This motion the Grand Master declared out of order. An appeal was taken from his decision, which he refused to entertain. A motion to declare the December proceedings null and void shared the same fate. A motion to rescind the proceedings in December shared the same fate.

4th. The majority who attended the February session, 1847, being prevented by the Grand Master from exercising their rights of legislation, appealed to the Grand

Lodge of the United States, with the consent of our State Grand Lodge; and the G. L. of the U. S., in September, 1847, set aside the decisions of the G. Master, as well as the action of December, 1846, and referred the form of constitution reported by the Convention, to the Grand Lodge of New York, with a direction to take up the same at the November session, 1847, and act upon the same, with full power to adopt or reject, or amend and adopt the same, as if regularly and formally before us for final action, pursuant to the old constitution.

5th. At said November session, 1847, the Grand Lodge of New York did take up the said form of constitution, and act upon the same, and by a vote of 202 ayes to 77 noes, amended and adopted the same, and declared that it should be in full force and effect from and after the close of that session, and that the constitution previously in force should be annulled, and of no further force and effect; and that this was so stated from the chair by the G. M. himself. The session closed 6th November, 1847.

6th. No appeal was taken from the action of our Grand Lodge to the G. L. of the U. S., nor was its consent to any such appeal asked. The mandate of our G. Lodge went forth, requiring all of its Lodges and members to observe and support the new constitution, so adopted.

7th. On the 1st of December, 1847, the G. Master of our Grand Lodge issued a proclamation which attempted to set aside the action of the Grand Lodge of November, by declaring that the old constitution was then, and would remain in full force, until the G. L. of the U. S. approved of the new constitution. An issue was thus presented to the Lodges and members in this State, whether they should obey the Grand Lodge or the Grand Master; and more than two thirds of the Lodges promptly decided to obey the Grand Lodge, and disregard the proclamation as a nullity, being founded on usurpation; neither the old or new constitution giving him the power by proclamation to nullify the legislation of the body which elected him.

8th. To prevent discord and confusion, a large number of Lodges applied to the Grand Sire to call a special session of the G. L. of the U. S., to settle the difficulties likely to follow from the proclamation. Instead of convening the constitutional body, created by the State Grand Lodges and Encampments, he convened a Board of Commissioners, created by himself, and sent them to New York to sit in judgment upon our Grand Lodge. No warrant being found in the constitution for such a body, the majority of the Order would not be represented before it, nor consent to abide by its decisions. It proceeded *ex parte*, and decided that the new constitution had not been legally adopted; thus exercising an appellate power, which even the Grand Lodge of the U. States could not exercise, without the consent of our State Grand Lodge.

9th. Before the decision of the Commission had been made, a small body of P. G's, with the Grand Master, held meetings in the city of New York, under the old annulled constitution, and had commenced the work of suspending and expelling Lodges and members, and of giving notice thereof to other jurisdictions; and also chartering Lodges in a manner not warranted by the new constitution.

10th. At the session of the G. L. of the U. S., in 1848, two sets of representatives presented credentials from the State of New York, one appointed in pursuance of the new, and the other in pursuance of the old constitution. That body, instead of being governed by the minutes of our Grand Lodge, assumed the power, without any appeal being before it, of investigating into the regularity of our proceedings, by evidence offered for the purpose of invalidating our minutes—a course of action without a parallel in the history of that body. On the last day, and almost the last hour of that session, a majority of that body admitted the representatives appointed under the old constitution, and resolved to recognize the body which appointed them as the only rightful Grand Lodge; thus, in effect, without a constitutional appeal, and without any warrant contained in the constitution, disfranchising more than two thirds of the Lodges in this State.

11th. In this condition were we placed at the last session of the Grand Lodge of the United States; more than one hundred Lodges declared expelled or suspended, and more than fifty declared spurious, for acting in obedience to the authority of the rightful Grand Lodge of this State and the mandates of the G. L. of the U. S. of 1847; and this declaration obtained by the exercise of usurped powers by the

Grand Master of this State, the Grand Sire in the recess of the G. L. of the U. S., and finally by the Grand Lodge of the U. S.

12th. A respectable minority of the G. L. of the U. S., believing the decision of that body wrong and unconstitutional, have tendered us their sympathy and support. Sustained thereby, we have continued our organization, and carry on the benevolent work of our Order. There are now upwards of two hundred and fifty Lodges working harmoniously under our jurisdiction. This large number are considered out of the pale of the Order by the officers of the G. L. of the U. S.; and yet our only fault has been a determined opposition to usurped powers, and an unwavering adherence to the written constitutions and laws of the Order.

If the efforts which have been made to crush the majority of the Order in this State should ultimately prove successful, then will encouragement be given elsewhere to minorities to bring discord and confusion upon their jurisdictions, by invoking the aid of proclamations of Grand Masters, and Grand Sires, and Grand Commissioners, to destroy the legislation of legally constituted Grand Lodges. We therefore feel called upon, as well out of regard to correct principles of government in our Order, as in reference to the peculiar situation in which we find ourselves placed, to invoke the attention of the Order in other jurisdictions to our condition, with a view that such instructions may be given to their Grand Representatives to the next session of the Grand Lodge of the United States, as will place us, who have committed no offence, in union and correspondence with the whole Order in the United States.

Respectfully submitted, in Friendship, Love, and Truth.

DANIEL P. BARNARD, *M. W. Grand Master.*
JETUR GARDINER, *R. W. Deputy Grand Master.*
ANDREW SAUL, *R. W. Grand Warden.*
WILLIAM H. H. PRALL, *R. W Grand Secretary.*
THEODORE A. WARD, *R. W. Grand Treasurer.*

GRAND ENCAMPMENT, I. O. O. F. OF CONNECTICUT.

SEMI-ANNUAL SESSION.

NEW HAVEN, Jan. 8th, 1850.

THE R. W. Grand Encampment, I. O. O. F. of Connecticut, convened this day in semi-annual session.

PRESENT:

M. W. JUNIUS M. WILLEY, *Grand Patriarch,*
M. E. CHOLWELL J. GRUMAN, *Grand High Priest,*
R. W. ORIGEN UTLEY, *Grand Senior Warden, pro tem.*
R. W. ELIPHALET G. STORER, *Grand Scribe, pro tem.*
R. W. SAMUEL BISHOP, *Grand Treasurer,*
R. W. FRANCOIS TURNER, *Grand Junior Warden, pro tem.*
R. W. WILLIAM E. SANFORD, *Grand Rep. to G. Lodge U. S.*
W. D. B. POTTER, *Grand Sentinel,*

and a representation from several of the subordinates under this jurisdiction.

By command of the M. W. Grand Patriarch, the Grand Officers who were present took their stations. The R. W. Grand Senior Warden and the R. W. Grand Scribe being absent, the M. W. Grand Patriarch appointed R. W. Grand J. W. Origen Utley, Grand Senior Warden, pro tem., Patriarch E. G. Storer, Grand Scribe, pro tem., and Patriarch François Turner, Grand Junior Warden, pro tem. The Throne of Grace was then addressed by the M. E. Grand High Priest, after which the Grand Encampment was opened in ample form.

The reading of the minutes of the annual session in July last was ordered by the G. Patriarch, and commenced by the G. Scribe, when, on motion of Patriarch S. H. Harris, the further reading was dispensed with, printed copies being in the hands of the members.

The M. W. Grand Patriarch appointed the following Committees, viz :

On Elections and Returns—Patriarchs Turner, Gruman, and Thrall; on Finance—Patriarchs Utley, Harris, and Leforge.

The Committee on Elections and Returns submitted the following report :

To the R. W. Grand Encampment of Conn.

The Committee on Elections and Returns have attended to the duties of their appointment, and beg leave to report as correct, the certificates of the following Patriarchs, viz :

Samuel B. Gorham,
Samuel Tolles, } of Sassacus, No. 1.
Calvin L. Hubbard,
Augustus Putnam, of Sowheag, No. 6.
Samuel E. Olmsted, of Kabaosa, No. 9.
Elizur T. Goodrich, of Connecticut, No. 11.
Edwin B. Dimock, } of Hinman, No. 13.
Samuel Watson,
William H. Treat, } Oasis, No. 16.
John L. Treat,

All of which is respectfully submitted.

F. TURNER, } *Committee.*
C. J. GRUMAN,

On motion, the report was accepted, and the several candidates therein named introduced and instructed in the Grand Encampment degree.

The M. W. Grand Patriarch submitted his semi-annual report, as follows :

R. W. Grand Officers and Patriarchs :

The return of the season that summons us together, finds us in circumstances in which we may congratulate ourselves upon quietness and prosperity. Nothing has occurred during the past term, calling for official interference, or interrupting the harmony which has generally existed in our State.

The returns from subordinate Encampments will exhibit the addition of a smaller number to this branch of the order than in terms past; but they will also show the financial condition of our Encampments to be healthy and encouraging.

On the 18th day of August, I received a petition from seven qualified Patriarchs residing in Meriden, asking for the establishment of the Patriarchal branch in that town. Having been long familiar with the zeal and efficiency of the Meriden brothers, and knowing no reason why the prayer of the petition should not be granted, I issued a dispensation, subject, of course, to your approval, and on the 6th day of September instituted " Oasis Encampment,

'No. 16," in ample form, and installed its officers. I was aided in these services by Grand Junior Warden Utley, and eleven Patriarchs of Sowheag Encampment. Six brothers were at that time received into the Patriarchal branch, and the same evening exalted to the sublime degree of the Royal Purple. The first officers of Oasis Encampment are, Wm. H. Treat, C. P.; John L. Treat, H. P.; Alden Peck, S. W.; George Redfield, Scribe; Andrew J. Smith, Treasurer; Joseph Gould, J. W. I would recommend that their dispensation be confirmed, and a charter granted in its stead.

On the 20th day of September, I made an official visit to Mount Hermon Encampment, No. 8, located in the city of Bridgeport. One candidate was at this time exalted to the sublime degree of the Royal Purple; and in justice to the members of this Encampment I deem it my duty to say that I never witnessed the degree conferred in a more dignified or impressive manner than on this occasion.

In view of the fact that many of our Encampments have ceased paying benefits, I would suggest the expediency of an alteration of Section 1st, Article V, of the Constitution for Subordinates, making the minimum amount of dues one dollar, instead of three, as at present provided.

I would also recommend that an addition be made to the By-Laws of this R. W. body, providing that whenever the Grand Patriarch may deem it needful to visit a subordinate Encampment, for purposes of discipline or counsel, and such subordinate is unable from its funds to pay the expenses of the Grand Patriarch, his necessary traveling expenses shall be defrayed by the Grand Encampment.

I would also recommend that our R. W. Grand Representative to the Grand Lodge of the United States be instructed to procure the regalia prescribed for that officer, at the expense of this R. W. body, said regalia to remain the property of this Grand Encampment, for the use of its future Representatives.

JUNIUS M. WILLEY, G. Patriarch.

On motion of G. Rep. Sanford, the report of the Grand Patriarch was accepted, and a charter granted to Oasis Encampment, No. 16, to be located at Meriden, in accordance with the recommendation therein contained.

On motion, it was resolved, that the report of the Grand Patriarch be referred to a committee of three, for a proper distribution of the subjects therein referred to.

The R. W. Grand Representative to the Grand Lodge of the United States submitted the following report:

To the R. W. Grand Encampment, I. O. O. F. of Conn.

Your Grand Representative to the R. W. Grand Lodge of the United States, respectfully reports, that he proceeded to the city of Baltimore a week previous to the annual session of that body in September last, and remained until its final adjournment.

The difficulties existing in our Order among the brethren in the

State of New York, seemed to render consultation among the Representatives advisable, previous to assembling in Grand Lodge ; for which purpose preliminary meetings were held at Barnum's Hotel, all of which were attended by your Grand Representative, which meetings were, in my opinion, of great benefit.

The resolutions passed by this Grand Encampment at its last session, relating to the powers of the Grand Lodge of the United States, were duly presented, and referred to the Legislative Committee. This course was taken by advice of Representatives who had attended previous sessions of the Grand Lodge, and were more familiar with its usual routine of business than myself. The committee, however, reported, that according to their appointment the resolutions could not properly come before them. As the great object of having the resolutions spread upon the journal had been secured, and any desirable action directly upon this subject would have been impossible at this time,—most of the Representatives being in favor of a special session, at which the constitution would be amended, and the powers of the Grand Lodge strictly defined,— I did not press their reference to any other committee.

Article XII of the Constitution of the Grand Lodge of the U. S. was so amended, that hereafter the expenses of Representatives are to be paid by that body ; the funds necessary for that purpose to be raised by assessment on each State Grand body, in proportion to the number of members under its jurisdiction. I was in favor of this alteration, because it is no more than just that those large constituencies which are located near the usual place of meeting of the Grand Lodge should share in the burden of supporting that organization, in proportion to their numbers, and of course their ability, which they have not heretofore done.

The following resolutions were adopted :

" *Resolved,* That when this Grand Lodge shall have passed upon the business brought and to be brought before it, instead of closing the present session, it shall adjourn to the second Monday of September, 1850, to meet at the city of Cincinnati, then and there to take into consideration the present Constitution of the Grand Lodge and Digest, and agree to report the same, with such alterations as may be deemed advisable ; which, having been agreed upon, shall be entered upon the minutes of the session as a proposition to amend the constitution, and shall lay upon the table until the next annual session of the Grand Lodge of the U. S., (which shall be held in the city of Cincinnati,) to be considered and acted upon by the Representatives to that session, in the manner and form prescribed by the present Constitution.

" *Resolved,* That at such adjourned session the Grand Lodge of the United States will not entertain any motion for, or transact any business except that mentioned in the above resolution."

Knowing that this Grand Encampment were strongly opposed to the exercise of power by the Grand Lodge of the U. S., other than that which had been " delegated to it by State jurisdictions, by and through which it was formed," and believing that in this way the assumption of such power might hereafter be prevented, I, with a large majority of the members of the Grand Lodge, favored the adoption of the above resolutions.

The following resolution was adopted :

" *Resolved,* That the Congressional Manual of Judge Southerland be and is hereby adopted for the government of the proceedings and debates of the Grand Lodge of the United States, so far as the same is applicable, and does not conflict with any of its special rules ; and that the same work be recommended to the Grand and subordinate bodies of the different States."

Also the following :

" *Resolved,* That no Representative can be recognized upon the floor of this Grand Lodge at any future session, unless clothed in the full regalia of a Grand Representative."

The New York difficulties were settled by dividing the State into two separate districts ; in doing which the Grand Lodge assumed a right of interfering in State jurisdictions, which, under ordinary circumstances, would not willingly be conceded by the Order in this State ; yet I felt compelled to vote in the way I did, for the purpose of correcting the improper legislation of a previous session.

WM. E. SANFORD, G. Rep.

On motion, it was voted, that the report of the Grand Representative be referred to the Committee on the Grand Patriarch's report. Patriarchs N. C. Hall, D. B. Potter, and W. H. Treat were appointed on said Committee.

The Committee of Finance submitted the following report, which was accepted :

To the R. W. Grand Encampment :

The Committee of Finance, having examined the accounts of the Grand Treasurer, report that there has been received, $93.42
Paid by Treas.,   90.74

Balance in hands of G. Treas., $2.68
All of which is respectfully submitted.

O. UTLEY,
S. H. HARRIS, } Com. of Finance.
J. H. LEFORGE,

New Haven, Jan. 8, 1850.

Patriarch Hall, from the Committee on the Reports of the Grand Patriarch and Grand Representative, submitted the following report :

To the Grand Encampment of Conn.

Your committee to whom was referred the reports of the Grand Patriarch and Grand Representative to the Grand Lodge of the U.

States, have had the same under consideration, and beg leave to recommend—

That so much of the Grand Patriarch's report as relates to the
Constitution of Subordinates and the By-Laws of this Grand Encampment, be referred to a committee of three :

That so much of said report as refers to regalia for our Representative to the Grand Lodge of the United States, be referred to a
committee of three :

Also, that the report of our Grand Representative be accepted
and spread upon the minutes of this R. W. body.

N. C. HALL,
D. B. POTTER, } *Committee.*
W. H. TREAT,

The above report was accepted, and the following committees appointed in accordance with the recommendation therein contained :

On so much of the G. Patriarch's report as relates to Constitution and By-Laws, Patriarchs N. C. Hall, O. Utley, and
E. B. Dimock.

On so much as relates to regalia for the Grand Representative, Patriarchs C. J. Gruman, E. Foster, and J. L. Treat.

The following bills, having been approved by the Finance
Committee, were ordered paid, viz :

J. M. Willey, for postage, ... ·	$1.62
P. Demick, for G. Scribe's salary, postage, &c., . .	28.50
T. J. Stafford, for printing, ...	29.00
J. H. Leforge, for preparing room, ...	3.00

Patriarch Turner, from the Committee on Returns, submitted the following report, which was accepted :

To the R. W. Grand Encampment of Conn.

The undersigned, committee on returns, beg leave to report, that
they have attended to the duty assigned them, and find that the returns of the following Encampments are correct, viz :

Sassacus, No. 1, . . .	dues paid,	$9.45
Sowheag, No. 6, ...	"	11.87
Kabaosa, No. 9, ...	"	4.55
Do. do. term ending Jan. 1849,	"	3.24
Charity, No. 10, ...	"	86
Connecticut, No. 11, . . .	"	11.89
Hinman, No. 13, ...	"	2.57
Montevideo, No. 15, . . .	"	3.35
Oasis, No. 16, : . . .	"	8.57

The returns of the other subordinate Encampments have not been
handed to your committee. All of which is respectfully submitted.

F. TURNER,
C. J. GRUMAN, } *Committee.*
R. THRALL,

Patriarch Gruman, from the Committee on Regalia, submitted the following report :

To the Grand Encampment, I. O. O. F. of Conn.

We your committee, to whom was referred so much of the report of the M. W. Grand Patriarch as relates to the regalia of the Representative of this Grand Encampment in the Grand Lodge of the United States, beg leave to report, that we have taken the subject into consideration, and are unanimously of the opinion that the recommendation of the Grand Patriarch was a proper one, and should be carried out by the Grand Encampment. We therefore offer the subjoined resolution.

C. J. GRUMAN,
E. FOSTER,   }   *Committee.*
J. L. TREAT,

Resolved, That Grand Representative Sanford be and hereby is authorized and instructed to procure suitable regalia, and that an order be drawn on the Grand Treasurer to pay for the same.

On motion, the report was accepted, the resolution adopted, and the committee discharged.

Patriarch Hall, from the Committee on Constitution and By-Laws, submitted the following report, which was accepted, and the resolutions adopted :

The committee to whom was referred so much of the Grand Patriarch's report as relates to the amendment of Art. 8th, Sect. 1st, of the Constitution of Subordinates, also so much as relates to the expenses of the Grand Patriarch when visiting the Subordinates, beg leave to report, that they have attended to the duties of their appointment, and would recommend the adoption of the following resolutions. All of which is respectfully submitted.

N. C. HALL,
O. UTLEY,   }   *Committee.*
E. B. DIMOCK,

Resolved, That Sec. 1st, Art. 5th, of the Constitution of Subordinates be amended by erasing the word " three," and substituting the word " one."

Resolved, That whenever, in the opinion of the Grand Patriarch, the welfare of the Order requires that he should visit any subordinate Encampment, and such Encampment is unable to pay the necessary expenses of such visit, said expenses shall be paid by this Grand Encampment.

P. G. Patriarch Thomas submitted the following resolution, which was adopted :

Resolved, That a committee be appointed to correspond with the several subordinate Encampments under the jurisdiction of this

Grand Encampment, upon the operation of the laws relating to benefits and initiation fees.

The Grand Patriarch appointed Patriarchs L. A. Thomas, P. Demick, and S. H. Harris, a committee under the above resolution.

Patriarch Heitmann submitted the following proposition for amending the Constitution of the Grand Encampment, which was laid over to the annual session to be held in July next :

We the undersigned hereby propose the following amendments to Article VI, Sect. 1, Constitution of Grand Encampment, viz :

Strike out, in second and third lines, the words " on the Tuesday next preceding the second Wednesday in July and January," and insert in lieu thereof, ——— ——— ——— ———. Also, insert at the end of said section, " and the semi-annual session shall only be held at the call of the M. W. Grand Patriarch."

January Session, Grand Encampment, 1850.

A. C. HEITMANN, ⎱ No. 1,
C. L. HUBBARD, ⎰
C. J. GRUMAN, No. 9,
D. B. POTTER, No. 10,
E. T. GOODRICH, No. 11.

No further business appearing, the Grand Encampment adjourned without day, and was closed in ample form.

Attest,

P. DEMICK, *Grand Scribe.*

CASH RECEIVED THE PRESENT TERM,

From Sassacus Encampment,	No. 1,	for dues,	.	.			$9.45
" Oriental,	"	" 2,	"	.	.	.	4.55
" Devotion,	"	" 5,	"	.	.	.	7.82
" Sowheag	"	" 6,	"	.	.		11.87
" Mount Hermon,		" 8,	"	.	.	.	5.92
" Kabaosa	"	" 9,	"	.	.	.	7.79
" Charity,	"	" 10,	"	.	.	.	86
" Connecticut,	"	" 11,	"	.	.	.	11.89
" Winsted,	"	" 12,	"	.	.	.	14.39
" Hinman,	"	" 13,	"	.	.	.	5.67
" Montevideo,	"	" 15,	"	.	.	.	3.35
" Oasis,	"	" 16,	"	.	.	.	8.57
" Sowheag	"	" 6, for cards,		.	.		1.56
" Oasis	"	" 16, "		.	.	.	75
" "	"	" 16, for charter,		.	.		30.00

GRAND ENCAMPMENT, I. O. O. F. OF CONNECTICUT.

ANNUAL SESSION.

New Haven, July 9th, 1850.

THE R. W. Grand Encampment, I. O. O. F. of Connecticut, convened this day in regular annual session.

PRESENT :

M. W. JUNIUS M. WILLEY, *Grand Patriarch.*
M. E. CHOLWELL J. GRUMAN, *Grand High Priest.*
R. W. GEORGE S. SANFORD, *Grand Senior Warden, pro tem.*
R. W. FRANCOIS TURNER, *Grand Scribe, pro tem.*
R. W. SAMUEL BISHOP, *Grand Treasurer,*
R. W. ORIGEN UTLEY, *Grand Junior Warden,*
R. W. WILLIAM E. SANFORD, *Grand Representative,*
W.   *Grand Sentinel.*

and a representation from several of the subordinate encampments under this jurisdiction.

By command of the M. W. Grand Patriarch, the Grand
Officers who were present took their stations. The R. W.
Grand Senior Warden and the R. W. Grand Scribe being ab-
sent, the M. W. Grand Patriarch appointed Patriarch George
S. Sanford as Grand Senior Warden, *pro tem.*, and Patriarch
F. Turner, Grand Scribe, *pro tem.*

The M. E. Grand High Priest then addressed the Throne of
Grace, and the Grand Encampment was declared opened in
ample form.

The minutes of the last semi-annual session was ordered by
the Grand Scribe, but on motion it was voted that the further

reading be dispensed with, as the report had been printed, and were on the table for distribution.

The following committees were appointed by the M. W. Grand Patriarch, viz:

On Election and Returns—Patriarchs E. G. Storer, George S. Sanford, and C. L. Hubbard.

On Finance—O. Utley, S. H. Harris, and J. H. Leforge.

The committee on Elections and Returns submitted the following report:

To the R. W. Grand Encampment of Connecticut:

The Committee on Elections have examined the certificates of the following Patriarchs, and find them entitled to be admitted to seats as members of the Grand Encampment:

Frederick P. Gorham, }
Elias T. Main, } of Sassacus, No. 1.
Alpheus S. Spencer, of Oriental, No. 2.
J. E. Bidwell, of Sowheag, No. 6.
Jesse Shadbolt, of Mt. Hermon, No. 8.
Wm. Oakes, }
Wm. R. Williamson, } of Connecticut, No. 11.
Philip Tucker, of Hinman, No. 13.
Lester Goodman, }
Ethel North, } of Montevideo, No. 15.
Joseph Gould, of Oasis, No. 16.
Orrin Benedict, of Devotion, No. 5.

All of which is respectfully submitted.

E. G. STORER, }
GEO. S. SANFORD, } *Committee.*
C. L. HUBBARD, }

On motion, voted that the report be accepted and the several candidates herein named declared to be entitled to seats in this Grand Encampment.

The above named Patriarchs, except Patriarch F. P. Gorham, being in attendance, were then introduced and instructed in the Grand Encampment degree.

The M. W. Grand Patriarch submitted his semi-annual report, as follows:

R. W. Grand Officers and Patriarchs:

The returning annual session calls *us* to give an account of our stewardship, and *you* to consult for the prosperity of the Encampments for which you legislate.

But little has been done by the Grand Patriarch, since the last session, and no occasion has existed for official interference. Of the little however that has been done, the following is a summary:

Immediately after the last semi-annual session, I appointed Patriarch John L. Roberts, D. G. P. for Mount Hermon Encampment, No. 8, and Patriarch —— Foster, D. G. P. for Montevideo Encampment, No. 15.

Upon the 8th day of February, I made an official visit to Palmyra Encampment, No. 3, and witnessed the conferring of the degrees on eight brothers.

On the 9th of the same month, I received a petition, in regular form, from seven qualified Patriarchs, residing in the town of Colchester, in New London County, praying for an Encampment to be located in that place.— Upon the recommendation of P. G. P. Brewer, and several of the officers and members of Palmyra Encampment, I issued a dispensation, subject to your approval, and on the 18th of the same month, assisted by P. G. Patriarch Brewer, G. Senior Potter, and several members of Palmyra Encampment, I instituted " Willey Encampment, No. 17," and installed the following officers:

Samuel A. Kellogg, *C. P.*; Alfred B. Pierce, *II. P.*; Solomon E. Swift, *S. W.*; George W. Rodgers, *Scribe;* Elisha C. Jennings, *Treas.*; J. L. Worthington, *J. W.*

I announced to this encampment that their first term would end with June, 1850. I would recommend that their dispensation be confirmed, and a charter issued in its stead.

On the 4th of the present month, I made an official visit to Charity Encampment, No. 10, and installed its officers in ample form.

Brother Patriarchs—In retiring from the position to which your partiality has exalted me, allow me to thank you for the many and repeated tokens of respect with which I have been honored, and to bespeak for my successor a portion of that candor and magnanimity which I have so liberally experienced at your hands.

JUNIUS MARSHALL WILLEY, Grand Patriarch.

NEW HAVEN, June 9th, 1850.

On motion of G. Representative Sanford, the report of the Grand Patriarch was accepted, and a charter granted to Willey Encampment, No. 17, to be located at Colchester, New London County.

The amendment to the Constitution, proposed at the semi-annual session in January last, by Patriarchs A. C. Heitmann, &c., was continued to the next session.

The following bills, having been approved by the Finance Committee, were ordered paid, viz:

Sassacus Encampment, for room rent for 3½ years, $17 50
T. J. Stafford, for printing, &c.,   .   .   9 00
Grand Patriarch, for expenses,   .   .   1 42
Jas. H. Leforge,   .   .   .   3 00
A. C. Heitinan, for stationery, &c.   .   .   4 55

The bill of Grand Scribe P. Demick, was laid over till the next session.

The Committee on Finance submitted the following report :

Grand Encampment in account with S. Bishop, Grand Treasurer.

1850.				Dr.
January 8.	To Cash paid G. Rep. Wm. E. Sanford,	.		$50 00
	" " J. M. Willey,	.	.	10 00
	" " D. B. Potter,	.	.	10 00
	" " C. J. Grumman,	.	.	5 00
	" " J. H. Leforge,	.	.	3 00
	" " J. M. Willey,	.	.	1 62
	" " P. Demick,	.	.	28 50
	" " T. J. Stafford,	.	.	29 00
				$137 12
July 9.	To balance from old Account,	.		10 50

1850.				Cr.
January 8.	By balance from old Account,	.	.	2 18
	Cash received for Dues, No. 1,	.	.	9 45
	" " " " " 2,	.	.	4 55
	" " " " " 5,	.	.	7 82
	" Cards, $1 56, for Dues, No. 6, $11 87,			13 43
	" received for Dues, No. 8,	.	.	5 92
	" " " " " 9,	.	.	7 79
	" " " " " 10,	.	.	86
	" " " " " 11,	.	.	11 89
	" " " " " 12,	.	.	14 39
	" " " " " 13,	.	.	5 67
	" " " " " 15,	.	.	3 35
	" " " Charter, " 16,	.	.	30 00
	" " " Cards, 75, 16, Dues, $8 57,			9 32
July 9.	Balance to new account,	.	. .	10 50
				$137 12

The Committee of Finance having examined the accounts of the Grand Treasurer, report that there has been received $126 62; paid by Treasurer, $137 12, amount advanced by Treasurer $10 50. All of which is respectfully submitted.

> O. UTLEY,　　}
> S. H. HARRIS,　} *Committee on*
> J. H. LEFORGE,　} *Finance.*

The time of election of officers for the ensuing year having arrived, the following nominations were made :

Grand Patriarch, C. J. Gruman.
Grand High Priest, O. Utley.
Grand Senior Warden, F. Turner, C. L. Hubbard.
Grand Scribe, A. C. Heitmann.
Grand Treasurer, Samuel Bishop.
Grand Junior Warden, Cunningham, Storer, Bidwell, and Tucker.

The Grand Encampment proceeded to ballot, and the following Patriarchs were declared duly elected to the several offices, to wit:

Cholwell J. Gruman, *M. W. Grand Patriarch.*
Origen Utley, *Grand High Priest.*
Calvin L. Hubbard, *Grand Senior Warden.*
Adrian C. Heitmann, *Grand Scribe.*
Samuel Bishop, *Grand Treasurer.*
Eliphalet G. Storer, *Grand Junior Warden.*

The Grand Officers were then successively presented to the M. W. Grand Patriarch, J. M. Willey, and installed in the respective offices to which they had been elected, with the appropriate ceremonies of the order.

M. W. Grand Patriarch Gruman appointed Patriarch P. S. Cunningham as Grand Sentinel, for the ensuing year, who was duly qualified for the office, and took his station.

On motion, it was voted that the usual number of reports of the proceedings of this session be printed for distribution.

No further business being offered for consideration, the Grand Encampment was closed in ample form.

FRANÇOIS TURNER, *Grand Scribe, pro tem.*

GRAND ENCAMPMENT, I. O. O. F. OF CONN.

SEMI-ANNUAL SESSION.

NEW HAVEN, JANUARY 7th, 1851.

THE R. W. Grand Encampment, I. O. O. F. of Connecticut convened this day in Semi-Annual Session.

PRESENT :

M. W. CHOLWELL J. GRUMAN, *Grand Patriarch.*
M. E. ORIGEN UTLEY, *Grand High Priest.*
R. W. CALVIN L. HUBBARD, *Grand Senior Warden.*
R. W. ADRIAN C. HEITMANN, *Grand Scribe.*
R. W. SAMUEL BISHOP, *Grand Treasurer.*
R. W. ELIPHALET G. STORER, *Grand Junior Warden.*
R. W. WILLIAM E. SANFORD, *Grand Representative.*
W. JAMES H. LEFORGE, *Grand Sentinel.*

and a constitutional representation from Subordinate Encampments under this jurisdiction.

By command of the M. W. Grand Patriarch, the Grand Officers took their stations.

The M. E. Grand High Priest then addressed the Throne of Grace, and the Grand Encampment was declared opened in ample form.

The reading of the minutes of the last annual session was commenced by the Grand Scribe, but on motion, the further reading was dispensed with.

The following Patriarchs were appointed a Committee on Credentials ; viz: William E. Sanford, Samuel H. Harris,. Peter L. Cunningham.

The following Patriarchs were appointed a Committee on the State of the Order ; viz: Lucius A. Thomas, William E. Sanford, François Turner.

23

The Committee on Credentials submitted the following report, which, on motion, was accepted, and the candidates therein named declared to be entitled to seats in this Grand Encampment.

To the R. W. Grand Encampment of Connecticut:

The Committee on Elections have examined the certificates of the following Patriarchs, and find them entitled to be admitted to seats as members of the Grand Encampment:

Benjamin Beecher, Jr, }
Samuel S. Bassett,   } of Sassacus, No. 1,
John G. Hayden, of Oriental, No. 2.
Lloyd E. Baldwin, of Palmyra, No. 3.
Samuel Lynes, of Kabaosa, No. 9.
A. G. Bradford, of Winsted, No. 12.
Jona. W. Pond, of Montevideo, No. 15.
George Redfield, of Oasis, No. 16.
John Wallace, of Excelsior, No. 18.

All of which is respectfully submitted,

WILLIAM E. SANFORD,)
S. H. HARRIS,   } *Committee.*
P. L. CUNNIGHAM.   )

On motion, the above named Patriarchs were introduced and instructed in the Grand Encampment Degree.

The following Patriarchs were appointed a Committee of Finance; viz: Philip Tucker, J. J. Twiss, Wm. H. Treat.

The attention of the R. W. Grand Encampment was called to the report of the M. W. Grand Patriarch, which was then submitted, as follows:

R. W. Grand Officers and Patriarchs:

It is with feelings of gratitude that I am enabled to greet you at this, the semi-annual session of the Grand Encampment of Connecticut.

I have to congratulate you on the uninterrupted harmony and prosperity of the subordinate Encampments of this jurisdiction. Since our last session the official business coming before me has been limited.

On the ninth day of September, I received a petition from seven qualified Patriarchs residing in Birmingham, town of Derby, praying that a Dispensation be granted, and asking for the establishment of the Patriarchal branch of our beloved Order, in that town. Having been long acquainted with some of the petitioners, and having received the highest testimonials as to the standing and qualifications of the others; after advising with the officers of the Grand Encampment, and knowing of no reason why the prayer of the petitioners should not be granted, I issued a dispensation, subject to your approval, and on the twenty-fifth day of September I instituted Excelsior Encampment, No. 18, in ample form, and installed its officers.

I was aided in these duties by C. P. Samuel Lynes, P. C. P. William E. Bissell, P. C. P. Thomas Warner, Jr., P. C. P. Edward C. Bissell, P. C. P. Samuel E. Olmsted, and P. C. P. George W. Smith, of Kabaosa Encampment, No. 9. We then had the pleasure of instructing five brothers in the Patriarchal and Golden Rule Degrees, and conferred the honors of the Royal Purple on two of the newly initiated Patriarchs.

The following are the Patriarchs I installed in their respective chairs of office. Sheldon Bassett, C. P., John Wallace, H. P., C. S. Jackson, S. W., H. Atwater, Scribe, Thomas Elms, Treasurer, M. Donnelly, J. W. From the known talent, ability and perseverance of the Patriarchs of Excelsior Encampment, I have no doubt that it will soon rank with the best and most flourishing Encampments in this jurisdiction ; and I most cheerfully recommend that a Charter be granted them in place of the Dispensation they now hold.

On the sixth day of December, accompanied by P. C. P. Thomas Warner, Jr., and C. P. Samuel Lynes, I made an official visit to Devotion Encampment, No. 6, held in the town of Danbury, for the purpose of giving instruction in the Degrees, and general work of our Order ; for their kind attention and courtesy they will please accept our thanks.

I would call your attention to the importance of having one hour of each session devoted to instruction in the Degrees and general work of the Subordinate Encampments, as it is of the utmost importance that the degrees should be conferred in a uniform manner—and that too, correctly.

I would also recommend that the Grand Scribe be requested to procure immediately, Books of Charges and Degrees, for the use of Subordinate Encampments that are only supplied in part ; also, that he procure blank commissions for D. G. P., as I think it of importance the D. G. P. be appointed for all Encampments, except where they have an Elective Officer of the Grand Encampment.

CHOLWELL J. GRUMAN,
Grand Patriarch.

On motion, the Report of the Grand Patriarch was accepted, and referred to a special committee of three, for distribution of subjects to appropriate committees. The chair, thereupon, appointed the following Patriarchs as said special committee : to wit : Samuel Lynes, Lloyd E. Baldwin, and Samuel H. Harris.

R. W. Grand Representative, William E. Sanford. submitted the following report, which was on motion, referred to the Committee on the State of the Order.

To the R. W. Grand Encampment, I. O. O. F., of Connecticut.

The undersigned having fulfilled the duty of his appointment, by representing your R. W. Body at the adjourned Session, and at the annual communication of the Grand Lodge of the United States, in September last, respectfully reports a brief abstract of such of the proceedings, as are most interesting to our members.

The appointed time for holding the adjourned Session was Sept. 9, 1850, at 9 o'clock, A. M. At that hour the Grand Sire took the chair, and decided after the calling of a roll, that no quorum was present. The same took place on the morning and afternoon of the next day, and so on till Friday the fifth day of the Session.

Contrary to the wishes of a large majority of those present, the Grand Sire would not allow any but the *individual* members of the last Annual Session to take their seats, though if the substitutes had been allowed to answer to the names of those whose places they filled, there would have been a quorum. Although so much time had been wasted, and so short a time remained, (as the Session must of necessity close on the next day,) a great number of propositions for amendment to the Constitution were acted upon, but as final action could only be had at the regular Session, it is unnecessary to report the acts of the adjourned.

The annual communication commenced on Monday the 16th of September, and closed on Friday the 20th.

In accordance with the recommendation of the Grand Sire, the assessment law was repealed, though the State Grand Bodies are not exonerated from paying the assessment already made.

The following was made a *By-Law* of the Grand Lodge of the U. S.

" The Grand Lodge of the United States will neither entertain nor consider any inquiry as to what are the laws or usages of the Order, unless the same be brought before the Body, by an appeal from the decision of a Grand Lodge or Encampment—or unless the same be presented by a Grand Lodge or Encampment."

A resolution was adopted, "directing the Grand Officers of Grand Encampments, to destroy the work of the P. O. Degrees of C. P. and H. P., and to certify such destruction to the Grand Corresponding and Recording Secretary."

By a vote of forty-eight to twenty-three, the eighth article to the Constitution was amended, to read as follows:

"Past Grand Sires shall be admitted to seats in this Grand Lodge with the power of debating, and making motions, but shall not have the privilege of voting, unless they be Representatives.

The Grand Lodge again by a large majority, as in 1848 and 1849, negatived the proposition to return to three months terms.

The following resolutions were adopted.

Resolved, That the pay of Representatives to, and Officers of this Body, (excepting those to whom stated salaries are allowed,) shall be three dollars per diem during their attendance upon the Sessions of the Grand Lodge of the United States.

Resolved, That in addition to the above, the said Representatives and Officers, shall also receive five cents for each mile traveled from their respective residences, to the place of meeting of the Grand Lodge of the United States and back again, the said mileage to be computed by the nearest mail route between said points.

Resolved, That the said per diem allowance and mileage shall be paid by the Grand Treasurer, on the certificate of the Grand Secretary; and these resolutions shall go into effect from and after the close of this communication; all laws inconsistent therewith, shall be from thenceforth repealed.

Resolved, That the Grand Secretary be directed to require cash payments for all orders from State Grand Lodges, and State Grand Encampments, for Books, Odes, Diplomas, Cards, &c.; and that no Representative from such State Grand Body, shall be allowed nor permitted to occupy a seat as a Representative upon this floor on and after this communication of the Grand Lodge of the United States, whose State Grand Lodge or Grand Encampment has not first paid all amounts due by said Grand Body to this Grand Lodge.

Resolved, That no Representative shall be permitted to occupy a seat on the floor of this Grand Lodge, whose State Grand Lodge or Grand Encampment shall not have paid the Representative tax, levied by the Constitution of this Right Worthy Body.

Resolved, That the By-Laws of this Grand Lodge be amended by striking out Article 12th.

Resolved, That a special Committee of three members be appointed to prepare an appropriate honorary degree, with an accompanying sign or signs and password, to be conferred upon the wives of Scarlet Degree members, who are in good standing in the Order, and that such Committee report such degree for consideration at the next communication of this Grand Lodge.

Resolved, That the claim set up by the R. W. Grand Lodge and Grand Encampment of Maryland, to the permanent seat of government of this Grand Lodge, is unfounded, and is not sustained by law or fact.

A Charter was authorized for a Grand Lodge in Florida.

Several Charters were also granted for Subordinate Lodges and Encampments, showing the Order to be in a very prosperous condition.

No report was sent from this Grand Encampment to the Grand Lodge of the United States.

The prices of Books and Cards, have been increased to defray the increased expenses of the Grand Lodge, in addition to which, the Representative tax is proposed to be changed from twenty to fifty dollars.

The undersigned acknowledges his great obligation to officers and members of the Grand Lodge of the U. S., also a number of the Fraternity and others resident in Cincinnati, for their kind attention and many favors during the Session, and subsequently, especially during a short but severe illness, a time when friendly acts seem doubly kind.

Respectfully,

WILLIAM E. SANFORD,
Grand Representative.

The following bills having been approved by the Finance Committee, were ordered paid ; viz :

A. C. Heitmann, - - - - - -	$29 19
William H. Stanley, - - - - -	7 33
Edward H. Augur, - - - - -	3 00
P. Demick, from last session, - - -	27 50
C. J. Gruman, - - - - - -	2 10
T. J. Stafford, - - - - - -	1 00

The special committee to whom was referred the Report of the M. W. Grand Patriarch, submitted the following report, which was accepted, and the resolutions adopted.

To the R. W. Grand Encampment of Connecticut:

The undersigned, your committee appointed on the report of the M. W. Grand Patriarch, beg leave to submit the following, as their

REPORT:

Resolved, That so much of the report as refers to the Charter of the new Encampment, No. 18, be referred to a special committee of three.

Resolved, That the Grand Scribe be and hereby is instructed to procure sufficient new working books, blank certificates and commissions.

Resolved, That one hour this afternoon after the transaction of the business of the Grand Encampment, be devoted to instruction in the work of the Patriarchal branch of the Order.

Respectfully,

SAMUEL LYNES,
LLOYD E. BALDWIN } *Committee.*
SAMUEL H. HARRIS. }

The chair appointed on the committee above named, the following Patriarchs; viz : Samuel S. Bassett, John G. Hayden and John Wallace.

The R. W. Grand Treasurer submitted the following Report, which, on motion, was referred to the Committee on Finance.

Grand Encampment in account with S. Bishop, Grand Treasurer.

1850,		Dr.
July 9.	To balance from old account, ...	$10 50
	" cash paid G. P. Willey, ...	10 00
	" " D. P. Potter, ...	10 00
	" " G. P. Willey, ...	1 42
	" " C. J. Gruman, ...	6 00
	" " Sassacas Encampment, No. 1. . .	17 50
	" " J. H. Leforge, ...	3 00
	" " A. C. Heitmann, ...	4 55
	" " Thomas J. Stafford, ...	9 00
		71 97
	Balance to new account, . .	45 80
		$117 77

1850.				Cr.
July 9.	By cash of No. 1 for Dues, ...			$25 51
	" " " 2 "			1 00
	" " " 5 "	$19 02, Cards, 62 cents,		19 64
	" " " 5 "			12 40
	" " " 9 "			8 10
	" " " 10 "			60
	" " " 11 "			6 05
	" " " 12 "			4 59
	" " " 15 " , ...			4 58
	" " " 16 "			5 30
	" " " 17 for Charter, . . .			30 00
				$117 77

The following petition from Winsted Encampment, No. 12, was received, and on motion referred to a select Committee of three ; the chair appointed L. A. Thomas, S. H. Harris, Lloyd E. Baldwin.

To the R. W. Grand Encampment of Connecticut :

Winsted Encampment, No. 12, located at Winsted, would most respectfully represent, that the affairs of our Encampment are in such a condition, that at our regular sessions we have hardly enough members in attendance to carry on our business; that there is not a quorum of members living in Winsted, and that from the fact that there are in Winsted two Subordinate Lodges who have always been at variance with each other, and that one of which have used and are using their powerful influence against the prosperity of said encampment, they not willing to unite themselves, and preventing brothers of neighboring lodges to unite with us. Feeling that we have struggled as long as we can to build up a prosperous and flourishing Camp in this place—that these adverse circumstances are lying like an incubus upon us, preventing our growth, chilling our interest, and destroying our influence, we passed the accompanying vote, believing that a change of location which will be more central, and free from the undeserved opposition we receive, and in our firm belief will be for the best interest of this branch of our beloved Order. We therefore humbly pray that our petition may be favorably heard and granted.

        In testimony whereof, we hereunto affix our hands and the
[L. s.]   Seal of our Encampment, this second day of January, one
        thousand eight hundred and fifty-one.

A. G. BRADY, C. P.
A. G. BRADFORD, Scribe.

  Copy of a vote passed by Winsted Encampment, No. 12, I. O. O. F., at its regular session, January 2, 1851 ;

  Voted, On motion of Patriarch D. W. Patterson of Winsted, and seconded by Warren Alvord of New Hartford, that this Encampment petition the Right Worthy Grand Encampment for the removal of Winsted Encampment, No. 12, from Winsted, to be located at Wolcottville.

    The Committee on Finance, to whom the report of the R. W. Grand Treasurer was referred, submitted the following, which was accepted.

To the R. W. Grand Encampment of Connecticut:

  The undersigned, Committee of Finance, have examined the account of the Grand Treasurer, and

REPORT

As follows: that he has received the sum of $117 77, during the past term, and paid out $71 97, which brings a balance to new account of $45 80.

  All of which is respectfully submitted.

PHILIP TUCKER, ⎫
J. J. TWISS,   ⎬ Committee.
WM. H. TREAT, ⎭

    The following resolution was presented, and referred to the Committee on the State of the Order.

    Resolved, That Section 5, Article 2d, Constitution for Subordinate Encampments, be amended by striking out the word "*five*" in the last line, and inserting in lieu thereof, the word "*two.*"

GEO. REDFIELD, of No. 16.

    The Committee on the State of the Order submitted the following report, which was accepted.

To the R. W. Grand Encampment of Connecticut:

  The Committee on the State of the Order have attended to the duties of their appointment, and beg leave to

REPORT:

That they have examined the following Returns, and found the same correct.

Sassacus Encampment, No.	1,	Dues,	-	-	-	-	$13	60
Oriental "	" 2,	"	-	-	-	-	1	00
Palmyra "	" 3,	"	-	-	-	-	1	00
Kabaosa "	" 9,	"	-	-	-	-	10	32
Winsted "	" 12,	"	-	-	-	-	2	20
Hinman "	" 13,	"	-	-	-	-	4	22
Montevideo (no seal,) "	15,	"	-	-	-	-	9	15
Oasis Encampment, "	16,	"	-	-	-	-	6	85
Willey "	" 17,	"	-	-	-	-	5	00
Excelsior "	" 18,	"	-	-	-	-	13	50

All of which is respectfully submitted.

L. A. THOMAS, ⎫
WM. E. SANFORD, ⎬ *Committee.*
FRAN. TURNER, ⎭

The committee on Charter for a new Encampment submitted the following report, which was accepted, and the accompanying resolution passed.

To the R. W. Grand Encampment of Connecticut :

The committee appointed to consider the propriety of granting a Charter to Excelsior Encampment, No. 18, beg leave to

REPORT

Favorably thereon, and recommend the adoption of the following resolution.

All of which is respectfully submitted.

SAMUEL S. BASSETT, ⎫
JOHN G. HAYDEN, ⎬ *Committee.*
JOHN WALLACE, ⎭

Resolved, That a Charter be, and is hereby granted to Excelsior Encampment, No. 18, I. O. O. F.

The Committee on the State of the Order, to whom was referred the amendment of the Constitution of Subordinates, proposed by Patriarch Redfield, submitted the following resolution, which was passed.

To the R. W. Grand Encampment of Connecticut :

The Committee on the State of the Order respectfully recommend the adoption of the following resolution submitted by Patriarch Redfield of No. 16.

Resolved, That Section 5th, Article 2d of the Constitution for Subordinate Encampments be amended by striking out the word "*five*" in the last line, and inserting in lieu thereof, the word "*two.*"

Respectfully submitted.

L. A. THOMAS, ⎫
WM. E. SANFORD, ⎬ *Committee.*
FRAN. TURNER. ⎭

The Committee to whom was referred the petition of Winsted Encampment, No. 12, submitted the following report and resolutions on that subject. The report was accepted and resolutions adopted.

To the R. W. Grand Encampment of Connecticut.

The Committee to whom was referred the petition of Winsted Encampment, No. 12, for change of location from Winsted to Wolcottville, respectfully

REPORT:

That they have had the subject under consideration, and are of the opinion that it will be for the interest of said Encampment, and the good of the Order, that the prayer of the petitioners be granted. The Committee therefore submit the following resolutions:

Resolved, That the location of Winsted Encampment, No. 12, be and is hereby removed from the village of Winsted, town of Winchester, to the village of Wolcottville, town of Torrington.

Resolved, That the Grand Scribe be and is hereby directed to send to Winsted Encampment, a copy of the above resolutions under seal of the Grand Encampment.

Respectfully submitted,

L. A. THOMAS,
S. H. HARRIS, } *Committee.*
LLOYD E. BALDWIN,

On motion, the Grand Encampment proceeded to instruction in the work of Subordinate Encampments.

The Committee on credentials made the following report, which was accepted, and the Patriarchs therein named admitted to seats.

To the R. W. Grand Encampment of Connecticut:

The Committee on Elections beg leave further to

REPORT:

That they have examined the certificates of Patriarchs Allen G. Brady, and P. H. Parsons of Winsted Encampment, No. 12, and find them entitled to be admitted to seats as members of this Grand Encampment.

S. H. HARRIS, } *Committee.*
P. L. CUNNINGHAM,

The Committee to whom was referred the communication of the R. W. Grand Representative, submitted the following report, which was read and accepted.

To the R. W. Grand Encampment of Connecticut.

The Committee on the State of the Order, have had the report of Grand Representative Wm. E. Sanford under consideration, and beg leave to request the attention of this R. W. Grand Body, to several of its features.

1st. The assessment law was repealed.

2d. The work of the P. O. Degrees of the Encampment, was directed to be destroyed, and official notice of said destruction given to the R. W. Grand Secretary of the Grand Lodge of the United States.

3d. The per diem allowance of the Representatives, was increased to $3 00, and the mileage to five cents per mile, to be computed by the shortest mail route.

4th. The claim of the R. W. Grand Lodge, and Grand Encampment of Maryland, was declared "not sustained by law or fact."

All of which is respectfully submitted,

L. A. THOMAS, } *Committee.*
FRANCOIS TURNER,

24

On motion, the proposed amendment to the Constitution of this Grand Encampment, which had been on the table since January Session, 1850—was again called up for consideration, when the Most Worthy Grand Patriarch, declared the same to be out of order ; from which decision, there being no appeal, the proposed amendment was withdrawn.

The following proposition to amend the Constitution of this Grand Encampment, was substituted, and laid over to the next regular Session.

The undersigned hereby propose the following amendments to the Constitution of the Grand Encampment.   To amend Art. VI, Sec. 1, by striking out the words *second* and inserting *third*, and striking out the words *and January*.   In the same article, by striking out the word *second* and inserting *first*, and by striking out *July and January*, and inserting *August*.

L. A. THOMAS, No. 1.
SAMUEL LYNES, NO. 9.

On motion the following resolution was adopted ; and Patriarchs Samuel H. Harris, A. C. Heitmann and E. G. Storer, were appointed said Committee.

Resolved, That a Committee be appointed to procure Blank Charters, for the use of this Grand Encampment.

Patriarch L. A. Thomas moved that a Committee be appointed, to enquire into the expediency of so placing the Patriarchal branch of the Order, as to induce all Past Grands to become members of that branch, so that the business of the whole Order might be conducted in the Grand Lodge, and thus do away with the necessity of State Grand Encampments; which motion was passed ; and the chair appointed on that Committee, Patriarchs L. A. Thomas, Junius M. Willey, and T. P. Abell.

On motion, it was ordered that the usual number of the proceedings be printed for distribution.

Motion to adjourn to next Annual Session, was sustained by ten yeas to seven nays.

No further business offering, the Grand Encampment was closed in ample form.

Attest,

A. C. HEITMANN,
Grand Scribe.

Abstract of Returns of the Subordinate Encampments under the jurisdiction of the R. W. Grand Encampment, I. O. O. F. of the State of Connecticut, from July, 1850, to January, 1851.

Name.	Initiated.	Adm. by Card.	Reinstated.	Rejected.	Withdrawn.	Suspended.	Expulsion.	Deaths.	Whole number	Revenue.
Sassacus, No. 1,	3	0	0	0	6	4	0	1	91	$136.00
Oriental, 2,	0	0	0	0	0	0	0	0	20	10.00
Palmyra, 3,	0	0	1	0	0	1	0	2	24	10.00
Unity, 4,										
Devotion, 5,	3	1	0	0	0	0	*1	0	48	88.42
Sowheag, 6,	0	0	0	0	0	0	0	0	48	53.00
Mount Hermon, 8,	1	0	0	0	0	0	0	0	26	36.50
Kabaosa, 9,	5	0	0	0	0	8	0	0	45	103.25
Charity, 10,										
Connecticut, 11,										
Winsted, 12,	0	0	0	0	0	0	0	0	39	22.00
Hinman, 13,	3	0	0	0	0	0	0	0	32	42.24
Wascussee, 14,										
Montevideo, 15,	7	0	0	0	0	0	0	0	46	91.50
Oasis, 16,	8	0	0	0	0	0	0	0	29	68.55
Willey, 17,	5	7	0	0	0	0	0	0	12	50.00
Excelsior, 18,	19	7	0	0	0	0	0	0	27	135.00
Total,	54	15	1	0	6	13	1	3	487	$846.46

* G. B. Trowbridge, for Forgery.

GRAND ENCAMPMENT, I. O. O. F. OF CONN.

ANNUAL SESSION.

NEW HAVEN, JULY 8th, 1851.

THE R. W. Grand Encampment, I. O. O. F. of Connecticut, convened this day in Annual Session.

PRESENT :

M. W. CHOLWELL J. GRUMAN, *Grand Patriarch,*
M. E. ORIGEN UTLEY, *Grand High Priest,*
R. W. CALVIN L. HUBBARD, *Grand Senior Warden,*
R. W. ADRIAN C. HEITMANN, *Grand Scribe,*
R. W. SAMUEL BISHOP, *Grand Treasurer,*
R. W. ELIPHALET G. STORER, *Grand Junior Warden,*
W. PETER L. CUNNINGHAM, *Grand Sentinel,*

and members from the several subordinates.

By command of the R. W. Grand Patriarch, the Grand Officers assumed their stations.

The M. E. Grand High Priest said an appropriate prayer, and the Grand Encampment was opened in ample form.

The Grand Patriarch announced the following Committees.

ON ELECTION AND RETURNS—Patriarchs L. A. Thomas J. J. Twiss and T. P. Abell.

ON THE STATE OF THE ORDER—Patriarchs Adna Whiting S. H. Harris, F. D. Ball.

ON FINANCE—Patriarchs J. J. Twiss, Wm. H. Treat and J. D. Gould.

The Grand Scribe commenced the reading of the minutes of the last session. On motion the further reading was dispensed with, the same having been published.

24

Finance Committee made report on the account of the R. W. Grand Treasurer—which on motion was ordered to lie on the table.

The committee on credentials made the following report, which on motion was accepted.

To the R. W. Grand Encampment, I. O. O. F. of Connecticut:

The Committee on credentials beg leave to

REPORT:

That they have examined the certificates of the following Patriarchs, and find them correct :—

Encampment, No. 1, Louis L. Beecher, P. C. P., S. L. Ford, P. H. P.
    "   " 5, Russel Bevans, P. C. P., W. H. Green, P. H. P., Charles Taylor, P. C. P.
    "   " 9, H. C. Randal, P. H. P., Platt Price, P. C. P.
    "   " 11, W. C. Armstrong, P. H. P.
    "   " 13, T. S. Hatch, P. H. P.
    "   " 15, Gad Norton, P. H. P.

The Committee also find the credentials of the following Patriarchs informal :—

Encampment, No. 6, L. B. Ward, P. C. P.
    "   " 18, C. C. Jackson, P. C. P., Thomas Wallace Jr., P. H. P.

All of which is respectfully submitted

L. A. THOMAS,
T. P. ABELL.

On motion it was ordered that Patriarch Ward of 6, and Patriarchs Jackson and Wallace of 18, be also admitted.

The special Committee appointed at the last Session, (pp. 182,) made the following report, which on motion was accepted and the Committee discharged.

To the R. W. Grand Encampment, I. O. O. F., of Connecticut.:

The undersigned appointed at the last Session, to inquire into the expediency of so placing the Patriarchal branch of the Order as to induce all Past Grands to become members of that branch, so that the business of the whole Order might be conducted in the Grand Lodge, respectfully

REPORT:

That after a careful consideration of the subject, they find one difficulty in the way of such an arrangement, that appears to preclude the expetcation of being able to accomplish so desirable a result. Most of the members of the Grand Encampment are not Past Grands, who must necessarily be excluded from a participation in the legislation appertaining to the Patriarchal branch ; and not only so, but a necessity would be virtually imposed upon Encampments of filling their two highest offices exclusively with Past Grands, to enable them to be represented in the business appertaining to the Grand Encampment. The Committee therefore find themselves unable to report any plan likely to accomplish the object contemplated.

L. A. THOMAS,
T. P. ABELL.

The Committee on the State of the Order made the following report, which was accepted.

To the R. W. Grand Encampment, I. O. O. F., of Connecticut:

The Committee on the State of the Order respectfully

REPORT:

That they have examined the Returns of the several Subordinates that
have been placed in their hands, and find those from Nos. 5, 6, 9, 13,
and 18 correct. The returns from Nos. 1 and 16, are deficient in names
of members, and No. 11 deficient in names and number of members.

There are no reports from Nos. 2, 3, 4, 8, 10, 12, 14, 15 and 17.

All of which is respectfully submitted,

ADNA WHITING,
S. H. HARRIS,
F. D. BALL.

The Report of the Committee on Finance taken up and
accepted.

To the R. W. Grand Encampment I. O. O. F., of Connecticut:

The undersigned Committee of Finance have examined the account of
the R. W. G. Treasurer, and

REPORT

As follows: that he has received the sum of $116 64 during the past term,
and that he had on hand $45 80, and has paid out $85 62, which brings a
balance to new account $76 82.

All of which is respectfully submitted,

J. J. TWISS,   } *Finance Committee.*
WM. H. TREAT, }

The proposed amendment to the Constitution, Art. VI,
Sec. 1, (page 182 printed Proceedings,) was taken up for consideration—and on motion, was indefinitely postponed.

The Committee appointed at the last Session to procure
Blank Charters for the use of this G. Encampment, reported
that they had attended to the duty of their appointment, and
had procured fifty Charters, at a cost of ten dollars; on motion,
report accepted and Committee discharged.

The following petition from Monte Video Encampment,
No. 15, was read, and on motion referred to a special Committee of three—Grand Patriarch appointed on said Committee Patriarchs F. Turner, L. A. Thomas and F. D. Ball.

To the R. W. Grand Encampment, I. O. O. F., of Connecticut:

Grand Officers and Representatives—Whereas, Monte Video Encampment, No. 15, I. O. O. F., located at Bristol, is laboring under many
disadvantages, among which are the following.

1st. Of being deeply involved, and paying a high rent, to meet the payment of which, together with our incidental expenses, absorbs all or nearly
all of our revenue.

2nd. On account of the low State of our finances, with no prospect of their being improved while we remain in our present locality, induces many of the Patriarchs to neglect the payment of dues, consequently our receipts are very limited.

3d. The virulent sectionalism which ever exists in the town of Bristol, is hanging like an incubus about the Patriarchal branch of our Order in this place.

4th. The indifference of the Patriarchs who reside in the vicinity of our Encampment Hall, is so great, that we are seldom, if ever able to open the Encampment, without the aid of Patriarchs from Plainville or Southington, or the remote parts of the town of Bristol.

5th. That under the present aspect of our affairs, it appears to us an unmistakable decree, that the R. W. Grand Encampment will at no distant day be in possession of the Charter and equipments of our Camp.

And in this our present state, we deem a new location indispensable to the health and prosperity of our Encampment.

We therefore pray your R. W. Grand Body to grant us leave to remove our Encampment from Bristol to the village of Plainville, in the town of Farmington.

Done by the Patriarchs of Monte Video Encampment at a regular meeting held in their Hall, in the town of Bristol, this fifth day of June, A. D. 1851.   CARLOS WELTON, *C. P.*
                                      ERASTUS FOSTER, *Scribe.*

The following bills having been approved by the Finance Committee, were presented, and on motion ordered paid.

A. C. Heitmann's bill $29 18, Wm. H. Stanley's bill for Printing, $16 16, T. J. Stafford's bill for Charters, $10 00, and C. L. Sage's bill for tyling, $3 00.

On motion, ordered, that the Grand Encampment now proceed to the nomination and election of Officers for the ensuing term.

The following Patriarchs were then nominated ; viz.

For Grand Patriarch, M. E. G. H. P. Origen Utley, R. W. G. S. W. Calvin L. Hubbard.

(Patriarch Utley withdrew his name as a candidate for Grand Patriarch, but was again nominated for that office.)

For Grand High Priest, R. W. G. S. W. Calvin L. Hubbard.

For Grand Senior Warden, R. W. G. J. W. Eliphalet G. Storer, Patriarchs A. Whiting, F. D. Ball, F. Turner, T. Wallace, Jr., J. Gould, William H. Treat, and Elias T. Main,

For Grand Scribe, R. W. G. S. Adrian C. Heitmann and Patriarch J. J. Twiss.

For Grand Treasurer, Samuel Bishop.

For Grand Junior Warden, Patriarchs Peter L. Cunningham, A. Whiting, L. B. Ward, E. T. Main, Philip Tucker, and J. Gould.

The Grand Patriarch appointed as Tellers, Patriarchs Abell and Thomas.

The Grand Encampment then proceeded to the election of Grand Patriarch for the ensuing term. The Tellers announced twenty-three ballots, of which

Patriarch Utley received 17.
"   Hubbard "   5.
"   Abell   "   1.

Whereupon Patriarch Utley was declared duly elected Grand Patriarch.

The Grand Encampment then proceeded to the election of Grand High Priest. The Tellers announced twenty-one ballots, of which

Patriarch C. L. Hubbard received 19.
"   E. G. Storer   "   2.

Whereupon, Patriarch Hubbard was declared duly elected Grand High Priest for the ensuing term.

The Grand Encampment then proceeded to the election of Grand Senior Warden. The Tellers announced twenty-six ballots, viz:

Patriarch Storer received 12.
"   Whiting   "   4.
"   Turner   "   4.
"   Ball   "   3.
"   Tucker   "   1.
"   Pratt   "   1.
"   Treat   "   1.

There being no choice, the Grand Encampment again proceeded to a ballot for Grand Senior Warden. The Tellers announced twenty-eight ballots cast, of which

Patriarch E. G. Storer received 18.
"   Whiting   "   5.
"   Ball   "   3.
"   Turner   "   2.

Whereupon Patriarch E. G. Storer, was declared duly elected Grand Senior Warden for the ensuing term.

The Grand Encampment then proceeded to the election of Grand Scribe. The Tellers announced twenty-seven ballots, of which

Patriarch Twiss received 13.
"   Heitmann "   12.
"   Main   "   1.

There being a miscount, as announced by the Tellers, a new count was had, when it appearing that Patriarch Twiss had received fourteen votes—he was declared duly elected Grand Scribe for the ensuing term.

The Grand Encampment then proceeded to the election of Grand Treasurer for the ensuing term. The Tellers announced sixteen ballots, of which

Patriarch Bishop received 15.
"   Whiting   "   1.

Patriarch Bishop having received a majority of the votes cast, was declared duly elected Treasurer for the ensuing term.

The Grand Encampment then proceeded to the election of Grand Junior Warden. The Tellers announced twenty-five ballots, of which

Patriarch Cunningham received 9.
"   Main,   "   5.
"   Whiting,   "   4.
"   Tucker,   "   2.
"   Turner,   "   2.
"   Ward,   "   1.
"   Taspe,   "   1.
"   Gould,   "   1.

There being no choice the Grand Encampment again proceeded to the election of Grand Junior Warden. The Tellers announced twenty-nine ballots. of which

Patriarch Cunningham received 21.
"   Whiting   "   4.
"   Main,   "   2.
"   Tucker,   "   2.

Whereupon Patriarch P. L. Cunningham was declared duly elected Grand Junior Warden, for the ensuing term.

The special Committee to whom was referred the petition of Monte Video Encampment, No. 15, made the following report, which on motion was accepted, resolutions passed and Committee discharged.

To the R. W. Grand Encampment, I. O. O. F., of Connecticut:

The Committee to whom was referred the petition of Monte Video Encampment, No. 15, for change of location from Bristol to the village of Plainville in the town of Farmington, respectfully

REPORT:

That they have had the subject under consideration, and are fully of opinion that it will be for the interest of said Encampment, and the good of the Patriarchal branch of our Order, that the prayer of the petitioners be granted. The Committee therefore submit the following resolutions:

Resolved, That the location of Monte Video Encampment, No. 15, be and is hereby removed from Bristol to the village of Plainville, town of Farmington.

Resolved, That the Grand Scribe be and is hereby directed to send to

Monte Video Encampment, No 15, a copy of these resolutions under the seal of this Grand Encampment.

Respectfully submitted,

FRANCOIS TURNER,
L. A. THOMAS,
FERRIS D. BALL.

On motion, the Officers elect were installed in ample form.

Attest,

A. C. HEITMANN, *Grand Scribe.*

Patriarch Harris offered the following resolution, which was on motion unanimously adopted.

Resolved, That the thanks of this R. W. Grand Encampment are due to Past Grand Patriarch Gruman, and the Right Worthy Grand Officers connected with him, for the past official year, for the faithful and impartial manner in which they have performed the duties of their office.

On motion. voted that one hour be devoted to instruction in the work of the Order; the Grand Patriarch called on Past Grand Patriarch Gruman to perform said duty, which was accordingly done.

On motion, voted that the thanks of this Right Worthy Grand Encampment, be presented to Past Grand Patriarch Gruman for his valuable instruction.

On motion, voted that the usual number of proceedings be published.

No further business offering, the Grand Encampment was on motion, adjourned sine die.

Attest,

J. J. TWISS, *Grand Scribe.*

SPECIAL SESSION.

NEW HAVEN, JULY 9, 1851.

Upon the call of the M. W. G. Patriarch, a special Session of the R. W. Grand Encampment, was held this day.

The Right Worthy Grand Patriarch presiding.

Grand Scribe J. J. Twiss resigned his office as Grand Scribe of this Encampment. Resignation accepted.

On motion it was voted, that we proceed to nomination for Grand Scribe. Whereupon Patriarch A. C. Heitmann was duly nominated. There being no further nominations it was voted that we proceed to an election of Grand Scribe.

Patriarchs Abell and Thomas appointed Tellers.

Patriarch A. C. Heitmann having received the majority, was declared elected Grand Scribe for the ensuing year. Patriarch J. J. Twiss appointed a Committee to wait upon Patriarch Heitmann, and inform him of his election. Patriarch Twiss retired, and then returned, accompanied by Patriarch Heitmann, who accepted the office to which he had been elected. Patriarch Heitmann being presented, was duly installed into the office of Grand Scribe for the ensuing year.

J. J. TWISS, *Grand Scribe.*

The following resolution was unanimously adopted.

Resolved, That the Grand Scribe be directed to forward to each Subordinate Encampment, a copy of the proceedings of this Grand Encampment, from its organization to the present time—also, a copy of the Constitution and By-Laws of this Grand Encampment.

Patriarch B. J. Watson Beach, was appointed D. G. P. of Connecticut Encampment, No. 11.

No further business appearing, the Right Worthy Grand Encampment adjourned sine die.

A. C. HEITMANN, *Grand Scribe.*

Grand Encampment in account with S. Bishop, Grand Treasurer.

1851.									Cr.	
July 9.	To cash paid A. C. Heitmann,	·	-	-	-	-	$29	18
"	"	"	C. L. Sage,	-	-	-	-	-	3	00
"	"	"	W. H. Stanley,	-	-	-	-	16	16
"	"	"	G. L. Hubbard,	-	-	-	-	4	00
"	"	"	L. P. Cunningham,	-	-	-	-	5	50
"	"	"	C. J. Gruman,	-	-	-	-	5	50
"	"	"	Thomas J. Stafford,	-	-	-	-	10	00

$73 34

1851.									Cr.	
July 9.	By cash of No. 1 for Dues,		-	-	-	-	$23	09
"	"	" 5	"	-	-	-	-	-	6	31
"	"	" 6	"	-	-	-	-	-	5	95
"	"	" 9	"	-	-	-	-	-	5	05
"	"	" 11	"	-	-	-	-	-	2	57
"	"	" 13	"	-	-	-	-	-	4	06
"	"	" 16	"	-	-	-	-	-	6	00
"	"	" 18	"	-	-	-	-	-	7	65

$60 70

DISTRICT DEPUTY GRAND PATRIARCHS

FOR THE PRESENT TERM.

Sassacus Encampment, No. 1, Samuel H. Harris.
Oriental " " 2, John G. Hayden.
Palmyra " " 3, James D. Mowrey.
Unity " " 4,
Devotion " " 5, F. D. Ball.
Sowheag " " 6, Residence of GRAND PATRIARCH.
Mount Hermon " " 8, Joseph Crosby.
Kabaosa " " 9, P. L. Cunningham.
Charity " " 10, William Meeker.
Connecticut, " " 11, Elihu Geer.
Winsted " " 12, A. G. Bradford.
Hinman, " " 13, Philip Tucker.
Wascussee " " 14, J. J. Twiss.
Montevideo " " 15, Ralph E. Perry.
Oasis " " 16, George Redfield.
Willey " " 17, Samuel A. Kellogg.
Excelsior " " 18, Charles C. Jackson.

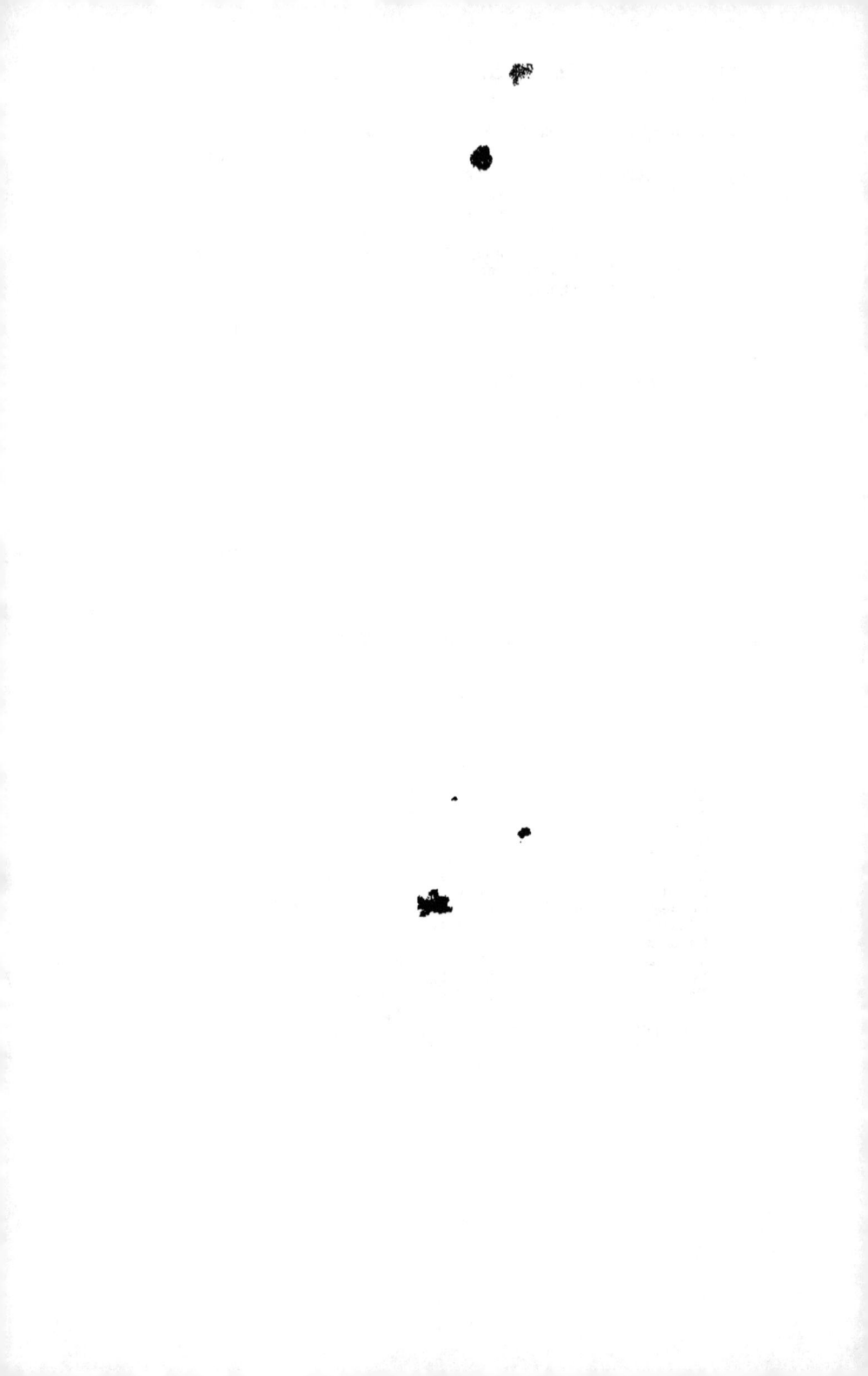

R. W. GRAND ENCAMPMENT, I. O. O. F. OF CONNECTICUT.

SEMI-ANNUAL SESSION.

NEW HAVEN, JAN. 13, 1852.

THE R. W. Grand Encampment, I. O. O. F. of Connecticut, convened this day in Semi-Annual Session.

PRESENT :

M. W. ORIGEN UTLEY,	*Grand Patriarch,*
M. E. CALVIN L. HUBBARD,	*Grand High Priest,*
R. W. A. C. HEITMANN,	*Grand Scribe,*
R. W. E. G. STORER,	*Grand Senior Warden,*

and a quorum of members.

By command of the M. W. Grand Patriarch, the Officers took their stations. The M. E. Grand High Priest said an appropriate prayer, and the G. Encampment was declared opened in ample form.

The Grand Scribe commenced reading the minutes of the last session, when, on motion, the minutes as printed were approved, with the exception of that part which declares that the amendment to the Constitution relative to one session of the Grand Encampment in each year was *indefinitely postponed ;* said minutes being amended so as to read, "*was laid on the table.*"

On motion, Voted, that when the G. Encampment adjourn, it be to the Tuesday preceding the 3d Wednesday of February, 1852, at 2 o'clock P. M.

On motion, the G. Encampment was adjourned.

25

ADJOURNED SESSION.

NEW HAVEN, Feb 17, 1852.

The R. W. Grand Encampment of Connecticut convened at 2 o'clock, according to adjournment.

PRESENT :

M. W. ORIGEN UTLEY,	*Grand Patriarch,*
M. E. CALVIN L. HUBBARD,	*Grand High Priest,*
R. W. SAMUEL BISHOP,	*Grand Treasurer,*
R. W. PETER L. CUNNINGHAM,	*Grand Junior Warden,*

and a quorum of members from the subordinates.

By command of the M. W. Grand Patriarch the Officers assumed their stations, and after the Throne of Grace had been addressed by the Grand High Priest, the Grand Encampment was opened in ample form.

The Grand Scribe being absent, the Grand Patriarch appointed Patriarch Lucius A. Thomas, Grand Scribe, *pro. tem.*

The minutes of Semi-annual Session, Jan. 13th, not being at hand, the reading was deferred.

The Grand Patriarch made the following appointments :

Committee on Credentials—Patriarchs J. M. Andrus of No. 1; John Wallace of No. 18 ; L. B. Ward of No. 6.

Committee on the State of the Order—Patriarchs J. M. Andrus of No. 1; John Wallace of No. 18 ; L. B. Ward of No. 6.

Committee on Finance—Patriarchs F. Turner of No. 1 ; P. L. Cunningham of No. 9 ; F. M. Brown of No. 16.

The Committee on Credentials submitted the following report, which was accepted :

To the R. W. Grand Encampment, I. O. O. F. of Connecticut:

The Committee on Credentials beg leave to report, that they have examined the certificates of the following Patriarchs and find them correct:

Frederick Botsford, *P. C. P.* } *No.* 1.
Robert Sizer, *P. H. P.*
Nathan Pratt, *P. C. P., No.* 2.
William J. Whipple, *P. C. P.,* } *No.* 13.
F. M. Brown, *P. H. P.,*
Alden Peck, *P. C. P.,* } *No.* 16.
Sidney P. Hall, *P. C. P.,*

All of which is respectfully submitted,

JONATHAN M. ANDRUS, }
JOHN WALLACE, } *Committee.*
LOUDON B. WARD, }

Whereupon, the above candidates were introduced and instructed in the Grand Encampment Degree, and took their seats.

The Grand Patriarch submitted the following report:

Right Worthy Grand Officers and Representatives:

By the goodness and mercy of an all-wise Providence, we are again permitted to assemble here in Grand Encampment, for the purpose of legislating for this branch of our beloved order in this State; and in accordance with previous custom, I will now submit for your consideration a brief report of my official acts since the last annual session.

In compliance with the desire expressed at the last session, that Deputy Grand Patriarchs should be appointed, I proceeded to appoint a Deputy Grand Patriarch for each subordinate Encampment under this jurisdiction, and forwarded them a dispensation.

From the reports received from several of those Officers, I am fully satisfied that they have generally performed their duties in a prompt and efficient manner.

In the month of August last, I received information through the Grand Scribe, that Unity Encampment, No. 4, had disbanded and become extinct. I immediately forwarded a communication to the last Officers of said Encampment, calling on them to surrender to the Grand Encampment their Charter, Books and other effects, as provided by the Constitution. They have since complied with the request and have forwarded to me their Working Books and Charter, which are now in the possession of the Grand Scribe.

On the 3d day of September, I received a communication from the Grand Scribe, informing me of the absence of R. W. Grand Representative Sanford, and that he would not return in season to attend the session of the Grand Lodge of the United States. I therefore appointed Past Grand Patriarch C. J. Gruman as a substitute to fill the vacancy, and directed the Grand Scribe to furnish him with the proper certificate.

The semi-annual Pass-Word was forwarded to each of the Deputy Grand Patriarchs previous to the first meeting in January.

At the last session of the Grand Lodge an amendment was made to its Constitution dispensing with the semi-annual session, and changing the time of holding the annual session from July to the third Wednesday in February.

In consequence of this arrangement, the subordinate Encampments were notified that the semi-annual session would probably be adjourned without transacting any important business, until the Tuesday preceding the 3d Wednesday in February, in order to accommodate those who might wish to attend the Grand Encampment and the Grand Lodge.

I would recommend that this Grand Encampment so amend its Constitution, as to hold but one session in each year, and that on the day previous to the session of the Grand Lodge.

Although our members have not increased the past term as rapidly as formerly, still I am happy to inform you that great harmony prevails in this higher branch of our ancient Order, throughout this State.

There has been no applications for Charters for new Encampments since our last session.

I cannot, in justice to my own feelings, close this report without expressing my thanks for the courtesy which has been extended to me since I have been elected to the honors of this station.

The duties imposed upon me I have endeavored to discharge according to the best of my ability, and certainly under the influence of the warmest love for our order. I therefore retire with thanks for your favors, and prayers for your individual and collective welfare.

O. UTLEY, *Grand Patriarch.*

The report of the Grand Patriarch was accepted and referred to a Special Committee, consisting of Patriarchs S. H. Harris and F. Turner of No. 1, and John Wallace of No. 18.

The bill of Grand Lodge of United States, $151.37, W. H. Stanley for Printing, and G. B. Bassett for Stationery, were presented and referred to Committee on Finance.

No record of the semi-annual session having been made, Patriarch Harris was appointed a Committee to prepare a record thereof.

On motion, the returns of subordinates were referred to the Committee on Credentials.

The Committee to whom was referred the report of the Grand Patriarch, submitted the following report, which was accepted:

To the R. W. Grand Encampment, I. O. O. F. of Connecticut:

The Committee to whom was referred the report of the M. W. Grand Patriarch, respectfully report, that they have had the same under consideration, and would recommend that the doings of the Grand Patriarch during the recess of the Grand Encampment be approved. The Committee find nothing in the Report of the Grand Patriarch requiring special action of this Grand Encampment, except the recommendation to alter the Constitution of the Grand Encampment so far as to have but one session of the Grand Encampment a year; which proposition the Committee would recommend to the favorable consideration of its members.

Respectfully submitted,
S. H. HARRIS,
JOHN WALLACE,   } *Committee.*
FRANC'S TURNER,

New Haven, Feb. 17, 1852.

The Committee on Finance submitted the following report, which was accepted, and the bills ordered paid.

To the R. W. Grand Encampment, I. O. O. F. of Connecticut, in semi-annual session:

The Committee on Finance beg leave to report, that they have examined the bills of George B. Bassett for Paper, $2.00; of Wm. H. Stanley for printing Circulars, $1.25, and find the same to be correct, and recommend that they be paid.

The Committee have also examined the bill presented by the Corresponding and Recording Secretary of the Grand Lodge of United States for taxes, &c., and presume it to be correct; but not having any way of ascertaining, the Committee would refer the same to the action of the Grand Encampment.

All of which is respectfully submitted,
FRANC'S TURNER,
P. L. CUNNINGHAM,   } *Committee.*
F. M. BROWN,

New Haven, Feb. 17, 1852.

The Committee to whom was referred the returns of subordinates, submitted the following report, which was accepted:

To the R. W. Grand Encampment, I. O. O. F. of Connecticut:

The Committee to whom was referred the returns of subordinates, respectfully report, that they have examined the returns of the said subordinates that have been placed in their hands and find those of Nos. 1, 2, 3, 5, 6, 15, 16, 18, correct.

There are no reports from 8, 9, 10, 11, 12, 13, 14, 17.

All of which is respectfully submitted,
JONATHAN M. ANDRUS,
JOHN WALLACE,   } *Committee.*
LOUDON B. WARD,

Patriarch Harris submitted the record of semi-annual session. [See p. 195.]

Motion to amend the amendment referred to in the record, by inserting February instead of August. Grand Patriarch ruled it out of order.

On motion, it was declared, that the amendment of record, made at the semi-annual session, was illegal and void.

The Committee of Finance submitted the following Report, which was accepted:

To the R. W. Grand Encampment, I. O. O. F. of Conn :

The Committee on Finance have examined the accounts of the Grand Treasurer, and beg to report the same to be correct, and that there is in his hands a balance of $64.18.

FRANC'S TURNER, }
P. L. CUNNINGHAM, } *Committee.*
F. M. BROWN, }

New Haven, Feb. 17, 1852.

On motion, a Special Committee, consisting of Patriarchs F. M. Brown of No. 13, C. L. Hubbard of No. 11, and S. Lynes of No. 9, was appointed to devise ways and means to increase the funds of the Grand Encampment.

Patriarch E. Augur's bill of $3 as Messenger, was ordered paid.

The Grand Patriarch submitted the following:

NEW YORK, Feb. 16, 1852.

ORIGEN UTLEY, ESQ., *Grand Patriarch :*

DEAR SIR AND BRO.:—Having removed from the State of Connecticut, I hereby tender my resignation of the Office of Grand Scribe.

Yours in F., H. and C.,

A. C. HEITMANN.

On motion, the resignation of Grand Scribe Heitmann was accepted.

Patriarch Turner offered the following amendments to the Constitution of the Grand Encampment, which were laid on the table under the rule :

The undersigned hereby propose the following amendments to the Constitution of the Grand Encampment.

To amend Art. VI, Sec. 1, by striking out the section and substituting the following: "The regular session of the Grand Encampment shall be held in each year on the Tuesday next preceding the third Wednesday of February, and special sessions shall be held at the call of the Grand Patriarch. And if there be any verbal amendments of the Constitution and By-Laws necessary to make them compatible with the foregoing amendment, the same are hereby ordered to be made and recorded by the Grand Scribe.

FRANC'S TURNER,
F. M. BROWN.

The Finance Committee reported in favor of paying the

bill of the Grand Scribe, A. C. Heitmann, also bills of Grand
Patriarch, Grand High Priest, and Grand Junior Warden, for
attendance on the sessions. Report accepted and bills ordered paid.

The following amendment to the Constitution of the Grand
Encampment was offered and laid on the table under the
rule :

Resolved, That the word *fifty* in Art. III, Sec. 7, of the Constitution, be stricken
out, and *thirty* substituted.

FRANC'S TURNER,
ADNA WHITING.

February 17th, 1852.

Patriarch Turner offered the following preamble and resolution, which after some discussion, were unanimously adopted :—

Whereas, the January session of this Grand Encampment was adjourned to
this day with a view to alter the Constitution so that the annual session should be
held hereafter on the Tuesday next preceding the third Wednesday of February, and

Whereas, the Grand Lodge of this State have so altered their Constitution as to
hold one annual session only, on the third Wednesday of February, and

Whereas, the expenses for holding two sessions annually are larger than the income of this Grand Encampment will justify, and

Whereas, the good of the Patriarchal Order in this State does not require more
than one session a year, and

Whereas, there seems to be errors in the wording of the amendments heretofore proposed, now therefore unanimously

Resolved, That this Grand Encampment now act upon the amendment of
Art. VI, Sec. 1, of our Constitution, as proposed at this session by Patriarchs Francois Turner and F. M. Brown.

Whereupon, the amendments to Art. VI, Sec. 1, were unanimously adopted.

No further business appearing, the Semi-annual Session
was closed in ample form, and the Grand Encampment adjourned without date.

Attest,

LUCIUS A. THOMAS,

Grand Scribe, pro tem.

ANNUAL SESSION.

NEW HAVEN, Feb. 17, 1852.

The Grand Encampment, I. O. O. F. of Connecticut convened this day in Annual Session, in accordance with the Constitution as amended at the Semi-annual Session :

PRESENT:

M. W. ORIGEN UTLEY,	*Grand Patriarch,*
M. E. CALVIN L. HUBBARD,	*Grand High Priest,*
R. W. SAMUEL BISHOP,	*Grand Treasurer,*
R. W. PETER L. CUNNINGHAM,	*Grand Senior Warden,*

and a quorum of members.

After prayer by the Grand High Priest, the Grand Encampment was opened in ample form.

The reading of the minutes of the Semi-annual Session was
dispensed with.

There being no candidates in waiting, the Grand Encampment proceeded to the nomination of officers, when the following nominations were made :

For Grand Patriarch—C. L. Hubbard of No. 11.

For Grand High Priest—P. L. Cunningham of No. 9, and
E. G. Storer of No. 1.

For Grand Senior Warden—F. Turner.

For Grand Scribe—L. A. Thomas of No. 1.

For Grand Treasurer—S. Bishop of No. 1.

For Grand Junior Warden—Adna Whiting of No. 15, and
F. M. Brown of No. 13.

For Grand Representative—O. Utley of No. 6, and C. J.
Gruman of No. 9.

The Special Committee, appointed at the Semi-annual Session, submitted the following report, which was accepted and
the resolution adopted :

To the R. W. Grand Encampment, I. O. O. F. of Conn.   .

The Special Committee appointed at the last adjourned session of this Grand
Encampment, to devise ways and means to relieve this Encampment of its indebtedness, beg leave respectfully to report, That the receipts of this Grand Encampment and the dues from the several subordinates are not sufficient to pay its
present indebtedness. Your committee find much difficulty in coming to a definite conclusion as to what should be the action of this Grand Encampment. They
would however recommend the adoption of the accompanying resolution.

All of which is respectfully submitted,

F. M. BROWN,   ⎫
C. L. HUBBARD, ⎬ *Committee.*
SAMUEL LYNES, ⎭

Resolved, That the Grand Scribe within the next sixty days be instructed to collect in the back dues to this Grand Encampment, and then ascertain the deficiency which exists between the indebtedness of this Grand Encampment and its funds on hand, and apportion the same among the subordinates pro capita and issue a circular stating the apportionment and the facts concerning the financial condition of this Grand Encampment, and request them to step forward and relieve our necessities.

The Grand Encampment then proceeded to the election of officers, when the following officers were elected :

CALVIN L. HUBBARD,	*Grand Patriarch.*
PETER L. CUNNINGHAM,	*Grand High Priest.*
FRANC'S TURNER,	*Grand Senior Warden.*
LUCIUS A. THOMAS,	*Grand Scribe.*
SAMUEL BISHOP,	*Grand Treasurer.*
ADNA WHITING,	*Grand Junior Warden.*
C. J. GRUMAN,	*Grand Representative.*

Whereupon, the Grand Officers were duly installed into their respective chairs by Grand Patriarch Utley.

No other business offering, the session was closed in ample form, and the Grand Encampment adjourned without day.

Attest,

LUCIUS A. THOMAS,
Grand Scribe.

PROCEEDINGS

OF THE

R. W. GRAND ENCAMPMENT, I. O. O. F. OF CONNECTICUT.

~~~~~~~~~~~~~~~

ANNUAL SESSION, 1853.

NEW HAVEN, Feb. 15, 1853.

THE R. W. Grand Encampment, I. O. O. F. of Connecticut, convened this day at 2 o'clock P. M. in Annual Session.

PRESENT:

M. W. CALVIN L. HUBBARD,	*Grand Patriarch,*	
M. E. P. L. CUNNINGHAM,	*Grand High Priest,*	
R. W. FRANCOIS TURNER,	*Grand Senior Warden,*	
R. W. LUCIUS A. THOMAS,	*Grand Scribe,*	
R. W. SAMUEL BISHOP,	*Grand Treasurer,*	

and a quorum of members.

In the absence of the Grand Junior Warden, the G. W. Patriarch appointed Patriarch S. H. Harris of No. 1, to that office, *pro. tem.*

By command of the M. W. Grand Patriarch, the Officers took their stations. The M. E. Grand High Priest performed his appropriate duties, and the Grand Encampment was declared opened in ample form.

The reading of the minutes of last session was dispensed with, and were approved as printed by the Grand Scribe.

The Grand Patriarch made the following appointments:

Committee on Credentials—Patriarchs F. M. Brown of No. 13, John Wallace of No. 18, and Nathan Pratt of No. 2.

Committee on the State of the Order—Past Grand Patriarchs W. E. Sanford and J. M. Andrus of No. 1, and Patriarch Lloyd E. Baldwin of No. 3.

Committee on Finance—Past Grand Patriarch J. M. Willey and Patriarch James Phelps of No. 2, and Benjamin Beecher, Jr., of No. 1.

The Committee on Credentials submitted the following report, which was accepted:

26

To the R. W. Grand Encampment, I. O. O. F. of Connecticut:

The Committee on Credentials beg leave to report, that they have examined the certificates of the following Patriarchs, and find them correct:

George W. Judd, *H. P.* and Erwin Shelly, *H. P.,* of No. 1.
James Phelps, *H. P.,* of No. 2.
H. H. Munroe, *C. P.* and S. O. Mead, *H. P.,* of No. 5.
Elbert Curtis, *C. P.,* of No. 9.
Benjamin Harlow, *H. P.,* of No. 10.
Newton F. Hart, *H. P.,* of No. 15.
Charles L. Grover, *C. P.,* of No. 16.
Chipman S. Jackson, *C. P.,* H. N. Hawkins, *H. P.,* William H. Thornton, *H. P.,* Robert R. Wood, *C. P.,* and S. P. Hubbard, *H. P.,* of No. 18.

All of which is respectfully submitted,

F. M. BROWN,   }
NATHAN PRATT, } *Committee.*
JOHN WALLACE, }

The following candidates were then introduced and instructed in the Grand Encampment Degree, viz:

George W. Judd and Erwin Shelly, No. 1, James Phelps, No. 2, H. H. Munroe, and S. O. Mead, No. 5, Elbert Curtis, No. 9, Benjamin Harlow, No. 10, Newton F. Hart, No. 15, Charles L. Grover, No. 16, Chipman S. Jackson, H. N. Hawkins, William H. Thornton, Robert R. Wood, and S. P. Hubbard, No. 18.

The semi-annual reports for July and January were referred to the Committee on the State of the Order.

The Grand Patriarch submitted the following report:

Right Worthy Grand Officers and Patriarchs:

Again, under the dispensation of a Benignant Providence, we are permitted to assemble in Annual Session under auspicious circumstances, to legislate for this branch of our beloved Order, and to devise means and measures for its existence and perpetuity.

In accordance with the custom and usage of our Order, I shall proceed to lay before you my official acts, and to recommend such measures as may, to my mind, seem necessary for the promotion of interests inseparably connected with the Order.

My official acts, I am pained to say, (owing to providential circumstances, and not within my control,) must, from necessity, be circumscribed in their recital.

The first of my official acts was to appoint D. D. G. Patriarchs, so far as I could procure nominations; and in some instances I appointed without nominations—none of which, I believe, have ever reported to me their official doings, with but one or two exceptions.

During the year my attention has frequently been called, by your Grand Scribe, to the position of delinquent Encampments, and a large majority of the Encampments in the State, I believe, may justly be classed under this head.

Whenever I have had personal acquaintance with any members of such Encampments, I have written them soliciting their coöperation in bringing about a better state of things. In some instances I have received letters, frankly saying that their Officers had not been installed for a year or more—and that there was no probability of anything being done to instill into their Encampments that interest so essential to their existence. In other instances my communications have not been answered.

The only official visit I have succeeded in making, was to Montevideo, No. 15, working at Plainville. I there found a large and energetic Encampment, truly filled with the spirit of F., L. and T., laboring with an energy entirely creditable to the high standing and character of its members; and I doubt not that their returns will show a more prosperous condition, considering its location, than any other Encampment in the State. I have tried in vain to visit some other Encampments, but have been unable to meet them, as some have not held any regular meeting for the last twelve months.

I would in this place call your attention to an abstract of reports, which will be presented to you for your consideration. It will be found, however, to be imperfect, for, with all the energy and perseverance of the Grand Scribe, he has not been able to procure the necessary returns to present you with anything like a perfect abstract.

I am happy to say, however, that this abstract shows a very prosperous state of affairs in some of our Encampments, whose energy and perseverance I hope may be imitated by all of the Encampments in the State. In connection with this abstract, I would call your attention to the great diversity which exists in the various Encampments in relation to initiation and yearly dues. For the good of all concerned, and the perpetuity of the Order in harmony, I deem it proper and expedient that a uniformity in these matters should prevail throughout this jurisdiction.

I would respectfully call your attention to the surrender of the charter of Winsted Encampment, No. 12. The books, charter and papers thereunto belonging, are all, I believe, in the hands of the Grand Scribe.

A petition for a new Encampment, in due form, to be located in Winsted. is now in the hands of your Grand Scribe, and will be presented for your consideration.

I would also call your attention to a petition of members of Sowheag Encampment, No. 6, for a removal of said Encampment from its present location in Middletown to Portland, and solicit for it your careful consideration.

I would also call your attention to a communication from the Grand Lodge of the United States concerning Resolutions passed by that Right Worthy Grand Body, and solicit for it, and the Resolutions, your deliberate consideration. They will be duly presented by your Grand Scribe.

Your attention is also invited to the last published proceedings of the Grand Lodge of the United States, of its last Annual Communication, and also to the proceedings of this Grand Body, both of which will be found upon the table of your Scribe.

Upon the whole, the condition of this Grand Encampment is in a better condition than it has been for some years past—it being to-day entirely free from debt, and having within itself resources sufficient to continue its operation for some time to come. But with you depends its future prosperity. It is with you to devise the ways and means for its future resources and its ability to meet its necessary expenses; to devise, if possible, the ways and means of restoring harmony where alienation exists, and to unite in stronger bonds, if possible, where F., L. and T. prevails.

Finally, you will accept my cordial thanks for your preference, which has placed me in this honorable and exalted position, regretting, as I do, that it has not been in my power to serve you more acceptably and more for your advantage. Hoping and trusting that your deliberations may be characterized by that spirit of harmony, candor and justice, which is so essential to the preservation of the bonds which unite us in universal brotherhood,

C. L. HUBBARD, *Grand Patriarch.*

On motion, the report of the Grand Patriarch was referred to a Special Committee, consisting of P. G. P. Willey, Patriarchs L. E. Baldwin of No. 3, and H. N. Hawkins of No. 18.

Petition for a Charter for a new Encampment to be located at Winsted, referred to Committee on the State of the Order.

The Committee on Finance submitted the following report, which was accepted :

To the R. W. Grand Encampment, I. O. O. F. of Connecticut:

The Committee on Finance beg leave to report, that they have examined the accounts of the Grand Treasurer, and find that there now remains in his hands, to be carried to new account, the sum of $57.18.

All which is respectfully submitted in F., H. and C.,

J. M. WILLEY, ⎫
JAMES PHELPS, ⎬ *Committee.*

New Haven, Feb. 15, 1853.

The Grand Scribe submitted the following report, which was accepted :

To the R. W. Grand Encampment, I. O. O. F. of Connecticut:

The embarrassed condition of the finances of the Grand Encampment at the time I entered upon the duties of Grand Scribe, was a source of much anxiety. With an entirely exhausted treasury, a debt owing to the Grand Lodge of the United States of one hundred and fifty dollars, the ordinary expenses of the session unprovided for, the Special Committee appointed by the Grand Encampment saw no means of relief but the taxation of the Subordinates.

A resolution adopted at the close of the last session directed the Grand Scribe to collect in back dues, and then apportion the amount of deficiency per capita amongst the different Encampments. In performing this duty, the Grand Scribe found that the great irregularity and tardiness with which the Subordinate Encampments had reported and paid their dues, had rendered many of the accounts obscure and doubtful. Several of the Encampments had not reported for a whole year, and the reports of others were so imperfect as to convey no information as to the condition of the Encampment. By a patient investigation and correspondence, I was enabled to approximate an adjustment, and to make such collection of back dues, as enabled me to pay the claim of the Grand Lodge of the United States, and meet all the other demands against the Grand Encampment, and as will appear by the report of the Grand Treasurer, leave a small balance in the treasury.

The imperfection of the blank used for the reports of Subordinates, and the imperfect manner in which they are filled out, have furnished so little information that my predecessors have not deemed it expedient to publish the tabular statement of their condition. For the term just closed, I have made some addition to the blank, requiring fuller information of the condition of the Encampments. Information also was asked for relative to the fees for initiation and dues, and the tariff of the various beneficiary payments in each Encampment. Tables of these are herewith submitted, together with tables of the reports of Subordinates since July, 1851.

The charter and effects of Winsted Encampment, No. 12, have been surrendered, and in accordance with the By-Laws, I issued cards to such of its members as were in regular standing at the time of its surrender, several of whom have united in a petition for a new Encampment at Winsted, which is herewith submitted.

Herewith is submitted a circular from the Grand Lodge of the United States, in reference to a proposed revision of the Constitution of that body. The present instrument was framed in the infancy of the Order, and requires many changes to adapt it to the field to which our Order is now extended.

LUCIUS A. THOMAS, *Grand Scribe.*

Appeal of William B. Hurd of No. 18, against the action of said Encampment, for refusing to reinstate him after having been suspended for non-payment of dues, referred to Special Committee on Grievance, consisting of Patriarchs S. Lynes of No. 9, B. Harlow of No. 10, and N. F. Hart of No. 15.

The Committee to whom was referred the report of the Grand Patriarch, submitted the following report, which was accepted :

To the R. W. Grand Encampment, I. O. O. F. of Connecticut:

The Committee to whom was referred the report of the M. W. Grand Patriarch, beg leave to recommend—

That so much of said report as relates to Winsted Encampment be referred to a Special Committee of three.

That so much of said report as relates to Sowheag Encampment be referred to a Special Committee of three.

That so much of said report as relates to a communication from the Grand Lodge of the United States be referred to a Special Committee of three.

All which is respectfully submitted in F., H. and C.,

J. M. WILLEY,   ⎫
L.·F. BALDWIN,   ⎬ *Committee.*
H. N. HAWKINS,   ⎭

New Haven, Feb. 15, 1853.

In accordance with the recommendation of the·Committee, the Grand Patriarch appointed the following Committees :

On Winsted Encampment, G. H. P. Cunningham, Patriarchs George W. Judd of No. 1, and H. H. Munroe of No. 5.

On Sowheag Encampment, Patriarchs Nathan Pratt of No. 2, S. B. Gorham of No. 1, and H. N. Hawkins of No. 18.

On communication from Grand Lodge of United States, Patriarchs S. Lynes and E. Curtis of No. 9, and Lloyd E. Baldwin of No. 3.

Petition for removal of Sowheag Encampment was referred to the Committee thereon.

The papers relative to the surrender of the Charter of Winsted Encampment were referred to the Committee thereon.

The communication from the Grand Lodge of the United States, relative to the amendment of its Constitution, was referred to the Committee thereon.

The Committee on the State of the Order submitted the following report, which was accepted :

To the R. W. Grand Encampment, I. O. O. F. of Connecticut:

The Committee on the State of the Order, to whom was referred the reports of Subordinate Encampments, respectfully report, that they have examined such papers as were placed in their hands, and found returns from Nos. 1, 2, 3, 5, 6, 8, 9, 10, 15, 16, and 18. There are no reports from Nos. 11, 13, 14, and 17.

All which is respectfully submitted,

W. E. SANFORD,   ⎫
LLOYD E. BALDWIN,   ⎬ *Committee.*
J. M. ANDRUS,   ⎭

The Committee on the State of the Order submitted the following report, which was accepted, and the Charter granted :

To the R. W. Grand Encampment, I. O. O. F. of Connecticut :

The Committee on the State of the Order, to whom was referred the petition of S. L. Wilder and other Patriarchs holding withdrawal cards from the Grand Scribe, for a Subordinate Encampment to be located at Winsted, and called Phenix Encampment, No. 19, would recommend that the prayer of the petitioners be granted.

All which is respectfully submitted,

W. E. SANFORD, }
LLOYD E. BALDWIN. } *Committee.*
JONATHAN M. ANDRUS, }

The Grand Encampment took a recess till 4½ o'clock.

4½ *o'clock P. M.*

The Grand Encampment was called to order by the Grand Patriarch.

The Special Committee on removal of Sowheag Encampment, No. 6, submitted the following report, which was accepted :

To the R. W. Grand Encampment, I. O. O. F. of Connecticut :

The Committee to whom was referred the petition of Benjamin Brainerd and others of Sowheag Encampment, in regard to removing said Encampment to Portland, beg leave to report, that said Encampment cannot be removed without a two-thirds vote of said Encampment.

All of which is respectfully submitted,

NATHAN PRATT. }
SAM. B. GORHAM, } *Committee.*
H. N. HAWKINS, }

On motión, the petitioners had leave to withdraw their petition.

The Special Committee on Grievance submitted the following report on the appeal of William B. Hurd. The report was accepted, and the resolution adopted.

To the R. W. Grand Encampment, I. O. O. F. of Connecticut :

The undersigned, your Committee on Grievance, to whom was referred the appeal of Patriarch Hurd, from the action of Excelsior Encampment, No.18, in having suspended him for non-payment of dues, and refusing to reinstate him upon application, beg leave to report—

That they have had the parties before them, have heard the facts upon both sides, and are of the opinion that the action of Excelsior Encampment, No. 18, in the case, has been perfectly legal and proper, and that Patriarch Hurd has no just cause of complaint. They would therefore respectfully submit the following resolution :

Resolved, That Patriarch William B. Hurd have leave to withdraw his appeal.

Respectfully, in F., H. and C.,

SAMUEL LYNES, }
NEWTON F. HART, } *Committee.*
BENJAMIN HARLOW, }

Charity Encampment, No. 10, asked advisement in the settlement of a claim held against it by Charity Lodge, No. 13. The subject was referred to the Special Committee on Grievance.

On motion, the Grand Encampment proceeded to the nomination and election of Officers, when the following nominations were made:

For Grand Patriarch—G. H. P. P. L. Cunningham.

For Grand High Priest—G. S. W. François Turner.

For Grand Senior Warden—Patriarchs John Wallace of No. 18, and F. M. Brown of No. 13.

For Grand Scribe—Lucius A. Thomas.

For Grand Treasurer—Samuel Bishop.

For Grand Junior Warden—Patriarchs Alden Peck of No. 16, F. M. Brown of No. 13, C. C. Jackson and John Wallace of No. 18.

The Grand Patriarch appointed Pat. S. B. Gorham and P. G. Pat. Andrus of No. 1, and E. Curtis of No. 9, tellers, and the Grand Encampment proceeded to ballot.

On balloting for Grand Patriarch, there were 20 votes cast, of which G. H. P. CUNNINGHAM had 18, and was declared duly elected Grand Patriarch for the year ensuing.

For Grand High Priest, there were cast 19 votes, of which G. S. W. TURNER had 17, and was declared elected Grand High Priest.

For Grand Senior Warden, 24 votes were cast, of which Patriarch John Wallace had 13, F. M. Brown 10, and blank 1. Whereupon Patriarch JOHN WALLACE was declared elected Grand Senior Warden.

For Grand Scribe, G. S. L. A. THOMAS received a unanimous vote, and was declared reëlected.

Grand Treasurer S. BISHOP was unanimously reëlected, and so declared.

On the two first ballots for Grand Junior Warden there was no choice. On the third ballot, Patriarch C. C. Jackson received 10 votes, Alden Peck 7, and F. M. Brown 1. Whereupon Patriarch C. C. JACKSON was declared duly elected.

The Finance Committee reported in favor of paying the following bills, which report was accepted, and the bills ordered paid, viz:

T. J. Stafford for Printing,	$12.00
W. H. Stanley for Printing,	18.27
George B. Bassett for Stationery,	5.50
E. Augur, O. Sentinel,	3.00

The Committee to whom was referred the communication of the Grand Lodge of the United States, submitted the following report, which was accepted :

To the R. W. Grand Encampment, I. O. O. F. of Connecticut:

The Special Committee to whom was referred the communication from the Grand Lodge of the United States, would recommend the appointment of a Committee of three to submit through the Grand Representation to the Grand Lodge of the United States at its next session, such amendments as in their opinion the wants of the Order require, or in their judgment they shall deem necessary.

All of which is respectfully submitted,

SAMUEL LYNES, ⎫
L. E. BALDWIN, ⎬ *Committee.*
ELBERT CURTIS, ⎭

The Grand Patriarch appointed as the Special Committee, Grand Scribe Thomas and Patriarchs S. Lynes of No. 9, and L. E. Baldwin of No. 3.

The following resolutions were on motion severally adopted :

Resolved, That a two-thirds vote shall be required to reinstate a suspended member of a Subordinate Encampment.

Resolved, That no person shall hold a seat in this Grand Encampment without presenting a certificate of membership at each session of his attendance.

Resolved, That the Grand Scribe be requested to publish, at the end of the printed proceedings of each session, the names of all the members of each Subordinate Encampment, who are entitled to seats in this R. W. Grand Encampment.

Resolved, That the Grand Scribe be empowered to take such steps as he may deem necessary to carry the above resolutions into effect.

On motion, the Grand Scribe was directed to draw orders on the Grand Treasurer for the payment of mileage of the Grand Officers.

The amendment of Art. III, Sec. 7, of Constitution of the Grand Encampment, laid on the table at a preceding session, (p. 200,) was called up and indefinitely postponed.

The Committee of Grievance reported that in their judgment the payment of one hundred dollars by Charity Encampment to Charity Lodge would be an equitable adjustment of the claim : accepted.

The Officers elect were then installed into their respective chairs in ample form, by G. P. Hubbard.

The following resolution was then adopted :

Resolved, That the thanks of this Grand Encampment are due and are hereby tendered to P. G. P. Hubbard, for the able and impartial manner in which he has presided over this Grand Encampment for the past year.

No further business offering, the Grand Encampment adjourned, and was closed in ample form.

Attest,

LUCIUS A. THOMAS, *Grand Scribe.*

GRAND TREASURER'S ACCOUNT.

Grand Encampment, I. O. O. F. in account with S. Bishop, Grand Trasurere.

1853.				Dr.
Feb. 14, To Cash paid Grand Lodge of United States,	·	·	·	$126.37
" " " P. L. Cunningham,	·	·	·	5.50
" " " . L. A. Thomas,	·	·	·	55.00
Feb. 15, " Balance to New Account,	·	·	·	57.18
				$244.05

1852.				Cr.
Feb. 17, By Balance from Old Account,	·	·	·	$37.82
1853.				
Feb. 14, " Cash of Grand Scribe,	·	·	·	206.23
				$244.05

27

Abstract of Semi-Annual Reports of Subordinate Encampments for Jan., 1851, to July, 1852.

No.	ENCAMPMENT	TOWNS	Initia'd	Ad. by C.O.	Reins'd	Withd.	Susp'd	Expell'd	Died	Whole No.	Receipts	Number	Initia'd	Ad. by C.O.	Reins'd	Withd.	Susp'd	Expell'd	Died	Whole No.	Receipts	Number	Initia'd	Ad. by C.O.	Reins'd	Withd.	Susp'd	Expell'd	Died	Whole No.	Receipts
			For the Term ending July, 1851.									**For the Term ending Jan., 1852.**										**For the Term ending July, 1852.**									
1	Sassacus	New Haven	11	0	0	2	13	0	0	85	230.96	1								84	165.50	1	3	0	0	0	4	0	0	83	206.51
2	Oriental	Essex	0	0	0	0	0	0	0	24		2								17	61.69	2		0	0	0	0	0	0	29	28.00
3	Palmyra	Norwich	1	1	0	0	0	0	0	35	33.00	3								13	10.65	3	3	0	0	1	0	0	0	13	7.50
5	Devotion	Danbury	0	0	0	1	0	0	0	47	63.12	5								11	40.62	5	4	0	1	1	1	0	0	12	04.40
6	Sowheag	Middletown	0	0	0	0	0	0	0	24	59.53	6							1	47	30.00	6	5	0	1	0	0	0	0	42	49.00
8	Mount Herman	Bridgeport	0	0	0	0	2	0	0	45	48.75	8								26	36.50	8	6	0	0	0	0	0	0	31	54.50
9	Kabaosa	Norwalk	0	0	0	0	0	0	0	28	50.50	9							2	44	62.63	9	9	0	0	0	4	0	0	0	74.82
10	Charity	Stonington	14	0	0	2	0	0	0		84.00	10								22		10	1	0	0	0	0	0	0	24	10.00
11	Connecticut	Hartford	0	1	0	0	0	0	0	26	25.79	11									27.25	11		0	0	0	0	0	0		
13	Hinman	Warehouse Point,	1	0	0	0	0	0	0	46	40.63	13		1								13	1	1	1	1	0	0	0	27	19.00
14	Wascusse	Stamford	1	0	0	0	0	0	0	34	78.09	15				1	3	1		57	173.50	14	0	0	0	0	12	0	0		
15	Montevideo	Plainville	4	1	0	0	2	0	0	12	59.87	16					3			35	16.00	15	2	2	0	0	0	0	0	46	43.50
16	Oasis	Meriden	0	0	0	0	0	0	0	33	6.00	17								14		16	2	0	0	0	0	0	0		32.66
17	Willey	Colchester	0	0	0	0	0	0	0			18								41	53.75	17	4	0	0	0	0	0	0		
18	Excelsior	Birmingham,	8	0	0	0	0	0	0		76.75	18										18		1	0	0	0	0	0		74.92
	TOTAL,		40	3	0	5	17	0	0	439	856.99		34	1	0;	2	23	2	4	470	721.99		24	1	3	3	21	0	0		694.81

Abstract of Semi-Annual Reports of Subordinate Encampments for Term ending January, 1853.

ENCAMPMENT.	Number	TOWNS.	Init'tes.	Ad. hyC.	Reins'd.	Withd.	Susp'd.	Expell'd.	Died.	Whole No.	Receipts	Benefits.	Expenses.	On hand	Initia'n. Fee.	Yearly Dues.	Fun'rl B Pat'chs.	Fun'rlB. Wife.	Weekly Benefit.
Sassacus,	1	New Haven,	3	1	0	0	4	0	0	82	169.50	47.00	63.03	1230.91	7.00	4.00	15.00	00	*2.00
Oriental,	2	Essex,	1	0	0	0	0	0	0	23	48.00	00	30.00	91.23	6.00	3.00	20.00	00	1.00
Palmyra,	3	Norwich,	0	0	0	0	0	0	0	12	16.50	16.25	15.63	114.42	10.00	1.00	15.00	00	
Devotion,	4	Danbury,	0	0	1	1	2	0	0		71.46	45.00	5.00	00	10.00	1.00	15.00	00	3.00
Sowleag,	5	Middletown,	0	0	2	1	1	0	0	42	29.00	14.00	15.00	00	10.00	3.00	15.00	00	
Mount Hernan,	6	Bridgeport,	2	0	0	0	0	0	0	31	21.00	00	00	00	6.00	3.00	15.00	00	
Kabaea,	8	Norwalk,	0	0	0	0	2	0	0	37	38.92	21.00	21.14	81.22	6.00	3.00	15.00	00	1.00
Charity,	9	Stonington,	0	0	0	0	5	0	0	30	21.00	00	15.00	34.85	6.00	1.00	15.00	10 00	1.50
Connecticut,	10	Hartford,	1	0	0	0	0	0	0	49	49.85		16.00	47.46	10.00	3.00	00	00	*6¼
Hinnan,	11	Warehouse Point,	1	0	0	0	0	0	0	30									
Wascusse,	13	Stamford,	3	0	0	0	6	0	0		67.70	00	28.87	97.64	6.00	2.00	00	00	00
Montevideo,	14	Plainville,	3	0	0	0	6	0	0		30.66	15.00	27.01						00
Oasis,	15	Meriden,																	
Willey,	16	Colchester,	1	1	0	0	0	0	0	42	63.74	90	22.02	107.49	7.00	2.00	15.00	00	1.00
Excelsior,	17	Birmingham,																	
TOTAL,			15	1	6	1	32	0	0	398	605.59	159.15	242.60	1805.22	80.00	26.00	125.00	10.00	

* After first week.

OFFICERS AND MEMBERS

OF THE

GRAND ENCAMPMENT, I. O. O. F. OF CONN,

OFFICERS FOR 1853.

M. W. PETER L. CUNNINGHAM, *Grand Patriarch.*
M. E. FRANCOIS TURNER, *Grand High Priest.*
R. W. JOHN WALLACE, *Grand Senior Warden.*
R. W. LUCIUS A. THOMAS, *Grand Scribe.*
R. W. SAMUEL BISHOP, *Grand Treasurer.*
R. W. C. C. JACKSON, *Grand Junior Warden.*
R. W. CHOLWELL J. GRUMAN, *Grand Representative.*

PAST GRAND PATRIARCHS.

*ROBINSON S. HINMAN, 1843.
WILLIAM E. SANFORD, 1843-4.
JOHN L. DEVOTION, 1844-5.
JONATHAN M. ANDRUS, 1845-6.
WILLIAM L. BREWER, 1846-7.
*MUNSON A. SHEPARD, 1847-8.
TOWNSEND P. ABELL, 1848.
LUCIUS A. THOMAS, 1848-9.
JUNIUS M. WILLEY, 1849-50.
CHOLWELL J. GRUMAN, 1850-51.
ORIGEN UTLEY, 1851.
CALVIN L. HUBBARD, 1852.

PAST GRAND HIGH PRIESTS.

CHARLES W. BRADLEY, 1843.
RICHARD S. PRATT, 1843-4.
JONATHAN M. ANDRUS, 1844-45.
WILLIAM L. BREWER, 1845-6.
*MUNSON A. SHEPARD, 1845-7.
TOWNSEND P. ABELL, 1847-8.
JUNIUS M. WILLEY, 1848-9.
CHOLWELL J. GRUMAN, 1849-50.
ORIGEN UTLEY, 1850-51.
CALVIN L. HUBBARD, 1851.
PETER L. CUNNINGHAM, 1852.

---

* Deceased.

MEMBERS.

Sassacus, No. 1, New Haven.

William E. Sanford,
Samuel Bishop,
Isaac Judson,
Jonathan M. Andrus,
Prelate Demick,
Newel C. Hall,
Lucius A. Thomas,
Elizur Hubbell,
Frederick Croswell,
Eliphalet G. Storer,
Noah Chandler,
Samuel H. Harris,
Lucius Peck,

James H. Leforge,
William H. Ellis,
Adrian C. Heitmann,
François Turner,
Samuel B. Gorham,
Samuel Tolles,
Elias T. Main,
Benjamin Beecher, Jr.,
Samuel Bassett,
Frederick Botsford,
Robert Sizer,
George W. Judd,
Erwin Shelley.

Oriental, No. 2, Essex.

Junius M. Willey,
John S. Dickinson,
James Phelps,

Alpheus S. Spencer,
John G. Hayden,
Nathan Pratt.

Palmyra, No. 3, Norwich.

John L. Devotion,
William L. Brewer,
H. H. Roath,

James A. Hovey,
Lloyd E. Baldwin.

Devotion, No. 5, Danbury.

William W. Bedient,
F. D. Ball,
A. Chichester,
H. N. Bennett,
Charles Taylor,

Samuel O. Mead,
Orrin Benedict,
Russel Bevans,
H. H. Munroe.

Sowheag, No. 6, Middletown.

Origen Utley,
James S. Parmelee,
Dennis Sage,
Townsend P. Abell,

William B. Casey,
Augustus Putnam,
James E. Bidwell.

Mount Hermon, No. 8, Bridgeport.

Joseph F. Crosby,
John L. Roberts,
George S. Sanford.

George G. Wheeler,
Jessee Shadbolt,
E. B. Stevens.

Kabaosa, No. 9, Norwalk.

Cholwell J. Gruman,
James A. Quintard,
Peter L. Cunningham,
George W. Smith,
Eli S. Quintard,

William E. Bissell,
Samuel E. Olmstead,
Samuel Lynes,
Henry C. Randle,
Elbert Curtis.

Charity, No. 10, *Stonington.*

Benjamin Harlow.

Montevideo, No. 15, *Bristol.*

Newton F. Hart.

Oasis, No. 16, *Bristol.*

Charles L. Grover.

Excelsior, No. 18, *Birmingham.*

Charles C. Jackson,	Thomas Wallace, Jr.,
Robert R. Wood,	William H. Thornton,
Chipman S. Jackson,	Horatio N. Hawkins,
John Wallace,	Samuel P. Hubbell.

.

PROCEEDINGS

R. W. GRAND ENCAMPMENT, I. O. O. F. OF CONNECTICUT.

ANNUAL SESSION.

NEW HAVEN, Feb. 14, 1854.

THE R. W. Grand Encampment, I. O. O. F. of Connecticut, convened this day.

PRESENT:

M. W.	P. L. CUNNINGHAM,	*Grand Patriarch,*
R. W.	FRANCOIS TURNER,	*Grand High Priest,*
R. W.	JOHN WALLACE,	*Grand Senior Warden,*
R. W.	LUCIUS A. THOMAS,	*Grand Scribe,*
R. W.	C. C. JACKSON,	*Grand Junior Warden,*
R. W.	CHOLWELL J. GRUMAN,	*Grand Representative,*

and members from the following Encampments, viz: Nos. 1, 2, 3, 5, 6, 8, 9, 15, 16, 18, 19, 20.

The Grand Encampment was opened in ample form, with the usual ceremonies.

The reading of the minutes of last session was dispensed with, having been printed, in which form they were approved.

The Grand Patriarch appointed the following Committees, viz:

Committee on Credentials—Patriarchs H. N. Hawkins of No. 18; Nathan Pratt of No. 2; Orlando Pease of No. 19.

Committee on the State of the Order—Patriarchs S. Lynes of No. 9; F. M. Brown of No. 13; S. H. Harris of No. 1.

Committee on Finance—Patriarchs O. Utley of No. 6; N. Chandler of No. 1; J. G. Hayden of No. 2.

The Committee on Credentials submitted the following report, which was accepted:

To the R. W. Grand Encampment, I. O. O. F. of Connecticut:

The Committee on Credentials beg leave to report, that they have examined the

28

certificates of the following Patriarchs, and find them correct, with the exception of the credential of Patriarch William L. Brewer, which is without seal of No. 3 :

Sassacus, No. 1—George W. Judd, Samuel H. Harris, Noah Chandler, Francois Turner, Lucius A. Thomas, James H. Leforge, Benjamin Beecher, Jr., Charles L. Sage, E. G. Storer, Samuel B. Gorham.

Oriental, No. 2—John G. Hayden, James Phelps, Nathan Pratt, George K. Stillman.

Palmyra, No. 3—William L. Brewer.

Devotion, No. 5—Stephen S. Bedient, S. Mallory.

Sowheag, No. 6—Origen Utley, James E. Bidwell.

Mount Herman, No. 8—George S. Sanford.

Kabaosa, No. 9—Charles Platt, Samuel Lynes, Elbert Curtis, Cholwell J. Gruman.

Charity, No. 10—Albegence Hyde.

Montevideo, No. 15—C. G. Thompson, Newton F. Hart, George B. Morse, William Hitchcock.

Oasis, No. 16—Alden Peck, Eldridge Hall, George E. Leonard.

Excelsior, No. 18—Chipman S. Jackson, H. W. Hubbard, John Wallace, James W. Fields, Charles C. Jackson, H. N. Hawkins, D. W. Boyd.

Phenix, No. 19—Phelps H. Parsons, S. T. Cook, Luman White, O. Pease.

Ansantawae, No. 20—William H. Warner, J. M. Andrus.

All which is respectfully submitted,

H. N. HAWKINS, } *Committee.*
NATHAN PRATT, }

New Haven, Feb. 14, 1854.

The following candidates were then introduced and instructed in the Grand Encampment Degree :

No. 1, Charles L. Sage; No. 2, George K. Stillman; No. 5, S. Mallory, Stephen S. Bedient; No. 9, Charles Platt; No. 10, Albegence Hyde; No. 15, George B. Morse, William Hitchcock, C. G. Thompson; No. 16, George A. Leonard, Eldridge Hall; No. 18, H. W. Hubbard, James W. Fields, David W. Boyd; No. 19, S. T. Cook, Luman White.

The Grand Patriarch submitted the following report :

To the Right Worthy Grand Encampment of Connecticut:

OFFICERS AND REPRESENTATIVES: Through the beneficence of Divine Providence, we are permitted, for the first time, to assemble within this new and beautiful Hall—recently dedicated to the principles of our beloved Order—for the purpose of reviewing the present condition of the Patriarchal Order in this jurisdiction, and to legislate for its future welfare ; and agreeable to the usual requirements of this Grand Body, I have the honor to submit the following brief report of my official acts, during the recess of this Grand Encampment.

By recommendations received for the office of Deputy Grand Patriarch, and aware of the responsibility and trust devolving on those that receive said appointment, as soon as practicable after the close of the last session, I forwarded Warrants to the following Patriarchs, viz: Grand High Priest Turner, Sassacus Encampment, No. 1, New Haven ; John G. Hayden, Oriental Encampment, No. 2, Essex Borough ; H. H. Roath, Palmyra Encampment, No. 3, Norwich ; Abraham Chichester, Devotion Encampment, No. 5, Danbury; Charles A. Newell, Sowheag Encampment, No. 6, Middletown ; George S. Sanford, Mount Hermon Encampment, No. 8, Bridgeport ; Nathan Platt, Charity Encampment, No. 10, Stonington ; F. M. Brown, Hinman Encampment, No. 13, Warehouse Point ; Chancey Ayres, Wascussee Encampment, No. 14, Stamford ; Adna Whiting, Montevideo Encampment, No. 15, Plainville ; John L. Ives, Oasis Encampment, No. 16, Meriden ; Grand Senior Warden Wallace, Excelsior Encampment

No. 18, Ausonia ; Orlando Pease, Phenix Encampment, No. 19, Winsted ; J. M. Andrus, Ansantawae Encampment, No. 20, Waterbury. The reports received from several of these officers bear testimony to the faithful discharge of their official duty.

I would recommend to your favorable consideration, the importance of requiring the Grand Patriarch to appoint, at *each annual* session, a Deputy Grand Patriarch, for each subordinate Encampment in this jurisdiction, and that said Deputy Grand Patriarch be required to report in writing to the Grand Patriarch an account of his official acts, on or before the first Tuesday in February, annually.

On the 28th day of February, I instituted Phenix Encampment, No. 19, at Winsted, and presented the *Charter* granted by this Right Worthy Body, at its last session, together with the lectures and charges necessary for its organization. On this occasion I received the assistance of Grand High Priest Turner, Grand Senior Warden Wallace, Past Grand Patriarch Andrus, of Sassacus Encampment, *C. P.* C. D. Cole, of Massoit Encampment, Boston, and a number of the officers and members from Excelsior Encampment, No. 18. After the institution, four brothers were initiated and exalted to the R. P. degree, and one admitted by card. The following Patriarchs were elected and installed into their respective chairs, for the term ending July, 1853, viz : Orlando Pease, C. P. ; P. H. Parsons, II. P. ; C. P. Newman, S. W. ; S. L. Wilder, Scribe ; S. T. Cooke, Treasurer ; L. White, J. W. The character and standing of the officers and members of Phenix Encampment, and the interest manifested by them in its work, leave no doubt of its ultimate success.

On the 14th of September, I received through the office of the Right Worthy Grand Scribe, a petition, accompanied by the Charter-fee and withdrawal-cards, from P. G. Patriarch J. M. Andrus, Patriarch George W. Benedict, and other Patriarchs, residing in the city of Waterbury, New Haven County, for an Encampment to be located at that place, to be known by the name and title of Ansantawae Encampment, No. 20. By recommendation from Grand Representative Samuel Lynes, Grand Scribe Lucius A. Thomas, and other distinguished members of our Order ; and from a personal knowledge of the high character and standing of the petitioners, I did not hesitate to grant a dispensation—*subject to your approval*—and on the 26th day of September, assisted by G. H. P. Francois Turner, G. S. W. John Wallace, G. Scribe L. A. Thomas, Grand Representative Samuel Lynes, G. J. Warden, C. C. Jackson, G. Sentinel Elbert Curtis, and several officers and members from Excelsior, Kabaosa, and Montevideo Encampments, I instituted the same, according to the laws and usage of the Order. The following officers were then elected and installed into their respective chairs in ample form—viz : D. S. Law, C. P. ; G. W. Benedict, H. P. ; G. H. Walters, S. W. ; E. L. Savage, Scribe : C. W. Johnson, Treasurer ; C. N. Upson, J. W.

Three brothers were on this interesting occasion initiated, advanced, and exalted to the sublime degree of the Royal Purple. This Encampment opens with the most flattering prospects of success, from its favorable location, and known reputation of its members for perseverance and enterprise. I doubt not it will soon occupy a high position as one of the leading branches of our Order.

The Grand Officers were on this occasion (also on their visit to Phenix Encampment) entertained with the most unbounded hospitality, courtesy and kindness.

I would respectfully recommend that the dispensation to Ansantawae Encampment, No. 20, be confirmed by a Charter.

Since the last meeting of this Grand Encampment, I have had the pleasure, either alone or in company with some distinguished officer or member of our Order, of visiting the following named subordinate Encampments, either to install their officers, to witness their work, or to give instructions in the work of this branch of Odd Fellowship—viz : Sept. 12, 1853, Phenix Encampment, No. 19, Winsted : Nov. 1, Oasis Encampment, No. 16, Meriden ; Nov. 3, Montevideo Encampment, No. 15, Plainville ; Nov. 10, Excelsior Encampment, No. 18, Birmingham ; Dec. 1, Sassacus Encampment, No. 1, New Haven ; Dec. 2, Devotion Encampment, No. 5, Danbury ; Feb. 1, 1854, Kabaosa Encampment, No. 9, Norwalk ; Feb. 3, Mount

Herman Encampment, No. 8, Bridgeport. Among these Encampments a considerable diversity of work was found to exist. Too many of our Encampments are apt to pay little or no attention to the detail of the work, and regard it as unimportant —forgetting that in this way arises nearly all the causes of errors and irregularities —producing a large number of *innovations upon the work* of our Order.

These errors were pointed out to the officers and members, and cheerfully corrected.

It is with pleasure and gratification that I have to report two additional subordinate Encampments, for the last year, and the Order, in the State—all things considered—in a healthy and prosperous condition. During my official visits I was received, as well as those that accompanied me, with courtesy, kindness and attention, for which I tender at this time my grateful acknowledgments to the officers and members of the several Encampments.

I would respectfully call your attention to the great *want of uniformity* in the *work* of Subordinate Encampments, and ask of you to adopt *measures* to remove this growing evil, and to establish the *correct work* of the Patriarchal branch of our Order, throughout the entire jurisdiction.

It is with feelings of regret that I have to report that the Charter of Connecticut Encampment, No. 11, has been reclaimed, which became forfeited by its neglect to forward proper returns to this Grand Encampment, for the two last years. On the third day of November, 1853, I received the Charter, Working Books, Record and Ledger of said Encampment—all of which are in the possession of the Grand Scribe. I would recommend that the usual certificates of membership be granted to the Patriarchs of Connecticut Encampment, entitled to the same.

I have been requested to bring to your notice the want of installation books in several of the Encampments. I would recommend to your consideration the propriety of procuring *two* Installation Books for each Encampment in this jurisdiction.

I beg leave to call your attention to the published proceedings of the last Session of the Grand Lodge of the United States, containing, among other important business, the report of the Special Committee appointed to report amendments to the Constitution of the Grand Lodge of the United States. It was thought expedient by that committee to report an entirely new Constitution, instead of proposing amendments to the one now in use. The interests of this Grand Encampment requires that this highly important subject should be investigated.

I would therefore recommend that a Committee be appointed for the purpose to report thereon.

The returns of subordinate Encampments will show a larger number of initiations than usual, and a more healthful condition. The financial affairs of the Grand Encampment, I take pleasure in saying, are in a favorable condition. It is free from all encumbrance. This prosperous condition is owing, in a great measure, to the *ever prompt and energetic Grand Scribe.*

The term of office, to which I have been exalted by the confidence and esteem of this Right Worthy Body, being near its close, I return my hearty and sincere thanks to the Officers and Representatives of this Grand Encampment, for the kindness, assistance and forbearance which they have shown me throughout the past year. And now may you, individually and collectively, be abundantly successful in your efforts to promote the best interests of the Patriarchal branch of our Order.

PETER L. CUNNINGHAM, *Grand Patriarch.*

New Haven, Feb. 14, 1854.

On motion, the report of the Grand Patriarch was referred to a Special Committee, and ordered to be spread on the records. The Grand Patriarch appointed as Special Committee thereon, Patriarchs J. M. Willey of No. 2; S. Maltby of No. 5; W. H. Warner of No. 20.

The Special Committee on the Grand Patriarch's report, submitted the following report, which was accepted :

To the R. W. Grand Encampment of the State of Connecticut :

The Committee to whom was referred the Report of the M. W. G. Patriarch, beg leave to recommend that so much of said Report as relates to charters for New Encampments, be referred to a Special Committee of three.

That so much as relates to Installation Books be referred to a Special Committee of three.

That so much as relates to the appointment of Deputy Grand Patriarchs be referred to a Special Committee of three.

And that so much as relates to uniformity in the work of the Order, be referred to a Special Committee of three.

All which is submitted in F., H. and C.

J. M. WILLEY,
S. MALLORY,   } *Committee.*
WM. H. WARNER, }

New Haven, Feb. 14, 1854.

In accordance with the recommendation of the Committee, the Grand Patriarch appointed the following Committees :

On so much as relates to New Encampments—Patriarchs G. S. Sanford of No. 8 ; Charles Platt of No. 9 ; J. E. Bidwell of No. 6.

On so much as refers to Installation Books—Patriarchs L. A. Thomas and S. H. Harris of No. 1, and G. S. Sanford of No. 8.

On so much as relates to Deputy Grand Patriarchs—Patriarchs Alden Peck of No. 16 ; D. W. Boyd of No. 18, and James Phelps of No. 2.

On so much as relates to uniformity in the work of the Order—Patriarchs E. G. Storer and S. B. Gorham of No. 1, and G. A. Leonard of No. 16.

The Committee on the State of the Order submitted the following, which was accepted :

To the R. W. Grand Encampment, I. O. O. F. of Connecticut :

The undersigned Committee on the State of the Order, to whom was referred the reports of Subordinates, beg leave respectfully to report that they have examined the reports of Encampments Nos. 1, 2, 3, 5, 6, 8, 9, 10, 15, 16, 18, 19, 20, for the two terms of the past year, and find them to be correct, with the exception of those of Nos. 15 and 20, which are deficient in seals. There are no reports from Nos. 13, 14 and 17, for the past year.

Respectfully submitted in F., H. and C.

SAMUEL LYNES, }
F. M. BROWN,   } *Committee.*
S. H. HARRIS,   }

Sundry bills were referred to the Committee on Finance.

The Committee on New Encampments submitted the following report :

To the R. W. Grand Encampment, I. O. O. F. of Connecticut:

"Your Committee, to whom was referred so much of the Grand Patriarch's report as relates to the institution of Ansantawae Encampment, No. 20, located at Waterbury, would respectfully recommend that the dispensation granted by the R. W. Grand Patriarch, be confirmed by a Charter from this R. W. Body.

GEO. S. SANFORD, ⎫
CHARLES PLATT, ⎬ *Committee.*
J. E. BIDWELL, ⎭

On motion, the Grand Encampment proceeded to the nomination and election of officers, when the following nominations were made:

For Grand Patriarch—G. H. P. Turner of No. 1, and G. S. W. Wallace of No. 18.
For Grand High Priest—G. S. W. Wallace of No. 18.
For Grand Senior Warden—G. J. W. Jackson of No. 18.
For Grand Scribe—G. S. Thomas of No. 1.
For Grand Treasurer—G. T. Bishop of No. 1.
For Grand Junior Warden—Patriarchs James Phelps of No. 2, S. Lynes of No. 9, S. B. Gorham of No. 1, and J. E. Bidwell of No. 6.
For Grand Representative—G. P. Cunningham of No. 9.

The Grand Patriarch appointed P. G. Patriarchs W. L. Brewer of No. 3, and J. M. Andrus of No. 20, tellers, when the Grand Encampment proceeded to the election of officers.

On balloting for Grand Patriarch, there were 33 votes cast, of which G. S. W. Wallace received 17, and G. H. P. Turner 16 votes. Whereupon G. S. W. Wallace of No. 18 was declared duly elected Grand Patriarch for the year ensuing.

Pending the ballot for Grand High Priest, the proceedings were stayed, and the ballot declared void.

Whereupon Patriarch Wallace declined the office of Grand Patriarch, and a new ballot was ordered for Grand Patriarch.

On balloting again for Grand Patriarch, Patriarch Turner had 26 votes, and Patriarch Wallace 14. Whereupon Patriarch Turner was declared duly elected Grand Patriarch.

On balloting for Grand High Priest, Patriarch Wallace was unanimously elected.

G. J. Warden C. C. Jackson was unanimously elected Grand Senior Warden.

G. Scribe L. A. Thomas, and Grand Treasurer S. Bishop, were unanimously reëlected.

Patriarch James Phelps was elected Grand Junior Warden.

P. G. Patriarch P. L. Cunningham was elected Grand Representative to the Grand Lodge of the United States.

The Committee thereon made the following report, which was accepted, and the resolution adopted.

To the R. W. Grand Encampment of Connecticut, I. O. O. F.:

Your Committee, upon so much of the Grand Patriarch's report as relates to the necessity of each subordinate Encampment under this jurisdiction being furnished with two copies of the form for Installation of Officers, would respectfully report, that they consider it expedient that each Subordinate Encampment be supplied with one extra copy of said form; but as the financial condition of this R. W. Body will not admit of so heavy a draft as would be required to furnish said books, they therefore recommend that each subordinate Encampment be required to supply themselves with one additional copy, to be supplied by the Grand Scribe.

Resolved, That each Subordinate Encampment, within this jurisdiction, be required to supply itself with one extra copy of the Installation form, immediately.

L. A. THOMAS, ⎫
GEO. S. SANFORD, ⎬ *Committee.*
S. H. HARRIS, ⎭

The Committee thereon submitted the following Report:

To the R. W. Grand Encampment, I. O. O. F. of Connecticut:

The Committee to whom was referred that part of the Grand Patriarch's report relating to a "want of uniformity in the work of the subordinate Encampments," respectfully report, that, in their opinion, the want of uniformity is chiefly owing to a neglect on the part of subordinates of the use of the authorized ritual of the Order, and a desire of introducing novelties. We therefore submit the following resolution:

Resolved, That it is hereby enjoined upon the Subordinate Encampments in this jurisdiction, to conform strictly to the work as laid down in the printed ritual, and that the visiting Grand Officers be requested to see the same carried out.

Respectfully submitted,

E. G. STORER, ⎫
SAML. B. GORHAM, ⎬ *Committee.*
GEO. E. LEONARD, ⎭

The question on the adoption of the report and resolution was divided—the report was accepted, but the resolution was rejected. On motion, the question which rejected the resolution was reconsidered, and the resolution was passed. The Committee thereon submitted the following report, which was accepted:

To the R. W. Grand Encampment, I. O. O. F. of Connecticut:

The Committee to whom was referred that portion of the Report of the Grand Patriarch relating to the appointment of Deputy Grand Patriarchs, respectfully report—That they have had the subject under consideration, and recommend the appointment, at each annual Session, by the G. Patriarch, of one D. G. Patriarchs for each Subordinate Encampment in this jurisdiction, and that said D. G. Patriarch be required to report in writing to the G. Patriarch an account of their official acts, on or before the first Tuesday in February, annually.

Respectfully submitted,

ALDEN PECK, ⎫
D. H. BOYD, ⎬ *Committee.*
JAMES PHELPS, ⎭

The Committee on Finance submitted the following report, which was accepted:

To the R. W. Grand Encampment, I. O. O. F. of Connecticut:

The Committee on Finance having examined the accounts of the Grand Treasurer, find the same correct, and that there remains in his hands a balance of One Hundred and Sixty-nine Dollars Twenty-seven Cents ($169 27,) to be carried to new account.

All of which is respectfully submitted, .

N. CHANDLER, ⎫ *Committee on*
O. UTLEY, ⎬ *Finance.*
J. G. HAYDEN, ⎭

The Committee on Finance, to whom was referred sundry bills, submitted the following report, which was accepted, and the bills ordered paid :

To the R. W. Grand Encampment, I. O. O. F. of Connecticut:

The Committee on Finance having examined the following bills, do report them correct:

T. J. Stafford's	bill	$38 04
W. H. Stanley's	"	1 50
George B. Bassett's	"	5 50
Com. of Quinnipiac and Harmony Lodges for rent of room..		5 00
L. A. Thomas's	bill	68 00
P. L. Cunningham's	"	8 39
E. Augur's bill, as Guardian		3 00

All of which is respectfully submitted in F., H. and C.

N. CHANDLER, ⎫ *Committee on*
O. UTLEY, ⎬ *Finance.*
J. G. HAYDEN, ⎭

P. G. P. Willey submitted the following resolution, which was unanimously adopted :

Resolved, That the thanks of this Grand Encampment be, and the same are hereby presented to P. G. Patriarch P. L. Cunningham, for the acceptable manner in which he has presided over this Body for the past year.

The Committee on the State of the Order reported that they had examined the By-laws of Ansantawae Encampment, No. 20, and recommended their approval. On motion, they were approved.

Grand Representative Gruman gave instruction in the work of the Order.

The Grand Officers were then installed by the Grand Patriarch in ample form.

The Grand Encampment was then closed with the usual form, and adjourned without day.

Attest,

LUCIUS A. THOMAS, *Grand Scribe.*

OF THE

PROCEEDINGS

OF THE

R. W. Grand Encampment, I. O. O. F. of Conn.

ANNUAL SESSION.

NEW HAVEN, Feb. 20, 1855.

The R. W. Grand Encampment, I. O. O. F. of the State of Connecticut, convened this day in annual session,

PRESENT :

M. W.	F. TURNER of No. 1,	*Grand Patriarch.*
M. E.	J. WALLACE of No. 18,	*Grand High Priest.*
R. W.	C. C. JACKSON of No. 18,	*Grand Senior Warden.*
"	L. A. THOMAS of No. 1,	*Grand Scribe.*
"	S. BISHOP of No. 1,	*Grand Treasurer.*
"	JAMES PHELPS of No. 2,	*Grand Junior Warden.*
"	P. L. CUNNINGHAM of No. 9,	*Grand Representative.*

and members from the following Encampments, viz : Nos. 1, 2, 5, 6, 9, 16, 18 and 20.

The Grand Encampment was opened in ample form, with the usual ceremonies.

The reading of the minutes of last session was dispensed with.

The Grand Patriarch appointed the following Committees :—

Committee on Credentials—Patriarchs E. G. Storer of No. 1, T. W. Wallace of No. 18, W. H. Warren of No. 20.

Committee on the State of the Order.—Patriarchs S. Lynes of No. 9, H. W. Hubbard of No. 18, N. Chandler of No. 1.

Committee on Finance—Patriarchs B. Boecher of No. 1, O. Utley of No. 6, S. S. Bedient of No. 5.

The Committee on Credentials submitted the following report, which was accepted :

To the R. W. Grand Encampment, I. O. O. F. of Conn.

The Committee on Credentials beg leave to report, that they have examined the certificates of the following Patriarchs, and find them correct:

29

Sassacus, *No.* 1—F. Turner, Samuel H. Harris, Samuel B. Gorham, Noah Chandler, E. G. Storer, Benj. Beecher, Jr., Lucius Peck, Frederick Botsford, Samuel Tolles, Samuel Bishop, Samuel Cleeton, Alfred W. Phelps, Robert A. Alling, Stephen M. Wier, William H. Stanley.

Oriental, *No.* 2—James Phelps, George K. Stillman, John G. Hayden, Wm. Gorton, Henry S. Russell.

Devotion, *No.* 5—Samuel O. Mead, Stephen S. Bedient, Edward D. Ritton, David B. Booth.

Sowheag, *No.* 6—Origen Utley.

Kabaosa, *No.* 9—Samuel Lynes, P. L. Cunningham, Wm. T. Craw.

Oasis, *No.* 16—Eldridge Hall, Thomas W. Badger.

Excelsior, *No.* 18—Charles C. Jackson, Thomas Wallace, Jr., John Wallace, H. W. Hubbard.

Ansantawae, *No.* 20—William H. Warner.

All of which is respectfully submitted,

E. G. STORER,
THOS. WALLACE, Jr., } *Committee.*

The following candidates were then introduced and instructed in the Grand Encampment Degree :

No. 1, Samuel Cleeton, Alfred W. Phelps, Robert A. Alling, Stephen M. Wier, Wm. H. Stanley ; No. 2, William Gorton, Henry S. Russell ; No. 5, Edward D. Ritton, David B. Booth ; No. 9, William T. Craw ; No. 16, Thomas W. Badger.

The Grand Patriarch submitted the following report :

PATRIARCHS : The report, which I have to present to you on this return of the regular session of this Grand Encampment, must, of necessity, be a very meagre one, owing to circumstances beyond my control. When your suffrages conferred upon me the honorable station which I have so imperfectly filled, it was my intention to devote part of my time to visiting the several Subordinate Encampments under this jurisdiction, so as to be able to judge by myself of the situation of each, and of the manner in which the degrees were conferred ; but in consequence of events ordered undoubtedly by an all-wise Providence for some useful purpose, I was cheated out of my good intentions, at the very time I was about to commence my visitations, and nothing was left to comfort me but the words of Job : God has given, God has taken away ; blessed be the name of the Lord ! and blessed be He who has preserved to me my health with a strong will and desire to work. I am confident that you will overlook my short comings, and this apparent neglect of my duty.

I am sorry that the several Deputies appointed at the last Session, have not sent their returns to me as yet. I should, perhaps, have found in them remarks that would call for some action on the part of this Grand Body ; however, being deprived of even this assistance, the only thing of interest to which I can call your attention at this time, is, the action taken by the Grand Lodge of the United States, at its last session, in regard to the degrees conferred in the Encampment. Resolutions of the Grand Lodges of Mississippi, Georgia, North Carolina and Delaware, were presented, instructing their Representatives to bring the subject of merging the Encampment degrees with those of the Lodge, so as to have a series of nine degrees in Odd Fellowship.

The subject was referred to a committee, who presented a long and elaborate report. On reading this, however, with the utmost attention, I am far from being convinced of the utility of the union or merger of the two branches. Many reasons presented in favor of it, seem to me rather to militate in favor of retaining the present organization of two distinct bodies. The strongest reason brought out to support the project seems to be that some consider the Encampment as too aristocratic, a body of a lofter distinction, which all are not permitted to reach, thereby destroying the equality which should reign among Odd Fellows. This sounds very well indeed, but although it may exist elsewhere, I have never remarked anything of the kind in my intercourse with those who do not belong to the Patriarchal Order.

The report, however, was accepted, and agreeably to the resolution accompanying it, a committee of five was appointed to prepare a report on the subject to be presented at the next session of the Grand Lodge of the United States.

This is the only matter of interest to this branch of Odd Fellowship that I find in the printed proceedings before me. For although there is a great deal of legislation and tinkering at the Constitution of the Grand Lodge and of the Subordinate Grand Lodges, yet this does not belong to the Encampment as such, and I must say that I would prefer to see less zeal to model and remodel the Constitution to suit the whim of some individuals, and more solid measures adopted for the good of the Order at large.

I have thus called your attention to this particular point, in order that you may take some action in the premises, if you see fit and proper to preserve the Encampment degrees as they *now are*, but I am afraid that even your representations would be in vain, for out of the five members of the committee, three have been selected from the States who have sent representations on the subject. My own opinion is that they had better leave well alone.

All of which is respectfully submitted in F. H. and C.

FRANS. TURNER, *G. Patriarch.*

On motion, the report of the Grand Patriarch was accepted and referred to a special committee, consisting of Patriarchs S. H. Harris of No. 1, G. K. Stillman of No. 2, and E. Hall of No. 16, and ordered to be spread on the records.

Grand Representative Cunningham submitted the following report, which was accepted and ordered to be spread on the records, and referred to the committee on the Grand Patriarch's Report:

To the Right Worthy Grand Encampment of Connecticut:

The undersigned your Representative to the R. W. Grand Lodge of the United States, having attended the recent session of that body, beg leave respectfully to report,

The R. W. Grand Lodge of the United States, assembled at the city of Baltimore, on Monday, September 4th, 1854, the M. W. Grand Sire, Wilmot De-Saussure presiding. The attendance was the largest ever convened of that R. W. Body. Numbering,

Officers and Members present, 104
Past Grand Sires,   "   3—107

All the States, Districts and Territorial Grand Lodges and Grand Encampments, except Florida, were fully represented, and the session was one of decided interest to the Order.

On the second day of the session, under a provision of the Constitution, the Grand Lodge proceeded to the election of officers, for the next term of two years, commencing on the 17th of September, 1855, the following is the result:

M. W. Grand Sire, WM. ELLISON, of Massachusetts;
R. W. D. Grand Sire, GEORGE RACE, of Louisiana;
R. W. Cor. and Rec. Sec., JAMES L. RIDGELY, of Maryland;
R. W. G. Treasurer, JOSHUA VANSANT, of Maryland.

There were three ballotings for Grand Sire, the principal candidates being Representatives Ellison of Massachusetts, Colfax of Indiana, and Barnard of N. New York. On the first ballot, out of ninety-six votes cast, Ellison received thirty-one, Colfax twenty, Barnard fifteen, scattering thirty. On the final ballot, ninety-six votes were cast, fifty-two for Ellison, thirty for Colfax, thirteen for Barnard, and one blank.

The following from the able report of the Grand Sire, shows the prosperous and onward progress of Odd Fellowship, with an increase from the last annual returns of one hundred and sixty-nine Lodges and Encampments, and eleven thousand (11,000) members.

" The returns from the various jurisdictions and bodies under the jurisdiction of this Grand Lodge, show a healthful condition of the Order, both in numerical strength and in financial prosperity. But most of all do they exhibit the liberal handed charity with which the distressed of our fraternity have been aided. The last annual report exhibited a total of 2,941 Lodges, a membership of 193,030, and a revenue of $1,209,228 90, of which $491,322 12 were expended for the relief of the sick, the burial of the dead, the aid of the widowed and the education of orphans. The report to be presented at this communication, will show about 3,110 Lodges; 204,000 members; $1,375,000 revenue, and $530,000 of expenditures for the benevolent purposes of our organization. Penetrating deep into the recesses of the North, and stretching northward toward the frozen regions of the Arctic Circle, as if emulous of the philanthropic efforts which science is making for the relief of the bold navigator, Sir John Franklin, and his gallant companions from their icy prison, charity too is seeking in those far off lands to relieve and comfort suffering humanity. Following the axe of the hardy pioneer, and bearing the best principles of civilization within its bosom, charity seeketh too in the westward, the opportunities of proclaiming good will towards men. Wafted by the wings of the wind to the Isles of the South, even there charity raiseth her standard, proclaiming to the tempest-tost mariner, rest from his labor and community with his brethren. Representatives, from Canada, from the Prairies of the West, from the Isles of the Pacific, charity reporteth to you of her deeds."

During the past year Grand Encampments have been organized in California and Texas, which will doubtless be represented at the next communication of the Grand Lodge of the United States.

The brethren of our Order in British North America, having relinquished the Supreme power in that Country to the Grand Lodge of the United States, such measures were taken at the recent session in regard to the membership of that jurisdiction, as will have a tendency to promote the general interest and prosperity of the Order. .The M. W. Grand Sire has been requested and authorized to pay an official visit to the brethren of British North America during the present year.

The Canadian Order of the Manchester Unity, has again made application during the past year, for a re-union with the Order in the United States. To this application the Grand Sire replied " that no treaty could be made, until the Manchester Unity, by a return to the ancient landmark, should remove the cause which had led to the disruption." The Grand Lodge unanimously approved this response of the M. W. Grand Sire.

. The Grand Lodge refused to change the terms from six to three months, by a decisive vote.

The most important business of the session, was the consideration of the proposed new constitution for the Grand Lodge of the United States. After several days were spent in amending its provisions, it was finally adopted by a vote of 87 to 6. It is believed that it will meet the general approval of the Order, as it vests in the several State Grand Bodies, much of the power which has heretofore been exercised by the Grand Lodge of the United States. Already a large number of amendments have been proposed to the new constitution, as follows:—Biennial sessions of the Grand Lodge; the extension of the term of Representatives from two to four years; an increase of Representatives according to membership in the Order; and to strike out Section 9, Article 1st, viz: "all power and authority in the Order not reserved to this Grand Lodge, by this constitution, is hereby vested in the various States, District and Territorial Grand Bodies."

The estimated revenue of the Grand Lodge of the United States, for the year 1854 and 5, will be $17,2'9 70, and the estimated expenses for the same period are $15,830 00.

Your attention is respectfully invited to the report of the legislative committee, upon the subject of a merger of the two branches of our Order. The following resolution offered by that committee, was adopted by 54 yeas to 41 nays:

Resolved, That the Grand Sire appoint a committee of five members of the Order, whose duty it shall be to prepare and report to the next session of the Grand Lodge, a plan merging the Subordinate Lodges and Encampments.

The Grand Sire appointed as that committee, Representatives W. L. Steel, of North Carolina; W. H. Tuthill, of Iowa; H. F. Askew, of Delaware; W. P. Russel of Vermont; and I. K. Connelly, of Mississippi.

The following resolution was also referred to the above named committee: "That said committee inquire into the expediency of so amending the written work of the Order, as to restore to the initiatory degree some of the effective ceremonies of the old work, and if said committee deem it expedient, that they report at the next session, the initiatory degree in a new form embracing the proposed amendment."

The following synopsis of the twelve decisions, made by the Grand Sire, during the recess, were unanimously confirmed:

1st. That a Grand Representative in a funeral procession, occupies such a position as the laws of the State in which the procession is organized, point out for offices.

2d. That there is no law of the Grand Lodge of the United States regulating the time when the holder of a card that has been rejected must lay off, before he can again offer it for deposit in the same State, and that the matter was left to the local laws of the several Grand Bodies.

3d. That application for degrees must be balloted for by the Lodge, open in the particular degree applied for, and the proceedings had by Lodges when open in the particular degree for the purpose of ballot or confirming degrees, were wholly distinct from ordinary Lodge proceedings, and were to be recorded in a distinct minute or record book. Each State jurisdiction to regulate the same, if no action by the State, then the law of the Grand Lodge of the United States to be in full force.

4th. That the authority of a Lodge to expel a member for non-payment of dues was governed by the local laws of the States, and that to publish a member thus expelled (other than reporting him to the State Grand Body) was a violation of the secrecy enjoined in respect to dealings of members one with another.

5th. That it was the duty of the N. G. and V. G. of a Lodge to be in possession of the work of the degree of Rebecca before their installation.

6th. That a Grand Patriarch was authorized to grant dispensation to exalt in localities remote from an Encampment, provided the nearest Encampment to the residence of the applicant assented thereto.

7th. That Chinese could be admitted into our Order if they came under the rule requiring a belief in a Supreme Being, the Preserver and Creator of the Universe.

8th. That a convention of Past Grands in the State of Maryland, for certain local purposes, was illegal.

9th. That there was no law of the Grand Lodge of the United States, forbidding the imposition of fines for non-attendance of members, but the spirit of the Order appears to be opposed to such fines.

· 10th. That the funds contributed for the building of a Hall at Honolulu could not be used to pay the rent of a Hall, but must be applied to the purpose intended.

11th. That where no local law provided therefore, an installed officer did not vacate his office by non-attendance, and should insufficient reason be given to the installing officer for the non-attendance of an officer elect upon an installation night, the instructions in the installation work appeared to indicate that the installing officer could require the Lodge immediately to elect an officer.

12th. That in the event of a N. G. failing to appear for installation for some time after the regular time, that the duties of such officer and appointment of subordidate officers would devolve on the V. G.

Also the following decisions were made by the Grand Lodge :

That members who withdraw from Subordinate Lodges, cannot retain their Encampment membership.

"That in all cases where a candidate for membership in a subordinate Lodge has been elected, but subsequent to his election and prior to his initiation, the Lodge shall become satisfied that he is unworthy, it shall be competent for the Lodge to annul such election and declare it void, provided, that notice of one week shall be given of the intention to move for such an amendment, and that it be done by a majority of two-thirds of the members present. `

The proposition to furnish each State with a book of diagrams, was rejected.

That the membership of a newly instituted Lodge is composed of only such number of the petitioners for the Charter who appear at the time, and assume before the instituting officer the obligations required by our laws, and the absentees can only gain admittance by withdrawing their cards from the hands of the Grand Officers, and applying in the usual mode for admission to membership by card.

No Grand Lodge or Grand Encampment, can confer degrees upon a member of another Grand Lodge or Grand Encampment, without the consent of the body to which the brother belongs, given under its seal. The Grand Master of one jurisdiction can confer the Past Official degrees on qualified Past Grands, on the written request of the Grand Master of another State, provided the request is accompanied by the request of the Grand Lodge to which such Past Grand belongs, authenticated according to law, but the Grand Lodge degree can only be conferred by a Grand Lodge."—See journal, pp. 1090, 1091.

The form of certificate adopted at the session of 1853, to be placed on the visiting cards, is ordered to be done by the Grand Secretary of the Grand Lodge of the United States.

The word "quarterly" in the charge books, was directed to be changed to "semi-annually" in all subsequent editions. All Encampment charge books hereafter printed, will contain the installation ceremony.

In closing this brief report, the undersigned would return his thanks to the Representatives of the R. W. Grand Lodge of Maryland, for their very liberal and hospitable entertainment. The entire session of the Grand Lodge of the United States was one of harmony and usefulness, and their deliberations are calculated to extend the beneficial influence of our beloved Order, throughout the entire jurisdiction. The only cause to mar the interest of the session, was the sad announcement of the death of Grand Representative Edwin P. Hunter, of the Grand Encampment of Virginia, who after attending the session for a few days, was suddenly cut down in his usefulness, and the Order is thus deprived of one of its most distinguished members, by a dispensation of Divine Providence.

Respectfully submitted in F. H. and C.

P. L. CUNNINGHAM, *Grand Representative.*

On motion, the Grand Encampment proceeded to the nomination of officers for the ensuing year, when the following nominations were made :

For Grand Patriarch—G. H. P. Wallace of No 18.
For Grand High Priest—G. S. W. Jackson of No. 18, E. G. Storer of No.
1, and J. Phelps of No. 2.
For Grand Senior Warden—J. Phelps of No. 2.
For Grand Scribe—G. S. Thomas of No. 1.
For Grand Treasurer—G. T. Bishop of No. 1.
For Grand Junior Warden—Patriarchs S. B. Gorham and S. H. Harris of No.
1, H. W. Hubbard of No. 18, E. Hall of No. 16, N. Chandler of No. 1, W. H.
W. Warner, S. S. Bedient of No. 5.

Patriarchs James Phelps and E. G. Storer declined the nomination for Grand High Priest, and Patriarch S. B. Gorham declined the nomination for Grand Junior Warden.

The Committee on Finance submitted the following report, which was accepted and the bills ordered to be paid :

To the R. W. Grand Encampment I. O. O. F. of Conn.

The Committee on Finance, having examined the following bills, do report them correct :

Wm. H. Stanley's bill,	- - - - - -	$10.50
C. J. Gruman's "	- - - - - -	12 00
Chas. Bradley's "	- - - - - -	3.00
L. A. Thomas's "	- - - - - -	51.69
T. J. Stafford's "	- - - - - -	14.50
		$91.69

All of which is respectfully submitted in F. H. and C.

O. UTLEY,   *Committee on*
S. S. BEDIENT,   *Finance.*

The Committee on the state of the order submitted the following report, which was accepted :

To the R. W. Grand Encampment I. O. O. F. of Conn.

The undersigned, Committee on the State of the Order, to whom were referred the reports of subordinates for the past year, beg leave respectfully to report, that they have examined the reports of Nos. 1, 3, 5, 8, 9, 16, 18 and 19, for the term ending July 5th, 1854, and find them correct, with the exception of those of Nos 5, 16 and 18, which were deficient in seals. There are no reports for that term from Nos. 2, 6, 10, 13, 14, 15, 17, 20.

We have also examined the reports of Nos. 1, 2, 3, 5, 6, 8, 9, 15, 16, 19 and 20, for the term ending January 3d, 1855, and find them correct, with the exception of those of Nos. 15, 18 and 20, which are deficient in seals. There are no reports from Nos. 10, 13, 14 and 17, for this term.

The Grand Encampment will observe that there have been no reports from Nos. 10, 13, 14 and 17, for the past year.

Respectfully submitted in F. H. and C.

SAMUEL LYNES,
H. W. HUBBARD,   *Committee.*
N. CHANDLER,

The Committee on Finance submitted the following report, which was accepted :

To the R. W. Grand Encampment I. O. O. F. of Conn.

The Committee on Finance, having examined the accounts of the Grand

Treasurer, find the same correct, and there remains in his hands Forty-one dollars and Seventy-six cents ($41.76) to be carried to new account.

All of which is respectfully submitted in F. H. and C.

B. BEECHER, Jr., }
O. UTLEY, } *Com. of Finance.*
S. S. BEDIENT, }

The Committee to whom was referred the reports of the Grand Patriarch and Grand Representative, submitted the following report, which was accepted :

To the R. W. Grand Encampment of Connecticut.

The special committee to whom was referred the report of the M. W. Grand Patriarch, and also the report of the R. W. Grand Representative to the Grand Lodge of the United States, would recommend that so much of said reports as refers to the mergence of the two branches of our Order, be referred to a special committee of three; and in connection with said mergence, they would also recommend that said committee take into consideration the expediency of amending the By-Laws of the Grand Encampment, by making the price to be paid as charter fee, *ten* dollars, instead of *thirty*, and that the fees for admission and dues to subordinate Encampments, shall be left with said Encampments. Respectfully submitted,

S. H. HARRIS, }
G. K. STILLMAN, } *Committee.*
E. HALL, }

The Grand Patriarch appointed as the Committee recommended, Patriarchs E. G. Storer of No. 1, James Phelps of No. 2, and Origen Utley of No. 6.

The Committee on Finance submitted the following report, which was accepted and the resolution adopted :

To the R. W. Grand Encampment I. O. O. F. of Conn.

The Committee on Finance, having considered the subject of paying the mileage of Grand Officers, do recommend that the practice be discontinued. They would therefore submit the following resolution.

All of which is respectfully submitted in F. H and C.

O. UTLEY, } *Committee*
S. S. BEDIENT, } *on Finance.*

Resolved, That the practice of paying mileage to the Grand Officers be hereafter discontinued.

The Grand Encampment proceeded to the election of officers. The Grand Patriarch appointed Patriarchs Cunningham and Utley, tellers.

On ballotting for Grand Patriarch, G. H. P. J. Wallace of No. 18 was unanimously elected and so declared.

On ballotting for G. High Priest, G. S. W. Jackson received 14 votes, and Patriarch E. G. Storer 5. Patriarch Jackson of No. 18 was thereupon declared to be elected Grand High Priest for the year ensuing.

On ballotting for Grand Senior Warden, G. J. W. Phelps was unanimously elected and so declared.

Grand Scribe Thomas and Grand Treasurer Bishop were re-elected.

On ballotting for Grand Junior Warden, Patriarch Harris of No. 1 received 13 votes, Scattering 6. Patriarch Harris was declared elected.

The Committee thereon presented the following report, which was accepted and the resolution adopted :

To the R. W. Grand Encampment of Connecticut.

The special committee to whom was referred so much of the reports of the M. W. Grand Patriarch and R. W. Grand Representative as relates to the merger of the patriarchal and subordinate branches of the Order, have had the subject under consideration, and beg leave to offer the following report, viz :—

The committee are of opinion, with the limited amount of time and attention they have been able to bestow on the subjects referred to them, that a merger of the two branches of the Order is inexpedient and impracticable, and they therefore recommend that the same be not done, and that the R. W. Grand Representative from this body in the Grand Lodge of the United States be requested to give his vote and use his influence against the same.

The committee also recommend the amendment of Art. I, Sec. 2d, of the By-Laws of this R. W. Grand Encampment, in relation to the price of charters, by striking out the word " thirty," and inserting " ten."

The committee also recommend the amendment of the Constitution for Subordinate Encampments, by erasing in Sec. 2d of Art. II, the words, " which shall not be less than six dollars," leaving it at the option of each Encampment to fix its own rate of initiation fees.

We recommend the adoption of the following resolutions.

Respectfully submitted in F. H. and C.

E. G. STORER,
JAMES PHELPS, } *Committee.*
O. UTLEY,

Resolved, That the 1st Sec. of Art. II, of the By-Laws of the Grand Encampment, be and hereby is amended, by striking out " thirty," and inserting "ten" dollars as the charter fee.

Resolved, That the 2d Sec. of Art. II, of the Constitution for Subordinate Encampments be amended by striking out the words, " which shall not be less ban six dollars "

The Grand Officers were then installed by the Grand Patriarch in ample form. Patriarch Lucius Peck of No. 1 was appointed Grand Guardian.

The following resolution was offered :

Resolved, That the Grand Scribe be directed to lay a per capita tax on each member of Subordinates, sufficient to meet the expenses of the Grand Encampment for the coming year.

After some discussion, the resolution was amended by substituting the following resolution, and as amended it was adopted :

Resolved, That the Grand Scribe be empowered to make an assessment on the Subordinate Encampments, to meet the expenses of the Grand Encampment, not exceeding 25 cents for each member.

The following resolution was unanimously adopted:

Resolved, That the thanks of this Grand Encampment be and the same are hereby presented to P. G. P. Frangois Turner, for the faithful and dignified manner in which he has presided over this body for the past year.

The following resolution was adopted:

Resolved, That Art. V, Sec. 2, of the Constitution for subordinate Encampments, be amended by striking out the following:—" But in no case shall the amount per week exceed one half the amount of dues paid per year."

The Committee on Finance submitted the following report, which was accepted and the resolution adopted:

To the R. W. Grand Encampment I. O. O. F. of Conn.

The Committee on Finance, having discovered an error in the settlement of the Grand Treasurer's account, July, 1849, would recommend the adoption of the following resolution.

Respectfully submitted in F. H. and C.

O. UTLEY, } *Com. on*
S. S. BEDIENT, } *Finance.*

Resolved, That the sum of one dollar be refunded to the Grand Treasurer, for an error that occurred in the settlement of his account, July, 1849.

The Grand Representative then gave instruction in the work of the Encampment.

After which, no other business offering, the Grand Encampment was closed in ample form, and adjourned without day.

Attest,

LUCIUS A. THOMAS, *Grand Scribe.*

GRAND TREASURER'S ACCOUNT.

Grand Encampment of Conn. I. O. O F. in ac't with S. Bishop, G. T.

1854.								DR.
Feb. 14,	To Cash paid E. Curtiss, G. S.		-		-		-	$3.80
"	"	"	P. Cunningham, G. P.		-		-	8.30
"	"	"	C. C. Jackson,	-		-	-	3.00
"	"	"	John Wallace,		-		-	3.00
"	"	"	Rent,		-		-	5.00
"	"	"	E. Auger,		-		-	3 00
"	"	"	T. J. Stafford,	-		-	-	12.00
"	"	"	W. H. Stanley,		-		-	1.50
"	"	"	L. A. Thomas, G. S.		-		-	68.37
1855.								
Feb. 19,	"	"	T. J. Stafford,	-		-	-	38.04
"	"	"	Grand Lodge of United States,	-			-	60.00
"	"	"	Balance to New Account,	-			-	41.76
								$247.86

1854.							CR.
Feb. 14,	By balance of Old Account,		-		-	-	$169.26
1855.							
Feb. 19,	" Cash received of G. S. Thomas,			-		-	78.60
							$247.86

Abstract of Semi-Annual Reports of Subordinate Encampments.

No.	Encampment	Location	For Term ending July, 1854.										For Term ending January, 1855.								
			Initiated	Ad. by C.	Reinsta'd	Suspen'd	Died	Whole No.	Receipts	Benefits	Expenses	On hand	Initiated	Ad. by C.	Suspen'd	Died	Whole No.	Receipts	Benefits	Expenses	On hand
1	Sassacus,	New Haven,	4		1	5	1	90	280.26	47.00	58.75	1591.16	4		3	1	93	184.56	99.00	61.07	1615.65
2	Oriental,	Essex,						11	4.00		1.20						17	25.41		20.00	107.76
3	Palmyra,	Norwich,						52	47.50	27.00	17.55	95.62	1	1			11	3.50		5.40	93.72
5	Devotion,	Danbury,										246.62					51	23.60		12.20	258.02
6	Sowheag,	Middletown,															28				178.81
8	Mount Herman,	Bridgeport,	2					31	35.50		32.80	115.32	1				31	20.62		32.05	103.89
9	Kabaosa,	Norwalk,						45	31.37		13.30	173.98	1		2		46	19.12		10.13	182.97
15	Montevideo,	Plainville,						35				110.47			10		44	35.00		23.50	11.50
16	Oasis,	Meriden,	9						68.21		29.79				1		36	18.08		9.88	121.67
18	Excelsior,	Birmingham,															46	41.63		32.90	123.08
19	Phœnix,	W. Winsted,	1			3		26	29.15			29.15		1	1		26			28.75	.40
20	Ansantawae,	Waterbury,		2				46	14.00	20.00	6.66	114.35	1		1		29	96.27		100.00	
	TOTAL,		16	2	1	8	1	336	509.99	94.00	160.05	2476.67	15	2	17	1	458	467.79	99.00	335.88	2797.47

R. W. GRAND ENCAMPMENT, I. O. O. F.

STATE OF CONNECTICUT.

----•••----

ANNUAL SESSION, 1856.

NEW HAVEN, Feb. 20, 1856.

The R. W. Grand Encampment, I. O. O. F. of Connecticut, convened this day in Annual Session, at 10 o'clock A. M.

PRESENT:

M. W. JOHN WALLACE of No. 18, *Grand Patriarch,*
M. E. C. C. JACKSON of No. 18, *Grand High Priest,*
R. W. JAMES PHELPS of No. 2, *Grand Senior Warden,*
R. W. LUCIUS A. THOMAS of No. 1, *Grand Scribe,*
R. W. S. BISHOP of No. 1, *Grand Treasurer,*
R. W. S. H. HARRIS of No. 1, *Grand Junior Warden,*
W. LUCIUS PECK of No. 1, *Grand Guardian,*

and members from the following Encampments, viz: Nos. 1, 2, 5, 6, 9, 16, and 18.

The reading of the minutes of the previous session was dispensed with.

The Grand Patriarch appointed the following Committees, viz:

Committee on Credentials—Patriarchs Thomas Wallace, Jr. of No. 18, Prelate Demick of No. 1, and J. W. Pond of No. 15.

Committee on the State of the Order—Patriarchs S. H. Harris of No. 1, A. Chichester of No. 5, and N. C. Hall of No. 1.

Committee on Finance—Patriarchs B. Beecher, Jr. of No. 1, T. W. Badger of No. 16, and Lucius Peck of No. 1.

The Committee on Credentials submitted the following report, which was accepted:

To the R. W. Grand Encampment, I. O. O. F. of Connecticut:

The Committee on Credentials beg leave to report, that they have examined the certificates of the following Patriarchs and find them correct:

Sassacus, No. 1—L. A. Thomas, S. Bishop, N. C. Hall, S. S. Bassett, B. Beecher, Jr., S. H. Harris, P. Demick, Lucius Peck, S. B. Gorham, F. Turner, F. Botsford, S. Cleeton, S. Tolles, E. G. Storer, T. C. Hollis, H. H. Peck, E. P. Church, P. L. Van Houton, W. H. Ellis.

Oriental, No. 2—J. G. Hayden, James Phelps, Gardiner K. Dickenson.

Devotion, No. 5—A. Chichester.

Sowheag, No. 6—H. P. Ransom.

Kabaosa, No 9—P. L. Cunningham.

Montevideo, No. 15—J. W. Pond.

Oasis, No. 16—Thomas W. Badger, Henry B. Sperry.

Excelsior, No. 18—John Wallace, C. C. Jackson, Thomas Wallace, Jr., R. R. Wood.

All which is respectfully submitted,

THOMAS WALLACE, Jr., ⎫
J. W. POND, ⎬ *Committee.*
P. DEMICK, ⎭

The following candidates were then introduced and instructed in the Grand Encampment degree:

No. 1, T. C. Hollis, H. H. Peck, E. P. Church, P. L. Van Houton; No. 2, G. K. Dickenson; No. 6, H. P. Ransom; No. 16, H. B. Sperry; No. 18, R. R. Wood.

The Grand Patriarch submitted his annual report, and, on motion, it was accepted and referred to a special Committee consisting of Patriarchs P. L. Cunningham of No. 6, J. G. Hayden of No. 2, and S. S. Bassett of No. 1.

Grand Representative Cunningham presented his report, which was accepted and referred to the Committee appointed on the Grand Patriarch's report.

The following report of the Committee on Finance was accepted, and the bills ordered paid:

To the R. W. Grand Encampment, I. O. O. F. of Connecticut:

The Committee on Finance have examined the accounts of the Grand Treasurer and find them correct, and that there remains in his hands $12.35 to be carried to new account.

They have also examined the following bills and find them correct:

G. B. Bassett's bill,.......................$ 2.00
Storer & Morehouse,...................... 16.56
L. A. Thomas,........................... 50.00
Chas. Bradley,........................... 3.00

$71.56

Respectfully submitted,

B. BEECHER, Jr., ⎫ *Committee on*
THOS. W. BADGER, ⎬ *Finance.*
LUCIUS PECK, ⎭

On motion, the Committee on Finance were directed to inquire into the expediency of making an assessment on the various subordinates.

A petition was received from Sowheag Encampment, No. 6,

asking leave to remove from Middletown to Portland. Referred to Committee on the State of the Order.

The Committee to whom was referred the reports of the Grand Patriarch and Grand Representative, submitted the following report, which was accepted:

To the R. W. Grand Encampment, I. O. O. F. of Connecticut:

The special Committee to whom was referred the reports of the Grand Patriarch and Grand Representative would respectfully recommend:

That so much of the Grand Patriarch's report as refers to the more general diffusion of information pertaining to this branch of our Order be referred to a committee of three;—and that so much as refers to the mergement and reorganizing the Degree Lodges, and authorizing the Encampment to confer the five Degrees, be also referred to a Committee of three.

That so much of the report of the Grand Representative as refers to finance be referred to a Committee of three; and that so much as refers to proposed amendments to the Constitution of the Grand Lodge of the United States, be referred to a Committee of three.

All of which is respectfully submitted in F., H. and C.

P. L. CUNNINGHAM,
J. C. HAYDEN,   } *Committee.*
S. S. BASSETT,

The Committee on Finance submitted the following report, which was accepted and the resolution adopted:

To the R. W. Grand Encampment, I. O. O. F. of Connecticut:

The Committee on Finance having taken into consideration the state of the finances of this R. W. Grand Body, beg leave to offer the following resolution:

Resolved, That the Grand Scribe be empowered to make an immediate assessment on the subordinate Encampments sufficient to meet the present indebtedness; and that hereafter he draw upon the subordinate Encampments at the close of each term for such amount as will defray the expenses of the Grand Encampment, said assessments to be levied equally, according to the number of members.

B. BEECHER, Jr.   } *Committtee on*
THOS. W. BADGER, } *Finance.*
LUCIUS PECK,

The Grand Patriarch announced the appointment of the following Committees:

On so much of the Grand Patriarch's report as refers to diffusion of information, Patriarchs James Phelps, G. K. Dickenson, and H. P. Ransom.

On so much of the Grand Patriarch's report as refers to mergement, &c., Patriarchs F. Botsford, R. R. Wood and H. B. Sperry.

On so much of the Grand Patriarch's report as refers to finance, Patriarchs B. Beecher, Jr., T. W. Badger, and Lucius Peck.

On so much of the Grand Representative's report as refers to the proposed amendments to the Constitution of the Grand Lodge of the United States, Patriarchs T. C. Hollis, H. H. Peck, and S. Cleeton.

On motion, the Grand Encampment proceeded to the nomination of officers for the ensuing year, when the following nominations were made:

For Grand Patriarch, G. H. P. Jackson of No. 18.
For Grand High Priest, G. S. W. Phelps of No. 2.
For Grand Senior Warden, G. J. W. Harris of No. 1.
For Grand Scribe, G. S. Thomas of No. 1.

For Grand Treasurer, G. T. Bishop of No. 1.
For Grand Junior Warden, Patriarchs H. H. Peck and F. Botsford of No. 1,
H. P. Ransom of No. 6, and J. G. Hayden of No. 2.
For Grand Representative, G. P. Wallace of No. 18.

The Committee on the State of the Order submitted the following report, which was accepted and the resolution adopted :

To the R. W. Grand Encampment, I. O. O. F. of Connecticut:

The Committee on the State of the Order, to whom was referred a resolution of Sowheag Encampment, No. 6, passed July 9, 1855, relative to the removal of said Encampment from Middletown to Portland, respectfully report that they have had the same under consideration, and would recommend the adoption of the subjoined resolution.

Respectfully submitted,

S. H. HARRIS, } *Committee on the*
A. CHICHESTER, } *State of the Order.*
N. C. HALL, }

Resolved, That whenever the R. W. Grand Patriarch shall have been duly notified that Sowheag Encampment, No. 6, at a meeting duly warned for that purpose, shall, by a major vote, decide to remove the location of said Encampment from Middletown to Portland, he be authorized to cause the same to be done.

Patriarch Cunningham offered the following resolutions, which were adopted :

Resolved, That our Grand Representative to the Grand Lodge of the United States be requested to use his exertions to procure the passage of a law by which members of a subordinate Encampment may retain an independent membership in the Encampment without the qualifications of being a member in good standing of a subordinate Lodge.

Resolved, That in the case of vacancies in the elective offices of a subordinate Encampment, and all qualified members refusing to accept office, the Encampment may elect royal purple members to office ;—provided, however, that a dispensation be obtained from the proper authority.

The Committee on Finance submitted the following report, which was accepted and the resolutions adopted :

To the R. W. Grand Encampment, I. O. of O. F. of Connecticut :

The Committee on Finance having taken into consideration so much of the report of the Grand Representative as refers to the finances of the Grand Lodge of the United States, beg leave respectfully to offer the following resolutions.

THOS. W. BADGER, } *Committee on*
LUCIUS PECK, } *Finance.*

Resolved, That the Grand Lodge of the United States be advised to curtail their expenses.

Resolved, That our representative be instructed to use his efforts to procure a repeal of the law whereby the Grand Lodge of the United States pays the mileage and per diem of the Grand Representatives, and a return to the old method of each Grand Body paying its own representatives.

The special Committee thereon submitted the following report, which was accepted :

To the R. W. Grand Encampment, I. O. O. F. of Connecticut :

The Committee to whom was referred so much of the Grand Patriarch's report as relates to the mergement of the Degree Lodge into the Encampment respectfully report that, after a careful consideration of the arguments both for and against the adoption of this mergement, we cannot recommend it as admissible.

All which is respectfully submitted,

F. BOTSFORD, } *Committee.*
R. R. WOOD, }

The Committee on the State of the Order submitted the following report, which was accepted :

To the R. W. Grand Encampment, I. O. O. F. of Connecticut:

The undersigned, Committee on the State of the Order, to whom was referred the reports of subordinates for the past year, beg leave respectfully to report, that they have examined the reports of Nos. 1, 2, 3, 5, 9, 15, 16, 18, for the term ending July, 1855, and find them correct, with the exception of No. 15, which is deficient in seal, and of No. 5, which has neglected to give the names of suspended members, of which there are ten. There are no reports from Nos. 8 and 20. Nos. 6 and 19 report no receipts.

They have also examined the reports of Nos. 1, 3, 5, 15, 16 and 18, for the term ending January, which are correct. Nos. 6 and 19 report no receipts. No. 20 reported two terms in one, correct except seal. No report from No. 8 for this term.

The Grand Encampment will observe that there have been no reports from No. 8 for the year, and that Nos. 6 and 19 report no receipts of any kind.

S. H. HARRIS,   } *Committee on the*
N. C. HALL,   } *State of the Order.*
A. CHICHESTER, }

The special Committee thereon submitted the following report, which was accepted and the resolution adopted :

To the R. W. Grand Encampment, I. O. O. F. of Connecticut :

The committee to whom was referred so much of the report of Most Worthy Grand Patriarch as relates to the "diffusion of information pertaining to our Order," have had the subject under consideration, and beg leave to submit the following resolution.

All which is respectfully submitted in F., H. and C.,

JAMES PHELPS,   }
G. K. DICKENSON, Jr. } *Committee.*
H. P. RANSOM,   }

Resolved, That for the purpose of diffusing information pertaining to the Order it is expedient that the Most Worthy Grand Patriarch visit all the subordinate Encampments in this jurisdiction in the course of his official term.

The special Committee thereon submitted the following report, which was accepted and the resolution adopted :

To the R. W. Grand Encampment, I. O. O. F. of Connecticut :

We, your Committee, to whom was referred so much of the Grand Representative's report as refers to the proposed amendment to the Constitution of the Grand Lodge of the United States, would most respectfully report that in their opinion the multitude of propositions to change the fundamental laws of the Grand Lodge of the United States, is calculated to injure the Order by rendering uncertain and unstable the laws and usages which guide us, and to produce confusion and dispute. They therefore recommend the adoption of the following resolution.

All which is respectfully submitted,

THOS. C. HOLLIS, }
HOMER H. PECK,   } *Committee.*
SAM'L CLEETON,   }

Resolved, That our Grand Representative be requested to use his influence to prevent any change in the Constitution of the Grand Lodge of the United States, until such time as the Order can become familiar with its features and form a judgment of its adaptation to its wants.

The Grand Encampment proceeded to the election of officers, when the following officers were chosen for the year ensuing:

C. C. Jackson, Grand Patriarch.

James Phelps, Grand High Priest.

S. H. Harris, Grand Senior Warden.

L. A. Thomas, Grand Scribe.

S. Bishop, Grand Treasurer.

J. Wallace, Grand Representative.

J. G. Hayden, Grand Junior Warden.

The officers were then installed in ample form by Grand Patriarch Wallace.

Patriarch Turner offered the following resolution, which was unanimously adopted.

Resolved, That the thanks of this Grand Encampment be, and the same are hereby presented to P. G. P. Wallace for the fidelity and zeal with which he has discharged the high office of Grand Patriarch of this Grand Body, and also the dignity he has displayed while presiding over our deliberations.

No other business offering, the Grand Encampment was closed in ample form.

Attest,

LUCIUS A. THOMAS, *Grand Scribe.*

PROCEEDINGS

OF THE

R. W. GRAND ENCAMPMENT, I. O. O. F.

OF THE

STATE OF CONNECTICUT.

ANNUAL SESSION, 1857.

NEW HAVEN, Feb. 17, 1857.

The R. W. Grand Encampment, I. O. O. F. of the State of Connecticut, convened this day in Annual Session.

PRESENT:

M. W. C. C. JACKSON of No. 18, *Grand Patriarch.*
M. E. JAMES PHELPS of No. 2, *Grand High Priest.*
R. W. S. H. HARRIS of No. 1, *Grand Senior Warden.*
R. W. L. A. THOMAS of No. 1, *Grand Scribe.*
R. W. S. BISHOP of No. 1, *Grand Treasurer.*
R. W. J. G. HAYDEN of No. 2, *Grand Junior Warden.*
R. W. JOHN WALLACE of No. 18, *Grand Representative.*
W. T. C. HOLLIS of No. 1, *Grand Guardian.*

The Grand Encampment was opened in ample form with the usual ceremonies.

On motion, the reading of the minutes of last session was deferred until after the initiation of new members.

The Grand Patriarch appointed the following Committees:

Committee on Credentials—John Wallace of No. 18, E. D. Ritton of No. 5, S. Bishop of No. 1.

Committee on Finance—B. Beecher, Jr. of No. 1, Thos. W. Badger of No. 16, W. H. Stanley of No. 1.

Committee on the State of the Order—S. B. Gorham of No. 1, O. Utley of No. 6, W. H. Martindale of No. 9.

The Committee on Credentials submitted the following report, which was accepted:

244 *Proceedings of Grand Encampment.* [Feb.,

To the R. W. Grand Encampment, I. O. O. F. of the State of Connecticut:

The Committee on Credentials respectfully beg leave to report, that they have examined the following certificates and find them correct:

Sassacus, No. 1—S. M. Weir, Wm. E. Sanford, T. C. Hollis, Robert A. Alling, Robt. Sizer, E. P. Church, S. Cleeton, L. L. Beecher, G. W. Judd, L. A. Thomas, E. Shelly, S. B. Gorham, E. G. Storer, S. Bishop, B. Beecher, Jr., P. Demick, S. S. Bassett, N. C. Hall, S. H. Harris, Noah Chandler. F. Turner, C. L. Sage, F. Botsford. S. Tolles, L. Peck, I. Judson, H. H. Peck, W. H. Stanley, B. L. Van Houton, Geo. Crabtree, M. B. Scott, D. E. Burwell.

Oriental, No. 2—James Phelps, J. G. Hayden.

Sowheag, No. 6—John Avery, O. Utley.

Kabaosa, No. 9—W. H. Martindale.

Oasis, No. 16—Thomas W. Badger.

Excelsior, No. 18—John Wallace, C. C. Jackson.

All which is respectfully submitted,

JOHN WALLACE, ⎱ *Committee on*
E. D. RITTON, ⎰ *Credentials.*
S. BISHOP,

The following candidates were then introduced and instructed in the Grand Encampment degree:

No. 1—Geo. Crabtree, M. B. Scott, D. E. Burwell. No. 6—John Avery. No. 9—Wm. H. Martindale.

The minutes of last session were then read and approved.

The reports of subordinates were referred to the Committee on the State of the Order.

The Grand Patriarch submitted his annual report, and, on motion, it was accepted and referred to a special Committee, consisting of Patriarchs S. Tolles, J. G. Hayden, D. E. Burwell.

Grand Representative Wallace submitted his report, which was accepted and referred to the Committee raised on the Grand Patriarch's report.

The Committee on Finance submitted the following report, which was accepted, and the bills ordered to be paid:

To the R. W. Grand Encampment, I. O. O. F. of Connecticut:

The Committee on Finance have examined the accounts of the Grand Treasurer, and find them correct, and that there remains in his hands $21.79 to be carried to new account.

They have also examined the following bills, and find them correct:—Chas. Bradley, guardian, $3. W. H. Stanley, $3.

Respectfully submitted,

B. BEECHER, Jr., ⎱ *Finance*
THOS. W. BADGER, ⎰ *Committee.*
W. H. STANLEY,

The Committee on the State of the Order submitted the following report, which was accepted:

To the R. W. Grand Encampment, I. O. O. F. of Connecticut:

The Committee on the State of the Order have examined the reports of the following subordinates for July, 1856, and Jan., 1857, viz., Nos. 1, 2, 3, 6, 9, 16, and 18.

Nos. 1, 2, 3, 6, and 16 they find correct. No. 9 is wanting in the seal of the Encampment, and is not signed by its officers. No. 18 is wanting in seal.

The January report of No. 9 is correct with the exception of wanting the seal.

Respectfully submitted in F., H. and C.

S. B. GORHAM, ⎫
O. UTLEY, ⎬ *Committee.*
W. H. MARTINDALE, ⎭

The Grand Encampment then proceeded to the nomination of Officers, when the following nominations were made:

For Grand Patriarch, G. H. P. James Phelps.

For Grand High Priest, G. J. W. S. H. Harris.

For Grand Senior Warden, G. J. W. J. G. Hayden.

For Grand Scribe, Lucius A. Thomas.

For Grand Treasurer, S. Bishop.

For Grand Junior Warden, T. W. Badger, T. C. Holles, B. Beecher, Jr., S. Tolles.

The special Committee, to whom was referred the reports of the Grand Patriarch and Grand Representative, submitted the following:

To the R. W. Grand Encampment, I. O. O. F. of Connecticut:

The special Committee, to whom was referred the reports of the Grand Patriarch and Grand Representative, would respectfully recommend,

That so much of the Grand Patriarch's report as refers to Deputy Grand Patriarchs be referred to a Committee of three.

That so much as refer to the expenditures of the Grand Lodge of the United States, and the amendment of the Constitution, offered by P. G. Sire Kennedy, be referred to a Committee of three.

That so much of the report of the Grand Representative as refers to the installation of officers in subordinate Encampments, be referred to a Committee of three.

All which is respectfully submitted,

S. TOLLES, ⎫
J. G. HAYDEN, ⎬ *Committee.*
D. E. BURWELL, ⎭

On motion, the report was accepted, and the following Committees appointed thereon:

On so much of the Grand Patriarch's report as refers to D. G. Patriarchs— Patriarchs T. C. Holles of No. 1, Thos. W. Badger of No. 16, M. B. Scott of No. 1.

On so much as relates to the amendment of the Constitution of the Grand Lodge of the United States—Patriarchs S. H. Harris of No. 1, J. G. Hayden of No. 2, John Wallace of No. 18.

On so much as relates to the report of the Grand Representative—Patriarchs F. Turner of No. 1, J. Phelps of No. 2, John Avery of No. 6.

The Grand Encampment then proceeded to election, when the following officers were chosen for the year ensuing:

James Phelps, Grand Patriarch.
S. H. Harris, Grand High Priest.
J. G. Hayden, Grand Senior Warden.
L. A. Thomas, Grand Scribe.
S. Bishop, Grand Treasurer.
S. Tolles, Grand Junior Warden.

The Grand Officers were then installed in ample form.

The Committee on Finance submitted the following report, which was accepted, and the resolution adopted :

To the R. W. Grand Encampment, I. O. O. F. of Connecticut :

The Finance Committee having taken into consideration the finances of this R. W. Grand Body, beg leave to offer the following resolution:

Resolved, That the Grand Scribe be authorized to levy assessments upon the several subordinates in this jurisdiction sufficient to meet the current expenses of the Grand Encampment, and that the first assessment be immediately raised.

BENJ. BEECHER,
THOS. W. BADGER, } *Committee.*
W. H. STANLEY,

The following amendment to the Constitution of the Grand Encampment was offered, and laid on the table till the next session :

Amend Art. VI., Sec. 6, by erasing all after the word Encampment, in second line, and adding the following—"a pro rata assesment on the number of its members sufficient to defray the expenses of the Grand Encampment, to be levied by the Grand Scribe."

SAMUEL B. GORHAM of No. 1,
JOHN WALLACE of No. 18.

The following resolution was unanimously adopted :

Resolved, That the thanks of this Grand Encampment be presented to P. G. Patriarch C. C. Jackson for the faithful discharge of his duties, and for his urbane and gentlemanly bearing while presiding over this Right Worthy Grand Body.

The following report was accepted, and the resolution adopted :

To the R. W. Grand Encampment, I. O. O. F. of Connecticut :

The special Committee appointed on so much of the Grand Patriarch's report as relates to the amendment to the Constitution of the Grand Lodge of the United States, beg leave to submit the following resolution.

Respectfully submitted,

S. H. HARRIS,
J. G. HAYDEN, } *Committee.*
JOHN WALLACE,

Resolved, That our Representative to the Grand Lodge of the United States be instructed to vote for the amendment to the Constitution of that Grand Body, offered by Grand Sire Kennedy, or any other proposition tending to lessen the expenses of that body.

The following report was accepted, and the resolution adopted :

To the R. W. Grand Encampment, I. O. O. F. of Connecticut :

Your Committee, to whom was referred so much of the Grand Patriarch's report as refers to D. G. Patriarch's, beg leave to offer the following resolution.

T. C. HOLLIS, ⎫
M. B. SCOTT, ⎬ *Committee.*
THOS. W. BADGER, ⎭

Resolved, That any D. G. P. failing to make his report to the Grand Patriarch before the first day of February in each year shall be excluded from a seat in this R. W. Grand Body.

The following report was accepted :

To the R. W. Grand Encampment, I. O. O. F. of Connecticut :

The Committee to whom was referred the subject of installation of officers, before the returns are made to the Grand Bodies, beg leave to submit the resolution of the Grand Lodge of the United States, as we think there is no getting over or around it.

" *Resolved*, That the officers of subordinate Lodges and Encampments shall not be installed nor furnished with the semi-annual pass word, unless the reports, returns, and moneys due from such Lodges and Encampments to their respective superior jurisdictions be actually in transit to the proper destination."

All which is respectfully submitted,

FRANCOIS TURNER, ⎫ *Committee.*
JOHN AVERY, ⎭

No further business appearing, the Grand Encampment was closed in ample form, and adjourned without day.

Attest,

LUCIUS A. THOMAS, *Grand Scribe.*

R. W. GRAND ENCAMPMENT, I. O. O. F.

STATE OF CONNECTICUT.

ANNUAL SESSION, 1858.

NEW HAVEN, Feb. 16, 1858.

The R. W. Grand Encampment, I. O. O. F. of the State of Connecticut, convened this day in Annual Session.

PRESENT:

M. W. JAMES PHELPS, *Grand Patriarch.*
M. E. S. H. HARRIS, *Grand High Priest.*
R. W. J. G. HAYDEN, *Grand Senior Warden.*
R. W. L. A. THOMAS, *Grand Scribe.*
R. W. S. BISHOP, *Grand Treasurer.*
R. W. S. TOLLES, *Grand Junior Warden.*

The Grand Encampment was opened in ample form, with the usual ceremonies.

The Grand Patriarch appointed the following Committees:

On Credentials—Patriarchs C. C. Jackson of No. 18, S. B. Gorham of No. 1, and G. K. Dickenson, Jr., of No. 2.

Committee on Finance—Patriarchs B. Beecher of No. 1, P. L. Cunningham of No. 9, and C. L. Sage of No. 1.

Committee on the State of the Order—Patriarchs E. G. Storer and Wm. H. Stanley of No. 1, and James R. Post of No. 2.

The Committee on Credentials submitted the following report, which was accepted:

To the R. W. Grand Encampment, I. O. O. F. of Connecticut:

The Committee on Credentials have examined the certificates of the following P. C. Patriarchs and P. H. Priests, and find them correct:

Sassacus, No. 1—P. C. Patriarchs E. G. Storer, C. L. Sage, M. B. Scott, Geo. Crabtree, S. M. Wier, Samuel Cleeton, D. E. Burwell, F. Botsford, S. H. Harris, B. Beecher, S. B. Gorham, S. Bishop, L. A. Thomas, W. H. Stanley, Edward A. Burgess, P. H. Priests T. C. Hollis, S. Tolles, F. Turner, A. G. Shears, Alfred W. Phelps, S. T. Scott.

Oriental Encampment, No. 2—P. C. Patriarchs James Phelps, Gardiner K. Dickenson, Jr., J. G. Hayden, James R. Post.

Kabaosa Encampment, No. 9—P. C. Patriarch P. L. Cunningham.

Excelsior Encampment, No. 18—P. H. Priest Thomas Wallace, Jr. P. C. Patriarchs R. R. Wood, C. C. Jackson, D. W. Boyd.

Respectfully submitted in F., H. and C.

C. C. JACKSON,
S. B. GORHAM,
G. K. DICKENSON, Jr.

The following candidates were then introduced and instructed in the Grand Encampment degree by the Grand High Priest, and took their seats as members:

No. 1, Patriarchs A. G. Shears, Alfred W. Phelps, Edward A. Burgess, S. T. Scott.

No. 2, James R. Post.

The minutes of last session were then read and approved.

On motion, Patriarchs S. B. Gorham and M. B. Scott of No. 1, and J. R. Post of No. 2, were appointed a Committee to bring forward the unfinished business of last session.

The reports of subordinate Encampments were submitted to the Committee on the State of the Order.

The Grand Patriarch submitted the following report:

R. W. Officers and Brethren:

We have again convened in Annual Grand Communication, to review the condition of the Patriarchal branch of our Order during the past year, and to deliberate upon and legislate with a view to its prosperity and usefulness for the future.

While it is a source of regret to be compelled to admit that the past has not been a year of advancement in the numerical force of this superior branch of Odd Fellowship, yet it is highly gratifying to be able to reflect, that in the amount of revenue, and the ability for discharging the important trust reposed in it, it is fully equal to the exigencies which press upon it; and an examination into the condition of its vital statistics demonstrates that these subordinate Encampments which maintain their organization, are in no degree less efficient, or less capable, than heretofore of fulfilling their legitimate obligations.

From the nature of surrounding circumstances, we must reasonably expect the patriarchal tents to embrace a comparatively small proportion of the Order at large; and while this is so, it is an agreeable fact which has attracted the attention of us all, that this proportion, whether greater or less, includes a large number of those who adhere to the Order from a sincere love of its principles—a devoted attachment to its forms and usages, and a steadfast determination to stand by them through evil as well as good report.

The record of my official acts during the year is necessarily brief, from the fact that little has been required of me to perform. I caused to be recommissioned the several Deputy Grand Patriarchs who had held these offices during the preceding year, and have no reason to doubt but that they have all faithfully discharged the duties which have devolved upon them, with the exception that they have failed to report to me in pursuance of the resolution of the last session of this R. W. Body. For this apparent breach of duty they perhaps ought to be held excusable, from the fact that the proceedings of the last session have not been published and distributed, for the want of funds in the treasury which could have been properly appropriated for that purpose. And in this connection I take the liberty to earnestly recommend the adoption of the proper measures to raise the necessary revenue to discharge the existing indebtedness of the Grand Encampment, procure the publication of the proceedings of the two last sessions, and defray the ordinary expenses of the current year.

I am informed we are in arrears to the R. W. Grand Scribe for his salary, which deficiency ought to be, and I trust will be, promptly provided for. He has with great fidelity and punctuality discharged the duties of his office, which have involved no small degree of care and labor; and he should not be required or expected to perform this duty without a reasonable and satisfactory compensation for that important and indispensable service.

I am not aware of the precise amount needed to place the Grand Encampment in easy and unembarrassed financial circumstances, but that information will doubtless be communicated by the Grand Scribe, who is familiar with statistics on that subject. But whether that sum be greater or less, I trust the requisite method will be pursued to discharge all our obligations for the past and present, and meet our necessary current demands. The Representative Tax was at the last session of the Grand Lodge of the United States raised from fifty dollars to seventy-five dollars, which of course adds twenty-five dollars to our necessary current yearly disbursements. The funds of the subordinate Encampments cannot be so properly applied in any other manner, as in that of liberating the Grand Encampment from its embarrassed circumstances, and I think it is their first duty, as I doubt not they will esteem it their highest privilege, to contribute from their ample substance, with cheerful alacrity, what shall be required of them for that laudable purpose.

There may be some diversity of opinion as to the most proper and equitable mode in which the finances of this body shall be relieved, and I leave it to your wisdom to devise that plan, whether by per capita assessment or otherwise, which shall in your judgment be best adapted to accomplish the purpose.

The resolution of the Grand Lodge of the United States increasing by thirty-three and a third per cent. the Representative Tax, was adopted as the most practicable mode of removing the financial pressure which had become burdensome upon that R. W. Grand Body. But while it essentially relieved them of their burden, it directly tended to add to the weight which was already bearing down the smaller and weaker of the State Grand Lodges and Encampments, and in this jurisdiction, and particularly by this Body, is severely felt; and I submit to you the question whether it is expedient to attempt, through your Representative, at the next session of the Grand Lodge of the United States, to procure a modification or repeal of that resolution.

A resolution was also adopted by the Grand Lodge of the United States at their last session, raising a special Committee to revise the entire secret work of the Order, and prepare and report to the next session a plan for merging the degrees; with suitable charges and lectures which would be appropriate after such mergement. This scheme is understood to originate with the large jurisdiction of Northern New York, and is but a repetition in a new form of the oft proposed, and as oft rejected, project of annihilating the Patriarchal branch, with perhaps a greater apparent prospect of success than heretofore.

If some practicable plan can be devised which will really be productive of good to the Order at large, and not oppressive upon the smaller jurisdictions, it may be best to adopt it; but in all such fundamental changes, there is serious danger that if relief is obtained in one direction, a corresponding injury will be inflicted in another; and it is especially to be apprehended that the proposed project will involve with it a change in the relative representation of the State Grand Bodies in the Grand Lodge of the United States; and we may very justly fear that no such change will be likely to take place except at the expense of the smaller jurisdictions.

All experience proves the tendency of greater and more powerful States and jurisdictions to encroach upon and take away the privileges of their weaker neighbors and coordinates, and to that tendency our Order furnishes no exception. We are well as we now are, and ought not to be compelled to hazard the consequences of a radical change of the character proposed, or indeed any change, that may involve such a result as I have predicted; and I respectfully suggest the propriety of instructing your Representative upon this, and the last preceding topic to which I have alluded, viz., the increase of the Representative Tax.

On the 14th of the last month, in company with Grand Scribe Thomas, I made an official visit to Excelsior Encampment, No. 18, located in the village of Birmingham, and installed their officers for the current term. The visit was in pursuance of an invitation from that Camp, which is the only subordinate in the jurisdiction from which I have received a like formal invitation. It gives me great pleasure to bear testimony to the thorough efficiency of that Encampment in the work of conferring the degrees, and the zeal and whole hearted energy displayed by the members of it in the discharge of their fraternal duties. While it numbers within its spacious tent those distinguished and active brethren who now give character and impulse to its work, there can be no doubt but that it will be sustained with credit to itself and honor to the jurisdiction, and will long continue to be what its fitly selected name implies, "a most excellent Encampment." The ceremonies of the interesting occasion were succeeded by a bountiful entertainment entirely characteristic of the hospitable patriarchs of "Excelsior," and I earnestly pray that their "shadows," individually and collectively, "may never be less."

My brethren, this branch of our cherished Order has seen brighter and more prosperous eras than the present; yet I trust no one for that reason seriously entertains the idea of the surrender of the charter of this Body, and the voluntary abandonment of everything under it. It is true, the shadows of adversity have for some time past been gathering about it, and the darkness of a perpetual night seemed to be preparing to brood over it. You are now its guardians, and with yourselves in a great measure rests the responsibility of its maintenance. Let not that responsibility be too lightly realized or insufficiently appreciated. Remember that seasons of adversity are propitious for making preparation for more favorable changes, and that we have the unfailing promise, that "those who sow in tears shall reap in gladness." That we have been more prosperous in time past, furnishes no good reason for discouragement. Every human institution has its period of advancement and retrogression. Even the divine system of Christianity has at times been apparently approximating to complete extinction, while literature, the arts and sciences, the civil law, and theories of rational civil government, have each been wrapped for ages in the mantle of oblivion, and each has subsequently revived, and risen with new power and beauty, seemingly invigorated and made resplendent by the adversity which had given them repose.

So, I trust, it will be with our institution. The good seed has been bountifully scattered on fruitful soil, and by the blessings of our Great High Priest will in due time produce an abundant harvest, "even an hundred fold." Its energies may for a period lie dormant, but when the causes of its present apparent decline shall have passed away, it will surely come forth with recuperated power; because it is founded in that Charity, and Hope, and Faith—in that Friendship, and Love, and Truth, which are divinely enjoined and ordained to be as imperishable as the stars.

Then let us rally to our Tents, and place around our Camps the Patriarchal virtues as the panoply of their defense; and as the ancient Patriarchs of Israel guarded and preserved the Sacred Ark of the Covenant, so let us cherish, protect, preserve, and perpetuate our sublime ritual—our mysterious symbalry—our valuable secrets—and our hallowed altars.

I have now only to add in conclusion, the expression of my sincere gratitude for the official honors which you have so liberally bestowed upon me, and only regret that my efficiency in carrying forward the benevolent work in which we are engaged, has not been more nearly commensurate with them. To make up for the deficiency, as far as may be, I pledge you my future energies in the cause, and trust we may yet be many times permitted to meet together in annual counsel, under the shadow of this tent, to labor for and advance this noble enterprise. And may the God of those holy Patriarchs, Abraham, Isaac, and Jacob, who holds in his hands the destiny of us all, watch over and defend us and our institution from all evil.

JAMES PHELPS, *Grand Patriarch.*

ESSEX, February 16th, 1858.

On motion, the Grand Patriarch's report was referred to a special Committee, consisting of Patriarchs D. E. Burwell and Wm. H. Stanley of No. 1, and G. K. Dickenson of No. 2.

A petition of sundry Patriarchs for an Encampment to be located at Hebron, was presented and referred to the Committee on the State of the Order.

The Committee on Finance submitted the following report, which was accepted, and the bills ordered paid.

To the R. W. Grand Encampment, I. O. O. F. of Connecticut:

The Committee on Finance having examined the accounts of the Treasurer find the same correct, and that there remains in his hands fifteen dollars and seventy-nine cents, to be carried to new account.

The Committee recommend the payment of the following bills: T. J. Stafford, $6.00; Wm. H. Stanley, $5.00; Geo. B. Bassett, $1.00; Grand Lodge of United States, $50.00; Chas. Bradley, $3.00; E. G. Storer, $1.00.

Respectfully submitted,

B. BEECHER, }
C. L. SAGE, } *Committee.*

The special Committee to whom was referred the Grand Master's report, submitted the following, which was accepted:

To the R. W. Grand Encampment, I. O. O. F. of Connecticut:

Your committee, to whom was referred the able report of the M. W. Grand Patriarch, beg leave to report that they have attended to their duty, and would recommend that so much as relates to the printing of the proceedings of the last two sessions, and the salary of the Grand Scribe, be referred to a special Committee of three.

That so much as relates to the representation tax in the Grand Lodge of United States, be referred to a special Committee of three.

That so much as refers to the resolution passed by the Grand Lodge of United States, raising a special Committee to revise the secret work of the Order, be referred to a special Committee of three.

Respectfully submitted in F., H. and C.,

D. E. BURWELL, }
W. STANLEY, } *Committee.*
G. K. DICKENSON, }

In conformity with the recommendation of the Committee the Grand Patriarch appointed the following Committees:

Committee on so much of Grand Patriarch's report as relates to printing proceedings, &c.—Patriarchs Thomas Wallace, Jr. of No. 18, A. G. Shears and S. T. Scott of No. 1.

On so much as relates to Representation tax—Patriarchs C. C. Jackson of No. 18, S. Tolles of No. 1, J. G. Hayden of No. 2.

On so much as relates to the revision of the work—Patriarchs G. K. Dickenson, Jr. of No. 2, R. R. Wood of No. 18, N. Chandler of No. 1.

The Committee thereon submitted the following report, which was accepted:

To the R. W. Grand Encampment, I. O. O. F. of Connecticut:

The Committee to whom was referred the minutes of the last annual communication for the purpose of bringing up unfinished business, would report, that they find an amendment to the Constitution of this Grand Encampment, offered by S. B. Gorham of No. 1, and John Wallace of No. 18, as follows:

"Amend Art. VI., Sec. 6, by erasing all after the word Encampment in second line, and adding the following—'a pro rata assessment on the number of members sufficient to defray expenses of the Grand Encampment, to be levied by the Grand Scribe."

Respectfully submitted in F., H. and C.,

S. B. GORHAM, ⎫
M. B. SCOTT, ⎬ *Committee.*
J. R. POST, ⎭

On motion, the amendment to Art. VI., Sec. 6, of the Constitution of the Grand Encampment was unanimously adopted.

The Grand Encampment then proceeded to the nomination of officers for the ensuing year, when the following nominations were made:

For Grand Patriarch—G. H. P. S. H. Harris.

For Grand High Priest—G. S. W. J. G. Hayden.

For Grand Senior Warden—G. J. W. S. Tolles.

For Grand Secretary—G. S. L. A. Thomas.

For Grand Treasurer—G. T. S. Bishop.

For Grand Junior Warden—Thos Wallace, Jr. and M. B. Scott.

For Grand Representative—P. G. P. C. C. Jackson.

The Committee on the State of the Order submitted the following report, which was accepted and the resolution adopted.

To the R. W. Grand Encampment, I. O. O. F. of Connecticut:

The Committee on the State of the Order, to whom was referred the petition of Patriarch Lucius J. Hendee and six other Patriarchs, praying for a charter for an Encampment to be located in the town of Hebron, County of Tolland, respectfully beg leave to report:

That they have had the said petition and accompanying documents under consideration, and are of opinion that the good of the Patriarchal branch of the Order in particular, and of Odd Fellowship in general, would be promoted by the establishment of an Encampment at the said location, and they therefore submit the following resolution.

Respectfully submitted in F., H. and C.,

E. G. STORER, ⎫
JAMES R. POST, ⎬ *Committee.*
W. H. STANLEY, ⎭

Resolved, That the prayer of the petition be and is hereby granted, and that a charter be issued in due form for an Encampment to be located in the town of Hebron, to be known by the name of Hebron Encampment, No. 21.

32

The special Committee thereon submitted the following report, which was accepted:

To the R. W. Grand Encampment, I. O. O. F. of Connecticut:

The Committee to whom was referred so much of the Grand Patriarch's address as relates to the printing of the proceedings of last session, and the salary of the Grand Scribe, respectfully report that the Grand Scribe be authorized to draw a sum sufficient to defray the expense of said printing and the arrears due him.

THOMAS WALLACE, Jr.,
A. G. SHEARS,   } *Committee.*
S. T. SCOTT,

The special Committee thereon submitted the following report, which was accepted, and the resolution adopted:

To the R. W. Grand Encampment, I. O. O. F. of Connecticut:

The Committee to whom was referred that part of the Grand Patriarch's report which relates to the appointment of a special Committee in the Grand Lodge of the United States to revise the secret work of the Order, and to take into consideration the propriety of a mergement of the degrees, beg leave to submit the following report:

While the Committee would recommend a cheerful acquiescence in any judicious revision of the secret work which may be made by the Grand Lodge of the United States, they are of the opinion that the virtual annihilation of the Patriarchal order, by the contemplated mergement of the degrees, would not be conducive to the highest interest of the Order. They would therefore submit the subjoined resolution.

G. K. DICKENSON, Jr.,
ROBERT R. WOOD,   } *Committee.*
N. CHANDLER,

Resolved, That our Grand Representative in the Grand Lodge of the United States, be instructed to oppose the mergement of the Patriarchal into the subordinate branch of the Order.

The special Committee thereon submitted the following report, which was accepted:

To the R. W. Grand Encampment, I. O. O. F. of Connecticut:

The Committee to whom was referred so much of the Grand Patriarch's report as refers to the action of the Grand Lodge of the United States in raising the representation tax from fifty to seventy-five dollars, have had the subject under consideration, and are of the opinion that it is unnecessary to take any action in the matter.

Respectfully submitted in F., H. and C.
C. C. JACKSON,
SAMUEL TOLLES,   } *Committee.*
J. G. HAYDEN,

The Grand Encampment proceeded to the election of officers for the year ensuing:

On balloting, the following officers were elected, viz:

S. H. Harris, Grand Patriarch.

J. G. Hayden, Grand High Priest.

S. Tolles, Grand Senior Warden.

L. A. Thomas, Grand Scribe.

S. Bishop, Grand Treasurer.

T. Wallace, Jr., Grand Junior Warden.

C. C. Jackson, Grand Representative.

The Grand Officers were then installed in ample form by G. P. Phelps.

On motion, the following was adopted:

WHEREAS, Grand Representative John Wallace, by severe illness, has been unable to present his report to this Grand Encampment, therefore

Resolved, That Grand Representative Wallace have leave to place his report on file, to be incorporated in the proceedings of this session, whenever his health will permit him to prepare the same.

Grand Patriarch Harris appointed Patriarch G. K. Dickenson of No. 2, Grand Guardian.

The following resolution was unanimously adopted:

Resolved, That the thanks of this Grand Encampment are hereby tendered to P. G. Patriarch James Phelps, for the able and satisfactory manner in which he has presided over its deliberations and discharged the duties of Grand Patriarch for the past year.

P. G. Representative Gorham then instructed the members of the Grand Encampment in the Patriarchal work.

The Grand Encampment then adjourned without day, and was closed in ample form.

Attest,

LUCIUS A. THOMAS, *Grand Scribe.*

R. W. GRAND ENCAMPMENT, I. O. O. F.

OF THE

STATE OF CONNECTICUT.

ANNUAL SESSION, 1859.

NEW HAVEN, Feb. 15, 1859.

The R. W. Grand Encampment, I. O. O. F. of Connecticut, convened this day at 2 o'clock in Annual Session.

PRESENT:

M. W. SAMUEL H. HARRIS, *Grand Patriarch.*
M. E. J. G. HAYDEN, *Grand High Priest.*
R. W. SAMUEL TOLLES, *Grand Senior Warden.*
R. W. LUCIUS A. THOMAS, *Grand Scribe.*
R. W. S. BISHOP, *Grand Treasurer.*

Patriarch O. Utley was appointed Grand Junior Warden, *pro tem.*

The Grand Encampment was opened in ample form with the usual ceremonies.

The reading of the record of the previous meeting was deferred until after the admission of candidates.

The Grand Patriarch appointed the following Committees:

Committee on Credentials—Patriarchs D. F. Burwell and Wm. H. Stanley of No. 1, and E. D. Ritton of No. 5.

Committtce on Finance—Patriarchs E. G. Storer and M. B. Scott of No. 1, and O. Utley of No 6.

Committee on the State of the Order—Patriarchs O. Utley of No. 6, G. L. Townsend of No. 20, and George Crabtree of No. 1.

The Committee on Credentials submitted the following report, which was accepted:

To the R. W. Grand Encampment, I. O. O. F. of Connecticut:

The Committee on Credentials, having examined the certificates presented, find the following Patriarchs correct and entitled to seats in the Grand Encampment, viz:

From *Sassacus,* No. 1—P. C. Patriarchs D. E. Burwell, S. T. Scott, Benj. Beecher, S. Bishop, W. H. Stanley, S. B. Gorham, E. G. Storer, L. A. Thomas, Geo. Crabtree, S. H Harris, David Botsford ; P. H. Priests M. B. Scott, Edwin Perkins, Thomas C. Hollis, Noah Chandler, Samuel Tolles.

Oriental, No. 2—P. C. Patriarchs James Phelps, John G. Hayden.

Devotion, No. 5—P. C. Patriarch E. D. Ritton.

Sowheag, No. 6—P. C. Patriarchs O. Utley, Chas. A. Newell ; P. H. Priest Sam'l B. Wetmore.

Ansantawae, No. 20—P. C. Patriarch Geo. L. Townsend.

Hebron, No. 21—P. C. Patriarch Jno. G. Page ; P. H. Priest Orrin C. White.

The following Patriarchs were then admitted and instructed in the Grand Encampment degree:

Sassacus, No. 1—P. C. Patriarch D. Botsford; P. H. Priests Edwin Perkins, M. B. Scott.

Sowheag, No. 6—P. C. Patriarch Chas. A. Newhall; P. H. Priest S. B. Wetmore.

Assantawae, No. 20—P. C. Patriarch George L. Townsend.

Hebron, No. 21—P. C. Patriarch Jonathan G. Page ; P. H. Priest Orrin C. White.

The record of proceedings of last session were read and approved.

The reports of subordinates were referred to the Committee on the State of the Order.

The Grand Patriarch submitted the following, being his annual report:

R. W. Grand Encampment, I. O. O. F. of Connecticut:

We are again, by permission of the Supreme Grand Patriarch, assembled within these walls, dedicated to the sacred principles of Friendship, Love and Truth, to take counsel together and to devise ways and means to promote the prosperity of this branch of Odd Fellowship, in this jurisdiction. Since we last met here, another year has passed away—has added its experience to the past, and furnished new incentives for renewed activity and increased energy in the noble work we have associated together to promote. In reviewing our blessings, we naturally turn to the great Author of them all, and whilst acknowledging His goodness, recognize our dependence on Him for a continuance of His protecting care and guidance.

That the Great Patriarch above looks approvingly on our efforts to extend the benign principles of our Order—principles designed to promote the happiness and social well-being of the human race, as well as to cultivate the noblest feelings of our nature—we have reason to believe, from the success which has heretofore crowned our efforts. Let us not, then, despair for the future, but buckle on our armor for renewed exertions in the cause of Friendship, Love and Truth, trusting that our efforts will meet with former success, and that the Patriarchal branch of Odd Fellowship will again flourish and blossom as the cedars of Lebanon.

For several years, Odd Fellowship has been gradually declining in Connecticut, until the number of Lodges has dwindled from eighty to about half that number. Consequently, it has been impossible to sustain several of the Encampments in this jurisdiction, and their charters have been surrendered ; so that we now number only *eight* in good standing, and the condition of some of these is such that it is feared they, too, will soon cease to exist. It becomes us, therefore, if possible, to devise means to sustain those Encampments now struggling for sustenance, and to encourage the formation of *new* ones, or this Grand Encampment will soon find itself without the constitutional number of subordinates requisite for its own existence.

. My official acts, during the past year, have necessarily been very limited— little having occurred beyond the regular duties of my station.

Soon after the commencement of my term of office, on consultation with our Right Worthy Grand Scribe, I forwarded commissions to the requisite number of brothers whom I thought would act as Deputy Grand Patriarchs of their respective Encampments—no Encampment having notified me of the nomination of a brother for that office, as recommended by resolution of this Grand Body.

Reports from only one of these officers have been received, and that report came to hand this day. It is to be hoped that hereafter those Patriarchs who may be commissioned as Deputy Grand Patriarchs, will make their reports in season for the Grand Patriarch to form some estimate of the condition of the Encampments under his jurisdiction.

It will be recollected that at the last session of this Grand Encampment a charter was granted to the requisite number of Patriarchs for an Encampment to be located in the town of Hebron. Early in April last, I was informed that our brother Patriarchs, who were to spread this new tent, had made the necessary arrangements, and were ready to have their Encampment instituted. Accordingly, the brothers were notified of the time the Grand Officers would meet them for that purpose, and on the 19th of April, accompanied by Grand Scribe THOMAS, P. C. P. WILLIAM H. STANLEY, P. H. P. ALONZO G. SHEARS, and Patriarch LEWIS P. MOREHOUSE, of Sassacus Encampment, No. 1, I proceeded to the town of Hebron, and instituted their Encampment, under the name of "HEBRON ENCAMPMENT, No. 21," and installed its officers for the term, which extended to January, 1859. The officers of this new Encampment, for the first term, were as follows: JONATHAN G. PAGE, C. P.; ORRIN C. WHITE, H. P.; HORATIO W. LITTLE, S. W.; EZRA L. BACKUS, Scribe and Treasurer ; LUCIUS J. HENDEE, J. W.

Owing to a severe storm on the afternoon and evening Hebron Encampment was instituted, no brothers were admitted to the mysteries of this branch of Odd Fellowship. This was much regretted by the Grand Officers, as well as the members of the Encampment. Such instruction, however, as the Grand Officers were able to give, was freely imparted and cordially received; and from the aptness of the brothers who were elected to office, we left them with the full belief that they would credibly impart the mysteries of the Encampment degrees to any brothers who should be admitted within their tent.

From the moral and social position of the Patriarchs who formed this new Encampment, and their zeal for the principles of our Order, as well as the reputation of the Odd Fellows of the district from which this Encampment is expected to be sustained, I have no doubt "Hebron Encampment, No. 21," will take a high rank, and be an honor to itself, as well as to this Grand Encampment.

I take pleasure in saying, that on this occasion the Grand Officers were received with open hands and warm hearts. The kindness and hospitality extended to us by our brothers of Hebron Encampment will long be remembered, I doubt not, by those who had the pleasure to be present.

At the regular meeting in July last, assisted by G. S. W. TOLLES, I installed the Officers of Sassacus Encampment, No 1. This Encampment is in a highly flourishing condition. The greatest harmony and good feeling prevails among its members, and the only strife between them seems to be, who shall most advance and best promote the principles of our universal brotherhood.

I would respectfully call your attention to the finances of this Grand Encampment It is well known to many of you that the Grand Encampment has not been able to meet its expenses for several years past. The Grand Scribe has not received any part of his salary for three years. This ought not so to be. So valuable an officer should be paid for his service*. While it would have been better to have devised means for that purpose when there were a large number of Encampments in existence, and more apparent zeal in the Order, I believe it is not yet too late to testify our appreciation of his invaluable services by liquidating our indebtedness to him. I would recommend this subject to your consideration.

The services of Grand Scribe Thomas have been so often alluded to and commended by my predecessors, as well as by distinguished Officers in the other branch of our Order, that it may seem an act of supererogation that I should allude to them. I cannot refrain, however, from testifying my obligations to him, and my appreciation of the zeal, industry and perseverance he has ever exhibited in behalf of the principles and objects of our beloved Order. A personal acquaintance and friendship of more than twenty-five years' standing, and an association with him of more than eighteen years in the cause of Odd Fellowship, enables me to judge of his worth, and forbids me to be silent on this occasion.

The report of the Grand Scribe will enable you to form some estimate of the condition of the several Encampments in this jurisdiction, and suggest what legislation is necessary for keeping our tents spread, until every brother in Connecticut has had an opportunity of reposing beneath their folds.

I have been favored with a copy of the proceedings of the last session of the Grand Lodge of the United States, and from a casual glance at it, I notice some legislation pertaining to the Encampment branch, and the usual number of amendments offered to the Constitution of the Grand Lodge of the United States, tending to the mergement of the two branches. The Report of our Grand Representative, however, will more immediately bring to your notice such action as may be necessary, in view of the legislation of the Supreme Head of the Order.

Although the subject of mergement has been frequently before the Grand Lodge of the United States, and has been as often defeated, yet there are a considerable number of the Order who are favorable to the project, and will use every exertion to accomplish their ends. It may be advisable, therefore, for this Grand Encampment to again express its opinion on this subject. I would recommend this matter to your consideration.

Sassacus Encampment, No. 1, at its regular meeting in December, passed a vote inviting the Grand Officers to be present and install its officers in January. Accordingly, in company with G. S. Warden Tolles and Grand Treasurer Bishop, I made an official visit to that Encampment, and installed its officers for the current term. We were deprived of the pleasure of the company and assistance of Grand Scribe Thomas, in consequence of his temporary illness. On this occasion the Grand Officers were received with that cordiality and good feeling characteristic of the brothers of this Encampment. After the regular duties of the evening, the brothers present partook of an entertainment provided for the occasion, and all seemed to feel that it was good for them to be there.

Those of us who were present at the last session of this Grand Encampment, missed one who, for some years past, had been with us at these annual meetings— and we were then pained and grieved to learn that his pleasant countenance and warm greeting would probably no more meet us here; that his musical voice would no more be heard in this sacred Hall, and that he would soon be summoned by the Supreme Grand Patriarch to render his final account. Our anticipations were soon, alas! sadly realized. But a few days passed, and the soul of our well-beloved Brother, P. G. Patriarch John Wallace, took its flight, and the tidings of his death came to us. This instance of mortality seriously affected this entire jurisdiction. At the time of his death, Brother Wallace was Grand Master of the Grand Lodge of Connecticut. The disease of which he fell a victim, was contracted while in the service of this Grand Encampment. As a Representative of this Grand Encampment, he attended the session of the Grand Lodge of the United States, in September, 1857, and while in Baltimore he was attacked with illness, from which he never entirely recovered.

Brother Wallace was always faithful to his duties, and ever watchful of the

true interests of our Fraternity—he was a *good* Odd Fellow. His manly form, un-
obtrusive deportment, and benignant demeanor, are vividly stamped on my mind.
In his death, our Order has sustained a great loss; but we have the consolation of
believing that he has gone to receive his reward, and that his memory will ever
be fresh in the minds of his brethren. But it is unnecessary for me to speak his
praise, or to enlarge upon the excellencies of his character. I would, however,
recommend some suitable expression of our feelings of respect and affection for
his memory.

Before closing this report, permit me, Patriarchs, to tender my grateful
acknowledgments to the members of this Grand Encampment, for the distinguished honor conferred on me by elevating me to this Chair, and for their kindness and courtesy since I have been an Officer of this Grand Body. It was not
without distrust of my abilities that I entered upon my duties; but knowing that .
I should be surrounded by Brothers who would look with indulgence upon my
imperfections, and that the mantle of charity would be thrown around me, I
assumed the responsibilities incident to the high and important station of Grand
Patriarch, with the full confidence that my short comings would not be visited
upon me. In laying aside the badges of Office, I shall not cease in my devotion
to the principles and requirements of our Order, and while life lasts, hope ever
to be found discharging the duties of a good Odd Fellow.

Patriarchs:—That all the business of this session may be conducted in the
spirit of brotherly love, and that, whether here or in our subordinates, there may
be no strife, but that noble emulation of who shall most advance and best extend
the principles and objects of our beloved Order, is my sincere hope and desire.

Respectfully submitted in F., H. and C.

SAMUEL H. HARRIS, *Grand Patriarch.*

NEW HAVEN, February 15, 1859.

The Grand Patriarch's report was accepted and referred to a
special Committee, consisting of Patriarchs E. G. Storer of
No. 1, G. L. Townsend of No. 20, and E. D. Ritton of No. 5.

The Grand Representative submitted the following report,
which was accepted and referred to the same Committee:

To the R. W. Grand Encampment, I. O. O. F. of Connecticut:

Your representative to the R. W. Grand Lodge of the United States, would respectfully report that he attended the session of that Grand Body held in Baltimore, September 20, 1858. The attendance was very large, there being Representatives from thirty-nine Grand Lodges and seventeen Grand Encampments,
two new Grand Lodges having been chartered since the last session, viz: Kansas and Nebraska. On the second day of the session the following officers were
elected for the term of two years:

M. W. Grand Sire, Samuel Craighead, of Ohio.
R. W. Deputy Grand Sire, E. H. Fitzhugh, of Virginia.
R. W. Grand Recording and Corresponding Secretary, J. L. Ridgely, of Mary-
land.
R. W. Grand Treasurer, Joshua Vansant, of Maryland.

The following, from the report of the Grand Secretary, shows the condition of
the Order.

No. of Lodges........................ 3,390
No. of members...................... 176,700
Amount of revenue................... $1,223,685
Amount paid for charitable purposes....... 440,259

I am sorry to say that there is a gradual decrease of Lodges and members in
the older jurisdictions, but it is made up in the rapid increase of the West.

The several Grand Bodies were authorized to confer upon their subordinates
the right to install their officers in public, provided that the ceremony is per-

formed by one or more of the Elective Grand Officers of such Grand Body—and provided that they use the form prescribed by the Grand Lodge of the United States.

Your attention is called to the report of the Committee on a Grand Celebration to be held in New York on the 26th day of April, 1859. Also, to the following resolution offered by Representative M'Auley:

Resolved, That the several Grand Bodies be requested to express their opinions, at the next annual session, as to what change, if any, it is desirable to make in the representation to, or meeting of the Grand Lodge.

Several amendments to the Constitution were laid over to the next session, most of them having reference to change of representation or mergement.

Respectfully submitted in F., H. and C.,

C. C. JACKSON.

The Committee to whom was referred the Grand Patriarch's report, submitted the following, which was accepted:

To the R. W. Grand Encampment I. O. O. F. of Connecticut:

The Committee to whom was referred the report of the Grand Patriarch, would respectfully report, that they have attended to their duty, and would recommend that so much of said report as relates to the condition of the subordinate Encampments in this jurisdiction be referred to the Committee on the State of the Order. That so much as relates to the indebtedness of the Grand Encampment be referred to the Committee on Finance. That so much as relates to the mergement, be referred to the Grand Representative. That so much as relates to the decease of Past Grand Patriarch Wallace, be referred to a special Committee of three.

Respectfully submitted,

E. G. STORER,
G. L. TOWNSEND, } *Committee.*
E. D. RITTON.

The Grand Patriarch appointed the following Committee on so much of his report as relates to the decease of Past Grand Patriarch Wallace—Patriarchs E. G. Storer of No. 1, Chas. A. Newell of No. 6, and M. B. Scott of No. 1.

The Committee on the State of the Order submitted the following report, which was accepted:

To the R. W. Grand Encampment, I. O. O. F. of Connecticut:

The Committee on the State of the Order respectfully beg leave to submit the following report:

Reports have been received for the term ending July 1st, 1858, from Nos. 1, 2, 6, 20, correct; No. 18 lacks signature of Chief Patriarch and seal. For the term ending January 1st, 1859, reports have been received from Nos. 1, 2, 5, and 6, correct; No. 18 lacks seal and signature of Chief Patriarch; Nos. 20 and 21 lack seal.

No reports have been received from the other Encampments.

Respectfully submitted in F., H. and C.,

O. UTLEY,
G. L. TOWNSEND, } *Committee.*
GEO. CRABTREE,

The Grand Encampment then proceeded to the nomination of officers for the ensuing year, when the following nominations were made:

For Grand Patriarch, Patriarchs J. G. Hayden and S. Tolles.

For Grand High Priest, Patriarchs Thomas Wallace, Jr. and M. B. Scott.

For Grand Senior Warden, Patriarchs T. C. Hollis and Chas. A. Newell.

For Grand Scribe, Patriarch L. A. Thomas.

For Grand Treasurer, Patriarch S. Bishop.

For Grand Junior Warden, Patriarch M. B. Scott.

Before proceeding to ballot, the following Patriarchs declined being candidates, viz:

J. G. Hayden for Grand Patriarch, M. B. Scott for Grand High Priest, and Chas. A. Newell for Grand Senior Warden.

On balloting, the following Grand Officers were elected for the year ensuing:

Samuel Tolles, Grand Patriarch.

Thomas Wallace, Jr., Grand High Priest.

Thomas C. Hollis, Grand Senior Warden.

Lucius A. Thomas, Grand Scribe.

Samuel Bishop, Grand Treasurer.

M. B. Scott, Grand Junior Warden.

The Committee on Finance submitted the following report, which was accepted and the resolution adopted:

To the R. W. Grand Encampment, I. O. O. F. of Connecticut:

The Committee on Finance, to whom was referred so much of the Grand Patriarch's report as refers to the finances of this Grand Body, have attended to their duty and beg leave to report, that as the Grand Scribe is authorized to levy on the several subordinates of this jurisdiction for such sum as may be necessary to meet the current expenses of this Grand Body, your Committee would respectfully recommend the adoption of the following resolution.

Respectfully submitted in F., H. and C.,

E. G. STORER, ⎫
O. UTLEY, ⎬ *Committee.*
M. B. SCOTT, ⎭

Resolved, That this Grand Body earnestly appeal to the several subordinates to meet promptly any call the Grand Scribe may make upon them for aid to defray the expenses of this Grand Body.

The Committee thereon submitted the following report, which was accepted and the resolution adopted:

To the R. W. Grand Encampment, I. O. O. F. of Connecticut:

The Committee to whom was referred the report of the Grand Representative respectfully report, that they have examined the same, and would recommend it for its brevity and good sense, and would also recommend to the Grand Encampment to adopt the following resolutions.

Respectfully submitted,

E. G. STORER, ⎫
G. L. TOWNSEND, ⎬ *Committee.*

Resolved, That in the opinion of this Grand Encampment some change should be made by the Grand Lodge of the United States, whereby its expenses may be reduced, and that biennial sessions is the most feasible and most likely to accomplish the object, and has the approval of this Grand Body.

Resolved, That in the opinion of this Grand Encampment public installations of officers would be injudicious and inexpedient in this jurisdiction at the present time.

The following report of the Committee on Finance was accepted:

To the R. W. Grand Encampment, I. O. O. F. of Connecticut:

The Committee on Finance having examined the accounts of the Treasurer find them correct, and that there remains in his hands $4.05 to be carried to new account.

O. UTLEY,
E. G. STORER, } *Committee.*
M. B. SCOTT,

The special Committee thereon submitted the following report, which was accepted and the resolutions adopted:

To the R. W. Grand Encampment, I. O. O. F. of Connecticut:

The Committee appointed to consider that portion of the Grand Patriarch's address which relates to the decease of Past Grand Patriarch and Grand Representative John Wallace, which occurred soon after the close of the last session of this Body, having attended to that duty, respectfully report:

That the melancholy event which has called into exercise the duties devolving upon your Committee, is one which has deeply and sadly affected the whole brotherhood in Connecticut. By this dispensation of Divine Providence, we are called to mourn the loss of one of the brightest ornaments and most substantial pillars of Odd Fellowship, not only in this jurisdiction but in the whole country. To say that he was highly esteemed and beloved as a citizen, a neighbor, and a Christian, is but to reiterate the expression of the whole community in which he lived.

Your Committee offer the following resolutions.

Respectfully submitted,

E. G. STORER,
C. A. NEWELL, } *Committee.*
M. B. SCOTT,

Resolved, That in the death of Past Grand Patriarch John Wallace, this Grand Encampment has sustained a loss which would seem irreparable, and which calls upon us to bow with humility to the will of our Heavenly Parent.

Resolved, That we extend to the family of our deceased friend the sympathy and condolence of this Grand Encampment.

On motion, it was ordered that a copy of the report and resolutions be sent to the widow of Brother Wallace.

The Grand Officers were then installed in ample form by Grand Patriarch Harris.

The following resolution was unanimously adopted:

Resolved, That the thanks of this Grand Encampment be and hereby are presented to Past Grand Patriarch S. H. Harris, for the able and faithful manner in which he has discharged the duties of his office.

The Grand Encampment then adjourned *sine die,* and was closed in ample form.

Attest,

LUCIUS A. THOMAS, *Grand Scribe.*

PROCEEDINGS

OF THE

R. W. GRAND ENCAMPMENT, I. O. O. F.

OF THE

STATE OF CONNECTICUT.

ANNUAL SESSION, 1860.

NEW HAVEN, Feb 14, 1860.

The R. W. Grand Encampment, I. O. O. F. of Connecticut, convened in Annual Session, in accordance with the Constitution.

PRESENT:

M. W. SAMUEL TOLLES, *Grand Patriarch,*
M. E. A. G. SHEARS, *Grand High Priest, p. t.*
R. W. E. G. STORER. *Grand Senior Warden, p. t.*
R. W. LUCIUS A. THOMAS, *Grand Scribe,*
R. W. SAMUEL BISHOP, *Grand Treasurer,*
R. W. M B. SCOTT, *Grand Junior Warden,*
W. G. L. TOWNSEND, *Grand Sentinel, p. t.*

and a delegation from six subordinate Encampments.

The Grand Encampment was opened in ample form, with the usual ceremonies.

The Grand Patriarch appointed the following Committees:

Committee on the State of the Order—Patriarchs O. Utley of No. 6, G. W. Benedict of No. 20, and R. R. Wood of No. 18.

Committee on Finance—Patriarchs James Phelps of No. 2, W. H. Stanley of No. 1, and C. C. Jackson of No. 18.

Committee on Credentials—Patriarchs W. E. Sanford of No. 1, G. W. Benedict of No. 20, and J. E. Bidwell of No. 6.

The Committee on Credentials submitted the following report, which was accepted:

To the R. W. Grand Encampment, I. O. O. F. of Connecticut :

The Committee on Credentials, having examined the certificates of members, find the following Patriarchs entitled to seats :

From *Sassacus*, No. 1—E. G. Storer, M. B. Scott, A. G. Shears, D. Botsford, D. E. Burwell, Lucius A. Thomas, Wm. H. Stanley, N. Chandler, S. Bishop, W. E. Sanford, W. W. White, J. R. Taylor.

Oriental, No. 2—James Phelps.

Sowheag, No. 6—O. Utley, J. E. Bidwell, J. Avery, C. A. Newell, S. B. Wetmore, Isaac Batten.

Excelsior, No. 18—C. C. Jackson, R. R. Wood.

Ansantawae, No. 20—G. W. Benedict, G. L. Townsend.

Hebron, No. 21—O. C. White, J. G. Page, L. J. Hendee.

Respectfully submitted,

W. E. SANFORD, ⎞
G. W. BENEDICT, ⎬ *Committee.*
J. E. BIDWELL, ⎠

The following Patriarchs were then admitted and instructed in the Grand Encampment degree :

No. 1, W. W. White, J. R. Taylor ; No. 6, Isaac Batten ; No. 21, L. J. Hendee.

The minutes of last session were then read and approved. The Grand Patriarch submitted his annual report :

To the R. W. Grand Encampment I. O. O. F. of Connecticut :

PATRIARCHS—In meeting together at this time to legislate for the Patriarchal branch of our Order, it is incumbent on me to report to you my official acts, as also to give such information as I may possess relative to the standing and condition of the Order under this jurisdiction.

During the time that I have had the honor to fill the office of Grand Patriarch of this Grand Encampment, I believe that no one can take exceptions to my official duties, from the fact that there has been none to perform.

As regards the condition of the several subordinates, I am compelled to refer you to the report of the R. W. Grand Scribe, he being the only officer that is cognizant of their doings. The fact that the proceedings of this Grand Encampment have not been published for the past several years, has placed me in rather an unpleasant position ; as the main source in which to gather statistics and general information, which every officer, and more particularly the Grand Patriarch, should possess. Such being the case, I have been compelled to leave all business at the discretion of the Grand Scribe, who I believe has worked faithfully, without fee or reward, to bolster up and sustain this Grand Body.

Some two years ago a resolution was passed to publish the back proceedings of this Grand Encampment, but I am informed by the Grand Scribe that the finances of the Grand Encampment have never allowed him to carry into effect said resolution. I would here suggest that should it be deemed advisable to keep up our State organization that some means should be devised to carry the resolution into effect.

Immediately after the adjournment of the Grand Lodge of the United States I received the following resolutions from the Grand Corresponding Secretary, directing me to promulgate the same to the several subordinates in this jurisdiction :

" *Resolved,* That all State Grand Officers, and officers of all subordinate Lodges and Encampments, are prohibited from signing any diploma, certificate, or card not issued by the authority of this R. W. Grand Body, to Brothers of the Order, and properly authenticated by the R. W. Grand Corresponding Secretary, written or engraved on the margin thereof.

" *Resolved.* That all diplomas, certificates, or cards, not issued by the authority of this R. W. Grand Body, which have been signed by any officer of a Grand or subordinate Body, are of no force or effect, and the same are null and void.

" *Resolved,* That the R. W. Grand Corresponding Secretary be requested to forward a copy of the foregoing resolutions to all State Grand Masters and Grand Patriarchs, immediately on the adjournment of this Grand Lodge, directing them to promulgate to their respective subordinates, the action of this Grand Lodge in relation to signing diplomas."

I take this occasion to tender my thanks to the Patriarchs for their uniform courtesy and kindness to me, while an Officer of this Grand Body—and in vacating the honorable post which their suffrages assigned me, I pledge myself to coöperate with them in anything which may add to the interest and advancement of the Patriarchal branch of our Order.

SAMUEL TOLLES, Grand Patriarch.

The Grand Patriarch's report was submitted to a special Committee, consisting of Patriarchs E. G. Storer of No. 1, C. A. Newell of No. 6, and C. C. Jackson of No. 18.

The Committee on Finance submitted the following report, which was accepted:

To the R. W. Grand Encampment, I. O. O. F. of Connecticut:

The Committee on Finance having examined the accounts of the R. W. Grand Treasurer, find them correct, and that there is in his hands a balance of $57.93 to be carried to new account.

Fraternally submitted,

JAMES PHELPS, ⎫
C. C. JACKSON, ⎬ Committee.
W. H. STANLEY, ⎭

. The Committee on the State of the Order submitted the following report, which was accepted and the resolution adopted:

To the R. W. Grand Encampment, I. O. O. F. of Connecticut:

The Committee on the State of the Order, having examined into the condition of the subordinates under this jurisdiction, beg leave to submit the following resolution.

Respectfully submitted,

O. UTLEY, ⎫
G. W. BENEDICT, ⎬ Committee.
C. C. JACKSON, ⎭

Resolved, That the various subordinate Encampments in this State be recommended to use greater efforts to increase their membership, and thereby restore the Grand Encampment to its former prosperous condition.

The Committee thereon submitted the following report, which was accepted:

To the R. W. Grand Encampment, I. O. O. F. of Connecticut:

The Committee to whom was referred the report of the Grand Patriarch, beg leave to report that they have examined the same, and are happy to be able to agree with the Grand Patriarch that no exceptions can be taken to his official acts during the term for which he was elected.

With regard to his suggestion that " *if it shall be deemed advisable to keep up our State organization,*" the proceedings should be printed, your Committee have been convinced that the contingency cannot be likely to occur. We therefore recommend that the resolution passed by this body some two years ago on the subject of printing the proceedings, be carried into effect whenever the necessary funds are on hand for that purpose.

Respectfully submitted,

E. G. STORER,
C. A. NEWELL, } *Committee.*
C. C. JACKSON,

The Grand Encampment proceeded to the nomination of officers for the year ensuing, when the following nominations were made:

For Grand Patriarch, T. C. Hollis of No. 1.

For Grand High Priest, M. B. Scott and A. G. Shears of No. 1.

For Grand Senior Warden, G. L. Townsend of No. 20 and J. E. Bidwell of No. 6.

For Grand Scribe, L. A. Thomas of No. 1.

For Grand Treasurer, S. Bishop of No. 1.

For Grand Junior Warden, D. Botsford of No. 1 and Isaac Batten of No. 6.

For Grand Representative, O. Utley of No. 6, S. H. Harris of No. 1, and Thomas Wallace, Jr., of No. 18.

On balloting, the following officers were elected:

T. C. Hollis, Grand Patriarch.

M. B. Scott, Grand High Priest.

G. L. Townsend, Grand Senior Warden.

L. A. Thomas, Grand Scribe.

S. Bishop, Grand Treasurer.

D. Botsford, Grand Junior Warden.

S. H. Harris, Grand Representative.

The Grand Patriarch elect not being present, Past Grand Patriarch Tolles was authorized to hold a special session of the Grand Encampment for the purpose of installing him.

Past Grand Patriarch Utley then presented the other officers elect, and they were installed in ample form by Grand Patriarch Tolles.

The following resolution was adopted:

Resolved, That the thanks of the Grand Encampment are hereby presented to Past Grand Patriarch Tolles, for the faithful manner in which he has discharged the duties of Grand Patriarch

The bill of Patriarch Charles Bradley, for services as Outside Sentinel, was presented and ordered paid.

No other business appearing, the Grand Encampment adjourned *sine die,* and was closed in ample form.

Attest,

LUCIUS A. THOMAS, *Grand Scribe.*

PROCEEDINGS

OF THE

R. W. GRAND ENCAMPMENT, I. O. O. F.

OF THE

STATE OF CONNECTICUT.

―――•••―――

ANNUAL SESSION, 1861.

NEW HAVEN, Feb. 19, 1861.

The R. W. Grand Encampment, I. O. O. F. of Connecticut, convened this day in Annual Session.

PRESENT:

M. W. T. C. HOLLIS, *Grand Patriarch,*
M. E. M. B. SCOTT, *Grand High Priest,*
R. W. G. L. TOWNSEND, *Grand Senior Warden,*
R. W. LUCIUS A. THOMAS, *Grand Scribe,*
R. W. S. BISHOP, *Grand Treasurer,*
R. W. C. L. SAGE, *Grand Junior Warden,*
W. S. CLEETON, *Grand Sentinel,*

and members from a quorum of Encampments.

The Grand High Priest addressed the Throne of Grace, when the Grand Encampment was opened in ample form. .

The Grand Patriarch appointed the following Committees:

Committee on Credentials—Patriarchs S. H. Harris, N. Chandler, George Crabtree.

Committee on Finance—Patriarchs S. Tolles, Charles W. Nott, J. W. Smith.

Committee on the State of the Order—Patriarchs E. S. Clark, Wm. Umberfield, C. L. Sage.

The Committee on Credentials submitted the following report, which was accepted:

To the R. W. Grand Encampment, I. O. O. F. of Connecticut:

The Committee on Credentials respectfully report, that they find the certificates of the following named Patriarchs correct, and that they are entitled to seats in the Grand Encampment:

Sassacus, No. 1—L. A. Thomas, M. B. Scott, Noah Chandler, S. H. Harris, C. L. Sage, Sam'l Cleeton, D. E. Burwell, S. T. Scott, George Crabtree, S. Tolles, T. C. Hollis, S. B. Gorham, S. Bishop, Ed. Perkins, C. W. Nott, A. G. Shears.

Ansantawac, No. 20.—E. S. Clark, J. W. Smith, Wm. Umberfield, George L. Townsend.

Respectfully submitted,

S. H. HARRIS,
N. CHANDLER, } *Committee.*
GEO. CRABTREE,

The following named candidates were then introduced, and instructed in the Grand Encampment degree, viz:

No. 1, Ed. Perkins, Charles W. Nott; No. 20, E. S. Clark, J. W. Smith, Wm. Umberfield.

The minutes of the last session were then read and approved.

The Grand Patriarch made a verbal report of his official acts, and referred with much feeling to the loss which the Order had sustained in the death of our Grand Junior Warden, David Botsford.

On motion, the Grand Patriarch's report was accepted and so much thereof as relates to the death of Grand Junior Warden Botsford, was referred to a special Committee, consisting of Patriarchs D. E. Burwell, S. T. Scott, and S. Cleeton.

Grand Representative Harris submitted his report, which was accepted and referred to the Committee appointed on the Grand Patriarch's report.

To the R. W. Grand Encampment, I. O. O. F. of Connecticut:

The undersigned, your Representative in the R. W. Grand Lodge of the United States, having attended the last session of that Grand Body, which convened in the city of Nashville, Tennessee, on the 17th of September last, respectfully submits the following as a synopsis of the most important proceedings of the session.

The R. W. Grand Lodge was temporarily organized in the Hall of the Odd Fellows of Nashville, on Monday, September 17th, the R. W. Deputy Grand Sire, EDWARD H. FITZHUGH, presiding, the Grand Sire being prevented from attendance by "circumstances of a public and private nature." All the other Grand Officers were present, and Representatives from twenty-three Grand Lodges and eighteen Grand Encampments. On taking the Chair the Deputy Grand Sire addressed the Grand Lodge in an able and graceful manner, announcing the absence of Grand Sire CRAIGHEAD, and that by the requirements of the Constitution the duty of filling his high place devolved upon him. He congratulated the members "that the great Senate of Odd Fellowship had met once more with unbroken ranks, the representatives of a united and prosperous brotherhood;" and he trusted that nothing would occur to disturb the harmony of the session, and "that under the smiles of an approving Providence our deliberations will result in advancing the common good of our Order."

The credentials of the new members were then received, referred to the appropriate Committee, and the Representatives present participated in the deliberations.

The large number in attendance at this session of the Grand Lodge—every jurisdiction except Oregon, I believe, being represented—speaks well for our beloved Order, and exhibits the deep interest felt throughout our extended jurisdiction for the advancement and welfare of an institution that has done so much to relieve the calamities and distresses of human life, and promote the elevation and happiness of mankind.

After the temporary organization, the Grand Lodge was put under charge of the Grand Marshal, and proceeded in a body, under an escort from a Committee of Arrangements and brethren from Nashville, to the State Capitol, and entered the Hall of the House of Representatives, the galleries of which were already crowded with ladies and gentlemen.

The Representatives and brethren of the Order being seated, the Grand Chaplain offered a prayer, when P. Grand E. D. Hancock, of Tennessee, was introduced, and on behalf of the Order in Nashville, addressed the Grand Lodge in an able and interesting manner. The remarks of Past Grand Hancock found a response, I doubt not, in the heart of every Odd Fellow present, as they were certainly appropriate to the occasion, and worthy of the distinguished brother.

After the address of P. G. Hancock, brother S. N. Hollingworth, Mayor of the City of Nashville, on behalf of that City, welcomed the Grand Lodge to Nashville, and cordially tendered the hospitalities of the City to its members.

The acting Grand Sire, Edward H. Fitzhugh, of Virginia, responded to the address of brother Hancock and the welcome of the Mayor in a most felicitous and appropriate manner—an address which would do credit to the most exalted patriot and statesman, as well as the most talented among our Order, and was a sufficient evidence that the confidence reposed in that worthy brother by the Grand Lodge in elevating him to the important and dignified station of Deputy Grand Sire, was well bestowed, and placed him high in the esteem of those who, for the first time, listened to his words.

The ceremony of reception being concluded, a benediction was pronounced by the Grand Chaplain, when the audience retired and the Grand Lodge proceeded to business.

The reports of the M. W. Grand Sire and the R. W. Grand Corresponding and Recording Secretary were read, the report of the Grand Sire giving the gratifying fact that the Order was generally in a prosperous condition, and that "the past year had exhibited a steady and healthy increase in numbers, resources and influence," and that "amid the convulsions and distractions which at times have disturbed our political systems, and while other organizations have been rent asunder, and still greater disasters were apprehended, our Order remained unimpaired and unthreatened."

The report of the Grand Corresponding and Recording Secretary is, as is usual with the reports of that Officer, an able and interesting document, giving a view of the operations of our Order during the past year, and showing that there is "abundant cause for gratitude to Almighty God for the continued favor which he has vouchsafed to our institution, not less signally displayed by the great prosperity which crowns our ministrations in behalf of humanity, than in the profound spirit of peace and harmony which characterizes the internal government of the Order in all its details, and hallows the relation of brotherhood which binds us together."

For a more full synopsis of the reports of the M. W. Grand Sire and R. W. Grand Corresponding and Recording Secretary, I would refer the Representatives to the printed proceedings of the Grand Lodge of the United States, now in possession of the Grand Encampment.

On Tuesday the Grand Lodge proceeded to the business of electing officers for the ensuing term, which resulted as follows:

P. G. Robert B. Boylston, of South Carolina, was elected Grand Sire, having received forty-seven votes, P. G. M. Edward H. Fitzhugh, of Virginia, receiving forty-six votes.

P. G. M. Milton Herndon, of Indiana, was elected Deputy Grand Sire, having received forty-three votes, Grand Marshal Isaac M. Tucker, of New Jersey, receiving forty-one votes.

The Grand Corresponding and Recording Secretary, and the Grand Treasurer, were unanimously reëlected to those offices.

The Grand Lodge resolved itself into a Committee of the Whole, Grand Representative Dwinelle, of Northern New York, in the Chair, to consider the proposed amendments to the Constitution, offered by P. G. Sire Kennedy, of Southern New York, last session, to the effect that no Grand Body shall have more than one Grand Representative in the Grand Lodge of the United States, at the same time, unless said Grand Body assume the payment of the *per diem* and mileage of an additional Grand Representative.

Also, that a Grand Lodge or Grand Encampment, who has more than one thousand members within its jurisdiction, shall be entitled to *two* votes in the Grand Lodge, and if less than one thousand members but *one* vote; but that no Grand Body shall have more than *one* Grand Representative at the same time.

Also the proposed amendment to the Constitution offered by Rep. Thayer, of South Carolina, that the Grand Lodge shall only hold biennial sessions.

After spending some hours in the consideration of these proposed amendments to the Constitution, the Committee rose. The acting Grand Sire having resumed the Chair, the Chairman of the Committee reported to the Grand Lodge that the Committee of the Whole recommended to the Grand Lodge the adoption of the first amendment proposed by Rep. Kennedy, and that they report back the others without action.

The report was accepted, and the amendments coming before the Grand Lodge for adoption, they were severally rejected by a decided vote.

The proposed amendment to the Constitution offered by Rep. Earl, of Ohio, that the Grand Lodge and Grand Encampment of any jurisdiction may be merged into one body, was indefinitely postponed.

All the other proposed amendments to the Constitution were also indefinitely postponed.

Your Grand Representative was constrained to vote against all of the proposed amendments, not doubting that he was conforming to the will of this Right Worthy Body.

On Wednesday the Grand Lodge in a body paid their respects to Mrs. JAMES K. POLK, widow of President POLK, whose remains lie entombed on the grounds of her mansion. This occasion was a source of much pleasure to all who had the happiness to be present, and one long to be remembered. On returning to the Hall it was

"*Resolved unanimously*, That this Grand Lodge hereby express the great pleasure derived from our visit to Mrs. James K. Polk, and tender to that estimable lady our unfeigned thanks for her very elegant and courteous reception."

On behalf of Mrs. Polk, Rep. Walker, of Tennessee, returned her sincere thanks to the members of the Grand Lodge, for what she was pleased to consider the distinguished honor paid her by them in their visit to her mansion, and assured the Grand Lodge that she will cherish the recollection of the event as one of the pleasantest and most agreeable of her life.

The Grand Lodge received and accepted an invitation from a Committee of Arrangements from the Order in Nashville, to participate in an excursion to the "Hermitage" and tomb of ANDREW JACKSON, and to partake of a collation which was to be provided on the grounds.

On Thursday, the members of the Grand Lodge availed themselves of the privilege so kindly extended to them by the brothers of Nashville, and proceeded in carriages, with a large number of the Order of Nashville and a band of music, to the home and grave of the beloved and honored patriot and hero, Gen. Jackson.

After spending some time in examining the grounds, the brethren partook of a bountiful entertainment, prepared under the direction of the Order in Nashville. After the dinner, a hickory arm chair, made of withs grown upon the "Hermitage" estate, was presented to the Grand Lodge by Dr. John M. Lawrence, the present custodian of the property belonging to the "Hermitage." The presentation was made in a neat speech from Rep. Walker, of Tennessee, to which the acting Grand Sire feelingly and appropriately responded.

This visit to the place where the illustrious soldier and patriot so long made his home; and spent so many happy years of his life, and where his ashes, as well as those of his beloved companion and kindred, repose, will long be remembered by the undersigned, as one of the most pleasant and hallowed events of his life.

The Grand Lodge held an evening session on Thursday, when the following resolution was adopted:—

" *Resolved,* That a Committee of ——— be appointed to report to the next session of this Body a revision of the secret work of the Order, having in view the various suggestions to that effect submitted to this Grand Lodge at this and previous sessions."

The M. W. Grand Sire appointed as the Committee on the above resolution, P. G. M. Frederick D. Stuart, of the District of Columbia; P. G. M. John W. Dwinelle, of Northern New York; and P. G. M. James B. Nicholson, of Pennsylvania.

Frequent revision of the secret work of our Order has by many been deemed injurious to our progress, while there has always been a large number who have believed that the work could be improved and made more interesting and profitable, and the many petitions which have been before the Grand Lodge for material changes, has at last induced that Grand Body to adopt the above resolution. The brothers appointed on the Committee are well qualified for their task, and they will probably present, as the result of their labors, at the next session of the Grand Lodge, something worthy of the high character they have attained for their intelligence and zeal for the Order.

I would recommend to the Grand Encampment some expression of their opinion on this subject.

Article ten of the By-Laws of the Grand Lodge was amended by adding thereto as follows:

" And in default of such returns being made and the dues thereon paid within ten days prior to the annual meeting of this Body, the Representatives from such delinquent Grand Lodges or Grand Encampments shall not be admitted to a seat in such annual meeting."

I would specially call the attention of the Grand Encampment to this important alteration of the By-Laws of the Grand Lodge. It will be seen from it that the Scribes of the several Encampments should be prompt in making their returns to the Grand Scribe, so that that officer can forward his report and dues to the Grand Corresponding and Recording Secretary in time to prevent your Grand Representative from being deprived of his seat in the Grand Lodge of the United States.

If this Grand Encampment has not sufficient law on the subject, I would recommend the adoption of some provision whereby Scribes shall make their returns within two months after each stated term.

A form of dedication of an Odd Fellows' Hall or Lodge Room and also a ceremony to be observed in laying corner stones, were adopted, which can be found in the printed proceedings of the Grand Lodge.

A large number of amendments to the Constitution was laid on the table, some of which are in the precise words of those rejected at this session. These amendments can be found in the printed proceedings of the Grand Lodge, and I would ask the attention of the Grand Encampment to the same, and some expression of their opinion relative to their adoption or rejection, that your Grand Representative, when he comes to vote on them, may not misrepresent your sentiments.

The following resolutions were unanimously adopted:—

" *Resolved,* That the thanks of this Grand Lodge are due and they are hereby tendered to R. W. Deputy Grand Sire Fitzhugh, for the very able, courteous, dignified and impartial manner in which he has discharged the unusually arduous duties of Grand Sire, during the present term.

" *Resolved,* That in consideration of these services, and of the services heretofore rendered this Grand Lodge, in all the departments of duty which he has been called upon to discharge and fill, the Grand Lodge recognize a debt of obligation which they propose in part to discharge by tendering this acknowledgment, and the additional request that he consent to sit for his portrait to embellish our Grand Lodge, and that an engraved likeness be made, to be inserted in the bound Journal, and that the Grand Secretary have the same carried into effect."

The business of the session having been concluded, the R. W. Grand Chaplain addressed the Throne of Grace, and the Grand Lodge was adjourned *sine die.*

Before closing this report—already too long—permit me to return to the officers and members of the Grand Encampment my thanks for electing me their Representative. I am under greater obligations, as when this honor was conferred I was not present, being prevented from attending the last session of the Grand Encampment by a severe domestic affliction. For your uniform kindness and confidence, I shall ever feel grateful, and pledge in return renewed devotion to the cause of Odd Fellowship.

SAMUEL H. HARRIS.

NEW HAVEN, Feb. 19, 1861.

The accounts of the Grand Secretary and Grand Treasurer were referred to the Committee on Finance.

The Committee to whom was referred the Grand Patriarch's report, submitted the following, which was accepted and the resolutions adopted:

To the R. W. Grand Encampment, I. O. O. F. of Connecticut:

We, your Committee to whom was referred so much of the Grand Patriarch's report as refers to the death of our late worthy brother, Patriarch David Botsford, respectfully report, that they have attended to their duty, and submit the following resolutions:

WHEREAS, It has pleased our all-wise Grand Patriarch to remove our worthy brother Patriarch David Botsford, Grand Junior Warden, from among us, in the prime of manhood and in the midst of usefulness in the community, exemplifying the all-wise teaching, that "in the midst of life we are in death;" therefore,

Resolved, That in the death of Patriarch Botsford the Order have lost a strong pillar, the brotherhood a faithful and untiring laborer, from whom the sick and the needy were never sent empty away.

Resolved, That while we mourn his loss we bow with reverence to the inscrutable ways of Providence, and humbly trust that in a higher and better world he reaps the reward of a good and faithful servant.

Resolved, That we tender to his bereaved family our sorrowing condolence in this their deep affliction, and commending them to the special aid and comfort of the brothers with whom he dwelt, we invoke the divine aid, support and guidance of Him who tempers the wind to the shorn lamb, and suffers not a sparrow to fall to the ground without His permission.

D. E BURWELL,
S. T. SCOTT, } Committee.
SAMUEL CLEETON,

The Committee to whom was referred the report of the Grand Representative, submitted the following, which was accepted and the resolutions adopted:

To the R. W. Grand Encampment, I. O. O. F. of. Connecticut:

We, your Committee, to whom was referred the able and interesting report of the R. W. Grand Representative, would report that they have attended to their duties, and would recommend to this Grand Body the passage of the following resolutions:

Resolved, That it is the duty of every member of this Grand Body to bring to the notice of his respective subordinate Encampment the unwarrantable and unnecessary delay of the Scribes of the several Encampments in making their returns to the Grand Scribe, and use their efforts to effect a change in the matter.

Resolved, That our Representative to the R. W. Grand Lodge of the United States be instructed to vote against all the Constitutional amendments offered at the last session of the Grand Lodge, except the one offered by Representative Hinkle of Kentucky, to change the day of meeting from Monday to Thursday.

D. E. BURWELL, }
S. T. SCOTT, } *Committee.*
SAM'L CLEETON, }

The Committee on Finance submitted the following report, which was accepted:

To the R. W. Grand Encampment, I. O. O. F. of Connecticut:

The Committee on Finance having examined the accounts of the R. W. Grand Treasurer and the R. W. Grand Scribe. find them correct, and that there remains in the hands of the R. W. Grand Treasurer a balance of $27.63 to be carried to new account.

Fraternally submitted,

SAMUEL TOLLES, }
CHAS. W. NOTT, } *Committee.*
J. W. SMITH, }

The Committee on the State of the Order submitted the following report, which was accepted:

To the R. W. Grand Encampment, I. O. O. F. of Connecticut:

The undersigned, Committee on the State of the Order, respectfully report— that from reports in the hands of the Grand Scribe, we arrive at the following information:

Present number of members as reported....   241

Funds on hand.......................$3,085.93

The above embrace reports from the following Encampments, viz: Nos. 1, 2, 6, 18, 20, and 21.

All of which is respectfully submitted,

E. S. CLARK, }
WM. UMBERFIELD, } *Committee.*
C. L. SAGE, }

The Grand Encampment proceeded to nomination and election, when the following officers were elected for the year ensuing:

M. B. Scott, Grand Patriarch.

G. L. Townsend, Grand High Priest.

J. W. Smith, Grand Senior Warden.

L. A. Thomas, Grand Scribe.

S. Bishop, Grand Treasurer.

C. L. Sage, Grand Junior Warden.

The Grand officers elect were then installed into their respective offices in ample form.

The Grand Patriarch appointed Patriarch Wm. Umberfield of No. 20, W. Grand Sentinel.

The following bills were accepted and ordered paid :

```
Grand Lodge of United States..............$75.00
Chas. Bradley, Outside Sentinel............  3.00
Wm. H. Stanley.........................  3.50
```

The following resolution was unanimously adopted :

Resolved, That the thanks of this Grand Encampment are hereby tendered to Past Grand Patriarch T. C. Hollis, and his associate officers, for the faithful manner in which they have performed their duties for the past year.

Grand Representative Harris then instructed the members in the work of the Encampment.

No further business appearing, the Grand Encampment was closed in ample form.

Attest,

LUCIUS A. THOMAS, *Grand Scribe.*

PROCEEDINGS

OF THE

R. W. GRAND ENCAMPMENT, I. O. O. F.

OF THE

STATE OF CONNECTICUT.

ANNUAL SESSION, 1862.

NEW HAVEN, Feb. 19, 1862.

The R. W. Grand Encampment, I. O. O. F. of Connecticut, convened this day in Annual Session, at 2 o'clock P. M.

PRESENT:

M. W. M. B. SCOTT, *Grand Patriarch,*
M. E. G. L. TOWNSEND, *Grand High Priest,*
R. W. J. W. SMITH, *Grand Senior Warden,*
R. W. LUCIUS A. THOMAS, *Grand Scribe,*
R. W. S. BISHOP, *Grand Treasurer,*
R. W. S. H. HARRIS, *Grand Representative,*
W. S. CLEETON, *Grand Sentinel, p. t.*

and a quorum of members of Encampments.

The Grand High Priest addressed the Throne of Grace, and the Grand Encampment was opened in ample form.

The Grand Patriarch appointed the following Committees:

Committee on Credentials—Patriarchs D. E. Burwell of No. 1, G. W. Benedict of No. 20, D. W. Boyd of No. 18.

Committee on Finance—Patriarchs C. W. Nott of No. 1, D. W. Boyd of No. 18, E. S. Clark of No. 20.

Committee on the State of the Order—Patriarchs S. H. Harris, E. G. Storer and Noah Chandler of No. 1.

The Committee on Credentials submitted the following report:

To the R. W. Grand Encampment, I. O. O. F. of Connecticut :

The Committee on Credentials respectfully report, that they have examined the certificates presented and find the following Patriarchs entitled to seats in the Grand Encampment, viz:

From *Sassacus*, No. 1—S. H. Harris, L. A. Thomas, W. H. Stanley, E. G. Storer, S. B. Gorham, S. Tolles, T. C. Hollis, D. E. Burwell, F. Botsford, C. W. Nott, J. R. Taylor, Noah Chandler, S. Bishop.

Sowheag, No. 6—O. Utley.

Excelsior, No. 18—D. W. Boyd, J. H. Barlow.

Ansantawae, No. 20—E. S. Clark, W. Umberfield, G. W. Benedict, G. L. Townsend, J. W. Smith.

D. E. BURWELL, ⎫
G. W. BENEDICT, ⎬ *Committee.*
D. W. BOYD,   ⎭

P. C. P. J. H. Barlow of No. 18, was then presented and instructed in the Grand Encampment degree.

On motion, the Rules of Order were amended by changing the order of the 5th and 6th sections of Article 1, so that the reading of the minutes shall be deferred until after the admission of candidates.

The Grand Patriarch submitted the following report, which was accepted and referred to a special Committee, consisting of Patriarchs O. Utley of No. 6, John H. Barlow of No. 18, Wm. H. Stanley of No 1.

To the R. W. Grand Encampment. I. O. O. F. of Connecticut :

OFFICERS AND PATRIARCHS:—Another year has passed away, and notwithstanding the many changes that have taken place since we last met by the favor of the Supreme Grand Patriarch of the Universe, we have again met beneath the shelter of the Grand Encampment's Tent to review the past, and from its lessons endeavor to learn wisdom for the future.

It has been customary for Grand Patriarchs upon retiring from office to make a report to this Right Worthy Grand Body of their official proceedings. This will be for me an easy duty, from the fact that my official doings have been very limited.

Shortly after the adjournment of this Grand Body at its last Annual Session, I made out and forwarded to the several Patriarchs, hereafter named, their commissions as Deputy Grand Patriarchs, viz Wm. Gorton of No. 2, J. E. Bidwell of No. 6, C. C. Jackson of No. 18, G. L. Townsend of No. 20, Albert Brown of No. 21,—these being the only Encampments who made their returns to this Grand Body at its last Annual Session, with the exception of Sassacus Encampment, No. 1, of which I am a member. I also wrote to the Encampment at Norwalk, inquiring into its condition, but received no reply.

In the month of June, I received an invitation from Ansantawae Encampment, No. 20, at Waterbury, to make them an official visit. Accordingly, at their first regular meeting in July, accompanied by Grand Junior Warden C. L. Sage, Grand Representative S. H. Harris, and by Grand Master Burwell, and several Patriarchs from No. 1, I made them an official visit and installed their officers. I found that Encampment in excellent working condition, and learned from its members that they were making additions to their numbers, and before leaving I fully realized that while Ansantawae Encampment, No. 20, is supported by as true Patriarchs as I met within their tents that evening, it must and will continue to flourish. And here let me improve the occasion to say, that for their unbounded hospitality, the kind and courteous treatment extended to us on that occasion, the Patriarchs of that Encampment will ever be held in grateful remembrance.

About the 11th of August, I received a letter from Grand Patriarch J. C. Smith of Illinois, stating that in the then existing state of the country he doubted the propriety of having the National Grand Lodge hold its Annual Session, and requesting me to write him my views on the subject, at the same time stating that he had directed the Grand Scribe of Illinois to withhold the dues of that Grand Body until he could communicate with Grand Patriarchs of the loyal States. I immediately communicated with Grand Scribe Thomas in reference to the matter, and was invited to attend a meeting of the Executive Council to be held August 23d, to consider the same matter. I was present at that meeting, and after due deliberation it was decided, that in our opinion, the majority of the loyal States agreeing, it was not advisable for the National Grand Lodge to hold its session, and it was decided to issue a circular to the several Grand Masters and Grand Patriarchs of the loyal States, to ascertain their views. A circular was accordingly issued by Grand Scribe and Secretary Thomas, which, being responded to, it was found that a large majority were in favor of a session. Another meeting of the Executive Council was called September 2d, at which I was present, as also your Grand Representative Harris, and finding that there would be a session of the National Grand Lodge, another circular was issued, (which is herewith submitted,) stating that our Representative would be present and our dues forwarded according to law.

A session of the National Grand Lodge was held, and for the proceedings of which I refer you to the Report of your Right Worthy Grand Representative Harris.

Upon the first Friday evening in January, I was present and installed the officers of Sassacus Encampment, No. 1.

The first week of the present month I addressed a letter to each of the Deputy Grand Patriarchs, reminding them to forward me their commissions and reports at the proper time ; also urging them to be present and endeavor to secure a good representation from their Encampments, at this session of this Grand Body. At the present writing I have received but two reports, one from D. G. Patriarch J. E. Bidwell of No. 6, and one from D. G. Patriarch Townsend of No. 20.

I think it would be of great benefit to this branch of our Order, if the Deputy Grand Patriarchs were required not only to report their official doings, but that semi-annually, or at least annually, they be required to report to the Grand Patriarch the state of the Order in their jurisdiction.

While it has been a year of general health in this jurisdiction, having lost but few of our members by death, it becomes my painful duty to announce to this Right Worthy Grand Encampment, that the founder of our beloved Order in this country, the Patriarch whom all loved and reverenced, Past Grand Sire Wildey, is no more.

Upon the 19th of October, 1861, in the city of Baltimore, the city where he organized the first Lodge of Odd Fellows in this country, the man who for forty-two years has labored for the prosperity of our beloved Order, was called from his labors here to rest in the Grand Encampment above. He died as he had lived, a true and faithful Odd Fellow.

In reference to the financial condition of this Grand Body, also for a recommendation for the necessary legislation on that subject, I beg leave to refer you to the report of our R. W. G. Scribe.

All of which is respectfully submitted in F., H. and C.,

M. B. SCOTT, *Grand Patriarch.*

Grand Representative Harris submitted the following report, which was accepted and referred to the Committee on the Grand Patriarch's report.

To the R. W. Grand Encampment, I. O. O. F. of Connecticut :

The undersigned, your Representative in the Grand Lodge of the United States, having attended the last session of that R. W. Grand Body, which convened in the city of Baltimore September last, and which continued in session four days, respectfully submits the following report:

The Grand Lodge assembled on Monday, September 16th, at 9 o'clock A. M. In the absence of the M. W. Grand Sire, R B. Boylston, of South Carolina, the chair was taken by the R. W. Deputy Grand Sire, Milton Herndon, of Indiana, and the Grand Lodge called to order. On calling the roll of officers and members, there were but fifteen Grand Lodges and seven Grand Encampments represented. A quorum not being present, by authority of the Constitution, the acting Grand Sire appointed a Committee on Credentials, who received and examined the credentials of the new Representatives, and on reporting it was found there were Representatives from a sufficient number of jurisdictions to proceed to business. No Representatives were present from the jurisdictions of Vermont, Kansas, Nebraska, South Carolina, North Carolina, Virginia, Louisiana, Alabama, Tennessee, Georgia, Mississippi, Texas, Florida, and Arkansas.

The acting Grand Sire then made a short but appropriate address, and with the sanction of the Grand Lodge appointed P. G. M. Frederick D. Stuart, of the District of Columbia, R. W. Deputy Grand Sire *pro tem.*, and P. G. M. W. H. H. Prall, of Northern New York, R. W Grand Marshal *pro tem.*

The Representatives were duly examined and declared qualified, and the business of the session commenced.

The report of the R. W. Grand Corresponding and Recording Secretary, as usual, is marked by his well known ability and careful elaboration. It shows that the duties devolving upon him for the past year have been faithfully performed, as far as possible. From this report we learn, that as far as reports had been received by the Grand Secretary, the Order is steadily progressing in usefulness, if not in numbers, and that "in view of the general prostration of all the monetary and business interests of the country, the Grand Lodge was in a much more gratifying condition of finance than could reasonably have been expected."

The deficiency in the receipts of the Grand Lodge, it was thought by the Grand Corresponding and Recording Secretary, could only be "overcome by a magnanimous act of personal sacrifice on the part of the Representatives themselves." In this opinion the Committee on Finance, it will be perceived, coincided, on making their report, with the addition, that said Committee recommended a reduction of the salaries of those Grand Officers who receive compensation for their services. Accordingly, the mileage of the Representatives was reduced from five to four cents per mile, the salary of the Grand Secretary from $1,200 to $1,000, and that of the Grand Messenger from $700 to $500. This reduction met the deficiency, and left the treasury in a better condition than for several years past.

On the morning of the second day of the session, Grand Secretary Ridgely sent a note to acting Grand Sire Herndon, saying that he felt himself wholly incapable of performing the duties of Grand Secretary, and asked him to appoint somebody in his place. The Grand Sire appointed *our* Grand Scribe, Representative L. A. Thomas, Grand Secretary *pro tem.* As the illness of brother Ridgely continued, he did not make his appearance again during this session, and Representative Thomas continued to discharge the arduous duties of that office till the adjournment. I need not say that Representative Thomas performed those duties with credit to himself and to the satisfaction of the Grand Lodge. While I could not but regret that I was deprived of the counsel and advice of my friend and colleague, I felt gratified with the honor conferred on him.

A number of appeals were decided at this session of the Grand Lodge; none, however, affecting this branch of the Order, but the following, viz.: "That the suspension by a Lodge for a definite period does not work absolute suspension in an Encampment, but operates only as a suspension dependent upon or during the period for which he may be held in suspension in his Lodge. During that suspension he has not the right to visit an Encampment or participate in its benefits; yet, if he should contiue to pay his dues during the period of his suspension, his restoration in his Lodge reinstates him in his Encampment, if the Encampment has failed to take cognizance of whatever misdemeanor may have been committed, and rests upon the action and punishment which may have been inflicted by the Lodge."

The amendment to the By-Laws of the Grand Lodge, requiring returns of Grand Bodies to be made "*within* ten days prior to the annual meeting of the Grand Lodge," and in default thereof Representatives should be deprived of their seats, passed at the session of 1860, was repealed, leaving the law to stand as formerly.

Copies of the digest of the Laws of the Order in Pennsylvania, were presented, on behalf of the Grand Lodge of Pennsylvania, to the Grand Lodge and the Bodies therein represented, and a vote of thanks passed for the same. This digest of the Laws of the Order in Pennsylvania, which is herewith presented, will be found a valuable compilation, and may prove useful to the business of this Grand Encampment.

The Committee on the Revision of the Work of the Order reported in secret session, that owing to several causes—one of the Committee being in California— they had not had a meeting, and of course could not make a final report. They had, however, in the performance of their duties, subdivided their labors as follows: To Rep. Stuart was assigned the Encampment work; to Rep. Dwinelle the Degrees; and to Rep. Nicholson the Initiatory work. Each of the Committee presented his views and intentions in relation to the special matter submitted to him, from which I am led to believe, as well as from the known ability of the Committee—no more competent Committee, I think, could have been selected— that when they have finished their labors, which will probably be at the next annual meeting of the Grand Lodge, the work of the Order will be so revised, amended and improved, that it will not only be a credit to themselves, but will be received with thankfulness and gratitude by every good Odd Fellow.

There being so large a number of jurisdictions unrepresented, a general conviction seemed to prevail, that no change or modification should be made in the organic laws of the Order; therefore no amendments to the Constitution of the Grand Lodge were adopted—all of those proposed at the last session being either indefinitely postponed or laid over to the next session.

Several new amendments to the Constitution were proposed, which I cannot transcribe here—as it would make this report too long—but to which I would refer you, in the printed proceedings now on your desks.

The only exciting question which arose during our deliberations, was, whether the next annual session of the Grand Lodge should be held in some other place than in the city of Baltimore. It was contended by some of the Representatives that Baltimore *might* be an unsafe place for the meeting of the Grand Lodge, and therefore such a contingency should be provided for. Your Representative had faith to believe that the unhappy dissensions and distractions which then and now encompass our whole country, will be happily settled before the time arrives for the next annual session of the Grand Lodge; or, if by that time peace and quietness do not again prevail over our once happy and glorious country, that Maryland will continue to remain loyal to the Government; and being unwilling to give cause of complaint or offense between the present and absent, voted against the various propositions for a change of place of meeting, not doubting by so doing I would meet with your approval.

All the exertions and eloquence of many of the most able members of the Grand Lodge—and there are in that Grand Body gentlemen whose ability and eloquence are not surpassed by those of any deliberative assembly of our country —having been ineffectual to secure the proposed change of place of meeting of the Grand Lodge—the last proposition, however, being defeated by a single vote, and that too by one Representative changing his vote from *yea* to *nay*—the following resolutions were unanimously adopted:—

"*Resolved*, That should circumstances justify the Grand Secretary, and if in his opinion the safety and security of the archives and books of the Grand Lodge may require it, he be authorized to remove the same to Philadelphia or New York.

"*Resolved*, That in the event of a probable interruption of the meeting of this Body in Baltimore, in 1862, the R. W. Deputy, (now acting Grand Sire,) Milton Herndon, be authorized to convene the Grand Lodge at some central and convenient place, sufficient notice to be given to the different jurisdictions."

The Committee on Finance, in their report, estimated the expenditure of the Grand Lodge, for the current year, at $12,070.12, and the revenue at $16,886.24 —thus exceeding the expenditure $4,816.12.

It is the opinion of your Representative that this estimate of receipts will be found to be far too great, and the expenditures of the fiscal year will, under the present state of our monetary affairs, equal, if not exceed, the actual receipts.

The Committee on Grand Bodies not Represented, in their report, expressed deep regret at the absence of Representatives from Grand Bodies not represented, and "believed that it was occasioned from necessity rather than choice;" that the "Grand Sire, who possesses, in an eminent degree, the esteem and affection of all Representatives who have been honored with his acquaintance, is only prevented from attending this session of the Grand Lodge by circumstances over which he has no control, and that the same reasons actuate a majority of other Representatives who are absent."

The Committee "entertained the hope, that by another session of the Grand Lodge all cause for their continued absence will be forever removed, and that their vacant seats will be again occupied, filling that void which all who have attended this session have sensibly felt, and making all hearts glad at so happy a reunion."

These sentiments met the unanimous response of the Grand Lodge. It could not have been otherwise with those Representatives who were present at the previous session. Many of the absent brothers were among the most distinguished members of the Order, and all who had the pleasure to meet them in Nashville, could not but regret that any circumstances should have occurred to prevent extending to them a fraternal greeting, and once more coöperate with them in legislating for the welfare of an Order which all of the absent seemed so much to have at heart.

Representative Escavaille, of Maryland, offered, and the Grand Lodge adopted, a preamble and series of resolutions, which will most probably meet the approval of all the members of the Order, and to which this Grand Encampment is respectfully referred. They will be found on pages 3373 and 3374 of the printed proceedings of the Grand Lodge.

The following resolution was unanimously adopted:—

"*Resolved*, That the thanks of the Grand Representatives be, and are hereby extended to the brethren of Baltimore, for the renewed acts of kindness and hospitality which the Representatives have received at their hands."

This was no unmeaning compliment, as all who have attended the sessions of that R. W. Grand Body in Baltimore, have reason to know. The courtesy and hospitality the brethren of Baltimore have heretofore extended to the members of the Grand Lodge, were on this occasion manifested, and the Representatives must ever bear fresh in their memory this pleasant incident of the last session.

There were present during this session of the Grand Lodge, Past Grand Sires THOMAS WILDEY and JOHN A. KENNEDY.

When Past Grand Sire WILDEY entered the Hall and took a seat, many of the Representatives gathered around him, anxious once more to grasp the hand and listen to the voice of the venerable Founder of our Order in America. As he recounted to the eager listeners the trials, vexations, and perplexities which he and his little band of noble men encountered before Odd Fellowship in this country was established on what might be considered a sure foundation, his voice trembled and he was much affected; but when he alluded to any of their successful undertakings, his eyes brightened and his countenance lightened up as with unwonted joy. But it was evident that the hand of age was pressing heavily upon the beloved and honored Patriarch; that soon we should see his form no more on earth. Little, however, did we think that in one short month the lightning would flash over our country that THOMAS WILDEY was dead! Such, alas! was the case, for on the 19th of October, surrounded by those he loved, he suddenly yielded up his life, and now sleeps in peace. Our sorrow for the loss of this beloved and worthy brother is indeed great; but it is not sorrow over one cut down in his prime, or in the midst of his days of usefulness:—he has been borne to his grave "as a shock of corn fully ripe." His burdens had been all borne—his trusts all discharged—his work was done! And *that* work, how noble, how glorious it was! When first begun, how little could he have anticipated its importance! How little could he have known that from the seed which he was then planting, would spring forth a tree, whose branches would overspread a whole continent, and under whose shade a whole nation would rejoice; that from golden California, from distant Oregon, from the islands of the Pacific, from wherever there is a brother to speak a word of comfort to the broken-hearted, to the widow or the fatherless—there *his* name will ever be held in grateful remembrance!—Brother—Patriarch—Sage—farewell!

From this imperfect synopsis of the business and acts of the last session of the Grand Lodge, it will be seen that nothing was done but what was "calculated to preserve our Order intact, wherever its benign influence had shed, wherever the banner of Odd Fellowship has been unfurled."

If there was ever a time since our banner was unfolded, when the sacred principles of our Order—Charity and Brotherly Love—should prevail, it is now;—now, when civil war, with all its attendant evils, exists in our once happy and united country—causing brother to lift his hand against brother, father against son, and son against father! Oh, may this internecine contention soon end! "May strife and discord be soon banished" from our land; may "the sword be turned into plowshares, and the spear into pruning hooks," and "the hearts of the people of this once peaceful and happy land" be gladdened by a "cloudless sky, a bright and genial sunshine, shedding peace, harmony, and joy over and throughout this widespread land!"

But while we deplore the present attitude of our nation, and pray that the God of Battles will protect the right, let us recollect what our Order teaches, and hope that now, more than ever before, Odd Fellowship will be a controlling influence in the land. Here, then, let *us* renew our vows of Friendship, Love and Truth, Faith, Hope and Charity, and extend the hand of forgiveness and brotherly love to the erring.

Before closing this, my last official communication, permit me again to return my thanks to the members of this Grand Encampment for the honors they have conferred, and the indulgence they have shown me. I am now, as ever, ready to unite and coöperate with them in anything which will extend the benign principles and objects of Odd Fellowship.

Respectfully submitted, in F., H. and C.,

SAMUEL H. HARRIS,
Grand Representative.

NEW HAVEN, Feb. 18, 1862.

The Committee thereon submitted the following report, which was accepted:

To the R. W. Grand Encampment, I. O. O. F. of Connecticut:

The Committee to whom was referred the reports of the M. W. Grand Patriarch and the R. W. Grand Representative would recommend that so much of the former as relates to the reports of the Deputy Grand Patrtarchs, be referred to a special Committee; that so much of both reports as relates to the death of Past Grand Sire Thomas Wildey, be also referred to a special Committee.

All of which is respectfully submitted,

O. UTLEY,
J. II. BARLOW,   } *Committee.*
WM. II. STANLEY,

The Grand Patriarch appointed the following Committees:

On so much of the Grand Patriarch's report as relates to Deputy Grand Patriarchs, Patriarchs S. B. Gorham of No. 1, E. S. Clark of No. 18, W. II. Stanley of No. 1.

On so much of the Grand Patriarch's and Grand Representative's reports as relates to the death of Past Grand Sire Wildey, Patriarchs G. L. Townsend of No. 18, E. G. Storer and S. Tolles of No. 1.

The Grand Encampment then proceeded to the nomination and election of officers, when the following nominations were made:

For Grand Patriarch, G. L. Townsend.
For Grand High Priest, J. W. Smith, O. Utley.
For Grand Senior Warden, F. Botsford.
For Grand Scribe, L. A. Thomas.
For Grand Treasurer, S. Bishop.
For Grand Junior Warden, D. W. Boyd.
For Grand Representative, T. C. Hollis, M. B. Scott.

Patriarch O. Utley declined the nomination for Grand High Priest.

On balloting, the following officers were elected for the year ensuing:

G. L. Townsend, Grand Patriarch.
J. W. Smith, Grand High Priest.
F. Botsford, Grand Senior Warden.
L. A. Thomas, Grand Scribe.
S. Bishop, Grand Treasurer.
D. W. Boyd, Grand Junior Warden.
M. B. Scott, Grand Representative.

The Committee on so much of the Grand Patriarch's and Grand Representative's reports as relate to the death of Past Grand Sire Wildey, submitted the following report, which was accepted:

To the R. W. Grand Encampment, I. O. O. F. of Connecticut:

The Committee to whom was referred so much of the reports of the Grand Patriarch and Grand Representative as refer to the death of Past Grand Sire Wildey, beg leave to submit the following resolutions.

Respectfully submitted in F., H. and C.,

G. L. TOWNSEND,
E. G. STORER,   } *Committee.*
SAM'L. TOLLES,

Resolved, That this Grand Encampment have learned with deep regret of the decease of our esteemed brother, Past Grand Sire Thomas Wildey, founder of the Order in this country, who departed this life in the city of Baltimore on the 19th of October last.

Resolved, That in the death of this venerable Pariarch our Order has lost an illustrious and highly cherished member—one whom we have long learned to venerate for his early and self-denying labor in behalf of Odd Fellowship and whose memory will ever be cherished by us and all true Odd Fellows in all time to come.

Resolved, That these resolutions be spread upon the minutes, and that the Grand Scribe be instructed to forward a copy to the family of the deceased.

The Committee on Finance submitted the following report, which was accepted:

To the R. W. Grand Encampment, I. O. O. F. of Connecticut:

We, your Committee appointed to examine the finances of this Grand Encampment, would respectfully report, that they have attended to the duties of the same, and would report as follows:

Amount of balance of last report... ....$27.63
Receipts from Encampments........................ 46.00

Total.................$73.63

The expenditures were as follows:
For Grand Encampment United States.......$75.00
" Printing............................ 1.25
" Outside Sentinel..................... 3.00—$79.25

Leaving a deficit of............. $5.62

To meet this indebtedness the Committee would recommend that the Grand Scribe increase the amount of assessments on the subordinates sufficient to meet the demand.

CHAS. W. NOTT,
D. W. BOYD, } *Committee.*
E. S. CLARK,

The Committee on so much of the Grand Patriarch's report as relates to Deputy Grand Patriarchs, submitted the following report, which was accepted and the resolution adopted.

To the R. W. Grand Encampment, I. O. O. F. of Connecticut:

The Committee to whom was referred so much of the Grand Patriarch's report as refers to the official returns of the Deputy Grand Patriarchs, have had the same under consideration, and would submit the following resolution.

All of which is respectfully submitted,

SAM'L. B. GORHAM,
W. H. STANLEY, } *Committee.*
E. S. CLARK,

Resolved, That the Deputy Grand Patriarchs be required to send to the Grand Patriarchs semi-annually a report of the state of the Order in their respective jurisdictions.

The Committee on the State of the Order submitted the following report, which was accepted:

To the R. W. Grand Encampment, I. O. O. F. of Connecticut:

The Committee on the State of the Order respectfully report, that they have examined the returns of Sassacus Encampment, No. 1, and find them correct; of Oriental, No. 2, which are correct, with exception of seal being pasted on; that no report has been received from Sowheag, No. 6, for the term ending July; and that the report of said Encampment for January, 1862, is correct, except it is without seal; that no report for July term of Excelsior Encampment, No. 18, has been received, and that the report of said Encampment for January, 1862, is correct, except it is without seal; that the reports from Ansantawae, No. 20, are correct, except that no seal is on the January report; that the reports from Hebron Encampment, No. 21, are correct, except that they are without seal.

The Committee find that there are 235 members reported; that six have been initiated; that five have been suspended, one has withdrawn, and one has died.

The amount of funds reported is $3,304.

Respectfully submitted,

S. H. HARRIS, }
N. CHANDLER, } *Committee.*
E. G. STORER, }

The Grand Officers elect were then installed into their respective offices in ample form.

The following resolutions were unanimously adopted:

Resolved, That the thanks of this Grand Encampment are due, and are hereby tendered to Past Grand Patriarch Merritt B. Scott, for the able and faithful manner in which he has discharged the duties of Grand Patriarch for the past year.

Resolved, That the thanks of this Grand Encampment be tendered to Quinnipiac and Harmony Lodges, for the gratuitous use of their Hall for the sessions of this R. W. Grand Body.

Representative Boyd announced the death of Past Chief Patriarch Calvin L. Russell, who fell at the battle of Roanoke Island. The subject was referred to a special Committee, consisting of Patriarchs D. W. Boyd of No. 18, E. S. Clark of No. 20, S. B. Gorham of No. 1.

The Committee submitted the following report, which was accepted and the resolutions adopted:

To the R. W. Grand Encampment, I. O. O. F. of Connecticut:

Your Committee to whom was referred the death of Patriarch C. L. Russell, respectfully beg leave to report:

That this Grand Encampment heard with deep regret the fall of Patriarch C. L. Russell, while gallantly leading the 10th Connecticut Volunteers onward at the battle of Roanoake Island.

Resolved, That this Grand Encampment extend to the widow and family our heartfelt sympathies in this sad event, and invoke the blessing of the Grand Patriarch above, "who doeth all things well," to rest his blessing on the widow and fatherless.

Resolved, That these resolutions be spread on the minutes of this Grand Encampment, and a copy be forwarded to the family, attested by the Grand Scribe.

Respectfully submitted,

D. W. BOYD, } *Committee.*
E. S. CLARK, }

Patriarch Harris then exemplified the work of the Order. The Grand Encampment was then closed in ample form.

Attest,

LUCIUS A. THOMAS, *Grand Scribe.*

34

PROCEEDINGS

OF THE

R. W. GRAND ENCAMPMENT, I. O. O. F.

OF THE

STATE OF CONNECTICUT.

ANNUAL SESSION, 1863.

New Haven, Feb. 17, 1863.

The R. W. Grand Encampment, I. O. O. F. of the State of Connecticut, convened this day in Annual Session.

PRESENT:

M. W. G. L. TOWNSEND, *Grand Patriarch,*
M. E. J. W. SMITH, *Grand High Priest,*
R. W. F. BOTSFORD, *Grand Senior Warden,*
R. W. L. A. THOMAS, *Grand Scribe,*
R. W. DAVID W. BOYD, *Grand Junior Warden,*
R. W. M. B. SCOTT, *Grand Representative,*

and Representatives from Nos. 1, 6, 18, 20.

The Grand High Priest addressed the Throne of Grace, and the Grand Encampment was opened in ample form.

The Grand Patriarch appointed as a Committee on Credentials, Patriarchs W. W. White and C. W. Nott of No. 1, and D. W. Boyd of No. 18.

The Committee on Credentials submitted the following report, which was accepted:

To the R. W. Grand Encampment, I. O. O. F. of Connecticut:

The Committee on Credentials respectfully report that they find the certificates of the following named Patriarchs correct, and that they are entitled to seats in the Grand Encampment.

Sausacus, No. 1—Samuel Cleeton, Noah Chandler, A. W. Phelps, L. A. Thomas, M. B. Scott, Samuel H. Harris, J. W. Hammond, John A. Hughes, Wm. W. White, Charles W. Nott, W. H. Stanley, Alonzo G. Shears, G. Crabtree, D. E. Burwell, F. Botsford, J. R. Taylor.

Excelsior, No. 18—John H. Barlow, David W. Boyd.

Ansantawae, No. 20—John W. Smith, George L. Townsend.

Souheag, No. 6—C. A. Newell, Origen Utley.

All which is respectfully submitted,

W. W. WHITE, ⎫
C. W. NOTT, ⎬ *Committee.*
D. W. BOYD, ⎭

Patriarchs J. W. Hammond and J. A. Hughes of No. 1, were then admitted and instructed in the Grand Encampment degree.

The Grand Patriarch appointed the following Committees :

Committee on the State of the Order—Patriarchs D. E. Burwell and George Crabtree of No. 1, and O. Utley of No. 6.

Committee on Finance—Patriarchs W. H. Stanley and Noah Chandler of No. 1, and C. A. Newell of No. 6.

The Grand Patriarch submitted his report, which was referred to a special Committee, consisting of Patriarchs S. H. Harris and M. B. Scott of No. 1, and O. Utley of No. 6.

To the R. W. Grand Encampment, I. O. O. F. of Connecticut :

OFFICERS AND REPRESENTATIVES:—Time, in his rapid flight, has completed another annual round, and in accordance with the provisions of our Constitution, we are again assembled in annual session.

Let us, before entering upon the important duties which are to engage our attention, pause a moment, to return our grateful thanks to the Grand Master of the Universe, through whose watchful Providence we have been spared to enjoy this reunion, and to invoke His blessing upon us while we legislate for the best interests of our beloved Order; "and may all our acts, begun, continued and ended in Him, redound to His glory, and the happiness of mankind."

As I look around this circle of Patriarchs, and recognize so many familiar faces, I search in vain for some, who in the years that are past have participated in our proceedings, zealous in every good word and work. Some are absent in the service of their country, foremost where duty calls. When next assembled in annual council, may we not hope to give them once more the fraternal grip and friendly greeting; and may the time soon come when

> "No more shall nation against nation rise,
> Nor ardent warriors meet with hateful eyes,
> Nor fields with gleaming steel be covered o'er,
> The brazen trumpets kindle rage no more ;
> But useless lances into scythes shall bend,
> And the broad falchion in a ploughshare end ;
> No sigh, no murmur, the wide world shall hear,
> From every face be wiped off every tear ;
> Peace o'er the world her olive wand extend,
> And white-rob'd innocence from heaven descend."

But there are those whom we have been wont to greet at our annual sessions, who will meet with us no more through all the future years. Death, who sunders the strongest and holiest of ties without remorse, has removed them from our councils. I trust I shall be pardoned for particular reference to two deceased members, of whom, from my intimate acquaintance with them, I am able to speak understandingly, and who, from their prominent position in the Order, are deserving of more than a passing notice. I refer to Grand Master Clark and Past Grand Master Benedict, both members of the Encampment and Lodge to which I belong.

In the death of these lamented brothers, our Encampment and the Order throughout the State have sustained a loss of no ordinary character. Among the original members of the Lodge and Encampment to which they were attached, for many years they had labored side by side for the advancement of the principles of Odd Fellowship, had been looked up to for counsel and relied upon for aid, had unsought, received from the subordinate and Grand Lodge, the highest honors in their gift, and had been faithful in the discharge of every trust. Both had been called to occupy the most honorable positions in the town and city governments, and had been selected by their fellow-citizens to represent them in the State Legislature. Both were present at the last meeting of the Grand Lodge and Grand Encampment,—both, we trust, are now enjoying the society of the Patriarchs of old, in that better land, whither, let us hope, our steps are tending.

Brethren, let us emulate their zeal in every good word and work, let us imitate their virtues, let us cherish their memory; so, when, like them, we shall be summoned, in the midst of our pilgrimage, to fold our tents and cross the swelling waters, we may decry with the eye of faith, beyond the tide, the promised inheritance, that "rest which remaineth for the people of God."

The record of my official acts will necessarily be brief, as but few subjects have demanded my attention.

Immediately after the adjournment of the R. W. Grand Encampment, I forwarded commissions to those brothers who had been recommended by the several subordinate Encampments for the office of Deputy Grand Patriarch. With one exception,—Deputy Grand Patriarch J. E. Bidwell, of No. 6,—I have received no report of their official doings, and am consequently unable to give any statistical information as to the condition of the patriarchal branch of the Order in this jurisdiction. For particulars as to the condition of the Encampments working under authority of this Grand Body, I must refer you to the report of our R. W. Grand Scribe.

It can hardly be expected that during the continuance of the unhappy troubles which now afflict our nation and overshadow every other interest, much progress can be made. I trust that we shall make no retrograde movement, and that when peace shall have again returned to our borders it will find our great brotherhood knit together more strongly than ever, ready to take the field with renewed vigor, and to march forth to conquests more glorious than those achieved by hostile cannon and bristling steel.

In September last I signed the credentials of Past Grand Patriarch M. B. Scott, of No. 1, who, at the last session, was elected as your Grand Representative to the Grand Lodge of the United States. The annual session was held in the city of Baltimore, commencing on the 15th day of September, Representatives being present from nearly every jurisdiction throughout the loyal States. I was gratified in looking over the daily journal, for which I am indebted to the courtesy of Grand Representative Scott, to notice the harmony which characterized the proceedings, and the fraternal spirit which marked the discussion of the various topics engaging the attention of the Grand Lodge. For the legislative doings of that Grand Body, I refer you to the report of your R. W. Grand Representative.

On the 4th of January, I received an invitation from Sassacus Encampment, No. 1, of New Haven, to be present at their next regular meeting, and install their officers. I immediately replied, accepting the invitation, and looked forward with much pleasure to the anticipated visit until the day previous to the time assigned, but was at last prevented from attending by unforeseen business engagements. The duties of Grand Patriarch were, however, ably performed by Grand High Priest Smith, and I was not surprised to learn through him that this, the oldest and largest Encampment in the State, numbering as it does so many zealous and influential members, is in a flourishing condition.

Near the close of January, I received a communication from brother Julius Attwood of Middlesex Lodge, No. 3, representing that Oriental Encampment, No. 2, now located at Essex, had for some time past been in a drooping condition and that its removal to its former location in East Haddam would build up the Encampment and advance the interests of the Order in that locality. He also stated that from conversation with members of the Encampment he was satisfied there would be no opposition to the removal. On referring to the proceedings of the Grand Encampment, July session, 1848, I find that on petition of 12 members of Oriental Encampment, being a majority thereof, stating that a unanimous vote had been passed in the Encampment in favor of such removal, the Grand Encampment changed its location from East Haddam so Essex.

While from the facts presented by the esteemed brother, I fully concur with him in the belief that the interests of the Encampment and the Order would be greatly promoted by its restoration to its original location, in view of the near proximity of the annual session of the Grand Encampment, I preferred that the same body which removed it to its present location should decide upon the application for its restoration.. I therefore replied to the communication in accordance with the tenor of the above, recommending him to take the proper steps to bring the subject before this Grand Body at its present session.

It is now several years since the Constitution for subordinate Encampments has been printed. In the meantime, some important amendments have been made, and as no journal of the proceedings has been printed since 1852, the subordinates are frequently at a loss to know whether they are working strictly according to the laws laid down for their government. I would suggest that the R. W. Grand Scribe be authorized to revise the Constitution and cause it to be printed in connection with the proceedings of this session or separately, as may be deemed advisable.

I would also recommend this Grand Body, at its present session, to investigate the subject of dues and benefits, believing as I do, that many of the feeble Encampments would be infused with new life and receive large accessions to their numbers if the former were made as low as possible and the latter entirely done away. I would not recommend any legislation affecting those Encampments which have a large accumulated fund, but since the beneficiary system is one of the features of the subordinate Lodges, the necessity for its incorporation into the Patriarchal branch does not exist. Many Encampments which have ceased working, might have been in a sound and healthy condition to-day had they not undertaken to pay liberal benefits, rendering it necessary to impose a large initiation fee and subjecting their members to an onerous taxation to sustain the system.

The Encampment with which I am connected, Ansantawae, No. 20, was revived a few years since, after a long slumber, the initiation fee reduced to a sum within the reach of all, and the dues cut down to the amount necessary to meet current expenses—no benefits to be paid. It was then placed in good working condition, new members flocked in, and since that time it has continued to thrive, while its influence upon the subordinate Lodge has been marked and salutary.

I trust you will give this important subject due consideration.

In conclusion, permit me, brethren and Patriarchs, to thank you for the unmerited honor you have conferred upon me in elevating me to this high position, and for the uniform courtesy which has marked your intercourse with me during my official term. And I only have to regret, that while my heart has been in the work, the pressure of my business engagements has been such that in the discharge of the duties of the office I have been unable to devote the time and attention which their importance demanded.

In resigning this chair to my successor, as I am soon to do, it is pleasant to feel that there is to be no sundering of the ties which unite us as brethren, and that I shall be permitted in the future, as in the past, though in a humbler sphere, to labor with you for the advancement of our beloved Order and for the diffusion of the glorious principles upon which it is founded.

And may He, without whose aid no human enterprise can permanently prosper, so smile upon and bless our labors, that amid the jarring of nations, the overturn of governments and the mutations of time, the institution of Odd Fellowship may be preserved to bless mankind and fraternize the world; and as we shall one by one be called from the scene of our earthly labors, may our places be filled by others, who shall, if possible, be more zealous in the dissemination of its benign influences.

G. L. TOWNSEND, *Grand Patriarch.*

NEW HAVEN, Feb. 17th, 1863.

The Grand Representative submitted his report, which was accepted and referred to a Committee, consisting of Patriarchs A. G. Shears, A. W. Phelps and J. W. Hammond of No. 1.

To the R. W. Grand Encampment, I. O. O. F. of Connecticut:

The undersigned, Representative of this Grand Encampment to the Grand Lodge of the United States, respectfully begs leave to report that he attended the session of that R. W. Grand Body, held at the city of Baltimore, commencing Monday, September 15th, 1862, at 9 o'clock, A. M. On that day the Grand Lodge was called to order by Milton Herndon, Deputy Grand Sire, who addressed the Grand Lodge, referring with much feeling to the death of Past Grand Sire Wildey, the venerated founder of the Order in this country, which will be found in the Journal of the session.

There was also embodied in the Grand Sire's report his official decisions, some of which being applicable to this branch of our Order, I beg leave to present to you in a condensed form.

The first decision in reference to "good standing" in the Lodge, in order to maintain membership in the Encampment, is well known to you all, as a reiteration of all our laws on that subject.

The second decision may not have been as generally understood; it is this—that the Grand Scribe being only the Clerk of the Grand Patriarch, is bound to obey his official behest and recognize a D. D. Grand Patriarch, although he knows him to be a member of a suspended Lodge.

The third is, that the Grand Scribe must recognize all offices of subordinates officially reported to him, until the matter has been settled by the Grand Encampment.

The fourth decision is, that the Grand Scribe is bound to recognize as legal members all that are officially reported to him.

The fifth decision is, that the Grand Master or Grand Patriarch has power to suspend a Lodge or Encampment for any act of insubordination, until the meeting of the Grand Body; and further, that a Grand Body has a right to raise revenue for its legitimate purposes by assessments on its subordinates.

There were twenty-four Grand Lodges and eleven Grand Encampments represented, which exceeded the number required for a quorum, and the Grand Lodge proceeded to business.

The Chair presented the following communication :

"*To the R. W. Grand Lodge, I. O. O. F. of the United States:*

"In accordance with a resolution of the Grand Lodge of Maryland, a eulogy upon the character and services of the late P. G. Sire Thomas Wildey, will be pronounced in this city on the morning of Tuesday, the 16th inst., at 10 o'clock, precisely.

"P. G. Master James L. Ridgely of Maryland, has been elected to perform the services indicated, and the Officers and Representatives of your R. W. Grand Body, as well as the Past Officers and Past Representatives, are respectfully invited to be present on the occasion."

On motion of Rep. Hanna of Illinois, it was resolved, that the invitation tendered be accepted.

The Grand Secretary and Grand Treasurer laid their reports before the Grand Lodge. From the Grand Treasurer's report I have taken the following items: The receipts for the past year have been $9,699.56, being but $890.55 less than last year.

There has been received from the estate of P. G. Sire Wildey, $1,000.00, making total receipts, $10,699.56. Balance on hand, as per last reports, $6,679.36, making $17,378.92. Disbursements amount to $9,216.27, leaving a balance of $8,162 65.

The Grand Treasurer also stated that the whole sum due the Grand Lodge from the estate of P. G. Sire Thomas Wildey, amounting to $5,551.50, would soon be paid into the Treasury.

At 10 o'clock, A. M., Tuesday, September 16th, 1862, the Grand Lodge, escorted by the Grand Lodge of Maryland, proceeded to the Front Street Theater, and listened to the eulogy on the life and labors of Past Grand Sire Thomas Wildey, delivered by our R. W. Grand Secretary, James L. Ridgely.

Of this eulogy it is unnecessary for me to speak. It is before you, and will do itself better justice than I can.

The Grand Lodge then proceeded to the election of Officers, with the following result :—Grand Sire, James B. Nicholson of Pennsylvania; Deputy Grand Sire, Wm. H. Young of Maryland; Grand Corresponding and Recording Secretary, James L. Ridgely of Maryland; Grand Treasurer, Joshua Vansant of Maryland.

The Legislative Committee presented the following resolutions:

"*Resolved,* That all term reports which may hereafter be made to Grand Bodies by their subordinates, shall contain, in their hand writing, the signature of the elective Officers thereof, and shall be carefully preserved by the Grand Scribes and Grand Secretaries."

"*Resolved,* That Grand Scribes and Grand Secretaries are hereby prohibited from delivering or transmitting visiting or withdrawal cards to any person whatever, or to any Encampment or Lodge, excepting upon the order in writing of an Encampment or Lodge, signed by its C. P., S. W. and Scribe, (in the case of an Encampment,) or by its N. G., V. G. and Secretary, (in the case of a Lodge,) and authenticated by the official seal of the Encampment or Lodge."

Representative Barry of Indiana, offered an amendment by striking out all the signatures required in second resolution, except the Scribe of an Encampment and Secretary of a Lodge, which was agreed to, and the resolutions were adopted.

An attempt was made by the Grand Lodge of Ohio to merge the Encampment Degrees, which was decided to be inexpedient, and that grave doubts existed of the power of the Grand Lodge to deprive Grand Encampments of their charter, except for violation of laws.

The amendments to the Constitution which were laid over at the last session, were again laid over until the next.

The Committee on mileage and per diem, reported in favor of paying the members four cents per mile.

Representative Saunders of Northern New York, moved to recommit the resolution to the Committee, with orders to strike out the word four and insert five, on which the yeas and nays were ordered, and resolved in the negative,—your Representative voting nay.

The Committee to whom was referred the subject of a Monument to P. G. Sire Wildey, reported a series of resolutions, which will be found on page 3,500 of the printed Journal.

The time now having arrived for the installation of Officers, the Grand Officers were duly installed, and after an eloquent speech by our Most Worthy Grand Sire, the Grand Lodge was adjourned " sine die."

Thus closed the session of the Grand Lodge of the United States for the year 1862, a session which was harmonious throughout; a session during which all the kindly feelings of our nature were called forth, and for the kindness, hospitality and brotherly love of which your Representative was a recipient from the Odd Fellows of Baltimore, I shall ever be deeply grateful.

All of which is respectfully submitted in F., H. and C.

M. B. SCOTT, *Grand Representative.*

On motion, the hour of half past four was assigned for the election of officers.

The Committee thereon submitted the following report, which was accepted :

To the R. W. Grand Encampment, I. O. O. F. of Connecticut:

The special Committee to whom was referred the report of the Grand Patriarch for the distribution of its subjects, would respectfully recommend that so much of said report as relates to the death of P. G. Masters George W. Benedict and Edward S. Clark, be referred to a Committee of three.

That so much of said report as relates to Oriental Encampment, No. 2, be referred to a special Committee of three.

That so much of said report as relates to the printing of the proceedings of the Grand Encampment, and of the Constitution of Subordinates, be referred to a Committee of three, and that so much as relates to dues and benefits, be referred to same Committee.

Submitted in F., H. and C.

S. H. HARRIS,
O. UTLEY,   } *Committee.*
M. B. SCOTT,

The Grand Patriarch announced the following Committees:

On so much of the Grand Patriarch's report as relates to the death of Grand Master Clark and Past Grand Master Benedict, Patriarchs A. G. Shears of No. 1, O. Utley of No. 6, and D. W. Boyd of No. 18.

On so much as relates to printing the Constitution of Subordinates, &c., Patriarchs S. H. Harris of No. 1, J. W. Smith of No. 20, and W. W. White of No. 1.

On so much as relates to Oriental Encampment, Patriarchs C. W. Nott, D. E. Burwell and F. Botsford of No. 1.

The Committee on the State of the Order submitted the following report, which was accepted:

To the R. W. Grand Encampment, I. O. O. F. of Connecticut:

The Committee on the State of the Order respectfully report that they have examined the returns of Sassacus, No. 1, Oriental, No. 2, Ansantawae, No. 20, and find them correct; Hebron, No. 21, correct, except seal; Sowheag, No. 6, returns for July, 1862, correct, but no report received for January, 1863; Excelsior, No. 18, made an annual report which is correct, except seal.

The Committee find the whole number of members reported, is 213; there have been initiated, 2; suspended, 13; died, 5; the amount of funds reported is $3,181.50.

All of which is respectfully submitted in F., H. and C.

D. E. BURWELL,
O. UTLEY,   } *Committee.*
GEO. CRABTREE,

The Committee thereon submitted the following report,
which was accepted:

To the R. W. Grand Encampment, I. O. O. F. of Connecticut:

Your Committee, to whom was referred the report of the R. W. Grand Representative, beg leave to report that they find nothing therein requiring special action by this Body. The report of the R. W. Grand Representative and his doings, they commend to your approval.

Submitted in F., H. and C.

ALONZO G. SHEARS,
A. W. PHELPS, } Committee.
J. W. HAMMOND,

The hour having arrived, the Grand Encampment proceeded to the nomination of officers, when the following nominations were made:

For Grand Patriarch, G. H. P. J. W. Smith.
For Grand High Priest, G. S. W. F. Botsford.
For Grand Senior Warden, G. J. W. D. W. Boyd.
For Grand Scribe, G. S. Lucius A. Thomas.
For Grand Treasurer, Rep. S. H. Harris.
For Grand Junior Warden, Rep. John H. Barlow.

On balloting, the nominees were all unanimously elected.

The Committee thereon submitted the following report, which was accepted and the resolution adopted:

To the R. W. Grand Encampment, I. O. O. F. of Connecticut:

We, your Committee appointed on so much of the Grand Patriarch's report as relates to Oriental Encampment, No. 2, of Essex, have attended to their duty, and would report the following resolution for adoption:

Resolved, That whenever the Grand Patriarch shall have been duly notified that Oriental Encampment, No. 2, at a meeting duly warned for that purpose, shall, by a major vote, decide to remove the location of said Encampment from Essex to East Haddam, he be authorized to cause the same to be done.

CHAS. W. NOTT,
F. BOTSFORD, } Committee.
D. E. BURWELL,

The Committee thereon submitted the following report, which was accepted:

To the R. W. Grand Encampment, I. O. O. F. of Connecticut:

We, your Committee, appointed to examine the finances of this Encampment, would respectfully report, that they have attended to the duties of the same and report as follows:

The amount of receipts from Encampments have been.................$79.50
The expenditures have been as follows:
To Grand Lodge of United States,............................$75.00
" Expenses of advertising funeral of Patriarchs Botsford and Pratt, 1.75
" Charles Bradley, Outside Sentinel,.......................... 3.00
" Deficit on report of 1862,.................................. 5.62

Total,...................................... 85.87

Leaving a deficit at this time, of.......................................$5.87

We also find that the following Encampments have made no reports for the following terms: Oriental, No. 2, from January to July, 1862; Sowheag, No. 6, from July to January, 1863; Excelsior, No. 18, from January to July, 1862.

To meet this indebtedness, the Committee would recommend that the Grand Scribe increase the amount of assessments on the subordinates, sufficient to meet the demands.

W. H. STANLEY,
N. CHANDLER,	} *Committee.*
C. A. NEWELL,

The Committee thereon submitted the following report, which was accepted:

To the R. W. Grand Encampment, I. O. O. F. of Connecticut:

The Committee to whom was referred so much of the M. W. Grand Patriarch's report as relates to the subject of printing the Constitution of subordinates, and of the proceedings of this session of the Grand Encampment; and also the matter relative to the dues and benefits of subordinates, respectfully report:

That they have given the subject due consideration; and while they would cheerfully recommend that the proceedings of this session of the Grand Encampment, as well as the Constitution of subordinates, be printed, did the finances of this Grand Encampment admit, yet they can simply advise that such amendments as have heretofore been or may be made at this session to the Constitution of subordinates, be printed and forwarded to the several subordinates.

S. H. HARRIS,
WM. W. WHITE,	} *Committee.*
J. W. SMITH,

Patriarch Harris submitted the following resolution, which was adopted:

Resolved, That Article V, Section 1, of Constitution for subordinates, be amended by striking out the words " a sum not less than three dollars to," and substituting " such sum as may."

The Committee thereon submitted the following report, which was accepted and the resolution adopted:

To the R. W. Grand Encampment, I. O. O. F. of Connecticut:

Your Committee, to whom was referred so much of the report of the R. W. Grand Patriarch as relates to the death of Patriarchs George W. Benedict and Edward S. Clark, beg leave to say, they have attended to this duty. They are deeply impressed by this visitation of Providence with the great loss sustained by this Grand Encampment, by our Fraternity in this State, and by the families respectively of our deceased brothers. We recommend the passage of the following resolutions:

Resolved, That our intercourse, year after year, with these beloved brothers, has increased our estimation of their worth, and their absence from our meetings produces a void sad to our hearts.

Resolved, That while thus we mourn, we are comforted by the thought and belief that theirs is now the kingdom of heaven, and that they cease from their labors.

Resolved, That we commend the bereaved families and relatives of our deceased brothers to God our Saviour, and that a copy of this report be transmitted to them by the Grand Scribe.

Respectfully submitted in F., H. and C.,
ALONZO G. SHEARS,
ORIGEN UTLEY,	} *Committee.*
DAVID W. BOYD,

The officers elect were then installed into their respective offices in ample form.

The Grand Patriarch appointed Patriarch J. R. Taylor of No. 1, Grand Sentinel.

Grand Representative M. B. Scott exemplified the work.

The following vote was passed unanimously:

Voted, That the thanks of this Grand Encampment are due and are hereby tendered to P. G. P. George L. Townsend, for the efficient and dignified manner which he has performed the duties of his office.

On motion, the Grand Scribe was requested to print the report of the Grand Patriarch, with other documents, at his discretion.

The Grand Encampment then adjourned *sine die.*

Attest,

LUCIUS A. THOMAS, *Grand Scribe.*

PROCEEDINGS

OF THB

R. W. GRAND ENCAMPMENT, I. O. O. F.

OF THE

STATE OF CONNECTICUT.

———◆◆◆———

ANNUAL SESSION, 1864.

NEW HAVEN, Feb. 16, 1864.

The R. W. Grand Encampment, I. O. O. F. of Connecticut, convened in Annual Session.

PRESENT:

M. W. J. W. SMITH, *Grand Patriarch,*
M. E. F. BOTSFORD, *Grand High Priest,*
R. W. D. W. BOYD, *Grand Senior Warden,*
R. W. LUCIUS A. THOMAS, *Grand Scribe,*
R. W. S. H. HARRIS, *Grand Treasurer,*
R. W. J. H. BARLOW, *Grand Junior Warden,*
W. J. R. TAYLOR, *Grand Sentinel,*

and Representatives from Encampments No. 1, 2, 6, 18 and 20.

The Grand Encampment was opened with the usual ceremonies, and by order of the Grand Patriarch was declared ready to proceed to business.

The Grand Patriarch appointed as Committee on Credentials, Patriarchs W. W. White and Noah Chandler of No. 1, and Wm. Umberfield of No. 20, who submitted the following report:

To the R. W. Grand Encampment, I. O. O. F. of Connecticut:

The Committee on Credentials beg leave to report that they have examined the certificates of the following named Patriarchs, and find them correct:

Sassacus, No. 1—D. E. Burwell, S. Cleeton, F. Botsford, T. C. Hollis, J. R.

Taylor, N. Chandler, W. W. White, S. H. Harris, L. A. Thomas, A. G. Shears, J. A. Hughes, E. L. Fairchild, P. B. Bebee.
Oriental, No. 2—Julius Attwood, W. M. Smith.
Sowheag, No. 6—S. B. Wetmore, O. Utley, J. E. Bidwell.
Excelsior, No. 18—D. W. Boyd, J. H. Barlow.
Ansantawae, No. 20—J. W. Smith, G. L. Townsend, Wm. Umberfield.

All of which is respectfully submitted,

W. W. WHITE,
N. CHANDLER, } *Committee.*
WM. UMBERFIELD,

The following candidates were then admitted and instructed in the Grand Encampment degree.

P. C. P. E. L. Fairchild, and P. H. P. P. B. Beebe of No. 1; P. C. P. Julius Attwood and P. H. P. Whitby M. Smith of No. 2.

The proceedings of the last session were then read and approved.

The Grand Patriarch announced the following Committees:

Committee on the State of the Order—Patriarchs D. E. Burwell of No. 1, S. B. Wetmore of No. 6, and G. L. Townsend of No. 20.
Committee on Finance—Patriarchs J. E. Bidwell of No. 6, S. Cleeton of No. 1, and J. Attwood of No. 2.

The Grand Patriarch submitted his annual report, which was accepted and referred to a special Committee, consisting of Patriarchs A. G. Shears and W. W. White of No. 1, and O. Utley of No. 6.

To the R. W. Grand Encampment, I. O. O. F. of Connecticut:

OFFICERS AND REPRESENTATIVES:—Reassembling in this our annual communication, our first duty is to render thanks to that kind Providence who ordereth all our steps in life, and watches over us for good; for that while kindred Grand Encampments in this our once happy country are by the wiles of designing and unscrupulous men debarred the privilege of mutual councils, we are permitted to meet as usual in peace and harmony in this beautiful city, to legislate for the best interests of our beloved Order, "under our own vine and fig tree, with none to molest or make us afraid."

For the result of our labors, as far as regards work and expenses, I refer you to the reports of our R. W. Grand Scribe and R. W. Grand Treasurer.

Immediately after the last session, I forwarded commissions to each of the Patriarchs who were nominated by their respective Encampments for the office of Deputy Grand Patriarch.

I regret to be obliged to state that I have received none but verbal reports from either of them.

In accordance with a vote of this Grand Encampment, a dispensation was granted in June, allowing Oriental Encampment, No. 2, to be removed from Essex to East Haddam.

On the 14th of July, assisted by R. W. Grand Scribe Thomas, R. W. Grand Treasurer Harris, R. W. Grand Representative Bidwell, Past Grand Patriarch Townsend and Patriarch Pond of No. 1, who is the present Grand Master of the Grand Lodge of Connecticut, I instituted said Encampment in its new location in ample form, and afterwards installed the newly elected officers.

From the character, standing and devotion to Odd Fellowship of the Patriarchs in East Haddam, I shall look for favorable reports from Oriental in the future.

Much credit is due to the energetic Patriarchs of that enterprising village, for the zeal which they have shown for the Order, and I would take this opportunity to thank them for the truly princely manner in which they received and entertained the Grand Officers and visiting Patriarchs on the occasion above alluded to.

By invitation, I visited Sassacus Encampment, No. 1, on the 8th of January, and assisted by M. E. Grand High Priest Botsford, R. W. Grand Scribe Thomas, and R. W. Grand Treasurer Harris, installed their officers in ample form.

It gives me great pleasure to state that this, the oldest Encampment in this jurisdiction, within whose folds are gathered so many Patriarchs of ripe experience, enlarged views, liberal and kindly feelings towards weaker Encampments, continues its onward march with its usual enthusiasm, and with increased numbers, seemingly undisturbed by the calamity which is upon the nation, and which so seriously embarrasses and retards the progress of other and smaller Encampments.

Ansantawae Encampment, No. 20, of which I am a member, has for the past year spent much time in a thorough and careful revision of its By-Laws, which will be presented to this Grand Body for examination and approval.

This Encampment has not increased in numbers since our last session. Already more than three-fifths of the members of Nosahogan Lodge, No. 21, are connected with it, but it is on a solid basis, and I am sure that their returns will in future be satisfactory. I installed their officers in July and January, in ample form.

Our Representative tax to the Grand Lodge of the United States seems excessive, it being the same as the amount paid by the largest Grand Encampments. Would not an appeal for a reduction of this tax be advisable?

I cannot close this report without alluding in terms of praise to the Patriarchs whose seats here are empty; to those who have left their happy homes with their lives in their hands for the defense of their country. Honorable mention is made of them in several instances by their superior officers, and our Order has reason to be proud of having such noble representatives in the very front ranks of our armies. Let us hope and pray that this terrible struggle for National life may immediately end in the putting down of all traitors who would undermine the glorious Union bequeathed to us by our fathers; then can our absent Patriarchs return with honors "thick upon them," feeling that they have not labored in vain, and that as true Odd Fellows they have been faithful to their country.

May He, before whom the nations are as a drop in the bucket, soon restore to us our united country, long to remain one and indivisible.

In conclusion, Officers and Representatives, let me tender you my sincere and heartfelt thanks for the high honor conferred in elevating me to this office, and for the uniform kindness, support and attention which I have received from each and all.

J. W. SMITH, Grand Patriarch.

NEW HAVEN, February 16th, 1864.

The Grand Scribe submitted his annual report, which was accepted and referred to the Committee on Finance:

To the R. W. Grand Encampment, I. O. O. F. of Connecticut:

OFFICERS AND REPRESENTATIVES:—The small number of Encampments now existing in this State, renders the financial requirements of the Grand Encampment somewhat onerous. Our expenses, however, are trifling, except in dues to the Grand Lodge of the United States.

For several years past I have found it exceedingly difficult to meet the payment of dues to the Grand Lodge of the United States. The income has been hardly sufficient to pay that claim alone, and only one-half of it became due in time to meet the payment, and although I was authorized to draw on the Encampments for such an amount as was necessary to meet the wants of the Grand Encampment, I continued to levy 10 cts. per capita each term, until last year, when I levied 25 cts., and I was then compelled to ask Sassacus and Ansantawae Encampments to advance me the whole years' dues, which was done with great alacrity, and for which I am under special obligations.

The present number of Patriarchs reported this session is as follows, viz. Sassacus, 128 ; Oriental, 19 ; Sowheng, 13 ; Excelsior, 29 ; Ansantawae, 30— Total, 219. A per capita tax of fifty cents. on this number, will yield $109.50. The Representative tax is $75, which will leave a balance of $34.50 for incidental expenses.

I have for several years discharged the duties of Grand Scribe without compensation, and am willing still to do the same, if such an addition can be made to our finances as will enable me to print the proceedings of the Grand Encampment.

I propose, therefore, to levy a per capita tax of fifty cents on the members of each Encampment, payable in July, to enable me to meet the tax levied by the Grand Lodge of the United States. In order to print the proceedings of the Grand Encampment, I propose to levy in January a tax sufficient, in addition to any surplus on hand, to pay the cost.

The reduction of the Encampment branch of our Order has kept steady pace with that of the Lodges,—three-fourths of the Lodges have become extinct, and three-fourths of the Encampments.

We must, therefore, look forward with interest, to the increase of membership in Lodges, as the harbinger of prosperity among the Encampments.

LUCIUS A. THOMAS, *Grand Scribe.*

The amended By-Laws of Ansantawae Encampment, No. 20, were presented and referred to the Committee on the State of the Order.

The Committee thereon submitted the following report, which was accepted :

To the R. W. Grand Encampment, I. O. O. F. of Connecticut:

The Committee to whom was referred the annual report of the M. W. Grand Patriarch, having attended to the duty of their appointment, would recommend that the subject of Representative Tax to the Grand Lodge of the United States, be referred to a special Committee of three.

All of which is respectfully submitted in F., H. and C.

A. G. SHEARS,
O. UTLEY, } *Committee.*
W. W. WHITE,

The Grand Patriarch appointed on the Committee recommended, Patriarchs S. H. Harris of No. 1, G. L. Townsend of No. 20, and J. E. Bidwell of No. 6.

The Grand Treasurer submitted the following report, which was accepted :

Grand Encampment, I. O. O. F. of Connecticut, in account with S. H. HARRIS, *Grand Treasurer.*

1863.	DR.	
Feb. 11. For cash paid Charles Bradley,............................	$ 3.00
" " " Grand Scribe, deficit last session,..............	5.87
Sept. 1, " " " Grand Lodge Tax,............................	75.00
Amount to new account,.......................	18.13

	CR.	$102.00
Feb. 16, By Cash from Grand Scribe,.....................$102.00		

Respectfully submitted in F., H. and C.

S. H. HARRIS, *Grand Treasurer.*

NEW HAVEN, February 16, 1864.

The Committee on the State of the Order submitted the following reports, which were accepted:

To the R. W. Grand Encampment, I. O. O. F. of Connecticut:

The Committee on the State of the Order, to whom was referred the reports of subordinates for the terms ending July 1st, 1863, and January 1st, 1864, beg leave to report,

That they had presented to them reports from Sassacus Encampment, No. 1; Oriental, No. 2; Sowheag, No. 6; Excelsior, No. 18; and Ansantawae, No. 20; all of which were found correct.

For the term ending July 1st, Sassacus, No. 1, reported, initiated, 2; reinstated, 1; withdrawn, 1; suspended, 2. For the term ending January 1st, initiated, 6; No. of members January 1st, 128; amount of funds, $3,196.47.

Oriental, No. 2, term ending January 1st, initiated, 12; admitted by card, 7; No. of members, 19; amount of funds, $50.22.

Sowheag, No. 6, No. of members January 1st, 13.

Excelsior, No. 18, term ending July 1st, initiations, 2; deceased, 1; term ending January 1st, initiations, 1; No. of members, 30; amount of funds, $11.99.

Ansantawae, No. 20, term ending July 1st, initiations, 7; withdrawn, 7; suspended, 1; No. of members, January 1st, 30.

Total initiations for the year ending January 1st, 30; reinstated, 1; admitted by card, 7; withdrawn, 8; suspended, 3; died, 1; present number of members, 220; increase of membership during the year, 26.

All of which is respectfully submitted in F., H. and C.

D. E. BURWELL, }
G. L. TOWNSEND, } *Committee.*
S. B. WETMORE, }

To the R. W. Grand Encampment, I. O. O. F. of Connecticut:

The Committee on the State of the Order, to whom was referred the amended By-Laws of Ansantawae Encampment, No. 20, beg leave to report:

That they have carefully examined said By-Laws, and find nothing therein inconsistent with the Constitution for subordinates, and would recommend their acceptance by this Grand Body.

Respectfully submitted in F., L. and T.

D. E. BURWELL, }
G. L. TOWNSEND, } *Committee.*
S. B. WETMORE, }

The Committee on Finance submitted the following report, which was accepted:

To the R. W. Grand Encampment, I. O. O. F. of Connecticut:

We, your Committee appointed to examine the finances of this Grand Encampment, respectfully report:

That they have attended to the duties of the same, and would report as follows:

Amount of receipts from Encampments have been........................$102.00
The expenditures have been as follows:
Paid Charles Bradley, Outside Sentinel,......................$ 3.00
"   Grand Scribe, deficit,............................... 5.87
"   "   Lodge, U. S. Representative Tax,................ 75.00   83.87
                                                          _____
                                                          $18.13

Your Committee have had the report of the Grand Scribe before them, and would recommend that the method of taxation of the subordinate Encampments proposed by him, be adopted by this Encampment; your Committee would also recommend the appropriation of a sufficient sum from the treasury of this

Grand Encampment to meet the Representative tax and any other bills now due, or that may become due the year ensuing, to the Grand Lodge of United States.

J. E. BIDWELL,
SAMUEL CLEETON, } <i>Committee.</i>
JULIUS ATTWOOD,

The following report was accepted :

To the R. W. Grand Encampment, I. O. O. F. of Connecticut :

The Committee to whom was referred so much of the Grand Patriarch's report as relates to the Representative tax to Grand Lodge of the United States, respectfully report :

That they have had the subject under consideration, and would recommend that our Grand Representative use his discretion with regard to the reduction of said tax, as now proposed in the Grand Lodge of the United States.

Respectfully submitted in F., II. and C.

S. H. HARRIS,
G. L. TOWNSEND, } <i>Committee.</i>
J. E. BIDWELL,

The Grand Encampment then proceeded to the nomination and election of officers for the year ensuing.

For Grand Patriarch, G. H. P. F. Botsford of No. 1.

For Grand High Priest, G. S. W. D. W. Boyd of No. 18.

For Grand Senior Warden, G. J. W. J. H. Barlow of No. 18.

For Grand Scribe, G. S. Lucius A. Thomas of No. 1.

For Grand Treasurer, G. T. S. H. Harris of No. 1.

For Grand Junior Warden, Patriarchs A. G. Shears of No. 1, J. Attwood of No. 2, and J. R. Taylor of No. 1.

For Grand Representative, P. G. Pat's J. W. Smith and G. L. Townsend of No. 20.

P. G. P. Townsend declined the nomination for Grand Rep.

On balloting, the following officers were elected :

F. Botsford, Grand Patriarch.

D. W. Boyd, Grand High Priest.

J. H. Barlow, Grand Senior Warden.

L. A. Thomas, Grand Scribe.

S. H. Harris, Grand Treasurer.

A. G. Shears, Grand Junior Warden.

J. W. Smith, Grand Representative.

The officers were then installed in ample form.

The following resolution was unanimously adopted :

Resolved, That the thanks of this Grand Encampment are due and are hereby most cordially tendered to Past Grand Patriarch John W. Smith, for the able, impartial and satisfactory manner in which he has discharged the highly responsible duties of Grand Patriarch for the past year.

The Grand Encampment then adjourned without day, and was closed in ample form.

Attest,

LUCIUS A. THOMAS, Grand Scribe.

35

PROCEEDINGS

OF THE

R. W. GRAND ENCAMPMENT, I. O. O. F.

OF THE

STATE OF CONNECTICUT.

———◆◆◆———

ANNUAL SESSION, 1865.

NEW HAVEN, Feb. 14, 1865.

The R. W. Grand Encampment, I. O. O. F. of Connecticut, convened this day at 2 o'clock, P. M., in accordance with its Constitution and By-Laws.

PRESENT:

M. W. FREDERICK BOTSFORD, *Grand Patriarch,*
M. E. D. W. BOYD, *Grand High Priest,*
R. W. J. W. BARLOW, *Grand Senior Warden,*
R. W. L. A. THOMAS, *Grand Scribe,*
R. W. S. H. HARRIS, *Grand Treasurer,*
R. W. A. G. SHEARS, *Grand Junior Warden,*
R. W. J. W. SMITH, *Grand Representative,*

and Representatives from five Encampments.

The opening ritual was read by the Grand High Priest, and the Grand Encampment was then opened in ample form.

The Grand Patriarch appointed as Committee on Credentials, Patriarchs Julius Attwood of No. 2, J. A. Hughes and E. L. Fairchild of No. 1.

The Committee submitted the following report, which was accepted:

To the R. W. Grand Encampment, I. O. O. F. of Connecticut:

The Committee on Credentials beg leave to report, that they have examined the certificates of the following Patriarchs and find them correct:

Sassacus, No. 1—S. Cleeton, W. H. Stanley, F. Botsford, A. G. Shears, L. A.

Thomas, J. A. Hughes, D. E. Burwell, N. Chandler, E. L. Fairchild, J. R. Taylor,
S. H. Harris, S. B. Gorham, P. B. Beebe, R. B. Dyar, S. D. Fairchild.
Oriental, No. 2—J. Attwood, H. R. Rogers.
Sowheag, No. 6—J. E. Bidwell, H. Leonard.
Charity, No. 10—A. Hyde, A. A. Palmer.
Excelsior, No. 18—D. W. Boyd, J. H. Barlow, Wm. E. Hine.
Ansantawae, No. 20—J. W. Smith, G. L. Townsend.
    All which is respectfully submitted,

JULIUS ATTWOOD, ⎫
J. A. HUGHES,   ⎬ *Committee.*
E. L. FAIRCHILD, ⎭

The following Patriarchs were then introduced and instructed in the Grand Encampment degree:

Sassacus, No. 1—P. B. Beebe, R. B. Dyar, S. D. Fairchild.
Sowheag, No. 6—H. Leonard.
Excelsior, No. 18—Wm. E. Hine.

The proceedings of last session were then read and approved.

The Grand Patriarch appointed the following Committees:

Committee on the State of the Order—Patriarchs J. H. Barlow of No. 18, J. E.
Bidwell of No. 6, and Noah Chandler of No. 1.
Committee on Finance—Patriarchs G. L. Townsend of No. 20, W. H. Stanley
and D. E. Burwell of No. 1.

The Grand Patriarch submitted his report, which was ac-
cepted and referred to a special Committee, consisting of
Patriarchs J. W. Smith of No. 20, A. G. Shears and J. R.
Taylor of No. 1.

OFFICERS AND REPRESENTATIVES:

Another year, with its joys and sorrows, has been numbered with the past
since our last meeting; and we are now, by Divine permission, again assembled
in annual Grand Encampment, to take counsel together, and to legislate for the
perpetuity and the best interests of the Patriarchal branch of our Order.

It is our first duty, therefore, as dependent beings, to raise our hearts in
gratitude to God for the innumerable mercies of the past year, and to invoke His
blessing on the work now in hand; to beseech him to grant us wisdom in counsel, and the spirit of fraternal courtesy, kindness, and justice in all our proceedings on this occasion.

Immediately after the close of our last Grand Encampment, I forwarded to the
several Patriarchs nominated in the Encampment reports, warrants empowering
them to act in their respective jurisdictions as "Deputy Grand Patriarchs" for
the current year.

In the month of April "Past Grand Master" John Greenwood, Jr., at present
residing in the city of New York, and formerly a member of an Encampment in
this State, (now defunct,) applied for a withdrawal card. His application was
granted, and the requisite papers forwarded to him by the R. W. Grand Scribe.

In May last I was informed that a number of Patriarchs in the borough of Stonington had decided to reopen "Charity Encampment, No. 10," of that place.
Business engagements preventing me from visiting them at that time, I addressed
them a congratulatory letter, and deputized Past Grand Master Philip Pond to
visit them at his earliest convenience—install their officers—give them instructions in the work of the Order—and to perform such other duties as, in his judgment, their circumstances should require. These duties were performed by him
on the 9th of June last, and his report to me of the proceedings on that occasion,

and the character of the men composing that Encampment, is such as to afford good grounds for the most sanguine hopes of its future.

On the evening of the same day, attended by the R. W. Grand Scribe and Grand Treasurer, and Patriarchs Morehouse and Kelsey, I visited "Excelsior Encampment, No. 18," of Birmingham. The cordial and hospitable manner in which we were received by the members of this Encampment, gave evidence of profitable study, on their part, of the great principle of the Patriarchal degree. The Grand Officers were received with the customary honors, and the degree of the Royal Purple conferred in our presence. I am happy to say that the work was correctly done, and in a manner highly creditable to the officers of that Encampment.

On the 1st of July, and also on the 6th of January last, I visited, officially, "Sassacus Encampment, No. 1," of New Haven, and installed its Officers in "ample form." It gives me great pleasure to state that the affairs of this Encampment are in a highly prosperous condition—with a rapidly increasing membership and fund.

I have received a report from "Deputy Grand Patriarch," James E. Bidwell, Esq., in which he speaks in very encouraging terms of the condition of Sowheag, No. 6.

I regret to say that this is the only report received up to the present time; and I take this opportunity to impress upon delinquent Deputies the importance of these reports. They are the annual history of subordinates, and as such are, in a great measure, the material from which the Grand Patriarch is to make up his report to the Grand Encampment of the state of the Order within its jurisdiction. They are also the channels through which much valuable information may be conveyed, and, perchance, suggestions made which might lead to legislation of vital importance to the stability and well-being of our institution.

On the 27th of January I addressed a letter to Gould D. Jennings, of Norwalk, District Deputy Grand Master, making inquiries as to the prospects for reopening the Encampment of that place. I have not as yet received his answer. I would suggest to this R. W. Body, whether some plan may not be devised that shall tend to revive the spirit of Odd Fellowship in the localities of the defunct Encampments, and thus result in their reorganization. This is a very desirable object, and worthy your careful consideration.

On the 4th of the present month I received a circular, accompanied with an engraved design of the "Wildey Monument," soliciting subscriptions to the Monument Fund from the several Encampments in this jurisdiction. I cheerfully commend this subject to your attention, in the belief that every true Odd Fellow will be gratified to have the opportunity to pay this tribute of respect to the memory of one to whom our institution is under so many obligations. To his energy, indomitable perseverance, and purity of character, are we indebted for our present high moral and social position. Let us emulate his virtues, and manfully carry on the great work of Love to our fellow man, which he, under so many difficulties and discouragements, so nobly commenced.

In the early part of September the M. W. Grand Sire, James B. Nicholson, of Philadelphia, announced his intention of visiting the Order in this city, on his way to attend the annual session of the R. W. Grand Lodge of the United States, to be held in Boston. The announcement was most enthusiastically received and a large committee of arrangements appointed to give to the Supreme Head of our Order a reception worthy of the man, and the exalted station which he occupied. Every detail was carried out with perfect success, and the whole affair was one long to be remembered by those who participated in its ceremonies. The Grand Sire addressed a large and intelligent audience in "Music Hall;" and the Order are under great obligations for the noble, manly, and eloquent exposition of its great principles and work. It was a stirring appeal to manhood's best feelings, and relit the fires of "Friendship, Love, and Truth" in many a heart long since cold and indifferent. It was the good seed sown, as we believe, on good ground, from which, we may be assured, we shall reap an abundant harvest in due time, if we faint not.

My attention has been called to a discrepancy between the practice of some subordinates and a decision of the M. W. Grand Sire, afterwards confirmed by the United States Grand Lodge, (see Vol. 4th, pages 3181, 3233, and 3266, Journal of Proceedings.) The decision to which I allude was called forth by the following question: "Is there any law or custom of the Order forbidding the holding of Encampment meetings but once a month, instead of once in two weeks, or weekly?" To which the Grand Sire replied: "Subordinate Encampments may, with the consent of their Grand Encampments, hold but one meeting per month, instead of two; but if the number be thus reduced, the official term of the officers should be extended to twelve months, as provided by law." I therefore present this subject for your consideration, and for such action as you may deem expedient.

My official duties have not been burdensome; on the contrary, through the courtesy and kindness of the Patriarchs, they have been made light and agreeable. My thanks are due to the Order generally, for the great respect and attention shown me on all occasions; and more especially are my acknowledgments due to our R. W. Grand Scribe and R. W. Grand Treasurer for good counsel and advice during my official term. Permit me, on this occasion, to congratulate you on the prosperous state of the Order. The great principles of love and good will to man have steadily advanced; the increase of members has been greater during this year than for several years past; and there is evidently a revival of interest in the good and benevolent work in which we are engaged. Let us "go on" with renewed energy, battling vigorously against all "impediments that meet us in the way," until there is no sorrow to soothe—no tear to dry.

The blood red cloud of war still darkens our national horizon; upon this subject, however, it is not my province to speak farther than to deplore its fearful consequences, and urge you, as good Odd Fellows and citizens, to give your hearty support "to the Government and its laws;" at the same time to implore "Him who ruleth in the armies of Heaven and among the inhabitants of the earth, to hasten the time when wars shall cease throughout the world, and unity, peace, and concord prevail throughout our land.

At the close of this session my official duties cease. I retire from the high and responsible station to which your suffrages elevated me, filled with a grateful sense of your kind consideration. Accept my heartfelt thanks for the numerous manifestations of good feeling during my official term. Accept also my sincere wishes for the health, happiness, and prosperity of each and all; and when we have done with all of earth, may the mantle of Charity be thrown over all our short comings and imperfections, and our departing souls be invested with that divine password that shall open to us the gates of Paradise, and admit us to those blest mansions above, prepared for us from the beginning,

FREDERICK BOTSFORD, *Grand Patriarch.*

NEW HAVEN, Feb. 14, 1865.

The Grand Scribe presented his report, which was accepted and referred to a special Committee, consisting of Patriarchs S. H. Harris of No. 1, D. W. Boyd of No. 18, H. Leonard of No. 6:

To the R. W. Grand Encampment, I. O. O. F. of Connecticut:

In my report of last session, I recommended an additional assessment of twenty-five cents, payable in July, for the purpose of meeting the immediate wants of the Grand Encampment in the payment of the dues to the Grand Lodge of the United States. This was sanctioned by the Grand Encampment, and I am happy to say the call was responded to with alacrity by the several subordinates and enabled me to transmit the dues to the national Grand Body without incon venience.

The payment accompanying the January reports has rendered us financially easy for our ordinary expenses, and the usual assessment of twenty-five cents per head for each term, will, I have no doubt, continue to keep us easy. An additional tax of twenty-five cents per annum, the same as last year, will, in two or three years, accumulate sufficient to enable us to print our proceedings. And this I regard as a matter of very great importance.

There has been a gratifying increase in the members of the Encampments. There have been thirty-two initiations, which with the resuscitation of Charity Encampment, No. 10, with fourteen members, makes the gain, since last session, forty-six, present number 266.

It would appear by the reports of some of the Encampments that they do not recognize the beneficiary principle, requiring no dues, and making no provision for benefits. The Grand Lodge of the United States has expressly decided, that as mutual help lies at the foundation of our institution, all working bodies must recognize the principle, and provide for it.

The entire work of the Order has been revised, and will probably be adopted at the next session of the Grand Lodge of the United States.

A special regalia has been adopted for the P. C. Patriarchs.

Only one Encampment, No. 2, contributed to the Wildey monument. This Encampment sent a noble subscription of twenty dollars.

On the 10th of January I received the working books of Wascussee Encampment, No. 14, of Stamford. I am indebted for this to Patriarch Geo. L. Lounds, who informs me that he hopes to be able to send me the charter upon the return of a Patriarch now absent.

This Encampment has not reported since 1850, and I have made several ineffectual attempts to obtain its effects.

LUCIUS A. THOMAS, Grand Scribe.

New Haven, Feb. 14, 1865.

The report of the Grand Representative was read and referred to the Committee on the State of the Order:

To the R. W. Grand Encampment, I. O. O. F. of Connecticut:

Officers and Representatives,—Having, as your Representative, attended the last annual communication of the R. W. Grand Lodge of the United States, held in Boston, Mass., on the 19th day of Sept., 1864, I would respectfully submit the following report:

The Grand Lodge was kindly and heartily welcomed to the Grand Lodge of Mass., by Grand Master W. E. Ford, in an eloquent speech tendering them the use of their elegant hall during the session.

The session of the R. W. Grand Body continued five days, during which time much business was transacted, and I will endeavor to give you a summary of such of the proceedings as directly relate to the Patriarchal branch of our Order.

At the calling of the roll each day no responses were heard from eleven jurisdictions. Should I again have the privilege of sitting in that R. W. Grand Body, may God, in his all-wise Providence, grant that I may be able to report to you that no "seat was empty," that the cause which prevented the attendance of Representatives from every part of our country had been removed.

The R. W. Corresponding and Recording Secretary reports that no Journal of Proceedings for the year 1863 had been received from this Grand Encampment.

MISAPPLICATION OF ENCAMPMENT OR LODGE FUNDS.

" Whereas a practice has grown up in some of the different State jurisdictions amongst the subordinate Lodges and Encampments holding charters from their respective State Grand Bodies of dividing the funds and property of the Lodge or Encampment (designed only for the use and benefit of brethren of the Order in sickness and distress) amongst the members thereof, that are neither disabled, sick, or in distress, contrary to the laws, usages, and customs of the Order from its earliest history;

" AND WHEREAS, by the terms and express language of the charters under which all working Lodges and Encampments are authorized to impose certain dues and collect contributions from their members, the power is conferred for the purpose of accumulating a fund for the benefit of 'sick brothers or brothers in distress;' that said funds are *trust funds*, and the Lodges or Encampments are but *trustees;* that said funds, having been contributed under and by authority of the charter, are for the objects and purposes therein expressed and for no other; and that any diversion from the real object or intention, as expressed in said charter or the laws of the body from which said charter emanated, is a wrongful and tortuous diversion of the funds so collected, and which has impressed upon it the great principle of *Trust, Benevolence and Charity;*

" AND WHEREAS the primary object of this Grand Lodge is to build up, protect, and perpetuate, to the latest time, a charity which shall command the admiration of the present and future generations with the fond hope of making it one of the noblest charities the world has ever seen; therefore,

" *Resolved,* That this Grand Lodge does hereby declare all attempts to divert the funds or property of a Lodge or Encampment from the objects and purposes for which they were in the name of our Order collected, by dividing or appropriating them to some other object or purpose before breaking up or surrendering their charter, to be wrong and dishonorable, and in direct violation of the *trust* which they have voluntarily assumed.

" *Resolved,* That the funds and property collected under and by authority of a charter duly granted to a Lodge or Encampment of the Independent Order of Odd Fellows are *trust funds,* and can be applied only to the objects for which they were collected, and that when a Lodge or Encampment shall fail from any cause to continue as a working body and yield up its charter, the money and property of whatever kind of which it may be possessed and belonging thereto must be surrendered up to and paid over to the State Grand Body from which it derived its authority, and that no diversion of the funds or property or other disposition of it, except for the legitimate objects of the Order, can or will be recognized or tolerated by this Grand Lodge.

" *Resolved,* That State Grand Bodies are directed to enact such laws as will most effectually put a stop to all such practices, and affix such penalties to the acts as will prevent any member participating therein, from ever again uniting with the Order, without first making due reparation therefor.

" *Resolved,* That when the laws of the Order shall be ineffectual for the purpose, the State Grand Bodies shall be justified in invoking the laws of the country to compel a surrender of the *trust funds* to the proper parties and objects.

" *Resolved,* That all State Grand Bodies, which have not heretofore legislated on this subject, are hereby directed to enact suitable and appropriate laws and regulations for the care of the funds and the property of defunct Lodges and Encampments; which shall thereafter become a separate *trust* or fund, to be employed and used under the direction of such Grand Body, or committee duly constituted by them, in aiding and assisting working Lodges and Encampments when in need of funds to sustain them in their organization.

" *Resolved,* That, for the pupose of enabling Grand Bodies the more effectnally to avail themselves of the means to obtain redress in the matters referred to, said Grand Bodies are hereby advised to obtain for themselves legislative acts of incorporation."

NON-BENEFICIAL MEMBERS.

" WHEREAS, from various causes, it at times has occurred that subordinate Lodges and Encampments, failing of success, have found it necessary or expedient to surrender their respective charters, and

" WHEREAS, in such cases, it has oftentimes happened that some of the members in such Lodges or Encampments have attained an age so advanced as to render it impracticable for them, in some of the jurisdictions, to obtain beneficial membership in other working Lodges or Encampments; and

" WHEREAS, in the judgment of this Grand Lodge, no detriment could, as a rule, arise to the Order by the admission, as non-beneficial members, into subordinate Lodges and Encampments, of brothers of advanced age who were in good standing at the time of the surrender of the charters of their respective Lodges and Encampments, upon such terms and conditions as may be prescribed by general or special laws of the respective State jurisdictions : therefore

"*Resolved*, That the several jurisdictions subordinate to this Grand Lodge are hereby recommended to provide such suitable legislation as may be requisite to enable working Lodges and Encampments to receive, as non-beneficial members, such members of defunct Lodges and Encampments as were in good standing at the time of the dissolution of their respective Lodges or Encampments, and who, by reason of their advanced age, are now ineligible to beneficial membership."

NON-AFFILIATED MEMBERS.

"WHEREAS a number of brothers in the several State jurisdictions have become *non-affiliated* with the Order by reason of the dissolution of their respective Lodges and Encampments, and, in consequence of old age, cannot again unite or renew their membership in the Order, and whereas means should be provided for at least a partial affiliation with the Order in such cases, be it therefore

"*Resolved*, That the several State jurisdictions be and they are hereby empowered to enact such laws as will enable brothers who have lost their membership by reason of the dissolution of Lodges and Encampments, and are unable in consequence of age, and from no other cause, to again connect themselves with the Order to the extent that they may become visiting brothers, and in the event of death, to be interred with the funeral ceremonies of the Order ; but in no case to become either active or honorary members of Lodges or Encampments.

"*Resolved*, As the sense of this Grand Lodge, that the foregoing may become effective, the State jurisdictions are hereby fraternally recommended to authorize their Grand Secretaries and Grand Scribes to communicate to brothers who may be situated as above described the term P. W., and to furnish them with a certificate setting forth that they were members in good standing of a defunct Lodge or Encampment, upon the payment of such fee as may be determined by law ; and in the event of the death of such brothers it shall be the duty of the M. W. Grand Master to delegate the officers of such Lodge in his jurisdiction as he may select to inter the remains of the brother with the funeral ceremonies of the Order.

"*Resolved*, That the several State jurisdictions are fraternally requested to form such auxiliary associations whereby a fund may be created for the benefit of brothers circumstanced as set forth in the foregoing preamble and resolutions."

As regards the courtesy, hospitality and attention received during our stay in Boston from the members of the Order there, I refer you to the following resolutions, which passed unanimously :

"*Resolved*, That thanks is a feeble word to express our gratification for the hearty welcome, generous hospitality, and liberal entertainment extended to us by our Boston brethren.

"*Resolved*, That their kindness, generosity, and liberality will abide in our memories as vividly and enduringly as the remembrance of the monuments which commemorate their heroes attest their appreciation of art and science, of their unrivaled memorials of the dead, and of the munificent evidences of their devotion to religion, philanthropy, and education.

"*Resolved*, That, as an earnest expression of our appreciation for the many acts of kindness and courtesy shown us by the most Worthy Grand Master, Officers, and brethren of the R. W. Grand Lodge of Massachusetts during the present session of the Grand Lodge, a copy of the resolutions submitted by Rep. BARRY, of Indiana, be engrossed and transmitted to the R. W. Grand Lodge of Massachusetts, attested by the seal and the signatures of the officers of this Grand Lodge."

The following officers were elected for 1864-5: Grand Sire, Isaac M. Veitch, of St. Louis, Missouri ; Deputy Grand Sire, James P. Sanders, of Yonkers, New

York; G. C. and R. Secretary, James L. Ridgely, of Baltimore, Maryland; Grand Treasurer, Joshua Vansant, of Baltimore, Maryland.

In conclusion, I sincerely tender you my earnest and heartfelt thanks for the high honor conferred in electing me to this office, and also for placing me in a position which allows me to wear the combined Royal Purple and Scarlet during my connection with this Order, which connection I fondly hope and trust will only be severed by death.

Yours in F., H. and C.,

J. W. SMITH, *Grand Representative.*

The Grand Patriarch appointed the following Committees:

On so much of the Grand Patriach's report as relates to the official term of officers of subordinate Encampments, Patriarchs D. E. Burwell and S. D. Fairchild of No. 1, and Julius Attwood of No. 2.

On so much as relates to Deputy Grand Patriarchs, Patriarchs J. H. Barlow of No. 18, J. E. Bidwell of No. 6, H. Leonard of No. 6.

On the Grand Scribe's report, Patriarchs S. H. Harris of No. 1, D. W. Boyd of No. 18, Horace Leonard of No. 6.

Patriarch J. W. Smith offered the following amendment to Art. I, Sec. 1 of the By-laws, which was unanimously adopted:

Strike out "two o'clock, P. M.," and insert "eleven o'clock, A. M."

The Committee thereon submitted the following report, which was accepted:

To the R. W. Grand Encampment, I. O. O. F. of Connecticut:

The Committee to whom was referred the report of the R. W. Grand Patriarch, would respectfully report, that they have attended to the duties assigned them, and would recommend that so much of said report as relates to Deputy Grand Patriarchs be referred to the Committee on the State of the Order.

So much as relates to official terms of officers of subordinate Encampments be referred to a special Committee of three.

So much as relates to the Wildey Monument Fund be referred to the Finance Committee.

J. W. SMITH,
A. G. SHEARS, } *Committee.*
J. R. TAYLOR,

The Committee on the State of the Order submitted the following report, which was accepted:

To the R. W. Grand Encampment, I. O. O. F. of Connecticut:

The Committee on the State of the Order would respectfully report that they have examined the reports of the following Encampments for the term ending July 1, 1864, and find the same correct:—Sassacus, No. 1; Oriental, No. 2; Sowheag, No. 6; Charity, No. 10; Excelsior, No. 18; Ansantawae, No. 20.

Also for the term ending Jan. 1, 1865, as follows:—Sassacus, No. 1; Oriental, No. 2; Sowheag, No. 6; Charity, No. 10; Excelsior, No. 18; Ansantawae, No. 20.

Respectfully submitted,

J. H. BARLOW,
J. E. BIDWELL, } *Committee.*
N. CHANDLER,

The Grand Treasurer submitted the following report, which was accepted:

Grand Encampment, I. O. O. F., in account with S. H. HARRIS, Grand Treasurer.

1864.	DR.		
Feb. 16. For cash paid Charles Bradley for tiling,..............			$2.00
1865.			
Sept. " " Grand Lodge of United States, Rep. Tax, .$75.00			
" " " " " " Books,.... 10.00			85.00
1865.			
Feb. 14. " " Grand Scribe........................			11.27
Amount to new account,................			99.61
			197.88

1864.	CR.	
Feb. 14. By balance of old account, ...$18.13		
1865.		
Feb. 15. By cash from Grand Scribe Thomas,..................179.75	197.88

Respectfully submitted in F., H. and C.,
SAMUEL H. HARRIS, *Grand Treasurer.*

NEW HAVEN, February 14, 1865.

The Committee on the State of the Order, to whom was referred the report of the Grand Representative, submitted the following report, which was accepted and the resolution adopted:

To the R. W. Grand Encampment, I. O. O. F. of Connecticut:

The Committee on the State of the Order, to whom was referred the report of the Grand Representative, would recommend that so much of said report as relates to the misapplication of the funds of Encampments, be referred to a special Committee of three.

On so much as relates to non-beneficial and non-affiliated members, the Committee offer the following resolution, and recommend its adoption.

Respectfully submitted,
J. H. BARLOW,
J. E. BIDWELL, } *Committee.*
N. CHANDLER,

Resolved, That the several Encampments under this jurisdiction be allowed to receive as non-beneficial members such members of defunct Encampments as were in good standing at the time of the dissolution of their respective Encampments, who by reason of their advanced age are ineligible to beneficial membership, on such terms as they may determine.

The Committee on Finance submitted the following report, which was accepted and the resolutions adopted:

To the R. W. Grand Encampment, I. O. O. F. of Connecticut:

The undersigned, Committee on Finance, to whom was referred the report of the R. W. Grand Treasurer, respectfully report that they have examined his books, together with those of the R. W. Grand Scribe, and find the same to be correct, and the sum of ninety-nine dollars and sixty-one cents in the hands of the Treasurer, to be carried to new account.

The following bills presented at this session of the Grand Encampment are approved by your Committee, and we would recommend their payment, viz:

Bill of Charles Bradley, for services as Sentinel this session,.....$2.00
" L. A. Thomas, Grand Scribe, for postage, from 1854 to 1864, 15.00
" T. J. Stafford, for printing blank Reports,.............. 8.00

Your Committee would respectfully recommend the adoption of the following resolutions.

Respectfully submitted in F., H. and C.,

> G. L. TOWNSEND, }
> WM. H. STANLEY, } *Committee.*
> D. E. BURWELL, }

Resolved, That the bills of Charles Bradley, L. A. Thomas and T. J. Stafford be ordered paid.

Resolved, That the Grand Scribe be authorized to forward, at the proper time, the annual Representative tax to the Grand Lodge of the United States.

On motion, the Grand Encampment proceeded to the nomination of officers, when the following nominations were made :

For Grand Patriarch, D. W. Boyd.

For Grand High Priest, J. H. Barlow.

For Grand Senior Warden, A. G. Shears.

For Grand Scribe, Lucius A. Thomas.

For Grand Treasurer, Samuel H. Harris.

For Grand Junior Warden, Albegence Hyde, J. Attwood, J. A. Hughes, and J. E. Bidwell.

The special Committee thereon submitted the following report, which was accepted and the resolution adopted :

To the R. W. Grand Encampment, I. O. O. F. of Connecticut :

Your Committee, to whom was referred so much of the R. W. Grand Patriarch's report as relates to the decision of the Grand Sire respecting holding meetings once a month by subordinate Encampments, have attended to their duty, and would recommend the passage of the following resolution.

Respectfully submitted,

> D. E. BURWELL, }
> S. D. FAIRCHILD, } *Committee.*
> J. ATTWOOD, }

Resolved, That officers of subordinate Encampments holding regular meetings only once a month, must hold their respective offices for one year.

The special Committee thereon submitted the following report, which was accepted and the resolution adopted :

To the R. W. Grand Encampment, I. O. O. F. of Connecticut :

The Committee to whom was referred the report of the Grand Scribe, beg leave to report that they have attended to that duty, and recommend the following :

That so much of the report as refers to an assessment of twenty-five cents for each term, and an annual tax of twenty-five cents, be adopted.

So much of the report as calls the attention of this Grand Encampment to benefits of subordinate Encampments, they have considered, and recommend the following resolution.

Respectfully submitted,

> S. H. HARRIS, }
> D. W. BOYD, } *Committee.*
> HORACE LEONARD, }

Resolved, That this Grand Encampment require all subordinate Encampments to recognize the paying of benefits.

The special Committee thereon submitted the following report, which was accepted and the resolution adopted :

To the R. W. Grand Encampment, I. O. of O. F. of Connecticut :

The Committee to whom was referred so much of the report of the Grand Patriarch as relates to D. G. Patriarchs, would recommend the adoption of the following resolution.

Respectfully submitted,

J. E. BIDWELL, } *Committee.*
J. H. BARLOW, }

Resolved, That all D. G. Patriarchs be required to make report of their official acts to the Grand Patriarch at least one week prior to the session of this Grand Encampment.

The following resolution was unanimously adopted :

Resolved, That the Past Grand Patriarchs of this Grand Encampment be requested to furnish portraits of themselves, to be hung upon the walls of the Grand Encampment Room.

The Grand Encampment then proceeded to the election of officers. On balloting, the following were elected :

D. W. Boyd, Grand Patriarch.

J. H. Barlow, Grand High Priest.

A. G. Shears, Grand Senior Warden.

L. A. Thomas, Grand Scribe.

S. H. Harris, Grand Treasurer.

J. E. Bidwell, Grand Junior Warden.

The following resolution was adopted :

Resolved, That the various Encampments in this jurisdiction be requested to contribute such sum as their funds will allow, or a contribution from among its members, to the Wildey Monument Fund.

The Committee thereon submitted the following report, which was accepted and the resolution adopted :

To the R. W. Grand Encampment, I. O. O. F. of Connecticut :

Your Committee to whom was referred so much of the report of the R. W. Grand Representative as refers to the action of the Grand Lodge of the United States, at its last session, relative to the division of funds of subordinate Lodges and Encampments among its members, beg leave to submit the following report:

Whereas the R. W. Grand Lodge of the United States having declared that all attempts to divert the funds or property of a Lodge or Encampment from the objects and purposes for which they were in the name of our Order collected, by dividing or appropriating them to some other object or purpose before breaking up or surrendering their charter, to be wrong and dishonorable, and in direct violation of the *trust* which they have voluntarily assumed ; and at the same session passed a resolution directing State Grand Bodies to enact such laws as will most effectually put a stop to all such practices, your Committee would respectfully recommend the adoption of the accompanying resolution.

Respectfully submitted in F., H. and C.,

G. L. TOWNSEND, }
SAMUEL B. GORHAM, } *Committee.*
WM. H. STANLEY, }

Resolved, That any member of a subordinate Encampment in this jurisdiction who shall have been guilty of consenting to the diversion of the funds or property of the Encampment to which he belongs, or other disposition of it, except for the legitimate objects of the Order, shall be suspended from membership in the Patriarchal branch of the Order, and be forever hereafter ineligible to membership in the same.

The officers elect were then installed into their respective offices by Grand Patriarch Botsford, in ample form.

The following resolution was unanimously adopted :

Resolved, That the thanks of this Grand Encampment are due, and most cordially tendered P. G. Patriarch FREDERICK BOTSFORD, for the able manner he has performed the duties of Grand Patriarch the past year, and for the ability with which he has presided over the deliberations of this R. W. Grand Body at this session.

No further business being before the Grand Encampment, it adjourned without day and was closed in ample form.

Attest,

LUCIUS A. THOMAS, *Grand Scribe.*

PROCEEDINGS

OF THE

R. W. GRAND ENCAMPMENT, I. O. O. F.

OF THE

STATE OF CONNECTICUT.

━━━━━━◆◆◆━━━━━━

ANNUAL SESSION, 1866.

NEW HAVEN, Feb. 20, 1866.

The R. W. Grand Encampment, I. O. O. F. of Connecticut, convened this day in Annual Session.

PRESENT:

M. W. D. W. BOYD, *Grand Patriarch,*
M. E. J. H. BARLOW, *Grand High Priest,*
R. W. A. G. SHEARS, *Grand Senior Warden,*
R. W. LUCIUS A. THOMAS, *Grand Scribe,*
R. W. S. H. HARRIS, *Grand Treasurer,*
R. W. J. E. BIDWELL, *Grand Junior Warden,*
R. W. J. W. SMITH, *Grand Representative,*

and Representatives from six Encampments.

The opening services were read by the Grand High Priest, when the G. J. Warden declared the Grand Encampment duly open.

The Grand Patriarch appointed as Committee on Credentials, Patriarchs J. W. Hammond, J. Attwood, C. A. Newell.

The Committee submitted the following report, which was accepted.

To the R. W. Grand Encampment, I. O. O. F. of Connecticut:

The Committee on Credentials beg leave to report that they have examined the credentials of the following named Patriarchs, and find them correct:

Sassacus, No. 1—S. H. Harris, M. B. Scott, Noah Chandler, Thos. C. Hollis, E.

L. Fairchild. A. G. Shears, W. W. White, L. A. Thomas, Frederick Botsford, Benj. Beecher, D. E. Burwell, J. W. Hammond, Wm. H. Stanley, J. R. Taylor, Alfred Holt, S. D. Fairchild, Sam'l Cleeton, Robert Sizer, George Crabtree

  Oriental, No. 2—Julius Attwood, W. M. Smith, Chas. II. Belden.
  Sowheag, No. 6—Samuel B. Wetmore, Chas. A. Newell, James E. Bidwell, Origen Utley, David Dickerson, Geo. II. Collins.
  Charity, No. 10—A. Hyde.
  Excelsior, No. 18—D. W. Boyd, J. H. Barlow.
  Ansantawae, No. 20.—J. W. Smith, T. I. Driggs, John II. Sandland, George L. Townsend.

Respectfully submitted,

J. W. HAMMOND,
J. ATTWOOD,   } *Committee.*
C. A. NEWELL,

The following named candidates were then introduced, and instructed in the Grand Encampment degree, viz:

No. 1, A. Holt; No. 2, Chas. II. Belden ; No. 6, Geo. II. Collins, David Dickerson; No. 20, T. I. Driggs, John H. Sandland.

The minutes of the last session were then read and approved.

The Grand Patriarch submitted his report, which was accepted and referred to a special Committee, consisting of Patriarchs Utley of No. 6, Driggs of No. 20, and Holt of No. 1.

To the R. W. Grand Encampment, I. O. O. F. of Connecticut:

REPRESENTATIVES—From the passing months we have again been called within this Grand Encampment, to legislate for the interest of our beloved Order; to exchange fraternal greetings, and to consider the best and greatest interest of the whole brotherhood.

The dark cloud of war that overhung our beloved land, at our last annual meeting, has, by the Providence of God, been swept forever from the horizon; the olive branch, with healing balm to a nation, has been accepted; through the length and breadth of the land comes the glad tidings of peace and a united country. While we rejoice in that peace, our hearts are bowed down for the nation's sorrow, for the fallen brave who-were united with us in this great and good work; in our memories ever green will we keep the bright recollections of our brothers and defenders, never forgetting the living records of true Odd Fellowship.

Pile on the noble deeds of her immortal sons ;
Pile on her sons, who noble battles for country won—
On her altars pile, a Wildey, a Father, a Washington.

"Leaving disputes and strifes to others," we will gird up our loins and go forth in the strength of our Order, recognizing "one law to bind all nations, tongues and creeds, and that law to be the law of universal brotherhood, when nation shall not lift up sword against nation, neither shall they learn war any more."

We have not only been blessed as a nation, but as an Order, and in our individual capacities, while the destroying angel of death has removed many of our brotherhood, we, as Representatives, are permitted to assemble ourselves within these sacred walls. For these and the manifold blessings which have been vouchsafed to us and our Order, let us with heartfelt gratitude and with prayer lift up our voices to our Father, that he may ever watch over us, guide our deliberations during the present assembling. Peace and harmony, fraternal fellowship and a steady increase has attended our Order; a lively interest is manifested in many of the Encampments.

Soon after the adjournment of the R. W. Grand Encampment, I appointed the several Deputy Grand Patriarchs, and their returns, so far as received, gives a good account of the several Encampments being prosperous and adding to their numbers.

On the 9th of June I received from the Grand Scribe a circular from the Grand Sire, requesting the coöperation of this Grand Encampment in the acceptance of the Wildey monument by the R. W. G. Lodge of the United States at Baltimore, September 20th, 1865. Not deeming it advisable to call the Grand Encampment, I appointed Grand Representative J. W. Smith as the representative from this Grand Body.

I would in this place call your attention to the expediency of creating the Elective Grand Officers as the Grand Executive Committee, with power to act in the intermission of this Grand Encampment.

On the 20th of September, I was in Baltimore at the unveiling of the Statue of Charity, and participated in the exercises. The whole proceedings, which have been so ably set forth by the R. W. Grand Lodge of the United States, needs no farther comment from me. In this connection I cannot but express my thanks to the Grand Representatives from this jurisdiction for their kindness and cordiality in which I was received by many members of the R. W. Grand Lodge of the United States.

On the 31st of October, by special appointment, I visited Sowheag Encampment, No. 6, at Middletown, where I was received by G. J. Warden Bidwell. I am sorry to report, I had not the pleasure to meet the Patriarchs, though by special appointment. There was no meeting of the Encampment. My thanks are due to Patriarch Bidwell for his kindness in showing me, so far as was in his power, the hall and other places of note.

On the 1st of November, I paid my respects to East Haddam for the purpose of visiting Oriental, No. 2, but for causes unexplained I was left to wander on in my journey without a guide. I had not the pleasure of seeing one familiar face. The darkness and the light were both alike to me, though I had taken measures to inform the Encampment and done what I could. There lacked a true ring of metal that should be found in the Patriarchal branch of our Order—for surely we should not be as sounding brass and as a tinkling cymbal.

November 15th, I visited Charity, No. 10, of Stonington; was received by Patriarchs A. P. Hyde and Harlow; found a good working Encampment. The Golden Rule and R. P. degrees were conferred with credit to them and the Order. Much interest is manifested, and I have no doubt her name and fame will be felt and known. I return my thanks to the Patriarchs of Charity for their kindness and courtesy.

On December 11th I visited Excelsior, No. 18, of Derby, in company with G. H. P. Barlow; the R. P. degree was conferred. The Encampment is in a prosperous condition.

On the 26th of December, 1865, I received a communication from Charity Encampment, No. 10, asking permission to have a public installation. I immediately answered that it would afford me the greatest pleasure to comply with their request were it in my power. The Grand Encampment, however, of Connecticut, having declined to sanction public installations, I was compelled to deny their request. I am of the opinion that public installations would be a great advantage to the Patriarchal branch of the Order, and would recommend the subject for your consideration.

On the 12th of January, 1866, by special invitation from Sassacus Encampment, No. 1, accompanied by G. H. P. Barlow, G. S. W. Shears and G. T. Harris, I visited and installed the officers into their respective chairs; after which a repast was served illustrative of the "hospitality" of Sassacus Encampment, reminding us "that the door of a Patriarch's Tent is never closed to a stranger in distress." Having refreshed the inner man, an hour was spent by the exchanging of sentiment, which was edifying and enjoyed by the Patriarchs. I cannot but have a feeling of pride for the prosperity and success of Sassacus; may her name be handed down to generations to come of her noble deeds in Faith, Hope and Charity. I return my grateful thanks to her for the many kind honors she has bestowed upon me.

For the financial condition of the Grand Encampment, I refer you to the report of the R. W. Grand Treasurer, and for a more full and complete returns to this R. W. Grand Encampment, I refer you most respectfully to the report of the R. W. Grand Scribe, with such practical suggestions as he may offer.

In closing my report, allow me to express my heartfelt thanks for the kindness and courtesy which I have received at your hands while in this honorable station. Imbued with the deepest feelings of our beloved Order, I retire feeling confident that I shall leave it in the hands of true exponents in Faith, Hope and Charity.

D. W. BOYD, *Grand Patriarch.*

NEW HAVEN, February 20th, 1866.

The Grand Patriarch appointed the following Committees :

Committee on the State of the Order—Patriarchs Townsend of No. 20, Scott of No. 1, Wetmore of No. 6.

Committee on Finance—Patriarchs Chandler of No. 1, Smith of No. 20, Botsford of No. 1.

Adjourned to 2 o'clock, P. M.

---

2 o'clock, P. M.

The Grand Encampment came to order.

The Grand Representative submitted his report, which was accepted and referred to a special Committee, consisting of Patriarchs Attwood of No. 3, Burwell and Holt of No. 1.

To the R. W. Grand Encampment, I. O. O. F. of Connecticut :

The R. W. Grand Lodge of the United States held its last session in Baltimore, Md., commencing Monday, September 18th, 1865, and closing Saturday, September 23d. Out of thirty-nine jurisdictions, thirty-four were represented—Lower Provinces of British North America, Oregon, North Carolina, Florida and Arkansas, being the only Grand Bodies unrepresented. It was a source of great gratification to all, to learn that the three last named were anxious to take part in the proceedings, and were only absent through causes which might have arisen ten years ago.

The following resolutions, as submitted by the Committee on Finance, were unanimously adopted:

"*Resolved*, That the Grand Lodge of the United States hereby remits the tax of the Grand Lodges and Grand Encampments of Virginia, North Carolina, South Carolina, Georgia, Alabama, Mississippi, Louisiana, Texas, and of Grand Lodges of Florida, Arkansas, and Vermont, for the years 1861, '62, '63, '64."

"*Resolved*, That the notes of Grand Lodge of Vermont for Representative tax for said four years, and notes of Grand Encampment of North Carolina given for taxes and supplies previous to 1861, be and hereby are canceled."

"*Resolved*, That the Grand Secretary be, and hereby is, authorized to furnish, upon reasonable credit, to such institutions, whatever supplies he may deem necessary during the current year."

The following resolution in regard to the secret work, was adopted :

"*Resolved*, That in order that the members of this R. W. Grand Body may vote

upon the revision of the work, in accordance with the wishes of their State Grand
Lodges and Encampments, Grand Representatives are hereby privileged to state
verbally to their Grand Bodies the main features of the proposed revision.

The following report of the Committee on the State of the Order, was accepted:

"The Committee on the State of the Order beg leave to report that they have
considered the question propounded by Representative Kirkup of Ohio, found on
page 3811 of the Journal, and report that a brother who has been expelled for
non-payment of dues or crime, from a Lodge which subsequently became extinct,
can only regain membership in the Order through the Grand Lodge to which the
Lodge he belonged to was subordinate; and this rule applies to the Patriarchal
branch of the Order."

The charter of the Grand Encampment of Delaware was restored on the 22d of
March, 1865.

A Grand Encampment has been chartered in West Virginia.

The Grand Encampments of Northern and Southern New York have been
united, under the name of the Grand Encampment of New York.

Article 22d of By-Laws in 25th line, Digest, page 18, the words "and aprons
as above described," were stricken out, and the words added, "trimmed with
yellow lace or fringe," so that so much of said By-Law as relates to the regalia of
the Past Chief Patriarchs, now reads as follows:

"Past Chief Patriarchs shall wear purple collars or sashes, trimmed with yellow
lace or fringe."

The Grand Lodge was honored by numerous invitations from various sources,
including those to banquets given by the City Government and the Merchants
and business men, all showing the high appreciation in which Odd Fellowship is
held in Baltimore.

In the opinion of Representatives who have been present at all the sessions for
many years, no more harmonious one than the last was ever held. Doubtless
many grateful and heartfelt thanks went silently up to the Giver of all good that
the members of our noble Order, though for a time separated, were not estranged
or divided.

In conclusion, Officers and Representatives, I again tender you my sincerest and
warmest thanks for the high honor conferred upon me in being chosen to represent you in the Grand Lodge of the United States.

Fraternally submitted,

J. W. SMITH, *Grand Representative.*

NEW HAVEN, February 20th, 1866.

The Grand Scribe presented his report, which was referred
to the Committee on the Grand Representative's report.

To the R. W. Grand Encampment, I. O. O. F. of Connecticut:

The quiet current of events in this branch of Odd Fellowship during the past
year, has hardly left occasion for a record. All my communications with the
subordinate Encampments have been of the most encouraging and harmonious
kind, and evidencing a sound and gratifying progress. The extra assessment on
the subordinates during the previous year has proved ample for its purpose, and
promises, with the advance of the Order, to keep us in good financial condition.

In compliance with the action of last session, in reference to the service of
officers, several of the Encampments have provided for holding their sessions
twice a month.

I am in receipt this morning of a communication from Brother Devotion of
Norwich, in reference to Palmyra Encampment, which, he thinks, (although not
now ready,) will soon be prepared to resume its work, and asks that authority
may be granted to reopen the Encampment. The communication is herewith
submitted.

The season of the year at which we hold our annual sessions is usually one of
the most inclement of the year. A very general feeling exists that it would be
better to change to some milder season. This subject will come up at the ses-

sion of the Grand Lodge, and that we may be able to hold our sessions as now, in immediate connection with that Grand Lodge, it will seem proper that we should take the initiatory steps for amending the Constitution for that purpose.

Respectfully submitted in F., H. and C.,

L. A. THOMAS, *Grand Scribe.*

The Committee on the Grand Patriarch's report submitted the following, which was accepted :

To the R. W. Grand Encampment, I. O. O. F. of Connecticut :

The Committee to whom was referred the report of the Grand Patriarch, having attended to the duty assigned them, beg leave to submit the following report:

That so much of the report as relates to the creating of an Executive Council, be referred to the Committee on the State of the Order.

That so much as relates to the visits to Sowheag Encampment, No. 6, and Oriental Encampment, No. 2, be referred to a special Committee of three.

That so much as relates to public installations, be referred to the Committee on the State of the Order.

All of which is respectfully submitted, in Faith, Hope and Charity,

O. UTLEY, ⎫
T. I. DRIGGS, ⎬ *Committee.*

The Grand Treasurer submitted the following report, which was accepted and referred to the Committee on Finance :

Grand Encampment, I. O. O. F. in account with S. H. HARRIS, *Grand Treasurer.*

1865.   DR.

Feb. 14. For cash paid Grand Scribe, for postage...............$15.00
        "   "   T. J. Stafford, for printing.............. 8.00
        "   "   Charles Bradley, for tiling .... 2.00—$25.00
1866.
Feb. 20 " amount on hand, to be carried to new account,....   74.61
                                                              ─────────
                                                                $99.61
                                                              ═════════

1865.   CR.
Feb. 14. By balance from old account,...................... $99.61

                Respectfully submitted, in F., H. and C.,
                                      S. H. HARRIS, *Grand Treasurer.*
New Haven, February 20, 1866.

Several bills were presented and referred to the Committee on Finance, who reported them correct, and they were ordered paid.

The following resolutions were presented and adopted :

Resolved, That hereafter it shall be the duty of the Grand Patriarch to make an official visit to each of the several subordinate Encampments of this jurisdiction at least once during his official term, or deputize some Patriarch to do so.

Resolved, That the other Grand Officers of this Grand Encampment be requested to accompany the Grand Patriarch or his deputy in said official visitations, whenever invited to do so.

The Grand Encampment then proceeded to the nomination of officers for the year ensuing, when the following nominations were made :

For Grand Patriarch, J. H. Barlow.
For Grand High Priest, A. G. Shears.
For Grand Senior Warden, J. E. Bidwell.
For Grand Scribe, L. A. Thomas.
For Grand Treasurer, S. H. Harris.
For Grand Junior Warden, T. I. Driggs of No. 20, Julius Attwood of No. 2, Albegence Hyde of No. 10, G. H. Collins of No. 6, C. A. Newell of No. 6.
For Grand Representative, F. Botsford of No. 1, D. W. Boyd of No. 18, J. W. Smith of No. 20.
On balloting, the following officers were elected :
J. H. Barlow, Grand Patriarch.
A. G. Shears, Grand High Priest.
J. E. Bidwell, Grand Senior Warden.
L. A. Thomas, Grand Scribe.
S. H. Harris, Grand Treasurer.
T. I. Driggs, Grand Junior Warden.
F. Botsford, Grand Representative.
The Committee on Finance submitted the following report, which was accepted :

The undersigned, Finance Committee, having examined the accounts of the Treasurer, find the same correct, and that there remains in his hands seventy-four dollars and sixty-one cents, to be carried to new account.

Respectfully submitted in F., H. and C.,

N. CHANDLER,
J. W. SMITH,   } *Finance Committee.*
FRED'K BOTSFORD,

The Committee thereon submitted the following report, which was accepted :

To the R. W. Grand Encampment, I. O. O. F. of Connecticut :

Your Committee, to whom was referred the reports of the Grand Representative and the Grand Scribe, respectfully report, that they find nothing in the report of the Grand Representative requiring any action of this Grand Body, but that in the report of the Grand Scribe in regard to communication from Patriarch Devotion, and also on the subject of changing the time of the sessions of this Grand Body, we respectfully offer the following resolutions.

Respectfully submitted in F., H. and C.,

J. ATTWOOD,
D. E. BURWELL,   } *Committee.*
A. HOLT,

Resolved, That whenever Palmyra Encampment signifies a desire to resume work, the Grand Patriarch be authorized to grant them all needful help and instruction to reopen their Encampment.

Resolved, That Article 6, Sec. 1 of the Constitution of the Grand Encampment be amended by striking out the word " February," in the third line, and insert the word "May" instead.

The first resolution was adopted, and the second resolution was laid on the table, in accordance with the Constitution.

The Committee on the State of the Order submitted the
following report, which was accepted:

To the R. W. Grand Encampment, I. O. O. F. of Connecticut:

The Committee on the State of the Order beg leave to report that they have
examined the returns from the following subordinate Encampments for the term
ending July 1st, 1865, and find them correct, viz: Sassacus, No. 1, Oriental, No.
2, Sowheag, No. 6, Excelsior, No. 18, Ansantawae, No. 20.   The returns from
Charity Encampment, No. 10, are correct, with the exception that the seal is
pasted on.

Correct returns have been received from the following Encampments for the
term ending January 1st, 1866: Sassacus, No. 1, Oriental, No. 2, Charity, No.
10, and Ansantawae, No. 20. In the returns of Excelsior Encampment, No. 18,
the signature of the Chief Patriarch is wanting. The returns of Sowheag Encampment, No. 6, for the last term have not come to hand.

The following summary will show the condition of the patriarchal branch in
this jurisdiction at the commencement of the present term: initiated, 23; admitted by card, none; expelled, none; suspended, 1; withdrawn, none; died, 1;
present number, 260; receipts for the year, $912.62; paid for expenses, $411.50;
relief, $240; present amount of funds, $3,659.90.

In looking over the returns, we notice that in several the names of the Past
Chief Patriarchs and Past High Priests are omitted, and a memorandum made
referring to previous reports for the list. As this, in many cases, might prove a
serious inconvenience, your Committee would recommend that in future the
names of the Past Officers be incorporated in the returns.

All which is respectfully submitted in F., H. and C.,

G. L. TOWNSEND,
M. B. SCOTT,   } *Committee.*
S. B. WETMORE,

The work of the Encampment was then exemplified by
Grand Representative Smith.

The Committee on the State of the Order submitted the following report, which was accepted and the resolution adopted.

To the R. W. Grand Encampment, I. O. O. F. of Connecticut:

The Committee on the State of the Order, to whom was referred so much of the
R. W. Grand Patriarch's report as relates to the public installation of officers,
have attended to their duty, and would recommend the adoption of the following resolution.

All of which is respectfully submitted in F., H. and C.,

G. L. TOWNSEND,
M. B. SCOTT,   } *Committee.*
S. B. WETMORE,

Resolved, That the subordinate Encampments be authorized to install their officers in public on first obtaining the consent of the R. W. G. Patriarch.

The Grand Scribe presented the following letter, with the
picture to which it refers:

WATERBURY, February 16th, 1866.

R. W. L. A. THOMAS, Grand Scribe:

Dear Sir and Brother:—I take pleasure in presenting to the R. W. Grand
Encampment, through you, a photographic picture of the officers and members
of the R. W. Grand Lodge of the United States, taken during their last session
in Baltimore.

Truly yours, in F., H. and C.,

J. W. SMITH, *Grand Representative.*

On motion, the following resolution was adopted:

Resolved, That the Grand Encampment accept with pleasure the beautiful picture of the members of the Grand Lodge, and that the thanks of this Grand Encampment are hereby tendered Grand Representative Smith for the elegant gift.

The Grand officers elect were then installed into their respective offices in ample form.

The following resolution was unanimously adopted:

Resolved, That the thanks of this Grand Encampment are due to Grand Patriarch Boyd, for the able and dignified manner in which he has discharged the duties of that office.

The Committee thereon submitted the following report, which was accepted:

To the R. W. Grand Encampment, I. O. O. F. of Connecticut:

We, your Committee, to whom was referred that portion of the M. W. Grand Patriarch's report referring to his visits to Sowheag Encampment, No. 6, and Oriental. No. 2, would respectfully report that in the case of Sowheag Encampment we find the letter of the M. W. Grand Patriarch making an appointment to visit, officially, said Encampment, was duly received and immediately answered by Patriarch Bidwell, informing him that it would be inconvenient to receive him at the time appointed, therefore no provision was made to comply with his appointment. In the case of Oriental, No. 2, no letter informing them of an official visitation has as yet been received.

Respectfully submitted in F., H. and C.,
FREDERICK BOTSFORD,)
J. W. SMITH,   } *Committee.*
D. E. BURWELL,)

No further business offering, the Grand Encampment was closed in ample form.

Attest,

LUCIUS A. THOMAS, *Grand Scribe.*

APPENDIX.

The copy for the following Reports was not found at the time of the printing of the proceedings of the sessions to which they respectively belong, but they are herewith inserted to make the record as complete as possible.

Report of Grand Patriarch John Wallace, at the Annual Session, 1856, omitted from page 238.

R. W. Grand Officers and Patriarchs:

We are again permitted to assemble in Annual Session, to review the past, examine our present position and thereby be the better enabled to adopt such measures as shall best promote the future prosperity of this branch of our Order, and the great object of our affiliation.

In accordance with a time-honored custom and the dictates of my own personal feelings, I take pleasure in laying before you a list of my official acts since the last meeting of this R. W. Grand Body. I say I take pleasure in the enumeration, from the fact that every act performed in my official capacity has been of a character highly calculated to produce the most pleasurable emotions. Not a single instance has occurred in which I have been called upon to settle a disputed point, or give an opinion, where any one has felt aggrieved by the decision.

As soon after the close of the last session as practicable, I issued commissions to the several Patriarchs regularly recommended to me, as suitable persons for the office of Deputy Grand Patriarch, to each of whom I intimated my intention to visit the Encampments in their several jurisdictions at a time mutually to be agreed upon. The result has been, that I have visited eight Encampments in different parts of the State, as follows:

On the 24th of May, accompanied by M. E. Grand High Priest Jackson, Grand Scribe Thomas, and Grand Junior Warden Harris, I visited Excelsior Encampment, No. 18, held at Birmingham, on which occasion two candidates were admitted into our family in a manner calculated to give them an exalted idea of our impressive ceremonies, and the Grand Officers in attendance assurance of the zeal, energy and devotion to the work, of the members of this young and vigorous Encampment. Happily chosen is their name, "Excelsior," and may they ever remember the words—"Onward"—"Go on."

On the 5th of June, in company with our Grand Scribe, I visited Oasis Encampment, No. 16, located at Meriden, where we witnessed the conferring of the three degrees. The special feature of this visit was the hearing the lectures and charges delivered by the C. P. (Brother George E. Leonard) without reference to the charge-book,—the only case of the kind witnessed in our several visits. The effect was calculated to make us wish we might hear the entire work, without reference to the text, and I feel assured this would soon be the case in most of our Encampments could the officers fully appreciate the beneficial effects of such a course.

On the 5th of July, accompanied by M. E. Grand High Priest Jackson, Grand Scribe Thomas, Grand Junior Warden Harris, and several Patriarchs from Excelsior, No. 18, I visited Sassacus Encampment, No. 1, of this city. On this occasion two candidates were admitted into full fellowship with us, at which time the teachings of our beautiful ritual were set forth in a manner highly calculated to produce a beneficial and lasting impression on the minds of the initiated. With the assistance of the Grand Officers present, I installed the officers of the Encampment for the current term, in ample form.

On the 6th of July, I visited Devotion Encampment, No. 5, located at Danbury, and witnessed the work in each of the degrees. I also installed its officers for the current term, in ample form. This Encampment, like several others in this jurisdiction, has suffered seriously in consequence of the general depression felt in all manufacturing districts during the past two years; yet I am happy to say, that the spirit manifested by the circle of Patriarchs, shows a *devotion* to the interests of the Order that will in due time bring forth its legitimate fruits.

On the 12th of July, assisted by M. E. Grand High Priest Jackson, I installed the officers of Excelsior Encampment, No. 18, in ample form.

On the 13th of August, I visited Phœnix Encampment, No. 19, at West Winsted. In consequence of a misunderstanding as to the time of my visit, I did not witness an initiation, but an opportunity was afforded for instruction and an interchange of ideas. I feel an assurance that the Order in Winsted is in safe hands, and that we shall hear glowing accounts from No. 19.

On the 26th of November, accompanied by M. E. Grand High Priest Jackson, Grand Scribe Thomas, and a number of Patriarchs from Excelsior, No. 18, I visited Kabaosa Encampment, No. 9, at Norwalk. On this occasion two candidates were admitted into our family through the formula set forth in our Ritual, and rarely has it been our pleasure to witness the "unwritten work" performed in a more acceptable manner, or better calculated to impress the mind with the important lessons taught by our ceremonies and symbols. This visit will long be remembered, not only because of the pleasure we felt in witnessing the work, but because we were made to feel that the Patriarchs of this Encampment practically illustrated in an eminent degree the lesson taught each of us when we first rested "beneath the covering of this tent."

On the 21st of December, accompanied by Grand Scribe Thomas, I visited Montevideo Encampment, No. 15, at Plainville. As no candidate was presented for initiation, we had ample opportunity for instruction, counsel, and that interchange of thought so necessary to unity of action in all great enterprises.

On the 1st of January last, accompanied by Grand Scribe Thomas, and Grand Senior Warden Phelps, I visited Oriental Encampment, No. 2, located at Essex. On this occasion, one candidate was admitted to our fraternal circle. In visiting this Encampment (older than this Grand Encampment) we were cheered with the assistance of a warm and enthusiastic band of Patriarchs, who demonstrated that time serves only to increase their love and devotion to the interests of the Order.

I feel an assurance that these several visits have been productive of much good, not only insuring a more uniform mode of working in our Encampments, but has had a tendency to cheer the faint-hearted, renew the vigor of the veteran and stimulate all to persevere with increased energy, in diffusing a knowledge of the principles of our Order. My own experience leads me to believe that a systematic course of annual visitation, by a properly qualified officer, would produce most favorable results. I cannot too strongly urge upon you the necessity of a more general diffusion throughout this jurisdiction of information pertaining to our Order. Ignorance begets Indolence, one of the worst evils we have to contend against, not only from without, but within the bosom of our own fraternal family. The most ardent and active in promoting the interests of Odd Fellowship, are almost uniformly those best informed in the work, and in relation to the doings of their brethren throughout the length and breadth of our land. My observation leads me to believe that zeal (in Odd Fellowship at least) is the sure companion of knowledge. I commend the subject to your careful consideration.

I congratulate you on the settlement (for the present at least) of the long vexed question of mergement, which has hung like an incubus over this branch of our Order for some time past, paralyzing, to some extent, the efforts of those who sought to promote and extend its influence and usefulness. If it is desirable to change existing arrangements, (as is contended by those favoring a mergement and reorganization of the Order,) the merging the Degree Lodge into the Encampment seems to me feasible, and much more desirable than the mergement of the Encampment into the subordinate Lodge. Authorize the Encampment to confer the five degrees, and such Lodges only as are without the district of an Encampment, and thus increase the amount of work and usefulness of this branch of our Order, without interfering in the least with the legitimate object of subordinate Lodges. Such an arrangement as is here suggested would not only be highly beneficial to the Encampment, but would relieve the Lodge of a portion of the work frequently performed in a very imperfect manner.

I cannot dismiss you to your labors without acknowledging my indebtedness to Grand Scribe Thomas, for much valuable information, aid and assistance rendered during the year past, and congratulating you on having so efficient and valuable an officer in the most responsible and important position in our jurisdiction.

In conclusion, allow me to return my sincere thanks to those with whom I have been brought in immediate contact during my incumbency of the exalted office your preference imposed on me.

JOHN WALLACE, *Grand Patriarch.*

New Haven, Feb. 20th, 1856.

Report of Grand Representative P. L. Cunningham, at the Annual Session, 1856, omitted from page 238.

To the R. W. Grand Encampment of Connecticut:

Your Representative to the R. W. Grand Lodge of the United States, having attended to the duty assigned him by this R. W. Body, beg leave respectfully to report:

The R. W. Grand Lodge of the United States assembled at the city of Baltimore, on Monday, the 17th of September, 1855, the M. W. Grand Sire Wilmot G. De Saussure, presiding.

The Officers and Representatives from thirty-five Grand Lodges (including one from Canada West, and one from Nova Scotia, admitted to this session for the first time,) and twenty-seven Grand Encampments, were in attendance.

The Order throughout the entire jurisdiction of the Grand Lodge of the United States is shown, by the reports of the Grand Sire and Grand Secretary, to be in a prosperous condition.

Warrants have been issued during the year, and charters granted, as follows:

For Grand Lodges.—Grand Lodge for the Lower Provinces of British North America, located at Halifax; Grand Lodge for Canada West, located at Brockville.

For Subordinate Lodges.—Olympia Lodge, No. 1, Olympia, Washington Territory; Nebraska Lodge, No. 1, Nebraska City, Nebraska; Phœnix Lodge, No. 3, Montreal, Canada East.

For Subordinate Encampments.—Walker Encampment, No. 6, Washington, Arkansas.

On the first day of the session, the officers of the past term retired, and those elected for the current two years, were installed.

A Special Committee was appointed by the Grand Lodge of the United States, at the session of 1854, to prepare and report a plan, merging the subordinate Lodge and Encampment. On this subject the Committee submitted their report, which was read and laid on the table, and no further action had thereon.

The most important business of the session, so far as the Grand Encampment is concerned, was the rejection of the proposed amendments to the Constitution, by Representative Glen of Georgia, page 2,351, having for its object to strike out Grand Encampment, wherever the same occurred in the Constitution.

The following resolution, in behalf of our afflicted brethren in Norfolk and Portsmouth, Virginia, was adopted by a unanimous vote:

Resolved, That the sum of three hundred dollars be and the same is hereby appropriated towards the relief of our suffering brethren in Norfolk and Portsmouth, the same to be forthwith disbursed by Special Committee of this R. W. Grand Body, in such manner as said Committee, after due inquiry, shall judge most expedient.

The finances of the Grand Lodge of the United States are not in a very flourishing condition; the estimated expenses for the current year are:

Estimated expenditure is... ....$18,245.25
"   revenue is.............................. 16,080.00

Leaving a deficit to be provided for of............... $2,165.25

To meet this deficiency, the Finance Committee have recommended that Article XIV of the Constitution be so amended as to provide that a Representative tax be levied of one hundred dollars, instead of fifty, as at present.

Also to amend Article XIV of the Constitution, by erasing the word "fifty," and inserting "seventy-five."

A resolution was adopted by a very close vote, reducing the pay of Representatives from *three* to *two* dollars per day, and their mileage from *five* to *four* cents.

The following decisions, made by Grand Sire Wilmot De Saussure, were confirmed:

That a member committing suicide, his family were not thereby debarred from benefits.

That the Grand Lodge of the United States had always refused to sanction public installations of Officers, and that Daughters of Rebekah were merely honorary in connection to the Order, and could not be present at the installation of Officers.

That a Grand Representative elect, taking a withdrawal card, thereby forfeits his office, although he afterwards deposits the card in another Lodge.

This decision, although confirmed, was subsequently, by resolution, so construed that it should not debar a Representative holding a seat in the Grand Lodge, from retaining such seat, should he withdraw from the Lodge of which he is a member for the purpose of connecting himself with another Lodge; provided not more than three months shall elapse between the times of withdrawal and deposit; and further provided, that no session of the Grand Lodge, either special or annual, shall be held in the interim.

That a subordinate Lodge violating the laws laid down by the Grand Lodge of the United States, and refusing to observe such laws, may be expelled therefor; and that the Grand Master, during the recess, may demand its charter.

That when visiting for installation purposes, a Grand Master was entitled to take the chair of the Noble Grand, but that when otherwise visiting, he was not entitled to the chair of right.

That a reconsideration of a ballot is inadmissible.

That a Noble Grand elect, having failed to appear for installation and forfeited (under the local laws) his office, the member elected and installed in his lieu is the Noble Grand of the Lodge.

That the correctness of giving two of the Patriarchal degrees upon the same evening, was to be determined by local legislation.

That it was improper to confer an Encampment degree upon one holding a withdrawal card from a subordinate Lodge.

Also the following decisions were made by the Grand Lodge:

A Grand Body, upon ascertaining that the qualifications set forth in a certificate under which a P. G. or P. C. P. has been admitted to membership in it, have been incorrectly stated, the certificate may be set aside and the seat found thereon, vacated.

It was decided that it is inexpedient to so alter the laws of the Order as to require all business to be transacted in the Scarlet Degree.

That the failure or neglect of a subordinate Grand Lodge to properly elect her Representatives, nor the commission of errors or irregularities in such election, do not relieve such subordinate from an obligation to pay her annual Representative tax.

That it is inexpedient to receive as a member, entitled to the social benefits of the Order, on his own proposition to renounce all pecuniary benefits, a person who, from advanced age, sickness or constitutional infirmity, is incapable of being received into full membership in a subordinate Lodge.

That when an applicant for membership is a citizen or subject of a foreign power, and only a temporary resident of the United States, he cannot be initiated into the Order.

As this report closes the official duties of your Representative, he would take this opportunity to return his sincere thanks for the many favors received from this R. W. Grand Encampment.

Respectfully submitted,

P. L. CUNNINGHAM, *Grand Representative.*

Report of Grand Patriarch Chas. C. Jackson, at the Annual Session, 1857, omitted from page 244.

Right Worthy Grand Officers and Representatives:

Another year has gone, and we are again permitted to assemble for the purpose of reviewing the past and to legislate, I trust, for the good and permanency of the Patriarchal branch of our Order in this jurisdiction.

Soon after the close of the last session I forwarded to those Patriarchs who had been reported to me as nominees their warrants as D. D. G. P., from whom, I regret to say, I have not received any reports.

At the last session of the Grand Encampment the Grand Patriarch was authorized to remove Sowheag Encampment, No. 6, from Middletown to Portland, whenever said Encampment at a meeting called for that purpose should so decide. I have not been apprised of any action by the Encampment on the subject.

On the 16th of January I received a communication from Grand Scribe Thomas, stating that Mount Hermon Encampment, No. 8, of Bridgeport had surrendered their charter, which, with their books and effects were in his possession, with the following note from the C. P. and Scribe, addressed to the Grand Patriarch:

Bridgeport, Jan. 9th, 1857.

To the M. W. Grand Patriarch of the Grand Encampment, I. O. O. F. of Conn.

DEAR SIR,—In pursuance of a vote passed unanimously by all the members of Mount Hermon Encampment, No. 8, I have this day forwarded to the Scribe of the Grand Encampment, the charter, books, &c., of said Mount Hermon Encampment, with a report up to the time of surrender of the charter, and the dues to the Grand Encampment. It was deemed advisable by the members of our Encampment to pursue this course, inasmuch as we were constantly falling in arrears in our work, with no prospect of any immediate improvement. We nevertheless hope that the time is not far distant when we may reclaim our charter, and be found, as we trust we have heretofore been, among the first ranks in this beautiful and beloved branch of our Order.

With great respect we remain in the bonds of F., H. & C.,

Yours,

JOHN STEVENS, *C. P.*
JOHN L. ROBERTS, *Scribe.*

By reference to the proceedings of the Grand Lodge of the United States it will be found that at their last session they increased the price of cards from ten to twenty cents, and other supplies twenty-five per cent. The reason assigned for this additional tax on subordinates is the increasing expenses of that Body, now amounting to over eighteen thousand dollars a year. I submit whether it would not have been better for the Order if they had devised some way to decrease this enormous expenditure.

I would recommend that our Representative be instructed to urge the passage of the amendment to the constitution offered by P. G. Sire Kennedy of New York.

C. C. JACKSON, *Grand Patriarch.*

Report of Grand Representative John Wallace, at the Annual Session, 1857, *omitted from page* 244.

To the R. W. Grand Encampment, I. O. O. F. of Connecticut:

Your Representative to the Grand Lodge of United States begs leave to report, that the Annual Communication of that R. W. Grand Body was held in the city of Baltimore in the month of September last, opening on the 15th and closing on the 22d day of that month. The undersigned was present at the opening of the session, and remained until the close of the fifth day, when information of sickness in his family compelled him to return home.

There were present Representatives from every Grand Body under the jurisdiction of the Grand Lodge of the United States, except Michigan, Minnesota and Canada West.

As a deliberative and legislative Body it has few equals in the United States, for the courteous bearing of its members, the amount of forensic talent displayed, and a strict adherence to parliamentary rule.

Although the session was held during one of the most exciting political contests ever witnessed in the United States, in which sectionalism was incorporated with party, more than ever before, and when the only sentiment in which the whole could agree was, "He who is not for us, is against us," yet in that sacred retreat all seemed to forget, for the time being, the animosities and strifes exciting the outer world, or if remembered, stimulating each to increased vigilance in promoting the principles of Friendship, Love and Truth—and, as if to seal and perpetuate a remembrance of the harmonizing influence of those principles on discordant elements, George W. Race of New Orleans, was *unanimously* elected Grand Sire, and by a majority of votes Timothy G. Senter, of New Hampshire, Deputy Grand Sire,—thus selecting the two highest officers in the Order from two extreme portions of the country.

Owing to a protracted illness Grand Sire Ellison, of Massachusetts, was not present. He however had prepared a very able and voluminous report, which was read, spread upon the record, and printed with the proceedings of the session, and will abundantly repay a careful perusal.

The absence of the Grand Sire would have been more seriously felt, had not the duty of presiding fallen to the lot of D. G. Sire Race (now Grand Sire elect.) His promptness of action, familiarity with parliamentary rule and usage, an intimate knowledge of the Constitution, By-Laws, and Rules of Order of the Grand Lodge, together with his dignified, courteous, and gentlemanly bearing, eminently qualified him for the important position he was so unexpectedly called upon to assume.

The following are the only decisions of the Grand Sire in which this branch of our Order is directly interested:

"6th. A Grand Representative has a right to introduce visiting brethren into either Lodge or Encampment in his jurisdiction, whether he be a Representative from his Grand Lodge or Grand Encampment."

The Grand Lodge modified this decision so as to limit the right of Grand Representatives to introduce visiting brethren into the subordinates of the *Body* they represented.

"15th. It has been enquired of me whether it is competent for a Grand Encampment or Grand Patriarch to grant a card to enable a Patriarch to join a subordinate Encampment, if the said Patriarch is at the time largely in arrears to a defunct Encampment.

"My reply was as follows: That a Grand Body has full power in the premises, not only in its resumption of the powers of a subordinate which has become extinct, but in its original control over all the members of the Order in its jurisdiction; even while a subordinate is in full operation a Grand Body may direct it to restore a suspended or expelled member without its consent.

"This discretionary power implies, of course, a wise and judicious investigation into the circumstances of every case presented."

The following resolutions were adopted, with others more immediately affecting Grand Lodges:

Resolved, That Grand Patriarchs and their Deputies be empowered to confer the degrees of a subordinate Encampment upon Scarlet Degree members of subordinate Lodges, for the purpose of organizing new Encampments, *provided* no subordinate Encampment be located within thirty miles of such new Encampment.

Resolved, That the officers of subordinate Lodges and Encampments shall not be installed nor furnished with the Semi-Annual pass-word, unless the reports, returns, and moneys due from such Lodges and Encampments to their respective superior jurisdictions be actually made and placed in the hands of the proper officer, or be actually in transit to the proper destination.

Resolved, That subordinate Lodges and Encampments, in reinstating members suspended for non-payment of dues, shall have power to remit in whole, or in part, the dues accruing during the suspension of such members.

Resolved, That all visiting and final cards shall hereafter be signed by the holders thereof, in the presence of the officer by whom the annual pass-word is communicated to such holders.

The question of mergement was agitated, and several resolutions offered tending to that object, all of which were voted down.

A mergement of some of the degrees in the Order may be desirable, and a more perfect consolidation of the entire work advisable, yet I feel convinced that a more feasible plan than any that has been offered, must be brought forward beford the Grand Lodge of the United States will so change the work as to blot out of existence thirty State Grand Bodies.

The subject of public installations was canvassed, and, although recommended by the Grand Sire in his report, the Grand Lodge withheld its sanction and refused to legalize the innovation.

Numerous amendments to the constitution, which had been offered at the previous session, came up for final action, all of which were voted down.

I cannot close this report, and do justice to my own feelings, without alluding to the very handsome manner in which the Representatives were entertained by the Fraternity of Maryland through their Grand Officers. Every day of the session we were reminded that they fully understood the first lesson taught each of us when we first "rested beneath the covering of this tent."

All of which is respectfully submitted,

JOHN WALLACE, *Grand Representative.*

Table showing the Number of Initiations and the Number in Membership in each Encampment, from 1855 to 1866, inclusive.

No.	NAME	LOCATION	1855 Init.	1855 No. Members	1856 Init.	1856 No. Members	1857 Init.	1857 No. Members	1858 Init.	1858 No. Members	1859 Init.	1859 No. Members	1860 Init.	1860 No. Members	1861 Init.	1861 No. Members	1862 Init.	1862 No. Members	1863 Init.	1863 No. Members	1864 Init.	1864 No. Members	1865 Init.	1865 No. Members	1866 Init.	1866 No. Members
1	SASSACUS	New Haven	11	100	17	114	4	111	10	114	16	115	17	130	4	131		122	2	122	11	133	23	154	19	170
2	ORIENTAL	Essex	2	19	2	20	1	20	1	20		11		11		7		7		7	9	21	1	22	5	27
3	PALMYRA	Norwich		11		11																				
5	DEVOTION	Danbury		50		50																				
6	SOWHEAG	Middletown		26		26		21	1	17	1	14		19	1	19		13		13	11	24		25	18	37
8	MOUNT HERMON	Bridgeport		21		21																				
9	KABAOSA	Norwalk	2	46		50																				
10	CHARITY	Stonington	3	28		28			3	23	1	24									2	16	7	23	8	30
15	MONTEVIDEO	Plainville		25		26																				
16	OASIS	Meriden	4	50		53																				
18	EXCELSIOR	Derby	1	26	4	18	1	51	3	40	3	34	4	36	5	30	2	32	2	29	4	33	3	30	3	33
19	PHENIX	Winsted		46	3	30		41	2	26	4	26	3	29		34		31	9	30	1	31	2	33	5	39
20	ANSANTAWAE	Waterbury			2				8	20		20	1	21		20										
21	HEBRON	Hebron																								
			23	448	28	447	6	244	25	264	25	244	25	246	10	241	2	205	13	201	38	258	37	287	53	336

PAST OFFICERS.

GRAND PATRIARCHS.

1.	ROBINSON S. HINMAN,	of No. 1,	New Haven,	from April, 1843, to July, 1848.
2.	WILLIAM E. SANFORD,	" 1,	New Haven,	" July, 1843, to July, 1844.
3.	JOHN L. DEVOTION,	" 3,	Norwich,	" " 1844, to " 1845.
4.	JONATHAN M. ANDRUS,	" 1,	New Haven,	" " 1845, to " 1846.
5.	WM. L. BREWER,	" 3,	Norwich,	" " 1846, to " 1847.
6.	MUNSON A. SHEPARD,	" 5,	Bethel,	" " 1847, to Feb. 1848.
7.	TOWNSEND P. ABELL,	" 6,	Middletown,	" Feb 1848, to July, 1848.
8.	LUCIUS A. THOMAS,	" 1,	New Haven,	" July, 1848, to " 1849.
9.	JUNIUS M. WILLEY,	" 2,	East Haddam,	" " 1849, to " 1850.
10.	CHOLWELL J. GRUMAN,	" 9,	Norwalk,	" " 1850, to " 1851.
11.	ORIGEN UTLEY,	" 6,	Middletown,	" " 1851, to Feb. 1852.
12.	CALVIN L. HUBBARD,	" 11,	Hartford,	" Feb. 1852, to " 1853.
13.	PETER L. CUNNINGHAM,	" 9,	Norwalk,	" " 1853, to " 1854.
14.	FRANCOIS TURNER,	" 1,	New Haven,	" " 1854, to " 1855.
15.	JOHN WALLACE,	" 18,	Derby,	" " 1855, to " 1856.
16.	CHARLES C. JACKSON,	" 18,	Derby,	" " 1856, to " 1857.
17.	JAMES PHELPS,	" 2,	Essex,	" " 1857, to " 1858.
18.	SAMUEL H. HARRIS,	" 1,	New Haven,	" " 1858, to " 1859.
19.	SAMUEL TOLLES,	" 1,	New Haven,	" " 1859, to " 1860.
20.	THOMAS C. HOLLIS,	" 1,	New Haven,	" " 1860, to " 1861.
21.	MERITT B. SCOTT,	" 1,	New Haven,	" " 1861, to " 1862.
22.	GEORGE L. TOWNSEND,	" 20,	Waterbury,	" " 1862, to " 1863.
23.	JOHN W. SMITH,	" 20,	Waterbury,	" " 1863, to " 1864.
24.	FREDERICK BOTSFORD,	" 1,	New Haven,	" " 1864, to " 1865.
25.	DAVID W. BOYD,	" 18,	Derby,	" " 1865, to " 1866.
26.	JOHN H. BARLOW,	" 18,	Derby,	" " 1866, to " 1867.

GRAND HIGH PRIESTS.

1.	CHARLES W. BRADLEY,	of No. 2,	East Haddam,	from April, 1843, to July 1843.
2.	RICHARD S. PRATT,	" 2,	East Haddam,	" July, 1843, to " 1844.
3.	JONATHAN M. ANDRUS,	" 1,	New Haven,	" " 1844, to " 1845.
4.	WILLIAM L. BREWER,	" 3,	Norwich,	" " 1845, to " 1846.
5.	MUNSON A. SHEPARD,	" 5,	Bethel,	" " 1846, to " 1847.
6.	TOWNSEND P. ABELL,	" 6,	Middletown,	" " 1847, to " 1848.
7.	JUNIUS M. WILLEY,	" 2,	East Haddam,	" " 1848, to " 1849.
8.	CHOLWELL J. GRUMAN,	" 9,	Norwalk,	" " 1849, to " 1850.
9.	ORIGEN UTLEY,	" 6,	Middletown,	" " 1850, to " 1851.
10.	CALVIN L. HUBBARD,	" 11,	Hartford,	" " 1851, to Feb. 1852.
11.	PETER L. CUNNINGHAM,	" 9,	Norwalk,	" Feb. 1852, to " 1853.
12.	FRANCOIS TURNER,	" 1,	New Haven,	" " 1853, to " 1854.
13.	JOHN WALLACE,	" 18,	Derby,	" " 1854, to " 1855.
14.	CHARLES C. JACKSON,	" 18,	Derby,	" " 1855, .o " 1856.
15.	JAMES PHELPS,	" 2,	Essex,	" " 1856, to " 1857.
16.	SAMUEL H. HARRIS,	" 1,	New Haven,	" " 1857, to " 1858.
17.	JOHN G. HAYDEN,	" 2,	Essex,	" " 1858, to " 1859.
18.	THOMAS WALLACE, Jr.,	" 18,	Derby,	" " 1859, to " 1860.
19.	MERITT B. SCOTT,	" 1,	New Haven,	" " 1860, to " 1861.
20.	GEORGE L. TOWNSEND,	" 20,	Waterbury,	" " 1861, to " 1862.
21.	JOHN W. SMITH,	" 20,	Waterbury,	" " 1862, to " 1863.
22.	FREDERICK BOTSFORD,	" 1,	New Haven,	" " 1863, to " 1864.
23.	DAVID W. BOYD,	" 18,	Derby,	" " 1864, to " 1865.
24.	JOHN H. BARLOW,	" 18,	Derby,	" " 1865, to " 1866.
25.	ALONZO G. SHEARS,	" 1,	New Haven,	" " 1866, to ". 1867.

GRAND SENIOR WARDENS.

1.	RICHARD S. PRATT,	of No. 2,	East Haddam,	from April, 1843, to July, 1843.
2.	ISAAC JUDSON,	" 1,	New Haven,	" July, 1843, to " 1844.
3.	WILLIAM L. BREWER,	" 3,	Norwich,	" " 1844, to " 1845.
4.	MUNSON A. SHEPARD,	" 5,	Bethel,	" " 1845, to " 1846.
5.	JOHN W. JOHNSON,	" 7,	Hartford,	" " 1846, to " 1847
6.	JUNIUS M. WILLEY,	" 2,	Essex,	" " 1847, to " 1848.

7. CHOLWELL J. GRUMAN, of No. 9, Norwalk, from July, 1848, to July, 1849.
8. WM. B. DAVIS, " 11, Hartford, " " 1849, to " 1850.
9. CALVIN L. HUBBARD, " 11, Hartford, " " 1850, to " 1851.
10. ELIPHALET G. STORER, " 1, New Haven, " " 1851, to Feb. 1852.
11. FRANCOIS TURNER, " 1, New Haven, " Feb. 1852, to " 1853.
12. JOHN WALLACE, " 18, Derby, " " 1853, to " 1854.
13. CHARLES C. JACKSON, " 18, Derby, " " 1854, to " 1855.
14. JAMES PHELPS, " 2, Essex, " " 1855, to " 1856.
15. SAMUEL H. HARRIS, " 1, New Haven, " " 1856, to " 1857.
16. JOHN G. HAYDEN, " 2, Essex, " " 1857, to " 1859.
17. SAMUEL TOLLES, " 1, New Haven, " " 1858, to " 1859.
18. THOMAS C. HOLLIS, " 1, New Haven, " " 1859, to " 1860.
19. GEORGE L. TOWNSEND, " 20, Waterbury, " " 1860, to " 1861.
20. JOHN W. SMITH, " 20, Waterbury, " " 1861, to " 1862.
21. FREDERICK BOTSFORD, " 1, New Haven, " " 1862, to " 1863.
22. DAVID W. BOYD, " 18, Derby, " " 1863, to " 1864.
23. JOHN H. BARLOW, " 18, Derby, " " 1864, to " 1865.
24. ALONZO G. SHEARS, " 1, New Haven, " " 1865, to " 1866.
25. JAMES E. BIDWELL, " 6, Middletown, " " 1866, to " 1867

GRAND SCRIBES.

1. WM. E. SANFORD, of No. 1, New Haven, from April, 1843, to July, 1843.
2. JOHN L. DEVOTION, " 8, Norwich, " July, 1843, to " 1844.
3. PRELATE DEMICK, " 1, New Haven, " " 1844, to " 1847.
4. LUCIUS A. THOMAS, " 1, New Haven, " " 1847, to " 1848.
5. PRELATE DEMICK, " 1, New Haven, " " 1848, to " 1850.
6. ADRIAN C. HEITMANN, " 1, New Haven, " " 1850, to " 1852.
7. LUCIUS A. THOMAS, " 1, New Haven, " " 1852—

GRAND TREASURERS.

1. SAMUEL BISHOP, of No. 1, New Haven, from April, 1843, to Feb. 1863.
2. SAMUEL H. HARRIS, " 1, New Haven, " Feb. 1863—

GRAND JUNIOR WARDENS.

1. THOS. C. BOARDMAN, of No. 2, East Haddam, from April, 1843, to July, 1843.
2. JOHN A. LATHROP, " 4, New London, " July, 1844, to " 1845.
3. JOHN W. JOHNSON, " 7, Hartford, " " 1845, to " 1846.
4. JUNIUS M. WILLEY, " 2, Essex, " " 1846, to " 1847.
5. CHOLWELL J. GRUMAN, " 9, Norwalk, " " 1847, to " 1848.
6. WM. B. DAVIS, " 11, Hartford, " " 1848, to " 1849.
7. ORIGEN UTLEY, " 6, Middletown, " " 1849, to " 1850.
8. ELIPHALET G. STORER, " 1, New Haven, " " 1850, to " 1851.
9. PETER L. CUNNINGHAM, " 9, Norwalk, " " 1851, to Feb. 1852.
10. ADNA WHITING, " 15, Plainville, " Feb. 1852, to " 1853.
11. CHAS. C. JACKSON, " 18, Derby, " " 1853, to " 1854.
12. JAMES PHELPS, " 2, Essex, " " 1854, to " 1855.
13. SAMUEL H. HARRIS, " 1, New Haven, " " 1855, to " 1856.
14. SAMUEL TOLLES, " 1, New Haven, " " 1856, to " 1857.
15. JOHN G. HAYDEN, " 2, Essex, " " 1857, to " 1858.
16. THOMAS WALLACE, Jr., " 18, Derby, " " 1858, to " 1859.
17. M. B. SCOTT, " 1, New Haven, " " 1859, to " 1860.
18. DAVID BOTSFORD, " 1, New Haven, " " 1860.
19. CHAS. L. SAGE, " 1, New Haven, " " 1861, to " 1862.
20. D. W. BOYD, " 18, Derby, " " 1862, to " 1863.
21. J. H. BARLOW, " 18, Derby, " " 1863, to " 1864.
22. ALONZO G. SHEARS, " 1, New Haven, " " 1865, to " 1865.
23. JAMES E. BIDWELL, " 6, Middletown, " " 1865, to " 1866.
24. T. I. DRIGGS, " 20, Waterbury, " " 1866, to " 1867.

GRAND REPRESENTATIVES.

1. ROBINSON S. HINMAN, of No. 1, New Haven, from July, 1843.
2. SAMUEL BISHOP, " 1, New Haven, " " 1844.
3. JOHN L. DEVOTION, " 8, Norwich, " " 1845.
4. JOHN GREENWOOD, Jr., " 5, Danbury, " " 1846.
5. WM. L. BREWER, " 8, Norwich, " " 1847.
6. T. P. ABELL, " 6, Middletown, " " 1848.
7. WM. E. SANFORD, " 1, New Haven, " " 1849 to 1851.
8. C. J. GRUMAN, " 9, Norwalk, " " 1852 to 1853.
9. PETER L. CUNNINGHAM, " 9, Norwalk, " " 1854 to 1855.
10. JOHN WALLACE, " 18, Derby, " " 1856 to 1857.
11. CHAS. C. JACKSON, " 18, Derby, " " 1858 to 1859.
12. SAMUEL H. HARRIS, " 1, New Haven, " " 1860 to 1861.
13. M. B. SCOTT, " 1, New Haven, " " 1862 to 1863.
14. JOHN W. SMITH, " 20, Waterbury, " " 1864 to 1865.
15. FREDERICK BOTSFORD, " 1, New Haven, " " 1866 to 1867.

www.ingramcontent.com/pod-product-compliance
Lightning Source LLC
Chambersburg PA
CBHW021114270326
41929CB00009B/871